Breaking GROUND

KEYS FOR SUCCESSFUL ONLINE LEARNING

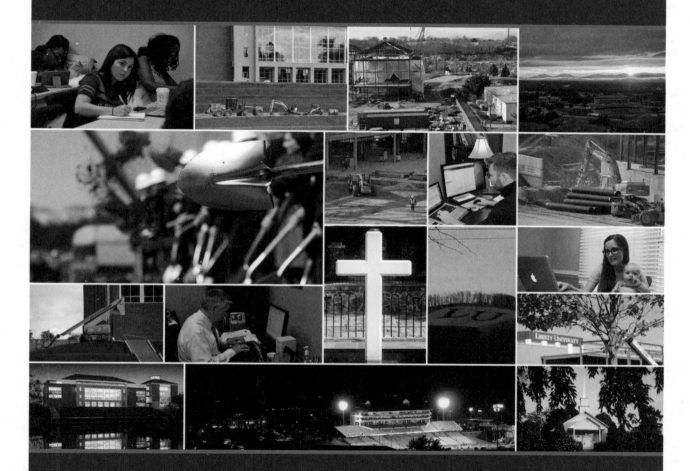

AMY SCOTT HASSENPFLUG | AARON D. TRAPHAGEN | JAMAICA JOHNSON CONNER

Liberty University

Kendall Hunt
publishing company

All Bible verses from the New International Version unless otherwise noted.

Cover images provided by the following:

Kevin Manguiob
Dave Moquin
Faith Perry
Chris Robinson
Les Schofer
Aaron D. Traphagen.

Kendall Hunt
publishing company

www.kendallhunt.com
Send all inquiries to:
4050 Westmark Drive
Dubuque, IA 52004-1840

CONTENTS

PREFACE

The development of your academic career is a lot like the construction of a building—you must build your education on a solid foundation. Upon this premise, we constructed the text, *Breaking Ground: Keys for Successful Online Learning*. This notion is nothing new. If you want to be successful in anything in life, you must begin with a purpose, building upon a firm foundation. Jesus even related this very principle to our spiritual walk with Him in Luke 6:48-49,

> *"Why do you call me, 'Lord, Lord,' and do not do what I say? As for everyone who comes to me and hears my words and puts them into practice, I will show you what they are like. They are like a man building a house, who dug down deep and laid the foundation on rock. When a flood came, the torrent struck that house but could not shake it, because it was well built. But the one who hears my words and does not put them into practice is like a man who built a house on the ground without a foundation. The moment the torrent struck that house, it collapsed and its destruction was complete"* (New International Version).

Jesus' message is clear throughout the simile: listen to His instruction and apply it if you want to have a lasting, strong relationship with Him. The same is true for your education; you must apply the guidance, instruction, and advice of your professors and those who have gone before you to achieve success in your academics.

Though there is nothing glamorous about forming the foundation because of the gritty, dirty nature of the work, the preparation and perspiration is critical so that the beautiful features of the structure last. Once a builder establishes that foundation, choosing the best materials and the most experienced team of builders makes all the difference in the strength and magnificence of the building. In I Corinthians 3:9-13, Paul explains this further,

> *For we are co-workers in God's service; you are God's field, God's building. By the grace God has given me, I laid a foundation as a wise builder, and someone else is building on it. But each one should build with care. For no one can lay any foundation other than the one already laid, which is Jesus Christ. If anyone builds on this foundation using gold, silver, costly stones, wood, hay or straw, their work will be shown for what it is, because the Day will bring it to light* (NIV).

As you "build with care," dig into the course materials, lessons, and resources that have been carefully selected for you. Enjoy collaborating with your classmates and your professor and share your own prayer requests and encouragement in the discussion board forums. Take advantage of every opportunity designed to make your academic experience and development rich and robust.

In the text, the analogy begins by comparing your school selection process to the beginning phase of a construction project when clients peruse model homes to find the perfect fit, and we conclude by celebrating the day you earn your degree, just like a client celebrates the day he accepts the keys from the builder. Each chapter contains four essential elements: a devotional, known as The Cornerstone; Key Concepts that highlight the academic objectives and instruction; a review and application section called Building Blocks; and finally, an explanation of resources, the Tool Box. Additionally, there are tips from former students, professors, and key leaders at Liberty University in the margins of each chapter. As you read each element of the text, our hope is that you recognize that not only is your academic career like a construction project, but your spiritual development is, as well. Ephesians 2:19-22 explains,

> *Consequently, you are no longer foreigners and strangers, but fellow citizens with God's people and also members of His household, built on the foundation of the apostles and prophets, with Christ Jesus Himself as the chief cornerstone. In Him the whole building is joined together and rises to become a holy temple in the Lord. And in Him you too are being built together to become a dwelling in which God lives by his Spirit.*

Once a building is constructed, it must be maintained, and though you may need to renovate or add-on down the road, the structure you began with is going to be the basis and main support in each of those scenarios. If your foundation is rooted in a faith in Jesus Christ and His teachings, your building will be resilient, as it undergoes spiritual growth and improvement. If your academic foundation is rooted in the lessons you will learn and apply throughout *Breaking Ground: Keys for Successful Online Learning*, you will be set up for academic success. With these principles in mind, we look forward to the day we will celebrate with you as you finally accept your key from the builder and earn your college degree.

Your authors,

Amy Scott Hassenpflug
Aaron D. Traphagen
Jamaica Johnson Conner

CONSTRUCTION KEY

Throughout this text, you will see symbols that represent different pieces of information, like student testimonials or professor tips. Use this legend as a visual guide to connect you to these valuable pieces of information.

IMAGE	TEXTUAL COMPONENT
	THE CORNERSTONE A brief devotional to begin each chapter, written by Jamaica Johnson Conner.
	KEY CONCEPT The main objectives of each chapter.
	PROFESSOR TIP Helpful tips from seasoned LUO faculty who teach INFT 101.
	STUDENT TESTIMONIALS Current and former LUO students share their tips for success.
	BUILDING BLOCKS A summary of each chapter.
	THE TOOLBOX A listing of helpful tools related to each chapter's topics.
	PERSONAL REFLECTION A place for you to reflect on the information presented in each chapter.

ACKNOWLEDGMENTS

Together, Amy, Aaron, and Jamaica would like to thank the following people for their invaluable contributions to this project:

Brad Burgess	Mark Heideman	Klaus Shmidheiser
Emily Foutz	John E. Johnson, Sr.	Lisa Stephens Taylor
Dr. Ron Godwin	Paula Oldham Johnson	Mark Tinsley
Paul Gormley	Wayne Patton	Mollie Yoder
Jennifer Griffin	Curtis Ross	INFT 101 Faculty
Dr. Ron Hawkins	Amanda Smith	
Dr. Emily Heady	Cari Smith	

Psalm 127:1, "Unless the LORD builds the house, the builders labor in vain. Unless the LORD watches over the city, the guards stand watch in vain" (NIV).

Amy, Aaron, and Jamaica thank the Lord for his protection, provision, and guidance throughout the construction of this textbook. Thank You, Lord Jesus, for being the Cornerstone of this project and the Cornerstone of our lives. We love you!

Amy:

Thank you to my wonderful family: Leon, Madeline, Rachel, Beau, Mom, and Bill. You each contributed to my ability to get this done and to my belief that it WOULD be possible, in due time! Rachel, you routinely demonstrate that more than 24 hours worth of work can go into each day. Thanks, I needed that! Maddy, you are my dog-walker, pasta-cooker, humorist, and perspective-maker. Thank you!! Leon, how could this even have been a dream without your encouragement and support? Thank you for your steadfast encouragement and love in this endurance event! I will cook again, sometime!

Linda Blair Milton, my tireless cheerleader who knows that an encouraging word is a priceless gift, THANK YOU for your many encouraging words along the way.

Dr. Yaw Adu-Gyamfi, you were the first to say to me, "Now write the textbook." Thank you!

To Jamaica and Aaron, thank you both for laughing when we could have cried! I love working with both of you.

Aaron:

Doug and Lee, thank you for allowing me to use your deck as a respite from the chaos.

Mark H. and Cari, thank you for all of the great discussions and debates regarding curriculum and instruction and for challenging my thinking.

Mark T. and Wayne, your friendship and advice have been invaluable.

Amy and Jamaica, I could not have asked to work with two more amazing people. Thank you for every minute of this experience.

Calista and Olivia, my little buddies. Thank you for your patience, your love, and for always knowing how to make me smile!

Lauren, you have done more for me than I could ever say thank you for. I love you until the end of time.

Jamaica:

Terry, thank you for your unfailing love, support, and goodness to me every day of our life together. Without you, I could not do what I do! I love you more than words can express.

Laura Grace and Marianna, thank you for inspiring me with your contagious giggles and addictive cuddles. I love you both so much!

Mom and Dad, thank you for your insightful contributions to this text and the wealth of knowledge that you brought to this project. Thank you for spending time with your grandbabies, so I could finish it! Thank you for falling in love with each other, with Liberty, and with the Lord, and for passing that legacy on to me. I love you both!

John, you are an inspirational and remarkable brother! Thank you for supporting me from miles away. I love you!

Lynn, thank you for living every day with a "never ever quit" attitude and for all of your help taking care of our girls! I love you!

Dr. Yaw, thank you for recommending me to be a part of this wonderful team. God blessed me abundantly through you!

Amy and Aaron, thank you for allowing me to work with you on this amazing project. I have loved collaborating with both of you!

For the Conner, Harmon, and Tomlin families; for the Cox, Johnson, Nicholson, Offenbacker, and Oldham families; for my dear friends Patricia Emmert, Emily Foutz, and Stacey Hester; for my team of babysitters: Jenny Harris, Emily Hine, Emily Cox, and Rebekah Cox (aka Aunt Dee Dee); for Michelle Martilla and your artistic advice; for my colleagues and friends in the College of General Studies; for my incredible team of professors, led by their incredible instructional mentors: Mary Dixon, Alissa Keith, and Katie Robinson; for my students, past and present—thank you all for all you do! You are a blessing to me!

Article Contributors

Brad Burgess
Emily Heady
John E. Johnson, Sr.
Paula Oldham Johnson
Wayne Patton
Lisa Stephens Taylor
Mark Tinsley

Student Contributors

Terry Conner
Emily Cox
Ruth Ferrell
Tim Harpe
Maddy Hassenpflug
Roger Nauss
Cheryl Palmer

Tip Contributors

Alexandra Barnett
Hanna Bruce
Betsey Caballero
T. Marcus Christian
Terry Conner
Jessica Cromley
Shaun Curran
Sherry Dickerson
Mary Marie Dixon
Lisa Eppard
Josh Gerstner
Tracey Good

Silvia Graham
Jennifer Griffin
David Hart
Mark Heideman
Stephanie Hobson
Kirsten Hoegh
Alissa Keith
Lucy LeRose
Nicole Lowes
Debra Magnuson
Michael Marrano
Kristy Motte
Ramona Myers
Sue Ocealis
Heather Patterson
Katie Robinson
Michael Shenkle
Barbara Sherman
Cari Smith
Katie Stewart
Joe Super
Nathaniel Valle
Jenny Walter
Terri Washer
Sherrie Welfel
Dustin Williams

Photography Contributors

Paula Johnson
Dave Moquin
Faith Perry
Aaron Traphagen

Liberty University Photographers

Joel Coleman
David Duncan
Bob Duval
Cali Lowdermilk
Kevin Manguiob
Les Schofer
LU Marketing

FOREWORD

The Journey . . .

Proverbs 15:22, "Plans fail for lack of counsel, but with many advisers they succeed" (NIV).

Wisdom literature, such as *Proverbs* and *Ecclesiastes,* is not meant to be lofty, but rather it is practical and seeks to show us how to best live our lives. Proverbs 15:22 has widespread utility and application. Along those lines, the passage truly points to the heart of the *Breaking Ground* text and its corresponding course.

If you look carefully at the verse, it presupposes a key aspect, that is, that a plan is in place. Without a plan, a hope, a vision, a dream, a mission, we are just arbitrarily going through the motions of existence. The good news is we all tend to have a plan, or plans. These ventures may just be laid out as vague goals or concepts. They may be well thought-out objectives with each step of the agenda meticulously thought through, a timetable established, and action points clarified.

Our personalities, strengths, and weaknesses all play into how we proceed with such tasks. Within the context of this study, the plan is for you to engage your educational goals, seek knowledge, earn your degree, improve your standing, and use your skills and gifts in your field. Clearly, such a mission requires a lot of thought and planning. If you are engaging this text, you are about to, or are currently, undertaking that mission. So what is your plan? Why are you here? What is the goal? How will you get there?

Often we set out to do something and may not be fully prepared. We may have pondered it greatly and committed to it, yet our level of readiness and ability to complete the task were not quite up to the challenge. That reality either made for a difficult journey or found us failing altogether. In our preparation of the plan, did we ask the right questions? Did we talk to the right people? Did we set ourselves up for success? Did we get a lay of the land? Yes, *the counsel* of others, who have been there before us and know the road ahead of us, is of great benefit.

A few years ago, I planned on kayaking the James River from Lynchburg to Richmond. This four day, 140-mile trek was my attempt to get away from computers, cell phones, and Blackboard and to reconnect with God and enjoy some quiet time in the abundant Virginia countryside. I planned the trip by studying the route, checking for dams, rough water, cities for resupplying along the route, and reviewing data on the flow of the river to determine what type of pace I could hope to maintain. I also sought the counsel of others who had had attempted similar trips. I read relevant books on the topic and spoke with people who had actually paddled those various sections of the river. I also sought the advice of friends who were much more astute in living in the bush than I. Given that my idea of camping was a nice hotel near the beach, I clearly could use some advice on this front.

It was in one of those conversations that two of my friends from Liberty University, and contributors to this text, joined the adventure. Mark Tinsley and Aaron Traphagen both had extensive military backgrounds and actually knew how to survive in the wild, unlike me. They also brought a wealth of knowledge in terms of the supplies we would need and a background in logistics for planning expeditions in the field. Granted, I had my own notions of what those aspects of the trip would require, but given their wisdom and experience in such matters, I listened and took note of their counsel. All of this planning and consideration yielded positive results. In sum, since that time, we have covered the James River from the headwaters up in the Blue Ridge Mountains all the way to Jamestown.

So with some planning, advice, and wise counsel, I not only have successfully completed the Lynchburg to Richmond phase, but now, I have also nearly paddled the entire James River. Were there difficulties along the way? Absolutely. But preparing, sharpening of skills (practice), knowing what was required, having a fall back plan, and depending on the available resources and expertise of others yielded success; that is the mission of this text. A team that knows the way and has been there before wants to set you up for success on your educational journey. For your part, this will require planning, assessing yourself, balancing your strengths and weaknesses, listening to the experts, and opening yourself up to being teachable. Some have a hard time taking wise counsel, but those who humble themselves for the sake of the mission will have a better journey.

In the spirit of the verse above, may you plan well, find and listen to wise counsel, and may you *succeed!*

God bless.

Wayne A. Patton
Associate Dean
The College of General Studies

Liberty University
Lynchburg, Virginia 2013

STUDENT TESTIMONIALS

These students have gone before you at Liberty University Online. Read their brief biographies below to find one that you most closely relate to as a student. Keep an eye out for that former student's comments throughout the text to guide you.

Cheryl, 30-something, graduate

Cheryl's Story:

"I am a single mother of two, a caregiver for my Mom (who is disabled), and I homeschool my son. Time is the hugest challenge that my situation has brought to my personal educational goals. I do not resent this. 'It is what it is.' However, someone always needs my attention and care. It is not usually small tasks either, as the 'time' thing in my situation has usually included doctor appointments, ER trips (sometimes all-nighters), or doctor follow-up appointments."

Emily, 19-year-old, freshman at Liberty University

Emily's Story:

"My name is Emily. I am an only child, and my parents are divorced. However, they would not be the same people together, and I have a great step family . . . I never had much discipline growing up, and I was never really good at disciplining myself so my first semester was rough trying to balance activities with school work. Honestly, I didn't do that well academically, so it was a hard lesson learned."

Maddy, 20-something, Liberty student

Maddy's Story:

"I am a 20-year-old 'traditional' college student, in my fourth year on campus. I have changed my major more than once, and have begun to take advantage of online classes in order to graduate in a more timely fashion. My main concern starting online classes was that I would completely forget about them, just because they would be unlike anything I had done before.

I mainly came to Liberty because of my scholarship from attending Liberty Christian Academy. There was also the comfort of not leaving home yet. Having been a student at LCA for most of my schooling, I was able to hear Dr. Falwell speak on multiple occasions. My favorite quote of his was one I heard often. When telling the story of how Thomas Road Baptist Church, LU, and LCA came to be, he would tell the students 'I walked this mountain; I claimed this land.'"

Roger, 50-something graduate of Liberty University with a MAT, 2011

Roger's Story:

"I was raised in New York to Christian parents and came to faith in Jesus Christ at an early age. Our church had many good role models and I felt truly blessed to enjoy a good relationship with them. Although neither of my parents had a high school education, they strongly believed their children should have a good education.

Dad was a bricklayer and the only breadwinner in the family. He worked very hard but he could only work if the weather cooperated or if there was a job. I remember one time when the construction trade collapsed and he was without work for nine months. He reminded us that God would take care of us and keep food on the table. In all that time, he never failed to tithe unto the Lord, even his unemployment check. Dad didn't want me to follow in his trade. He wanted me to develop talents in serving the Lord, so he didn't teach me the masonry skills.

After high school, I really didn't know what I wanted to do with my life. I wanted to go to college but my family couldn't afford to send me. I worked for about a year and then was laid off on Christmas Eve. "What should I do now?" I prayed. I felt the urge to apply to a Christian college about a half-hour from home. What did I have to lose? Shortly thereafter, I received an acceptance letter. God provided state and federal tuition grants, part-time jobs, and I made it through school without owing any money.

My educational journey had only begun. Within two years I was married and off to seminary for a Master of Divinity degree. Again God had provided and I graduated debt free.

Over 20 years of pastoral ministry had passed and I was becoming tired out; I needed a ministry change. So I asked the Lord, how can I use my ministry gifts to serve people? Teaching was always a strong point in my life. Both major and minor concentrations were in religious education; and in pastoral ministry, opportunities abound for teaching all educational levels. So, I applied to Liberty University

I had heard about Liberty University for many years. Dr. Falwell often invited pastors to refer qualified students to the college with reduced tuition incentives. Furthermore, LU had a great education department that was certified by several accrediting agencies. So, I applied and was accepted into the MAT program (Master of Arts in Teaching and Learning). I believed that I could use my gifts and abilities to positively influence young people in a public education setting as a licensed and certified teacher.

In May 2011, I graduated with a dual endorsement in Secondary Education—History and Special Education K–12 General Curriculum. One week before the fall term began I was hired as a special education teacher for Pittsylvania County, VA. That's not bad for a 52-year-old career changer."

Ruth, LU employee, completing her degree after raising children

Ruth's Story:

"Because I was a single mom with three children to raise, I did not have the opportunity to get a college education until they were older, and I accomplished an associate's degree from Central Virginia Community College, one class at a time for a few years. Once I became employed with Liberty and my children were grown, my personal goal was to work toward a bachelor's degree. If it wasn't for online courses and being able to take them from home, I never would have been able to accomplish this goal. During the time I was taking online courses, my father became ill, and I had to skip a term, sometimes two, but I was able to get back on track when I could return."

Terry, 30-something graduate of Liberty University with an MA, 2007

Terry's Story:

"My situation is not unique; before I went to LU, I was in a company that I loved. The environment was great, I was able to have good balance with work and family, and I genuinely liked what I was doing. However, I had been at the company for many years, and it appeared that I'd hit a ceiling as far as my advancement went. I came to Liberty to get input from experts outside of my company to expand my understanding of business. I could have certainly gone to any other university, but Liberty's mission aligned with my Christian beliefs, so I came here and haven't regretted the choice."

Tim, 20-something, Active Duty Marine

Tim's Story:

"My name is Corporal Timothy W. Harpe, II. I am a married, active duty Marine finishing my last few classes before I graduate. Some of the biggest challenges with taking college courses and being active duty is field duty and deployment. It was definitely difficult to submit course work when I was in the field without internet or cell phone service for days and sometimes weeks. It can also be difficult to do course work when you are in a different time zone. The difficulty is that when I get off work, I have maybe an hour to submit homework because of the time zone difference. . . . Being married and completing course work can also have its own set of challenges. Typically, when my wife wanted to do something, I had to do course work, but when I had completed all of my course work, she did not want to do anything."

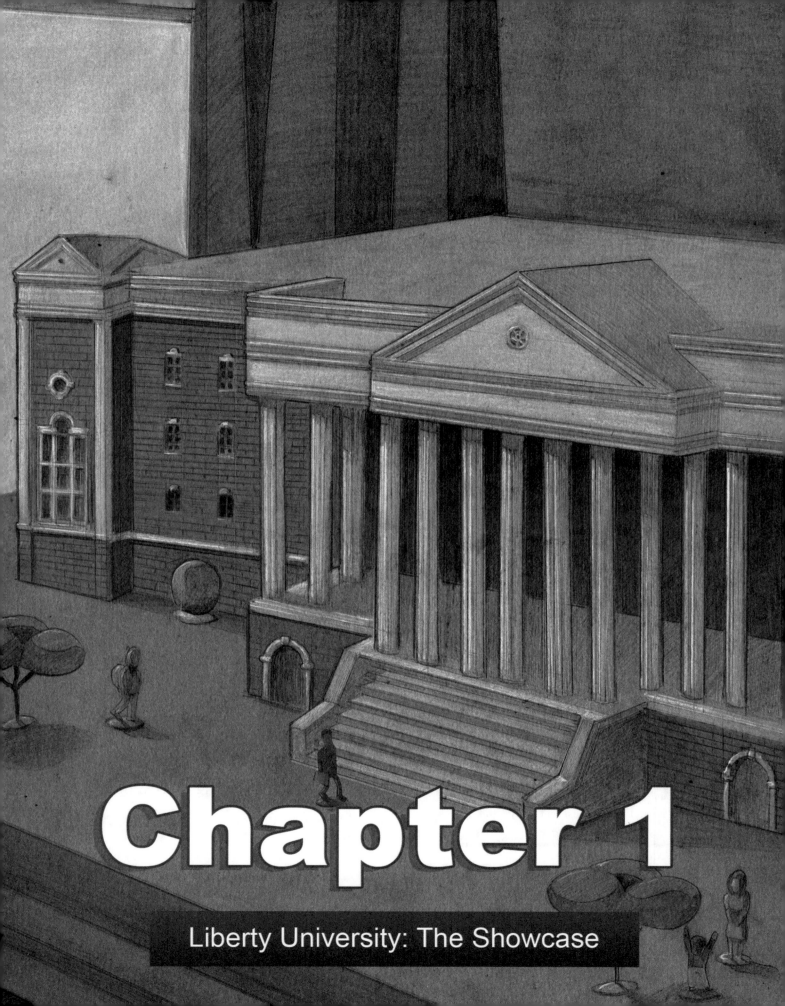

Chapter 1

Liberty University: The Showcase

In this chapter, you will:

- Acquaint yourself with Liberty University's history.
- Identify Liberty University's core values.
- Examine the way you view the world.
- Generate ideas to implement a Biblical worldview.

SHOWCASE HOME

As Matthew 7:24–27 explains, a home must be built on a firm foundation to withstand the elements. Before the construction process starts, however, builders often recommend that their clients tour showcase homes to discover what they like best. As you pursue your college education, you must also build on a solid foundation, and finding the perfect school for you is the best place to start. We know Liberty University Online is the best place for you! Liberty University Online offers a Christ-centered, liberal arts education in a flexible, engaging, and interactive format. We welcome you to our showcase as you begin the building process of your academic career.

© 2013 by Lightspring. Used under license of Shutterstock, Inc.

Matthew 7:24-27,
"Therefore everyone who hears these words of mine and puts them into practice is like a wise man who built his house on the rock. The rain came down, the streams rose, and the winds blew and beat against that house; yet it did not fall, because it had its foundation on the rock. But everyone who hears these words of mine and does not put them into practice is like a foolish man who built his house on sand. The rain came down, the streams rose, and the winds blew and beat against that house, and it fell with a great crash" (New International Version).

THE CORNERSTONE

The Vision: Year One

Habakuk 2:2–3, "And the Lord answered me, and said, Write the vision, and make it plain upon tables, that he may run that readeth it. For the vision is yet for an appointed time, but at the end it shall speak, and not lie: though it tarry, wait for it; because it will surely come, it will not tarry" (King James Version).

In 1971, Dr. Jerry Falwell spread his vision of a Christian college to "train young champions for Christ" across the East Coast of the United States. During that first year, Paula Johnson was one of the first 235 students who came to the Lynchburg Baptist College to share in the humble inception of Falwell's vision. In the following narrative, she shares how the Lord led her to Lynchburg Baptist College, now Liberty University, and how that vision impacted her life.

Having made new friends in my freshman year at a college in the Midwest, I was not very excited to hit the road with my family for summer travels. I wanted to stay in town and hang out with my new college buddies.

Photo courtesy of Les Schofer and courtesy of Liberty University.

Aerial view of the original Thomas Road Baptist Church on Thomas Road in Lynchburg, VA.

But, as usual, the whole family was expected to go along in my Dad's bus for his summer tour. Being the child of a gospel singer had its perks and its drawbacks. Leaving town this particular summer seemed like a drawback to me.

One of our first stops this summer of 1971 was in a little town in the foothills of the Blue Ridge Mountains in Virginia. I was familiar with several little towns in Virginia as we had spent other summers in the area, but I had never been to Lynchburg. I was impressed with its charming neighborhoods with homes fronted by amazing electric blue hydrangeas and pink-red climbing roses.

Dad pulled our big bus up in front of Thomas Road Baptist Church. I jumped down the bus steps and onto the heat of the blacktop on the parking lot. Dad took me through a side door into the sanctuary of the church where we were welcomed by a gust of air conditioning. And there, my Dad, Doug Oldham, introduced me to pastor Jerry Falwell. Dad said, "Jerry, this is my daughter, Paula," and Dr. Jerry stretched out his big paw for a handshake.

Photo courtesy of Liberty University.

Paula Johnson and Jerry Falwell at the Jerry Falwell Museum opening in 2003.

Unbeknownst to me, at the same time, he placed his hand near my back, so that when he kicked my feet out from under me during the handshake, he could catch me and help me gently fall to the floor.

Needless to say, this was the most unusual handshake from a preacher I had ever received! There I was, laying on the floor of the sanctuary with my dad and Jerry Falwell laughing and looking at me. I said, 'So! This is how it is going to be?' Still laughing, Dr. Jerry reached down and pulled me to my feet and gave me a big bear hug. As I look back over the 42 years since that moment, that is how our friendship was . . . full of the unexpected, slightly scary moments and an affectionate helping hand.

As we traveled the summer months with Dr. Falwell, Dr. Elmer Towns, and others, Dad would sing in the rallies or services and Dr. Falwell would preach and share his vision of starting a new Bible college in Lynchburg. As a 17-year-old girl, I spent a lot of time rolling my eyes at my mother with my cynical attitude. Who would want to go to a college with no professors, no classrooms, no campus, no traditions, nothing?

Near the end of the summer the last rally to raise money and recruit students for the new Lynchburg Baptist College was held at the Pate Chapel at the Thomas Road Baptist Church in Lynchburg. Having heard the spiel many times over the summer, I paid little attention as Dr. Towns explained the academic goals of the new college. Dad sang another song and then Dr. Falwell took the pulpit. He spoke of his vision for the college . . . to train young champions for Christ, to change the world by educating young Christians to go into every conceivable field of endeavor ... lawyers, doctors, teachers, preachers, mechanics, entertainers, missionaries, pilots, artists, musicians . . . the list went on and on.

I had zoned out a bit thinking of my own life . . . where was I headed? What would I do for Christ in my lifetime? At just about that time I heard the Voice of God . . . (no kidding) . . . say, 'Go.'

I knew without a shadow of a doubt God wanted to me to come to the 'nothing college' I had ranted about all summer long. And so, I came to this new school. And we did have nothing. Dr. Towns managed to convince a few quality professors to teach. Our classes met in the Sunday school rooms of Thomas Road Baptist Church. The 'campus' was the parking lot and hallways of the church. We had no cafeteria, so some of us walked more than a mile in the evenings up a steep Thomas Road hill to Burger King or Pizza Hut. We did our laundry at the local laundromat.

My first 'dorm room' (I use that term loosely) was in the basement of the oldest part of the church facility. It had a cement floor, a cot, a brown metal folding chair, a used dresser, and a closet. Or, at least I thought it was a closet. When I opened the closet door, before me stood the building's old boiler. I looked around for the bathroom and was told it was out the door, up the outside steps through the courtyard, into another building, up the steps and down the hall. Convenient.

As little as we had in the way of a campus or dorms, we more than made up in a passionate approach to living for Christ. Everyone who came was at the new college because God had led him or her there. We were a motley bunch, but we loved the Lord more than fancy college facilities. And we were given hands-on experience. If a student was there for a communications diploma, they were put in front of the camera in the church services or behind the camera or up in the control room or in the editing suite. If you were there to become a missionary, you were spending breaks in foreign lands reaching souls for Christ and building churches. If you were going to be a preacher or singer, you were traveling to other churches on the weekends, singing and preaching.

Photo courtesy of Thomas Road Baptist Church.

In the first year, this building, formerly owned by the Donald Duck bottling company, served as the dorm for Lynchburg Baptist College.

Dr. Falwell urged us on, prayed with us, encouraged us, opened doors of opportunity for us; he personally paid for our trips overseas, paid for our lunches. He poured his life into us and pulled us along to help make the vision of this new school a reality.

Now, 43 years later, sometimes after work, I leave the beautiful campus of Liberty University where I work as the curator for the Jerry Falwell Museum and drive up the mountain to an overlook. As the sun sets over the 6,000-acre campus of Liberty University, I look over what God has done through the life of Jerry Falwell, and I thank God for His blessings. And I thank Him for giving Jerry Falwell the vision of Liberty University.

I pray your life will be changed by your experience with Liberty University as dramatically and powerfully as mine was years ago. And, if God said, 'Go' to you, I am sure it will be!

As Paula Johnson shared, Dr. Falwell's vision for Liberty University has come to fruition in the beautiful campus, the competitive residential and online academic programs, the qualified and Spirit-filled faculty and administration, and the remarkable body of students training to be effective "Champions for Christ." Just as the Lord led Paula to Liberty University those many years ago, He has also led you to take part in the vision, and God's best is yet to come! ". . . as it is written: 'What no eye has seen, what no ear has heard, and what no human mind has conceived'—the things God has prepared for those who love him," I Corinthians 2:9 (NIV).

Photo courtesy of Kevin Manguiob and courtesy of Liberty University.

"As the sun sets over the 6,000-acre campus of Liberty University, I look over what God has done through the life of Jerry Falwell, and I thank God for His blessings."

Acquaint Yourself with Liberty University's History

II Corinthians 3:17,
". . . where the Spirit of the Lord is, there is Liberty" (KJV).

Dr. Jerry Falwell, founder

"If America is to remain free, we must raise up a generation of young people who are trained as witnesses for Christ and voices for righteousness who can call this nation back to God and back to the principles upon which it was built. We must bring America back to God and back to greatness. We can only do it by helping young people find purpose in life in Christ" (Falwell, 2008, p. 145).

Appropriately nicknamed "the World's Most Exciting University," the professors and leadership of Liberty University have trained men and women toward academic excellence since 1971. At the school's inception, Dr. Jerry Falwell and Dr. Elmer Towns determined that this college would be different than any other; this college would prepare young Christians to be successful and to make a difference in their chosen professions. They determined that Lynchburg Baptist College would be a place where the Spirit of the Lord would dwell, and the Spirit of the Lord is "alive and well here at Liberty University" all these years later (Falwell, 2007). Along with a variety of academic, athletic, and spiritual programs, Liberty University offers support to students through first-class facilities and valuable resources.

Photo by Kevin Manguiob. Courtesy of Liberty University.

Liberty University's Hancock Welcome Center and Williams Stadium aglow as the sun sets into the Blue Ridge Mountains.

Notable Academic and Institutional Advances

Then . . .	Now . . .
In 1971, 235 students attended Lynchburg Baptist College.	Over 100,000 residential and online students attend Liberty University.
In that first year, co-founder, Dr. Elmer Towns, was the only full-time professor.	Now, about 3,000 full-time and adjunct professors teach for Liberty University.
In the 1970s, Lynchburg Baptist College offered students many opportunities to use what they had learned in their field in a meaningful way: communications (camera crew), hospitality (flight attendants), recruitment (singing teams), and evangelism experiences.	Relevant learning experiences have continued today at Liberty University, with internship programs in various fields, student teaching placements, medical and mission outreach experiences, cinematic and theatre arts opportunities, and much, much more!
During 1971 to 1973, students were awarded certificates of completion instead of degrees.	Lynchburg Baptist College began conferring degrees in 1974.
	In 1980, Liberty University earned accreditation from the Southern Association of Colleges and Schools.
	Liberty University now offers over 206 degree programs.
In 1975, the school changed its name to Liberty Baptist College.	In 1984, the school changed its name to Liberty University.
Liberty University School of Lifelong Learning (LUSLL) began in 1985. This correspondence program offered students the opportunity to earn a degree at a distance. Students could choose from three different degree options.	Liberty University Online now offers over 166 degree programs!
In Liberty University's short life, there have been four presidents, including Dr. A. Pierre Guillermin, Dr. John M. Borek, and Dr. Jerry Falwell, Sr.	Today, Jerry Falwell, Jr. proudly serves as Liberty University's president.

Dr. Jerry Falwell, founder

"I am convinced that if we will attend to the depth of our ministry, God will attend to its breadth" (Falwell, 1997, p. 265).

Rev. Jonathan Falwell, Pastor of Thomas Road Baptist Church

"Whenever he [Dr. Jerry Falwell] mentioned the words 'Liberty University,' somewhere in that conversation was 'training young champions for Christ.' It wasn't a flippant phrase that he just happened to come up with—it's something that was purposeful, intentional and it was often" (Bible, 2009, Training champions for Christ section).

Athletic Programs

Photo courtesy of Liberty University.

Liberty's fans pack Williams Stadium for a night of football and fireworks.

Dr. Elmer Towns, co-founder

"I was excited about what we could do to reach the world for Jesus Christ, and because of Dr. Falwell and his vision, I got excited about what we have done in the past and what we can do in the future, and I am so thrilled to have been a part of Liberty University and what God has done here" (Liberty University News Service, 2014).

Then . . .	Now . . .
In 1971, the school colors were green and gold.	In 1975, the school colors changed to the ones students wear today to show their school spirit: red, white, and blue.
Basketball was Lynchburg Baptist College's first sports team.	Liberty University's sports teams include basketball, football, softball, baseball, soccer, hockey, volleyball, track, rowing, swimming, tennis, and more. 20 different teams are a part of the NCAA Division I program. There are 32 Club Sports teams and an intramural program. (Liberty University, 2014, *About Liberty*)
"Knowledge Aflame" is the school's motto, and that is how Liberty University's sports teams became known as the Flames. The eagle mascot of the Liberty University Flames, Sparky, was born August 20, 1971.	Sparky fiercely supports the Flames at each athletic event and welcomes a hi-five, picture snapshot, or a hug when walking throughout campus. Sparky is even the star of his own children's book, *Sparky's ABC Adventure*.
At the first basketball game, only 20 people cheered the Flames.	Today, Flames fans pack each sport facility to support the different teams. Pat Summit, former women's basketball coach, stated, "We have grown the game of women's basketball, each and every day along the way supported by the best fans in the country. No doubt." Summit earned the title of the "winningest basketball coach in NCAA men's and women's history" (Woolfolk, 2012).
In 1973, Chip Smith made the first touchdown on the football team coached by Rock Royer.	Today, the Jerry Falwell Museum in DeMoss Hall showcases the football that began a long history of touchdowns. Currently, Turner Gill leads Liberty University's fierce football team.

Spiritual Programs

Then . . .	Now . . .
Dr. Falwell's vision for a Christian college committed to a Christ-centered education began in 1971.	Dr. Falwell's vision continues in each residential and online classroom as professors share with their students their love for the Lord and each subject they teach.
Students attended Thomas Road Baptist Church for Sunday services, including Dr. Elmer Towns' Sunday School class.	Liberty University students worship the Lord at Thomas Road Baptist Church, Liberty University 's Campus Church, and many local churches in the Lynchburg area.
Students attended Thomas Road Baptist Church for all chapels and assemblies.	Liberty University hosts convocation on Mondays, Wednesdays, and Fridays at the Vines Center. Online students can view the services through streaming or recorded format on LU's website. Another way for online students to stay connected to the physical campus and to receive spiritual encouragement is through Liberty Online Communities.
On January 21, 1977, the students attended a prayer meeting in the snow on what is now Liberty Mountain. Robbie Hiner sang the song, "I Want that Mountain."	In 2012, over 5,000 Liberty University students, faculty, and staff gathered at the groundbreaking site for the Jerry Falwell Library to pray over the new construction and to reflect on God's blessings and provision over the years at Liberty University. In January 2014, Liberty University held a dedication service for the new Jerry Falwell Library. (Bible, 2012)

Photo courtesy Bob Duval. © Liberty University.

Photo courtesy Les Schofer. © Liberty University.

In the early days, students met in a tent to attend worship services and convocation.

Ruth, LU employee, completing her degree after raising children

Ruth's Story:

Q: *What brought you to Liberty University?*

A: "I had an application with Liberty for two years before they called me. It was a God thing because the company I had previous worked for was closing, and I would have been without a job. I had always wanted to be a teacher, but because I had a family to raise and educate, there was no time or money for me to do so. Liberty was the closest to being a teacher I would ever get, and it has been a blessing being a servant to the faculty and students since I have been here for 25 years."

Student Facilities

Photo courtesy of Liberty University.

Students can enjoy study or fellowship time in the Hancock Welcome Center.

President Jerry Falwell, Jr.

"As part of Liberty's Christian mission we have sought to make Christian education affordable and accessible to as many individuals as possible. Liberty University online has achieved that objective like nothing else could" (Falwell, 2014).

A. Pierre Guillermin, first president of LU

"The history of Liberty University has been and continues to be a chronology of miracles and accomplishments . . . From its very inception, Liberty has been a very dynamic organization. And while other colleges and universities have been built on years of calculated steps, Liberty has always advanced in leaps and bounds. What is happening today is really a great testament to Dr. Falwell's vision and to the team that eventually put all this together" (Menard, 2012).

Then . . .	Now . . .
In 1971, the dorm rooms were in different houses on Thomas Road in Lynchburg, VA as well as in the basement of the Donald Duck Bottling Company building that was the first Thomas Road Baptist Church sanctuary.	On Liberty Mountain, beautiful brick dorms house students comfortably, with new construction for Residence Halls set for completion in the fall of 2014.
In the second year, the dorms were housed on Treasure Island on the James River in Lynchburg, VA, and in the Old Virginian Hotel.	
In 1971, Elmer Towns held a journalism class in his office. Eight students brought in folding metal chairs to make themselves comfortable in the makeshift classroom.	Liberty University's classes are now held in various buildings, such as Arthur S. DeMoss Learning Center, Towns Religion Hall, and Green Hall. Smart Classrooms in each building feature LCD projectors and screens.
Dr. Jerry Falwell loved Thomas Jefferson's architecture and wanted to infuse that into the style of all of Liberty University's buildings. He started by having an architect use one of Jefferson's designs to develop the octagon-shaped building that served as the home for Thomas Road Baptist Church from 1969 to 2006.	Buildings inspired by Thomas Jefferson's architecture can be found all over the campus. Such buildings include Arthur S. DeMoss Learning Center, Towns-Alumni Lecture Hall, Hancock Welcome Center, and the Center for Medical and Health Sciences.
In 1971, Dr. Falwell flew over Candler's Mountain Road (the site of what is now Liberty University's campus) in a helicopter. At the time, he was just interested in 60 acres of timbering land. He asked the real estate agent accompanying him if the owners of the property would be willing to sell it. When the owners were ready to part with the land, Dr. Jerry wrote a personal check of $10,000 earnest money and asked them to wait until the end of the week to cash the check. By the end of the week, the check was good!	Liberty University now owns over 7,000 acres of land and has built many first-class facilities to generate a comfortable and recreational home away from home for Liberty University's residential students: Liberty Mountain Snowflex Center, Barrick-Falwell Lodge, Williams Stadium, the Vines Center, LaHaye Ice Rink, David's Place, Tower Theatre, LaHaye Student Union, Jerry Falwell Library, and many more. (Liberty University, 2014, *About Liberty*)

Then . . .	Now . . .
Fundraising built Liberty University.	Donors such as A. L. Williams, Jerry Vines, Dan Reber, Jimmy Thomas, Tim LaHaye, Arthur S. DeMoss, Jerry Falwell, the Tilley family, David Green, and many others, along with alumni and ministry supporters, have made each construction project possible.

Leadership Legacy

Since 1971, Liberty University's resources, facilities, academic, athletic, and spiritual programs have benefited each student's academic experience, bringing Dr. Jerry Falwell's vision to fruition. In order to appreciate the remarkable achievements and growth of Liberty University, it is important to recognize the life and legacy of its founder, Dr. Jerry Falwell and its current president, Jerry Falwell, Jr. Dr. Ronald S. Godwin, Liberty University's Senior Vice President for Academic Affairs and Provost, elaborates further:

> Liberty University exists today because of one of the most gifted and talented pastors and leaders of our generation. During his entire ministry Dr. Jerry Falwell demonstrated the heart of a pastor, the keen mind of a world-class educator, and the courage and vision of a great citizen statesman. His greatest passion was to establish a Christian university that would be for protestant Christians what Brigham Young is for Mormons and Notre Dame is for the Roman Catholics. Today America, the world, and Christians everywhere are the beneficiaries of his vision and incredibly tenacious faith.

> Safely beyond its struggles to survive during its pioneer years, and now enjoying the visionary and yet prudent leadership of Chancellor Jerry Falwell, Jr., Liberty is continuing to dramatically expand its facilities, programs, and enrollments. Already it has become the largest private Christian University in the world (Falwell, J. & Godwin, R., 2014.)

Take some time to get to know Liberty University's founder, Dr. Jerry Falwell and his son, President Jerry Falwell, Jr. These men have invested their lives, wisdom, and experience to ensure that students of all ages have a quality Christian education.

Dr. Elmer Towns, co-founder

"Some of the greatest spiritual leaders have been motivated by a great vision" (McKay, 2009).

President Jerry Falwell, Jr.

"Liberty was a school that wasn't supposed to happen. Everybody said a conservative Christian school could not survive—but we did" (Falwell, 2014).

President Jerry Falwell, Jr.

"As part of Liberty's Christian mission, we have always sought to make Christian education as affordable and as accessible for as many individuals as possible . . . Liberty University Online is achieving this objective every day, making the dreams of tens of thousands of men and women come true" (Menard, 2013).

Photo courtesy of Liberty University

Jerry Falwell passed away on May 15, 2007, at age 73. He was married to Macel Pate Falwell for 49 years. They had three children: Jerry, Jr., now President of Liberty University; Jeannie, Chief of Surgery at Hunter Holmes McGuire, VA Medical Center in Richmond, Virginia; and Jonathan, senior pastor of Thomas Road Baptist Church; and eight grandchildren.

Emily, 19-year-old, freshman at Liberty University

Q: *What brought you to Liberty University?*

A: "Liberty was always in my mind . . . I knew God was calling me to Liberty and I had to follow . . . Once coming to Liberty, I realized it was the best decision I could have made, and obviously, it was since God led me here."

Jerry Falwell . . . a legacy of faith.

Then . . .

Falwells have lived in Virginia since the first "Fallwell" ancestors arrived on the shores of Chesapeake Bay in the early 1600s. Over the centuries they made their way up the mighty James River through Goochland County and on to Buckingham County, where an ancestor who lived there served in the Revolutionary War.

The Falwells were of sturdy stock and their personalities were as strong as the great hickory trees that forest the Blue Ridge Mountains of Virginia. Tough and resilient, the family prospered in the New World.

In 1850, Jerry Falwell's great-grandfather, Hezekiah Carey Falwell, moved up the James and bought 1,000 acres of land in Campbell County. True Southerners at heart, Hezekiah used his farm's bounty to feed Confederate soldiers and his skills as a wheelwright to fix their wagons and shoe their horses. His son, Charles William (Charlie) Falwell, built a large dairy farm on his portion of the family land.

Charlie was married to the very beautiful Martha Catherine Bell Falwell. Photographs of her show a slim, dark-haired beauty, dressed in a very fashionable white Victorian dress. When she died of cancer at an early age, Charlie turned his back on God forever.

Their son, Carey Hezekiah, must have sensed his father's anger and bitterness toward the Lord. Carey was high-spirited, talented, and energetic. He was not a church-going man, but he married the beautiful and gentle Helen Beasley, who had been raised by her parents, King David and Sallie Beasley, in the ways of the Lord. King David saw to it that his 14 children were in the Baptist Church in the tiny town of Hollywood, Virginia, every Sunday morning.

Carey began to build a business empire in Campbell County and a reputation as a tough entrepreneur, who worked tirelessly to provide the best of the best for his young family. Helen presented Carey with a son and two girls. Rosha, the youngest girl, was the apple of her father's eye. When she died at age ten from appendicitis, Carey, no doubt remembering the loss of his mother and his own father's reaction, turned his heart away from the Lord. Two years after Rosha's death in 1933, Carey and Helen welcomed twins into their home. Jerry and Gene Falwell brought joy back into the Falwell household.

Carey doted on his twin boys while overseeing his many business ventures. He sold bootleg whiskey during the Prohibition years from his many Falwell service stations to raise working capital. He built and operated the popular Merry Garden Dance Hall. He brought big name celebrities into town for the entertainment of the community, such as the Tommy Dorsey Orchestra, Houdini, Claude Thornhill, and Jack Teagarden.

(continues)

(continued)

So, when Jerry Falwell, son of Carey, was saved in 1952 at the Park Avenue Baptist Church, is it any wonder that the people of Lynchburg, Virginia, had a difficult time believing that a preacher could come from such a family?

As a young teenager, Jerry Falwell saw a real change in his father after Carey accepted Christ on his deathbed. This transformation had an impact on the young man, as did his mother's faithful Christian life. Each Sunday morning, as she served her big Southern breakfasts to her twins, Helen was sure to have the family radio playing Charles Fuller's "The Old-Fashioned Revival Hour." Those songs and sermons laid the foundation for Jerry's salvation.

Following his years at Baptist Bible College, Jerry returned to Lynchburg and founded the Thomas Road Baptist Church in 1956. Starting with just 35 adults and their children, Thomas Road Baptist Church grew by leaps and bounds. Jerry Falwell was not only a man of prayer—he was also a man of action. He determined to knock on 100 doors a day to meet new families, to pray for their needs, and to invite them to church. Like his father, Jerry did things in a big way.

In 1956, just months after founding the church, Jerry began a radio and television ministry. His "Old Time Gospel Hour" program, which was the broadcast of the Sunday morning services of the Thomas Road Baptist Church, has led millions to Christ and became the longest continually running televised religious program in America.

Jerry Falwell began to build ministries. The first was the Elim Home for Alcoholics, which he built in memory of his father who had died of alcoholism. From there he built the Treasure Island summer youth camp and reached thousands of children for Christ. Then, seeing a need for Christian Education, he founded Lynchburg Christian Academy (now Liberty Christian Academy), and in 1971, he founded Lynchburg Baptist College, now known as Liberty University. He would go on to establish the Liberty Godparent Home and Adoption Agency to help unwed mothers.

In the 1980s, Jerry Falwell, influenced by the great Christian apologist, Francis Schaeffer, entered the political arena by establishing, with other Christian leaders, the Moral Majority. Their fervent endeavors ultimately led to the election of Ronald Reagan as President of the United States.

Jerry left politics and returned his attention full time to Thomas Road Baptist Church and her ministries. Liberty University had grown from 235 students in 1971 to tens of thousands. His strong, Godly leadership led the university to become the largest Christian university in the world. Jerry bought land on the other side of the mountain where he grew up and where his great-grandfather, Hezekiah Falwell, had purchased 1,000 acres in 1850, to build the campus of Liberty University.

Jerry Falwell became a national leader, seen by millions weekly on television talk shows, but his real passion was being pastor of Thomas Road Baptist Church and "training young Champions for Christ" as a Christian educator.

Written by Paula Johnson, Curator of the Jerry Falwell Museum.

Dr. Elmer Towns, co-founder

"Vision is for an appointed time . . . wait for it because it will surely come" (McKay, 2009).

Dr. Jerry Falwell, founder

"You are never really fulfilled in life until you recognize your vision and fulfill it" (Falwell, 1997, p. 480).

On October 3, 1987, Jerry Falwell, Jr. married Becki Tilley in the little white Prayer Chapel on the campus of Liberty University. Together, over the years, they have renovated a charming farmhouse in the country-side outside of Lynchburg, Virginia. They have three children, Trey (Jerry Falwell, III), Wesley, and Caroline. The Falwells are generous and loving people, who open their home for the Senior Class picnic each year. Their investment in students' lives can also be witnessed as they share in enthusiasm and school spirit while attending sport events and cheering on the Flames!

Jerry Falwell, Jr. . . . realizing the vision.

Now . . .

Liberty University President, Jerry Falwell, Jr., has taken on the task of transforming the Liberty campus above and beyond anything previously envisioned. To see the fast-paced building program that is now underway is nothing short of amazing and a credit to the vision of Liberty's founder, Dr. Jerry Falwell.

President Falwell grew up in the home of Liberty's founder, Dr. Jerry Falwell, Sr., and saw first-hand the growth of the university from a tiny Baptist Bible college founded in 1971 to the largest Christian university in the world. From the time he was a young boy, Jerry Jr. soaked up the wisdom and business sense he would need to run a university with more than 100,000 residential and online students.

President Jerry Falwell, Jr. attended Liberty Christian Academy and Liberty University, graduating with a Bachelor of Arts in Religious Studies in 1984. He then went on to attend the University of Virginia School of Law, and in 1987, he obtained a Juris Doctor degree and became licensed to practice law that same year. Jerry Jr. began to work closely with his father to help develop and manage the university.

Following his father's passing, Jerry Jr. became deeply involved in the planning and construction of improvements on campus, explaining that "All of these buildings and programs are ultimately and primarily about building lives—the lives of our students and the lives of those they will impact."

When you walk this campus, there is a sense that this place is different. It is alive with the hum of construction equipment working on more than 30 major construction projects currently underway. It is also alive with the excitement of thousands of Christian students attending classes, meeting and studying together . . . making plans to change their world.

Often labeled "the world's most exciting Christian university," one cannot make a visit to the campus without sensing the feeling that something big, something ordained, and something blessed by God is happening in Lynchburg, Virginia.

One of the newest and largest construction projects is the Jerry Falwell Library. Named for the founder, Dr. Jerry Falwell, this new state-of-the-art facility will meet the needs of generations to come. The library will have an automated robotic retrieval system for the catalogue of books, conventional stacks of books, reading rooms, study rooms, and a food court.

(continues)

(continued)

Other projects being completed in the months to come include the new Center for Medical and Health Sciences building, new improvements to the Equestrian Center, the first of many new ten-story residence halls, a larger chapel suitable for weddings, a new softball stadium, and improvements to the hiking and biking trails on the mountain. The projects, too many to list, are adding to the rich collegiate experience offered at Liberty University.

Convocation speakers challenge and motivate Liberty University students. Convocation guest speakers have included President and CEO of Samaritan's Purse Franklin Graham, football standout Tim Tebow, Kay Arthur, former House Speaker Newt Gingrich, inspirational speaker Joni Eareckson Tada, Jim Bob and Michelle Duggar of "19 Kids and Counting," Donald Trump, U.S. Rep. Michelle Bachmann, neurosurgeon Dr. Ben Carson, former Governor Mike Huckabee . . . the list goes on and on. Students are challenged on a weekly basis by successful Christian and world leaders to become the best they can be with the help of the Lord.

President Falwell understands that every aspect of a student's life is important, from academic classes to recreational facilities. Each aspect of student life is being enriched, with spiritual leadership chosen carefully, buildings erected and improved, convocation and commencement speakers chosen with today's challenges in mind, and new physical and recreational facilities being added. The student who attends Liberty will leave with not only a first-class education, but also with a rich and varied experience that gives the student a foundation for the future.

When Liberty's founder, Dr. Jerry Falwell, passed away just a week before commencement exercises were held in May of 2007, the first words his son, President Jerry Falwell, Jr., spoke to the thousands upon thousands of people gathered at that momentous occasion were, "Liberty University is alive and well!"

Today Liberty is more alive than any time in its short 43-year history. President Falwell is leading Liberty into a bright and amazing future. We are excited to have you as a part of Liberty University!

Written by Paula Johnson, Curator of the Jerry Falwell Museum.

Terry

My favorite quote from Dr. Falwell is "Sometimes the rabbit has to climb the tree." This is a quote that was used a lot in the early years of Liberty as a metaphor for having to do a task, regardless of our own limitations. The university accomplished many things through the grace of God, so that rabbit climbed the tree.

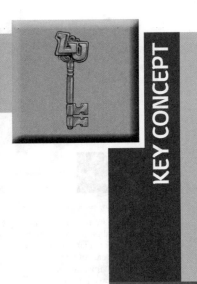

KEY CONCEPT

Identify Liberty University's Core Values

I Timothy 4:7–9,

"Have nothing to do with godless myths and old wives' tales; rather, train yourself to be godly. For physical training is of some value, but godliness has value for all things, holding promise for both the present life and the life to come. This is a trustworthy saying that deserves full acceptance" (NIV).

Dr. Ron Hawkins, Vice Provost of Liberty University

"Liberty is about impacting the culture. Equipping men and women with the knowledge, values, and skills to impact the culture for Jesus Christ" (Menard, 2012).

Terry

Q: *What brought you to Liberty University?*

A: "I was looking for a school that not only taught up-to-date information in my field of study but also taught it from a Christian perspective. Ethics is a hot topic in the realm of business now, and I wanted to complete a degree at a university that was rooted in longstanding biblical beliefs."

As Timothy 4:7–9 explains, Christians should strive for godliness in every area of their lives. Liberty University's core values reflect the truth of God's Word. These reflections of God's truth can be found in Liberty's Mission Statement, which includes the Philosophy of Education, the Statement of Mission and Purpose, and the Doctrinal Statement. Take some time to familiarize yourself with Liberty's value system and see how it lines up with your own.

Mission Statement

Philosophy of Education

Liberty University is a Christian academic community in the tradition of evangelical institutions of higher education. As such, Liberty continues the philosophy of education that first gave rise to the university, and that is summarized in the following propositions.

God, the infinite source of all things, has shown us truth through scripture, nature, history, and above all, in Christ.

Persons are spiritual, rational, moral, social, and physical, created in the image of God. They are, therefore, able to know and to value themselves and other persons, the universe, and God.

Education, as the process of teaching and learning, involves the whole person, by developing the knowledge, values, and skills that enable each individual to change freely. Thus it occurs most effectively when both instructor and student are properly related to God and each other through Christ.

Statement of Mission and Purpose

Maintaining the vision of the founder, Dr. Jerry Falwell, Liberty University develops Christ-centered men and women with the values, knowledge, and skills essential to impact the world.

Through its residential and online programs, the university educates men and women who will make important contributions to their workplaces and communities, follow their chosen vocations as callings to glorify God, and fulfill the Great Commission.

Liberty University will:

1. Emphasize excellence in teaching and learning.

2. Foster university-level competencies in communication, critical thinking, information literacy, and mathematics in all undergraduate programs.

3. Ensure competency in scholarship, research, and professional communication in all graduate programs.

4. Promote the synthesis of academic knowledge and Christian worldview in order that there might be a maturing of spiritual, intellectual, social and physical value-driven behavior.

5. Enable students to engage in a major field of study in career-focused disciplines built on a solid foundation in the liberal arts.

6. Promote an understanding of the Western tradition and the diverse elements of American cultural history, especially the importance of the individual in maintaining democratic and free market processes.

7. Contribute to a knowledge and understanding of other cultures and of international events.

8. Encourage a commitment to the Christian life, one of personal integrity, sensitivity to the needs of others, social responsibility and active communication of the Christian faith, and, as it is lived out, a life that leads people to Jesus Christ as the Lord of the universe and their own personal Savior. (Liberty University Board of Trustees, 2010, *Mission statement*)

Approved by the Liberty University Board of Trustees, November 12, 2010

Ruth

Q: *What is your favorite Dr. Falwell quote?*

A: "'Don't quit!' What a testimony that was for me during the 4–5 years I took online courses."

Doctrinal Statement

We affirm our belief in one God, infinite Spirit, creator, and sustainer of all things, who exists eternally in three persons, God the Father, God the Son, and God the Holy Spirit. These three are one in essence but distinct in person and function.

President Jerry Falwell, Jr.

"Many universities abandoned their original Christian mission when they achieved academic and athletic prominence. Often, the founding principle was compromised because of financial needs and pressure from donors who did not share the founding values of the institution. We believe that God has blessed Liberty University financially so this pattern is not repeated here" (Falwell, 2014).

Cheryl, 30-something, graduate

Q: *What brought you to Liberty University?*

A: "I was first interested in Liberty U because it was one of the first universities to work around my hectic schedule. I very simply would not have been able to further my education in a brick-and-mortar environment."

A. Pierre Guillermin, first president of LU

"Liberty has made a tremendous impact all over the world and it will continue to be a very strong Christian institution, so long as it is consistent and committed to its Christian faith . . . That really is what makes it distinctive. To my knowledge there is not another university in the world that has had such an impact because of its Christian orientation" (Menard, 2012).

We affirm that the Father is the first person of the Trinity and the source of all that God is and does. From Him the Son is eternally generated and from Them the Spirit eternally proceeds. He is the designer of creation, the speaker of revelation, the author of redemption, and the sovereign of history.

We affirm that the Lord Jesus Christ is the second person of the Trinity, eternally begotten from the Father. He is God. He was conceived by the virgin Mary through a miracle of the Holy Spirit. He lives forever as perfect God and perfect man: two distinct natures inseparably united in one person.

We affirm that the Holy Spirit is the third person of the Trinity, proceeding from the Father and the Son and equal in deity. He is the giver of all life, active in the creating and ordering of the universe; He is the agent of inspiration and the new birth; He restrains sin and Satan; and He indwells and sanctifies all believers.

We affirm that all things were created by God. Angels were created as ministering agents, though some, under the leadership of Satan, fell from their sinless state to become agents of evil. The universe was created in six historical days and is continuously sustained by God; thus it both reflects His glory and reveals His truth. Human beings were directly created, not evolved, in the very image of God. As reasoning moral agents, they are responsible under God for understanding and governing themselves and the world.

We affirm that the Bible, both Old and New Testaments, though written by men, was supernaturally inspired by God so that all its words are the written true revelation of God; it is therefore inerrant in the originals and authoritative in all matters. It is to be understood by all through the illumination of the Holy Spirit, its meaning determined by the historical, grammatical, and literary use of the author's language, comparing Scripture with Scripture.

We affirm that Adam, the first man, willfully disobeyed God, bringing sin and death into the world. As a result, all persons are sinners from conception, which is evidenced in their willful acts of sin; and they are therefore subject to eternal punishment, under the just condemnation of a holy God.

We affirm that Jesus Christ offered Himself as a sacrifice by the appointment of the Father. He fulfilled the demands of God by His obedient life, died on the cross in full substitution and payment for the sins of all, was buried, and on the third day He arose physically and bodily from the dead. He ascended into heaven where He now intercedes for all believers.

We affirm that each person can be saved only through the work of Jesus Christ, through repentance of sin and by faith alone in Him as Savior. The believer is declared righteous, born again by the Holy Spirit, turned from sin, and assured of heaven.

We affirm that the Holy Spirit indwells all who are born again, conforming them to the likeness of Jesus Christ. This is a process completed only in Heaven. Every believer is responsible to live in obedience to the Word of God in separation from sin.

We affirm that a church is a local assembly of baptized believers, under the discipline of the Word of God and the lordship of Christ, organized to carry out the commission to evangelize, to teach, and to administer the ordinances of believer's baptism and the Lord's table. Its offices are pastors and deacons, and it is self-governing. It functions through the ministry of gifts given by the Holy Spirit to each believer.

We affirm that the return of Christ for all believers is imminent. It will be followed by seven years of great tribulation, and then the coming of Christ to establish His earthly kingdom for a thousand years. The unsaved will then be raised and judged according to their works and separated forever from God in hell. The saved, having been raised, will live forever in heaven in fellowship with God. (Liberty University Board of Trustees, 2010, *Doctrinal statement*)

Approved by the Liberty University Board of Trustees, November 12, 2010

Ruth

Q: *How does your worldview fit in with the message and purpose of LU?*

Q: "Training Champions for Christ at LU is part of our job in being a testimony to each and every one we come in contact with."

Liberty's Mission Statement clearly outlines a value system that embraces a biblical worldview. The Philosophy of Education, the Statement of Mission and Purpose, and the Doctrinal Statement all reinforce an allegiance and commitment to Jesus Christ in all arenas of life. Dr. Ronald S. Godwin echoes this as he explains, "Without apology our mission is to educate Champions for Christ who are prepared to also utilize their education to become lifelong agents of cultural transformation and exponents of the Great Commission. To this end we are both grateful and proud that Liberty graduates are increasingly taking their place in positions of leadership in America and around the globe" (Falwell, J. & Godwin, R., 2014). In your choice to attend Liberty University, evaluate how your values align with Liberty's Mission Statement because the instruction you receive here will shape you as you develop skills for your future profession and as you develop and strengthen your walk with Christ.

Roger, 50-something graduate of Liberty University with a MAT, 2011

Why attend Liberty University?

"I received a world-class education from qualified faculty. Online classes provided flexibility, affordability, and convenience. The school had my major and helped me to achieve my goals. And most importantly, it approached my major from a biblical worldview."

Examine the Way You View the World

I John 1:5–7,
"This is the message we have heard from him and proclaim to you, that God is light, and in him is no darkness at all. If we say we have fellowship with him while we walk in darkness, we lie and do not practice the truth. But if we walk in the light, as he is in the light, we have fellowship with one another, and the blood of Jesus his Son cleanses us from all sin" (English Standard Version).

Cheryl

What is your worldview?

"I am a fervent Christian. Thusly, I follow the Bible, trust Jesus, and love God. Because of this, my worldview fits in seamlessly with the message and purpose of LU."

Roger

Q: *What is your worldview? How does that fit in with the message and purpose of LU?*

A: "I believe that all truth is God's truth. He spoke this universe into existence and gave us the manual for life in the Bible. God's Word provides all that we need for life and godliness. A biblical worldview is theologically internally consistent, makes total sense of life's questions and provides the means whereby one can live a fulfilled, blessed and productive life. Only when we come to understand that we were made for God's pleasure and purposes, and we align our passions, will, and desires to God, can we reach our full potential. Liberty's purpose blends wonderfully with my worldview because LU seeks to glorify God by training champions for Christ. I desire to fulfill God's purposes through my vocation."

What do you value in life? What is important to you? Your values impact the choices that you make in life and how you view the world around you. They contribute to your world view. Your values may be different from others, but that doesn't make your ideals any less valuable or vice versa. Knowing where you stand on an issue and your reasoning for it is necessary for character building and growing in your interpersonal relationships and in your relationship with Christ.

VALUES CHECKLIST

Assessing Your Personal Values

Use the following checklist to begin to think about what values are important to you. Place a checkmark next to any value that is important to you. There are no right or wrong answers. If you think of other values that are important to you, add them to the bottom of the list.

✓ Having financial security
___ Making a contribution to humankind
___ Being a good parent
✓ Being honest
✓ Acquiring wealth
✓ Being a wise person
✓ Becoming an educated person
✓ Believing in a higher power (God)
___ Preserving civil rights
___ Never being bored
✓ Enjoying life and having fun
✓ Making something out of my life
✓ Being an ethical person
✓ Feeling safe and secure
✓ Having a good marriage
✓ Having good friends
✓ Having social status
___ Being patriotic
___ Having power
✓ Having good morals
___ Being creative
✓ Having control over my life
✓ Growing and developing
✓ Feeling competent
✓ Feeling relaxed
___ Having prestige
✓ Improving society
✓ Having good mental health
✓ Being a good athlete
✓ Enjoying the present moment
✓ Maintaining peace of mind

✓ Having good family relationships
___ Preserving the environment
✓ Having the respect of others
___ Becoming famous
✓ Happiness
___ Freedom and independence
✓ Common sense
✓ Having pride in my culture
___ Doing community service
✓ Achieving my goals in life
✓ Having adventures
___ Having leisure time
✓ Having good health
✓ Being loyal
✓ Having a sense of accomplishment
___ Participating in church activities
✓ Being physically fit
___ Helping others
___ Being a good person
✓ Having time to myself
✓ Loving and being loved
✓ Being physically attractive
✓ Achieving something important
✓ Accepting who I am
✓ Appreciating natural beauty
✓ Using my artistic talents
✓ Feeling good about myself
✓ Making a difference
___ Other: _____
___ Other: _____
___ Other: _____

REFLECTION

What is your most important value? Why is it important to you? Values are what are most important to you; they are your highest principles. They provide the road map to your success and happiness. You will face important turning points along life's journey. Should I go to college? What will be my major? What career will I have? Whom should I marry? What job should I take? Where shall I live? You can find good answers to these questions by being aware of your values and using them to make decisions and guide your actions. If your decisions follow your values, you can get what you want out of life.

The first step is knowing your values. You may need some time to think about your values and change them if they are not right for you. What values were you taught as a child? What values do you want to keep as an adult? Look around at people that you admire. What are their values? What values have you learned from your religion? Are these values important to you? Ask your friends about their values and share yours. Revise and rethink your values periodically. Make sure your values are your own and not necessarily values that someone has told you were important. When you begin to think about values, you can come up with many things that are important. The key is to find out which values are most important. In this way, when you are faced with a choice, you will not be confused. You will know what is most important to you.

Knowing about values is not enough. It is important to act consistently with your values and to follow them. For example, if people value health but continue to smoke, they are saying one thing but doing another. If they value family but spend all of their time at work, they are not acting consistently with their values. As a result, they might find that their family is gone and they have lost something that is really valuable.

Use your actions to question or reaffirm your values. Do you really value your health and family? If so, take action to preserve your good health and spend time with your family. It is necessary to periodically look at your patterns of behavior. Do you act out of habit or do you act according to what is important to you? Habits might need to be changed to get what you value most out of life. In times of doubt and difficulty, your values can keep you going. If you truly value getting a college education, you can put in the effort to accomplish your goal. When you have doubts about whether you can be successful, examine your values again and remind yourself of why you are doing what you are doing. For example, if you value being an independent business entrepreneur, you will put in the effort to be successful. If you value being a good parent, you will find the patience and develop the skill to succeed. Reminding yourself of your values can help you to continue your commitment to accomplishing your goals.

By knowing your values and following them, you have a powerful tool for making decisions, taking action, and motivating yourself to be successful.

Generate Ideas to Implement a Biblical Worldview

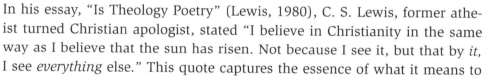

Philippians 4:7–9,
"And the peace of God, which passeth all understanding, shall keep your hearts and minds through Christ Jesus. Finally, brethren, whatsoever things are true, whatsoever things are honest, whatsoever things are just, whatsoever things are pure, whatsoever things are lovely, whatsoever things are of good report; if there be any virtue, and if there be any praise, think on these things. Those things, which ye have both learned, and received, and heard, and seen in me, do: and the God of peace shall be with you" (King James Version).

In his essay, "Is Theology Poetry" (Lewis, 1980), C. S. Lewis, former atheist turned Christian apologist, stated "I believe in Christianity in the same way as I believe that the sun has risen. Not because I see it, but that by *it*, I see *everything* else." This quote captures the essence of what it means to have a biblical worldview, approaching the world through the lens of God's camera, His Word. Having a biblical worldview encompasses what you take in to your heart and mind and what you pour out into the lives of others.

Taking It All In

When you were growing up, did you ever hear the phrase "garbage in—garbage out?" I certainly did, especially as my teachers explained reasons why I shouldn't watch certain TV shows or read different books. The concept was clear cut: If I watched a show with profanity, sooner or later that profanity would become a part of my vocabulary, a part of me. Proverbs 23:7a confirms this, "For as a man thinketh, so is he" (KJV).

Part of getting a quality liberal arts education involves studying a wide array of content, both Christian and secular. So, how do you approach the culture with a biblical worldview and avoid the culture influencing and defining you? The answer is also clear cut: Take

© 2013 by Simon Bratt. Used under license of Shutterstock, Inc.

"I believe in Christianity in the same way I believe that the sun has risen. Not because I can see *it*, but that by it, I see *everything* else," C.S. Lewis.

in the information, let it add to your learning, but filter everything through God's Word. Ask yourself these questions while studying:

1. What message is the author trying to communicate?

2. Do I agree/disagree with the author's message? Why?

3. What does the Bible say about the author's point of view?

4. What does the Bible say about my point of view?

5. How does all of this information impact me?

Thinking critically through your learning process will not only help you grow as a scholar, but it will also strengthen your faith. Finally, pray for discernment as you approach your studies, and the Holy Spirit will guide your heart and mind. Philippians 4:4–9 affirms this, "Rejoice in the Lord always. I will say it again: Rejoice! Let your gentleness be evident to all. The Lord is near. Do not be anxious about anything, but in every situation, by prayer and petition, with thanksgiving, present your requests to God. And the peace of God, which transcends all understanding, will guard your hearts and your minds in Christ Jesus. Finally, brothers and sisters, whatever is true, whatever is noble, whatever is right, whatever is pure, whatever is lovely, whatever is admirable—if anything is excellent or praiseworthy—think about such things. Whatever you have learned or received or heard from me, or seen in me—put it into practice. And the God of peace will be with you" (NIV).

Pouring Into Others

Living a life that reflects a biblical worldview involves absorbing information through God's truth, and it also involves what you pour into the lives of others. Galatians 5:13-26 explains this concept beautifully:

> You, my brothers and sisters, were called to be free. But do not use your freedom to indulge the flesh; rather, serve one another humbly in love. For the entire law is fulfilled in keeping this one command: "Love your neighbor as yourself." If you bite and devour each other, watch out or you will be destroyed by each other.

> So I say, walk by the Spirit, and you will not gratify the desires of the flesh. For the flesh desires what is contrary to the Spirit, and the Spirit what is contrary to the flesh. They are in conflict with each other, so that you are not to do whatever you want. But if you are led by the Spirit, you are not under the law.

> The acts of the flesh are obvious: sexual immorality, impurity and debauchery; idolatry and witchcraft; hatred, discord, jealousy, fits of rage, selfish ambition, dissensions, factions and envy; drunkenness, orgies, and the like. I warn you, as I did before, that those who live like this will not inherit the kingdom of God.

© 2013 by R. Gino Santa Maria. Used under license of Shutterstock, Inc.

Jesus gave us the perfect example of what it means to show love and goodness to others when He washed His disciples' feet (Read John 13 in the New Testament.).

But the fruit of the Spirit is love, joy, peace, forbearance, kindness, goodness, faithfulness, gentleness and self-control. Against such things there is no law. Those who belong to Christ Jesus have crucified the flesh with its passions and desires. Since we live by the Spirit, let us keep in step with the Spirit. Let us not become conceited, provoking and envying each other. (NIV)

What do you pour into the lives of others? When faced with a trying situation, do you respond in the flesh or do you respond with the fruit of the Spirit? You may be thinking, "It depends on what kind of situation it is." That's a very honest response because we all have our buttons that when pushed bring us to a breaking point. It is human nature to respond in the flesh, especially when someone pushes those sensitive buttons, so it is critical that you cover yourself in prayer and fill yourself with the fruit of the Spirit.

Cheryl

Q: *What do you value in life?*

A: "I value many things in life. However, the top five of my values all revolve around my faith base and my family."

Bearing Fruit

Love

The first fruit of the Spirit mentioned in Galatians 5 is love. The *Merriam-Webster Dictionary* defines love as a "strong affection for another arising out of kinship or personal ties" *(Merriam-Webster.com*, 2013). Love, however, is so much more than a strong affection. In I John 4:8, we learn that God is love; love is forgiveness, acceptance, and sacrifice.

Corrie ten Boom's story serves as a profound example of a believer pouring out love into the lives of others. In her book, *The Hiding Place*, Corrie tells of her family's bravery when they hid people in their home during the Jewish Holocaust to help them escape Nazi cruelty. When the Nazis discovered the ten Boom's kindness, they raided the home and dragged the family and those in hiding away to concentration camps. Ultimately, Corrie and her sister Betsie were sent to Ravensbruck Death Camp in Germany. Betsie died there, but Corrie lived to tell their story.

After World War II, Corrie went around Germany speaking to people about the love of Jesus and His forgiveness. After one of her talks, a man approached her and told her that he was a guard at Ravensbruck. He thanked her for her message, stretched out his hand to shake hers, and asked for her forgiveness. Corrie remembered this man as one of the cruelest guards in the camp, and she wrestled with extending forgiveness to him. The outcome follows in her words:

> It was at a church service in Munich that I saw him, a former S.S. man who had stood guard at the shower room door in the processing center at Ravensbruck. He was the first of our actual jailers that I had seen since that time. And suddenly

Shannon Bream, Liberty alumna and American journalist for Fox News in her address to Liberty graduates at the 40th commencement ceremony

"In order for people to care about the message of God's love, they first have to believe that you—the messenger— care about them. Human beings have not only spiritual needs, but practical and physical needs too" (Menard, 2013).

it was all there—the roomful of mocking men, the heaps of clothing, Betsie's pain-blanched face.

He came up to me as the church was emptying, beaming and bowing. "How grateful I am for your message, Fraulein," he said. "To think that, as you say, He has washed my sins away!" His hand was thrust out to shake mine. And I, who had preached so often to the people in Bloemendaal the need to forgive, kept my hand at my side.

Even as the angry, vengeful thoughts boiled through me, I saw the sin of them. Jesus Christ had died for this man; was I going to ask for more? Lord Jesus, I prayed, forgive me and help me to forgive him. I tried to smile; I struggled to raise my hand. I could not. I felt nothing, not the slightest spark of warmth or charity. And so again I breathed a silent prayer. Jesus, I prayed, I cannot forgive him. Give me Your forgiveness.

As I took his hand the most incredible thing happened. From my shoulder along my arm and through my hand a current seemed to pass from me to him, while into my heart sprang a love for this stranger that almost overwhelmed me. And so I discovered that it is not on our forgiveness any more than on our goodness that the world's healing hinges, but on His. When He tells us to love our enemies, He gives, along with the command, the love itself (ten Boom, 1971).

When put to the ultimate test, Corrie ten Boom chose to pour out love into the life of her former persecutor. Her relationship with Jesus Christ made this impossible action a possibility.

Emily

Q: *What do you value in life?*

A: "I value relationships with people, whether they are with friends, family, or a significant other."

Personal Reflection

How have you extended love to those around you? How can you extend love to those around you who may not deserve it?

I believe love can look like encouragement and brightening those around me by pulling out of them their best. Esteeming others first.

Joy

Merriam-Webster defines joy as "a feeling of great happiness" (*Merriam-Webster.com*, 2013). Legendary evangelist, Billy Graham elaborates further, "Joy cannot be pursued. It comes from within. It is a state of being. It does not depend on circumstances, but triumphs over circumstances. It produces a gentleness of spirit and a magnetic personality" (Goodreads, Inc., 2014,

Billy Graham: Quotes). A beautiful Christian lady, who triumphed over her own circumstances and lives a life of joy, is Joni Eareckson Tada.

When Joni was 18 years old, she injured herself in a swimming accident in Chesapeake Bay, resulting in quadriplegia. Confined to a wheelchair, Joni fought feelings of anger and depression, but her faith in Jesus Christ and God's promise to give her a "hope and a future" (Jeremiah 29:11) helped her overcome her circumstances and approach life with joy. Joni began painting with a brush between her teeth. Today, she's an accomplished artist, author, speaker, and wife. She also founded Joni and Friends, an outreach designed to "advance disability ministry and changing the church and communities around the world" (Joni and Friends: International Disability Center, 2009–2014).

God has your future in the palm of His hand and has your best interests at heart. Regardless of your circumstances, He wants you to live in joy, just as Joni has, "Jesus went without comfort so that you might have it. He postponed joy so that you might share in it. He willingly chose isolation so that you might never be alone in your hurt and sorrow. He had no real fellowship so that fellowship might be yours, this moment. This alone is enough cause for great gratitude!" (Goodreads, Inc., 2014, *Joni Eareckson Tada: Quotes*).

Personal Reflection

~ What brings you joy in life? What circumstances do you find stunt your joy? How can you overcome those circumstances and embrace life with a joyful spirit?

Being with people and creating adventures.
Feelings of loneliness, having no one to count
on. Find people and create relationships

Peace

Catholic friar, St. Francis of Assisi, lived a life of peace, which according to Merriam-Webster is "a state of tranquility or quiet: as a freedom from civil disturbance . . . freedom from disquieting or oppressive thoughts or emotions . . . harmony in personal relations" (*Merriam-Webster.com*, 2013). Born into a well-to-do family, Francis abandoned a life of financial security and embraced a life of poverty, longing to live the way Christ lived. Men and women alike responded to the gospel message and Francis' way of life, which led to the establishment of the Franciscan Orders: the Friars Minor, Order of St. Clare, and the Third Order. Francis even braved the conflict of the Crusades in an effort to share the message of peace and Christ's love with Muslims in Egypt. He even managed to deliver this message of peace to the Sultan of Egypt, al-Kamil and earned his respect, giving "him permission (it is said) to visit the sacred places in the Holy Land" (Brady, I. C., OFM., 2014). St. Francis lived a life that bore many fruits, and his prayer invokes God's peace in all areas of life:

> Lord, make me an instrument of Thy peace;
> where there is hatred, let me sow love;
> where there is injury, pardon;
> where there is doubt, faith;
> where there is despair, hope;
> where there is darkness, light;
> and where there is sadness, joy.
>
> O Divine Master,
> grant that I may not so much seek to be consoled as to console;
> to be understood, as to understand;
> to be loved, as to love;
> for it is in giving that we receive,
> it is in pardoning that we are pardoned,
> and it is in dying that we are born to eternal life.
>
> Amen.
>
> (World Prayers Project, nd.)

Ruth

Q: *What do you value in life?*

A: "My children and family come second to God, being a testimony to them and loving them as God loves me."

Personal Reflection

Where do you find peace in times of conflict? How can you extend the peace of God to others?

I find peace in thankfulness.
Help them understand that they have
a friend.

Forbearance

The fruit of the Spirit, forbearance, is "the quality of someone who is patient and able to deal with a difficult person or situation without becoming angry" according to Merriam-Webster (*Merriam-Webster.com*, 2013). Forbearance means the same as the words patience, tolerance, and endurance. Dr. Martin

Luther King, Jr. is a prime example of a Christian who showed forbearance to others in the midst of dark circumstances, like the segregation in America before the Civil Rights Movement.

In the 1950s, King served as a Baptist minister. He spearheaded the Civil Rights Movement, which led to the Civil Rights Act of 1964 and the Voting Rights Act of 1965. He won the Nobel Peace Prize in 1964. In 1968, before King could see the full fruition of his dream of peace and equality, he was assassinated (The Biography Channel Website, 2014, *Martin Luther King, Jr.*).

King's "I Have a Dream" and "I've Been to the Mountaintop" speeches are iconic pieces of American history, inspiring and beautifully written and delivered, especially in the context of the cultural conflicts King faced. His words continue to inspire others today to endure through difficult times, "If you can't fly then run, if you can't run then walk, if you can't walk then crawl, but whatever you do you have to keep moving forward" (Goodreads, Inc., 2014, *Martin Luther King, Jr.: Quotes*).

Shannon Bream, Liberty alumna and American journalist for Fox News in her address to Liberty graduates at the 40th commencement ceremony

"Now is not the time to stand silently by as your most deeply held beliefs are being questioned in the public square. Speaking up is rarely easy when the world is actively waiting to discredit and misconstrue what you have to say—but we have Christ as our model" (Menard, 2013).

Personal Reflection

Who in your life tests your patience? How can you inspire them with your forbearance and endurance?

My family usually tests my patience and the people I interact with at work. Practice Patience.

UNDER CONSTRUCTION

Kindness

The definition of kindness is compassion for others. Bono, lead singer of U2, walks in compassion in his walk with Christ. In his own words, he explains compassion and Christianity, "To me, a faith in Jesus Christ that is not aligned with the poor . . . it's nothing" (Hardaway. J.E. and Epictrek.com, 2009). Bono aligns himself with the poor, hurting, and hungry as a humanitarian and activist raising awareness and funds for disease prevention and education through relief concerts and organizations, such as RED, ONE, and EDUN (TED Conferences LLC., 2014). His passion and compassion for others is seen in his actions and through his words, as he encourages others to extend compassion, "God is in the slums, in the cardboard boxes where the poor play house. God is in the silence of a mother who has infected her child with a virus that will end both their lives. God is in the cries heard under the rubble of war. God is in the debris of wasted opportunity and lives, and God is with us if we are with them" (Compassion International, Inc., 2014).

Personal Reflection

How have you shown compassion to those around you who are hurting? How can you extend kindness to others?

I extend kindness but not always in the form of meeting someone's need.

Goodness

Goodness is the fruit of ministry. Catholic nun and missionary, Mother Teresa, led a life full of ministry, as she reached out to the people in the slums of Calcutta (Kolkata), West Bengal, India. Originally a teacher and principal at St. Mary's School for Girls in Calcutta, Mother Teresa felt the Lord Jesus calling her to a life of ministry to the poorest of the poor. She founded the Missionaries of Charity Sisters to work toward this end, "Let us touch the dying, the poor, the lonely and the unwanted according to the graces we have received and let us not be ashamed or slow to do the humble work" (Brainy Quote, 2014). Mother Teresa established a school, "a leper colony, an orphanage, a nursing home, a family clinic and a string of mobile health clinics" (The Biography Channel Website, 2014, *Mother Teresa*) to care for the "dying, the poor, the lonely, and the unwanted." She traveled across the globe extending care and developing ministries for those in dire need. In 1979, she received the Nobel Peace Prize for her humanitarian efforts, which she continued until her death in 1997.

Personal Reflection

What ministry work do you do? In what ministries would you like to get involved? How does/could your investment in ministries bless the lives of others?

I would like to get involved in a ministry associated with girls and young women.

Faithfulness

Merriam-Webster explains that faithfulness is "having or showing true and constant support or loyalty; deserving trust; keeping your promises or doing what you are supposed to do" (*Merriam-Webster.com*, 2013). Known for his classic devotional work, *My Utmost for His Highest*, Oswald Chambers never knew fame during his lifetime, though he had published a few works. While studying the arts at the University of Edinburgh, he felt called to pursue ministry studies. During his lifetime, he served the Lord faithfully as a teacher, a speaker, and a chaplain during World War I. He died at the young age of 43, resulting from complications of an emergency appendectomy (McCasland, Ed., 2014). About faithfulness and integrity Chambers said, "It is a great thing to see physical courage, and greater still to see moral courage, but the greatest to see of all is spiritual courage; oh, to see a person who will stand true to the integrity of Jesus Christ no matter what he or she goes through!" (Joni and Friends: International Disability Center, 2009–2014).

Personal Reflection

In what areas of your life have you been faithful? How might the people in your life benefit from your faithfulness in all circumstances?

I have been faithful in being true and honest with myself and those around me. The benefits others receive is honesty and truth.

Self-Control

The final fruit of the Spirit is self-control. Self-control is "restraint exercised over one's own impulses, emotions, or desires" according to Merriam-Webster (*Merriam-Webster.com*, 2013). Francis A. Schaeffer was a noted author, philosopher, theologian, apologist, and missionary to Switzerland. While he and his wife, Edith, served as missionaries, they began a ministry called L'Abri, which means "The Shelter." Francis and Edith invited people to take shelter in their Swiss chalet. At L'Abri, the Schaeffers gathered together with their guests, offering them food and conversation, specifically to find answers to their questions about philosophy, theology, and other relevant topics of concern.

Opening up their home to strangers was an adventure that required restraint over their own reactions, especially when people took advantage of their hospitality. Schaeffer explained, "In about the first three years of L'Abri all our wedding presents were wiped out. Our sheets were torn. Holes were burned in our rugs. Indeed once a whole curtain almost burned up from somebody smoking in our living room . . . drugs came into our place. People vomited in our rooms" (Christianbook.com, LLC., 2014). These challenges did not deter the Schaeffer's; they continued to welcome people into their home and ministry. As a result, the L'Abri ministry grew and exists internationally today. In his book *Art and the Bible,* Schaeffer explains what it means to have self-control through any circumstance, "When a man comes under the blood of Christ, his whole capacity as a man is refashioned. His soul is saved, yes, but so are his mind and his body. True spirituality means the lordship of Christ over the total man" (Goodreads, Inc., 2014, *Francis August Schaeffer: Quotes*).

Personal Reflection

In what way(s) have you exercised self-control in your life? What areas of your life require self-control? How can the people in your life (your family and friends) benefit from your ability to show restraint in your reactions to things that upset you?

I have self-control in my eating habits
and physical health habits
They will only benefit if they apply
the same Practices.

Biblical Worldview: Implementation

Approaching the world through the lens of the Bible's truth can change your life and the lives of those around you remarkably. In order to generate this change, you must first know Jesus Christ as the Lord and Savior of your life (for more information about making this decision, see "Our Altitude and Our Salvation" in the Final Cornerstone of this text). You must also remember to use scripture to filter all that your mind takes in and remember to pray for discernment through the process. Additionally, find little ways that you can show love, joy, peace, forbearance, kindness, goodness, faithfulness, and self-control to others in your life, for in doing so, you will also be sharing those fruits with Jesus, just as the scripture states, "The King will reply, 'Truly I tell you, whatever you did for one of the least of these brothers and sisters of mine, you did for me'" (Matthew 25:40, NIV).

BUILDING BLOCKS

As you look back on your decision to begin online education with Liberty University, what factors did you consider? Were you looking forward to the final outcome or considering the milestones of personal growth along the way? Did you consider the investment of time, money, and family resources, and weigh them against the long-term benefits? Perhaps you looked at how you would work out the details of tuition and financial aid, books and course offerings.

Dr. Falwell often described his "BHAGs," or big, hairy, audacious goals. He felt that God was leading him, and he simply pursued the path laid out ahead of him. Those goals were ones that he never swerved from, once they were crystallized, and he was galvanized into action to pursue them. Reviewing what you read in this chapter about the founding of what would become Liberty University, would you expect what you see when you evaluate the school today? Many people have big dreams, but few live out the accomplishments that Dr. Falwell was able to realize. Thinking about where you are in life, do you have audacious goals? Are you sensitive to God's leading in your life?

Liberty University does not have a hundred-plus year history like many of the prestigious universities around the United States or around the world. This university has developed only since 1971. That is a relatively brief period for such incredible growth, but God has had His hand on our university. We know that many students come to Liberty University *because* they want an education that is distinctively Christian. We also understand that some students come to us despite the fact that we are founded and guided by God's design and direction. What worldview guides your thinking? It may be that you have never considered this before, but we believe you are learning here with us as part of God's design.

On what foundations have you built your life to date? Read the following verse. Psalm 19:14 "Let the words of my mouth, and the meditation of my heart, be acceptable in thy sight, O Lord, my strength, and my redeemer" (KJV). Is this a verse that you can pray?

In the New Testament book of Romans, we read in 12:2, "Do not conform to the pattern of this world, but be transformed by the renewing of your mind. Then you will be able to test and approve what God's will is—his good, pleasing, and perfect will" (NIV). If we are pursuing God's will, described in that verse as "good" and "perfect," we will not necessarily be doing things that others expect. Just as Dr. Falwell frequently found himself outside of the expectations of others, what differences might that bring to your life? How will that influence your work as a college student?

Personal Reflection

Read the story of Joshua at the Battle of Jericho in Joshua 6:2-20. What evidence can you see of the Israelite's dependence on God to achieve what might be described as a "big, hairy, audacious goal"?

They were clueless on what they were doing. All they had was to put their trust in what God was saying and the history of His absurd requests and his faithfulness to fulfilling them.

TOOL BOX

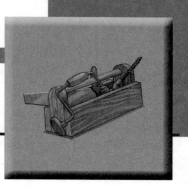

More about Liberty

- **About Liberty**—Only so much can be summed up in a single chapter, especially when you are talking about a campus where so much is continuously happening. To learn more about Liberty University and to keep up-to-date with the latest happenings, check out these resources (www. liberty.edu/aboutliberty/).

- **Social Media**—Keep up-to-date with all of the latest happenings at Liberty by liking us on Facebook, following us on Twitter, or connecting through a number of other social media outlets.

- **The Liberty Journal**—Liberty University's official journal, published each semester. As a student you can subscribe for free print copies or read online (www.liberty.edu/libertyjournal/).

- **Athletics Department**—Become a fan of your university's sports teams. Follow football, soccer, swimming, or tour the various athletic facilities on campus (www.liberty.edu/flames/).

- **LU Quick Facts**—Check out the latest statistics about Liberty (www. liberty.edu/index.cfm?PID = 6925).

- **Then & Now**—Browse through a library of photos showing how the campus looked in the beginning and how it looks now (www.liberty.edu/ index.cfm?PID = 22854).

- **Story of the Mountain**—View an interactive timeline of Liberty University that takes you from 1971 until present day (www.liberty.edu/aboutliberty/index.cfm?PID = 25314).

Student Resources

- **Blackboard Tutorials**—The Center for Curriculum Development continuously develops new tutorials aimed at helping students navigate the Blackboard learning management system where all of Liberty's courses are housed (www.liberty.edu/academics/cafe/?PID = 20252).

- **Information Technology**—Liberty's IT department works continuously to maintain all of the technology with which students interface, and also offers additional services. Through the IT department you can access a personal help desk agent to troubleshoot problems with your computer, search for self-help topics on things like how to set up email on your smart phone, and even shop a virtual storefront where Liberty students can buy computers and software at significantly reduced prices (www. liberty.edu/index.cfm?PID = 180).

- **Academic Advising**—Liberty University employs an army of highly trained academic advisors to assist and guide you through your academic journey. You can reach an advisor by email, chat, or even a personal phone call (www.liberty.edu/online/academic-advisors/).

Additional resources, and links to specific sites, worksheets, and apps can be located by accessing the Breaking Ground website:

www.breakinggroundlu.com

References

Bible, M. (2009). *Championing the vision: Jonathan Falwell leads TRBC into its second generation.* Retrieved from http://www.liberty.edu/libertyjournal/index.cfm?PID = 15758&section = 3&artid = 736.

Bible, M. & Liberty University News Service. (2012). *Liberty University honors founder Dr. Jerry Falwell at library groundbreaking.* Retrieved from http://www.liberty.edu/index.cfm?PID = 18495&MID = 49773

The Biography Channel Website. (2014). *Martin Luther King, Jr.* Retrieved from http://www.biography.com/people/martin-luther-king-jr-9365086.

The Biography Channel website. (2014). *Mother Teresa.* Retrieved from http://www.biography.com/people/mother-teresa-9504160?page = 1.

Brady, I. C., OFM. (2014). *The Franciscan rule.* Retrieved from http://www.britannica.com/EBchecked/topic/216793/Saint-Francis-of-Assisi/2421/The-Franciscan-rule.

Brainy Quote. (2014). *Mother Teresa quotes.* Retrieved from http://www.brainyquote.com/quotes/authors/m/mother_teresa.html#fTYUl2gKCrXZStIe.99.

Christianbook.com, LLC. (2014). *Meet Francis Schaeffer.* Retrieved from http://www.christianbook.com/html/authors/581.html.

Compassion International, Inc. (2014). *Famous quotes about children.* Retrieved from http://www.compassion.com/child-advocacy/find-your-voice/famous-quotes/.

Faithfulness. (n.d.). In *Merriam-Webster.com.* Retrieved from http://www.merriam-webster.com/dictionary/faithfulness.

Falwell, J. (1997). *Falwell: An autobiography.* Lynchburg, VA: Liberty House Publishers.

Falwell, J. (2007). *Liberty University Commencement address.* Liberty University, Lynchburg, VA.

Falwell, J. (2014). *Press quotes.* Retrieved from http://www.liberty.edu/aboutliberty/index.cfm?PID = 26726.

Falwell, J. & Godwin, R. (2014). *Message from the president and the provost.* Retrieved from http://www.liberty.edu/index.cfm?PID = 27045.

Falwell, M. (2008). *Jerry Falwell: His life and legacy.* New York, NY: Howard Books.

Forbearance. (n.d.). In *Merriam-Webster.com.* Retrieved from http://www.merriam-webster.com/dictionary/forbearance.

Fralik, M. (2011). *College and career success.* Dubuque, IA: Kendall Hunt Publishing Company.

Goodreads, Inc. (2014). *Billy Graham: Quotes.* Retrieved from http://www.goodreads.com/author/quotes/40328.Billy_Graham?page = 2.

Goodreads, Inc. (2014). *Francis August Schaeffer: Quotes.* Retrieved from http://www.goodreads.com/author/quotes/601678.Francis_A_Schaeffer?page = 2.

Goodreads, Inc. (2014). *Joni Eareckson Tada: Quotes.* Retrieved from http://www.goodreads.com/author/quotes/3715.Joni_Eareckson_Tada.

Goodreads, Inc. (2014). *Martin Luther King, Jr.: Quotes.* Retrieved from http://www.goodreads.com/author/quotes/23924.Martin_Luther_King_Jr.

Hardaway. J.E. and Epictrek.com. (2009). *Quotes: Bono.* Retrieved from http://epictrek.com/Epictrek/BonoQuotes.html.

Joni and Friends: International Disability Center. (2009–2014). About us. Retrieved from http://www.joniandfriends.org/about-us/.

Joni and Friends: International Disability Center. (2009–2014). Joni's favorite quotes. Retrieved from http://www.joniandfriends.org/jonis-corner/jonis-favorite-quotes/.

Joy. (n.d.). In *Merriam-Webster.com*. Retrieved from http://www.merriam-webster.com/dictionary/joy.

Lewis, C.S. (1980). Is Theology poetry? In Lewis, C.S., *The Weight of Glory*. New York, NY: Harper Collins.

Liberty University. (2014). *About Liberty*. Retrieved from http://www.liberty.edu/aboutliberty/

Liberty University. (2014). *Doctrinal statement*. Retrieved from http://www.liberty.edu/index.cfm?PID = 6907.

Liberty University. (2014). *Then and now photo gallery*. Retrieved from http://www.liberty.edu/index.cfm?PID = 22854

Liberty University Board of Trustees. (2010). *Mission statement*. Retrieved from http://www.liberty.edu/aboutliberty/index.cfm?PID = 6899.

Liberty University News Service. (2014). *Chancellor Falwell announces Towns will step down for sabbatical*. Retrieved from http://www.liberty.edu/news/index.cfm?PID = 18495&MID = 97080.

Love. (n.d.). In *Merriam-Webster.com*. Retrieved from http://www.merriam-webster.com/dictionary/love.

McCasland, D. (Ed.). (2014). *Oswald Chambers' bio*. Retrieved from http://utmost.org/oswald-chambers-bio/.

McKay, Dominique. (2009). *Dr. Elmer Towns speaks at convocation*. Retrieved from http://www.liberty.edu/news/index.cfm?PID = 18495&MID = 5840.

Menard, D. (2013). *40th Commencement: Celebrating historic accomplishments, continuous growth*. Retrieved from http://www.liberty.edu/aboutliberty/index.cfm?PID = 24995&MID = 91512.

Menard, D. (2012). *From vision to reality*. Retrieved from http://www.liberty.edu/libertyjournal/index.cfm?PID = 24995&MID = 56752.

Menard, D & Liberty University News Service. (2012). *Liberty Online now 80,000 strong*. Retrieved from http://www.liberty.edu/news/index.cfm?PID = 18495&MID = 56836.

Peace. (n.d.). In *Merriam-Webster.com*. Retrieved from http://www.merriam-webster.com/dictionary/peace.

Self-Control. (n.d.). In *Merriam-Webster.com*. Retrieved from http://www.merriam-webster.com/dictionary/self-control.

TED Conferences LLC. (2014). *Speakers Bono: Musician, activist*. Retrieved from http://www.ted.com/speakers/bono.html.

Woolfolk, A. (2012). *Vol's Pat reaches the summit*. Retrieved from http://www.liberty.edu/champion/2012/04/editorial-vols-pat-reaches-the-summitt/

World Prayers Project. (nd). *Title of document*. Retrieved from http://www.worldprayers.org/archive/prayers/invocations/lord_make_me_an_instrument.html.

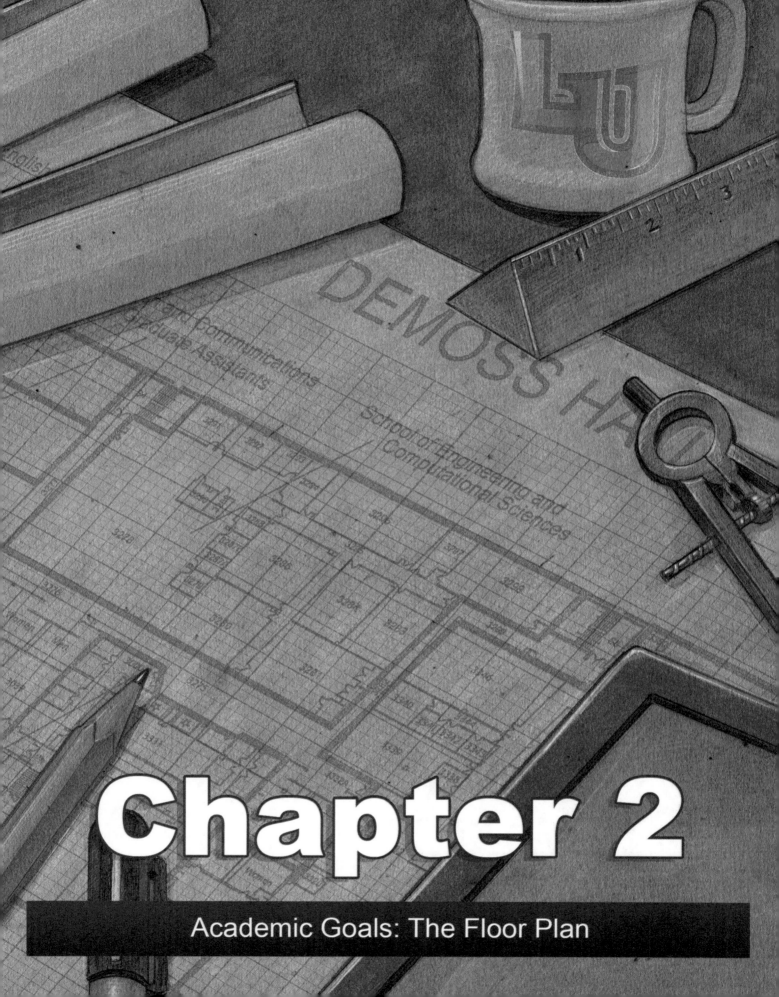

Chapter 2

Academic Goals: The Floor Plan

In this chapter, you will:

- Define success.
- Establish educational goals.
- Assess your self-awareness.
- Identify areas of motivation.
- Strategize motivation maintenance.
- Determine valuable, goal-setting character traits.

THE FLOOR PLANS

Establishing educational goals is a critical step to college success. Much like designing the floor plans of a new home, goal setting must take place during the beginning stages. With an established floor plan, a contractor has the ability to begin the building process, taking into consideration the homeowner's preferences for the location and size of every room, window, door, and closet. As you begin your academic career, determine worthwhile goals and draft a realistic plan toward completion of each goal.

© 2013 by Imagewell. Used under license of Shutterstock, Inc.

Jeremiah 29:11,
"For I know the plans I have for you," declares the Lord, "plans to prosper you and not to harm you, plans to give you hope and a future" (NIV).

THE CORNERSTONE

Psalms 37:4, "Take delight in the Lord, and He will give you the desires of your heart" (NIV).

Dr. Falwell, founder of Liberty University, used to tell his students they needed to choose a BHAG for their lives, a Big Hairy Audacious Goal. My mom attended Liberty University in 1971 when it was called Lynchburg Bible College. She learned, very quickly, the merit in Dr. Falwell's BHAG message, and when she became a mother, she extended that message to her children as well.

When my brother, John, and I were children, we watched the Wonderful World of Disney on Sunday nights with Mom and Dad. We did not watch a lot of television, so this was a real treat. John and I would camp out on the floor in front of the TV and eat a small bowl of freshly popped popcorn and drink a cold glass of orange juice (weird combination, I know, but it worked). Mom and Dad would join us for the feature presentation. I remember being so excited as Tinker Bell would fly to the top of Cinderella's Castle and set off the fireworks in the opening credits. Mom would say, "One of these days, kids, we're going to get you to Disney World. You can see that castle and Tinker Bell for yourself." John and I would smile, sip our orange juice, and take in yet another story, this time brought to life through the TV screen. For Mom, the promise of taking us to Disney World was a BHAG; it involved many years of planning and saving.

Finally, when I was a teenager, she took us to Disney World's Magic Kingdom. We rode Dumbo, Snow White's Scary Adventures, Peter Pan, and Mr. Toad's Wild Ride. We went on the Jungle Cruise and climbed the Swiss Family Robinson Tree House. We rode the Pirates of the Caribbean and visited the Enchanted Tikki Room. We braved the mountains: Splash Mountain, Big Thunder Mountain, and Space Mountain. As the close of the day drew near, we took in the wonder of Main Street USA and Cinderella's Castle, lit up brilliantly with twinkle lights. John and I anxiously awaited Tinker Bell's appearance in the distance, remembering Mom's promise that Tinker Bell would wave her wand and the fireworks would begin.

© 2013 by Gladskikh Tatiana. Used under license of Shutterstock, Inc.

What is your BHAG?

As we waited, however, Mom heard thunder in the distance. She panicked; all she could think about was getting us back to the car safely without risking our lives dodging thunderbolts in the vast parking lot. She ushered us quickly out of the park, and we missed Tinker Bell. It was not until we got on the ferry departing the Magic Kingdom that Mom realized the thunder she heard was actually just the fireworks show at EPCOT. We missed witnessing Tinker Bell light up the sky, and for my part, I began to doubt that the fairy even existed.

After that experience, we teased Mom over the years about Tinker Bell's flight, telling her that she must have imagined it from our nights of watching it happen on the Wonderful World of Disney when we were younger. Despite our taunts, she insisted that Tinker Bell really flew to the Castle and set off fireworks; we just missed it.

Nine years after our Disney trip, I was engaged to be married. When my fiancé (now husband), Terry, told me and my parents that he was taking me to Disney World for our honeymoon, Mom's response was, "Great! Now you can see Tinker Bell!" Knowing the story, Terry laughed; we all did.

Cut to the honeymoon—as Terry and I made our way down Main Street USA after a fun-filled day in the park, we grabbed some ice cream. With our delicious treat in hand, we walked toward the exit to beat the crowds to our bus. All of the sudden, Jiminy Cricket's voice echoed through the loud speaker announcing the fireworks show. We turned around just in time to see Tinker Bell, gleaming brightly and flying toward the highest turret of the Castle. Terry and I looked at each other, our eyes wide with wonder and amazement, glistening with tears.

My Mom had told us the truth over the years, and her BHAG was realized in that precious moment shared between a new husband and wife. It was almost 20 years in the making, yet she did not give up, much like the Parable of the Persistent Widow in Luke 18:1–8,

"Then Jesus told his disciples a parable to show them that they should always pray and not give up. He said: 'In a certain town there was a judge who neither feared God nor cared what people thought. And there was a widow in that town who kept coming to him with the plea, 'Grant me justice against my adversary.' For some time he refused. But finally he said to himself, 'Even though I don't fear God or care what people think, yet because this widow keeps bothering me, I will see that she gets justice, so that she won't eventually come and attack me!' And the Lord said, 'Listen to what the unjust judge says. And will not God bring about justice for his chosen ones, who cry out to him day and night? Will he keep putting them off? I tell you, he will see that they get justice, and quickly. . . .'" (NIV)

Just as the widow kept after the judge, Mom persisted in her playful vision for her children. Through taunts and disbelief, she was unshaken.

Dr. Falwell used to say, "You do not determine a man's greatness by his talent or wealth, as the world does, but rather by what it takes to discourage him" (Falwell, 1997, p. 43). What is your BHAG? Whatever it may be, whether it is academic, professional, spiritual, or personal, do not be discouraged; do not give up! In Psalms 37:4, you are promised, "Take delight in the Lord, and He will give you the desires of your heart" (NIV). Your persistence will pay off, and when it does, rejoice in the wonder and amazement of that precious moment.

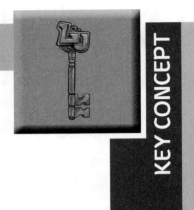

Define Success

Micah 6:8,
"He has shown you, O mortal, what is good.
And what does the Lord require of you?
To act justly and to love mercy
and to walk humbly with your God" (NIV).

Dr. Jerry Falwell, founder

"God never called anyone to be a quitter. The word 'retreat' should not be in the Christian's vocabulary. The only way is upward and onward for the Lord" (Falwell, 1997, p. 150).

Ruth

Q: *What is a favorite Bible verse that has kept you focused on your goals?*

A: Philippians 4:13, "I can do all things through Christ who strengthens me."

What Does Being "Successful" Mean to You?

"Achieving a desired outcome" is how success is commonly defined. The word success derives from the Latin root successus, meaning "to follow or come after" (as in the word succession). Thus, by definition, success involves an order or sequence of actions that lead to a desired outcome. The process starts with identifying an end (goal) and then finding a means (sequence of steps) to reach that goal (achieving success). Goal setting is the first step in the process of becoming successful because it gives you something specific to strive for and ensures that you start off in the right direction. Studies consistently show that setting goals is a more effective self-motivational strategy than simply telling yourself that you should try hard and do your best (Boekaerts, Pintrich, & Zeidner, 2000; Locke & Latham, 1990).

By setting goals, you show initiative—you initiate the process of gaining control of your future and taking charge of your life. When you take initiative, you demonstrate what psychologists call an internal locus of control: you believe that the locus (location or source) of control for events in your life is inside of you, rather than being external, or outside of you and beyond your control—for instance, determined by such factors as innate ability, luck, chance, or fate (Rotter, 1966; Carlson, Buskist, Heth, & Schmaltz, 2007). They believe that success is influenced more by attitude, effort, commitment, and preparation than by natural ability or inborn intelligence (Jernigan, 2004).

Research has revealed that individuals with a strong internal locus of control display the following characteristics:

1. Greater independence and self-direction (Van Overwalle, Mervielde, & De Schuyer, 1995);

2. More accurate self-assessment (Hashaw, Hammond, & Rogers, 1990);

3. Higher levels of learning and achievement (Wilhite, 1990); and

4. Better physical health (Maddi, 2002; Seligman, 1991).

An internal locus of control also contributes to the development of another positive trait that psychologists call self-efficacy—the belief that you have power to produce a positive effect on the outcomes of your life (Bandura, 1994). People with low self-efficacy tend to feel helpless, powerless, and passive; they allow things to happen to them rather than taking charge and making things happen for them. College students with a strong sense of self-efficacy believe they're in control of their educational success and can take control of their future, regardless of their past or current circumstances.

People with a strong sense of self-efficacy initiate action, exert effort, and sustain that effort until they reach their goals. If they encounter setbacks or bad breaks along the way, they don't give up or give in; they persevere or push on (Bandura, 1986; 1997). They don't have a false sense of entitlement— that they're entitled to or owed anything; they believe success is something that's earned and the harder they work at it, the more likely they are to get it.

Students with a strong sense of academic self-efficacy have been found to:

1. Put considerable effort into their studies;

2. Use active-learning strategies;

3. Capitalize on campus resources; and

4. Persist in the face of obstacles (Multon, Brown, & Lent, 1991; Zimmerman, 1995; 2000).

Students with a stronger sense of self-efficacy also possess a strong sense of personal responsibility. As the breakdown of the word responsible implies, they are "response" "able"—that is, they believe they are able to respond effectively to personal challenges, including academic challenges.

Dr. Elmer Towns, co-founder

"The real secret to Jerry's faith was that he refused to focus on the problem. He focused on Jesus" (Falwell, 2008, p. 88).

© 2013 by Greg Epperson. Used under license of Shutterstock, Inc.

People with a strong sense of self-efficacy initiate action, exert effort, and sustain that effort until they reach their goals.

Roger

Q: *What is a favorite Bible verse that has kept you focused on your goals?*

A: "My life verse has always helped me to focus on the greater organizer of my life. Philippians 1:6 says 'He who has begun a good work in you will bring it to completion till the day of Christ Jesus.' God started me out on this journey of faith years ago and he will finish the work he is doing in my life. I can rest in His good will and His timely direction."

Dr. Jerry Falwell

"It is my conviction that whatever is required to make a good Christian also makes a good citizen" (Falwell, 1997, p. 379).

For example, studies show that students who convert their college degrees into successful careers have two common characteristics: personal initiative and a positive attitude (Pope, 1990). They don't take a passive approach and assume good positions will fall into their laps; nor do they believe they are owed a position simply because they have a college degree or credential. Instead, they become actively involved in the job-hunting process and use various job-search strategies (Brown & Krane, 2000).

From *Thriving in College and Beyond,* 3/e by Joseph B. Cuseo, Aaron Thompson, Michele Campagna and Viki S. Fecas. Copyright © 2013 by Kendall Hunt Publishing Company. Reprinted by permission.

Establish Educational Goals

> Proverbs 9:9–11,
> "Instruct the wise and they will be wiser still; teach the righteous and they will add to their learning. The fear of the Lord is the beginning of wisdom, and knowledge of the Holy One is understanding. For through wisdom your days will be many, and years will be added to your life" (NIV).

Strategies for Effective Goal Setting

Motivation begins with goal setting. Studies show that people who neglect to set and pursue life goals are prone to feelings of "life boredom" and a belief that their lives are meaningless (Bargdill, 2000). Goals may be classified into three general categories: long-range, mid-range, and short-range, depending on the length of time it takes to reach them and the order in which they are to be achieved. Short-range goals need to be completed before a mid-range goal can be reached, and mid-range goals must be reached before a long-range goal can be achieved. For example, if your long-range goal is a successful career, you must complete the courses required for a degree (mid-range goal) that will allow you entry into a career; to reach your mid-range goal of a college degree, you need to successfully complete the courses you're taking this term (short-range goal).

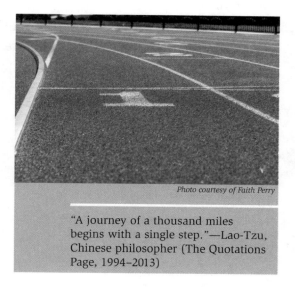

Photo courtesy of Faith Perry

"A journey of a thousand miles begins with a single step."—Lao-Tzu, Chinese philosopher (The Quotations Page, 1994–2013)

This process is called means-end analysis, which involves working backward from your long-range goal (the end) and identifying the order and timing of the mid-range and short-range subgoals (the means) that need to be taken to reach your long-range goal (Brooks, 2009; Newell & Simon, 1959).

Setting Long-Range Goals

Setting effective long-range goals involves a process that has two components: (1) self-awareness, or self-insight into who you are now, and (2) self-projection, or a vision of what you want to become. When you engage in both of these processes, you're able to see a connection between your short-range and long-range goals.

Cheryl

Q: How did you determine your goals for college study?

A: "My goals for college study revolved around my desire to understand people. However, I wanted my undergrad to be through a Christian filter."

Q: What goals did you set up for yourself when entering college?

A: "I had quite a gap between beginning college, and returning to complete my degree. My FIRST goals I set for myself upon returning to my undergrad, was to complete it. It was a HUGE goal for me, and I had to focus on one assignment, and one class . . . at a time."

Maddy

Q: *How did you determine your goals for college study? Did you begin with your goals set, or did they take shape as you made progress? How did you refine your goals?*

A: "When I graduated high school, I had goals set, but they've completely changed since that time. I've changed my major, and have even started pursuing hobbies that could develop into different careers. The refining of my goals has been a large amount of trial and error."

Dr. Elmer Towns

"You must go out and fulfill your dream. An idea is never yours until you write it down" (McKay, 2009).

Terry

Q: *How did you determine your goals for college study?*

A: "I started out with a large goal, to earn an upper level position at work. From this I developed a series of goals, or a roadmap, to reach that goal."

Q: *Did you begin with your goals set, or did they take shape as you made progress?*

A: "Some took shape as I got into the program and learned what I could handle and what was difficult for me."

Long-range goal setting enables you to take an approach to your future that is proactive—acting beforehand to anticipate and control your future life rather than putting it off and being forced to react to it without a plan. Research shows that people who neglect to set goals for themselves are more likely to experience boredom with life (Bargdill, 2000). Setting long-range goals and planning ahead also helps reduce feelings of anxiety about the future because when you give forethought to your future, you gain greater power to control it—i.e., you develop a stronger sense of self-efficacy. As the old saying goes, "To be forewarned is to be forearmed."

Remember that setting long-range goals and developing long-range plans doesn't mean you can't adjust or modify them. Your goals can undergo change as you change, develop skills, acquire knowledge, and discover new interests or talents. Finding yourself and discovering your path in life are among the primary purposes of a college education. Don't think that the process of setting long-range goals means you are locking yourself into a premature plan and reducing your options. Instead, long-range goal setting just gives you a map that provides you with some sense of direction about where you're going, which can also provide you with the ignition and motivation to get going.

From *Thriving in College and Beyond*, 3/e by Joseph B. Cuseo, Aaron Thompson, Michele Campagna and Viki S. Fecas. Copyright © 2013 by Kendall Hunt Publishing Company. Reprinted by permission.

Assess Your Self-Awareness

II Corinthians 4:15–18,

"All this is for your benefit, so that the grace that is reaching more and more people may cause thanksgiving to overflow to the glory of God. Therefore we do not lose heart. Though outwardly we are wasting away, yet inwardly we are being renewed day by day. For our light and momentary troubles are achieving for us an eternal glory that far outweighs them all. So we fix our eyes not on what is seen, but on what is unseen, since what is seen is temporary, but what is unseen is eternal" (NIV).

Steps in the Goal Setting Process

Effective goal setting involves a four-step sequence:

1. **Awareness of yourself.** Your personal interests, abilities and talents, and values;

2. **Awareness of your options.** The range of choices available to you;

3. **Awareness of the options that best fit you.** The goals that are most compatible with your personal abilities, interests, values, and needs;

4. **Awareness of the process.** The steps you need to take to reach your chosen goal.

Discussed in the next sections are strategies for taking each of these steps in the goal-setting process.

Emily

Share a realistic goal.

"Start studying for a test at least three days prior to a test."

Share an unrealistic goal.

"Being able to finish all your work for all your classes in one or two days is unrealistic."

Step 1. Self-Awareness

The goals you choose to pursue say a lot about who you are and what you want from life. Thus, self-awareness is a critical first step in the process of goal setting. You must know yourself before you can choose the goals you want to achieve. While this may seem obvious, self-awareness and self-discovery are often overlooked aspects of the goal-setting process. Deepening your self-awareness puts you in a better position to select and choose goals and to pursue a personal path that's true to who you are and what you want to become.

Alissa Keith

"Take charge/responsibility of your own education. No one cares more about your educational success than you; figure out now how you will complete your educational journey."

No one is in a better position to know who you are, and what you want to be, than you. One effective way to get to know yourself more deeply is through self-questioning. You can increase self-awareness by asking yourself questions that can stimulate your thinking about your inner qualities and priorities. Effective self-questioning launches you on an inward quest or journey to self-insight and self-discovery, which is the essential first step to effective goal setting. For example, if your long-range goal is career success, you can launch your voyage toward achieving this goal by asking yourself thought-provoking questions related to your personal:

- **Interests.** What you like to do;

- **Abilities and talents.** What you're good at doing; and

- **Values.** What you believe is worth doing.

The following questions are designed to sharpen your self-awareness with respect to your interests, abilities, and values. As you read each question, briefly note what thought or thoughts come to mind about yourself.

Your Personal Interests

1. What tends to grab your attention and hold it for long periods of time? *People (curiosity) interactions*

2. What sorts of things are you naturally curious about and tend to intrigue you? *how things work, How to better myself*

3. What do you enjoy and do as often as you possibly can? *read / go to coffee shops*

4. What do you look forward to or get excited about? *Relationships*

5. What are your favorite hobbies or pastimes? *Baking, Reading, working out*

6. When you're with friends, what do you tend to talk most about or spend most of your time doing? *Being together; discussing like and topics on our minds.*

7. What has been your most stimulating or enjoyable learning experience? *Going to school*

8. If you've had previous work or volunteer experience, what jobs or tasks did you find most enjoyable or stimulating? *working with kids, Leading, taking risks*

9. When time seems to fly by for you, what are you usually doing? *Working, being with loved ones, working out*

10. When you choose to read, what topics do you read about? *History, Christian literature, school books*

11. When you open a newspaper or log on to the Internet, where do you tend to go first? *Facebook / social media, research (self improvement)*

12. When you find yourself daydreaming or fantasizing about your future life, what's going on or what are you doing? *Married, working, interacting with clients, kids, housing (big)*

"Know thyself"

—Socrates

BREAKING GROUND

Personal Reflection

From your responses to the preceding questions, identify one long-range goal you could pursue that's compatible with your personal interests. In the space that follows, write down the goal and your interests that are compatible with it.

Working with clients/friends. One of my goals is to have a private practice with my family being my priority. I also want to maintain a healthy life physically, mentally, and spiritually.

Your Personal Abilities and Talents

1. What seems to come easily or naturally to you? *Solutions or answers for situations*

2. What would you say is your greatest personal strength or talent? *Bringing a realistic perspective to life*

3. What do you excel at when you apply yourself and put forth your best effort? *Anything*

4. What are your most advanced or well-developed skills? *Wisdom*

5. What would you say has been the greatest accomplishment or achievement in your life thus far? *Discovering and developing who I am*

6. As you reflect on your life, what are you most proud of, or what do you take the most pride in doing? *Going back to school*

7. Do others come to you for advice or assistance? If so, why do you think that is? (i.e. because I am a good listener I can keep a secret . . . etc.) *Because they know I will be straight with them*

8. What would your best friend or friends say is your best quality, trait, or characteristic? *Listening, being honest with them*

9. When you had a strong feeling of being successful after you had done something, what was it that you did? *Screamed, celebrated, shared my success.*

10. If you've received awards or other forms of recognition, what did you do to earn them? *I worked and put in time and effort*

11. In what types of learning tasks or activities have you experienced the most success? *working out.*

12. In what types of courses do you tend to earn the highest grades? *All N/A*

Tim

Share a realistic goal.

"A realistic goal for anyone in the military is to complete one course each term. It is possible to complete more, depending on your workload at work. However, one class per sub term is definitely doable."

Share an unrealistic goal.

"For military personnel, it is definitely not wise to take on a full 15 credit hour semester while on active duty. Doing so will stress the individual, and it will show in their course work."

Emily

Q: *How did you determine your goals for college study?*

A: "After finding out that my study habits were not benefiting me that's when I determined what would work. I was not allowing enough time for studying and preparation. So now I know that it is necessary to keep up with what all is due that month then plan which days to study for what and when to start working on an assignment so that I do not have to do it all the day it is due."

Personal Reflection

From your responses to the preceding questions, identify a long-range goal you could pursue that's compatible with your personal abilities and talents. In the space that follows, write down the goal and your abilities and talents that are compatible with it.

Counseling. I listen well and am honest I bring answers and solutions to situations.

Your Personal Values

1. What matters most to you? *Being recognized*

2. If you were to single out one thing you stand for or believe in, what would it be? *Truth the way it is supposed to be*

3. What would you say are your highest priorities in life? *To achieve success and a name of recognition*

4. What makes you feel good about what you're doing when you're doing it? *Helping others. Studying*

5. If there were one thing in the world you could change, improve, or make a difference in, what would it be? *Empowering people to fully them.*

6. When you have extra spending money, what do you usually spend it on? *Bills, Shopping gifts*

7. When you have free time, what do you usually spend it on? *Internet surfing*

8. What does "making it big in life" mean to you? *Recognition, (socially) Having a family & wealth*

9. How would you define success? (What would it take for you to feel that you were successful?) *Debt paid off, being able to spend money w/o it effecting other circumstances*

10. How would you define happiness? (What would it take for you to feel happy?) *Being fully Myself.*

11. Do you have any heroes or anyone you admire, look up to, or believe has set an example worth following? If yes, who and why? *Cesar. He inspires me to be my best and Creates a desire to improve myself*

12. Which of the following four personal qualities would you want to be known for? Rank them in order of priority to you (1 = highest, 4 = lowest).

_2_ Smart   _4_ Creative

_3_ Wealthy   _1_ Caring

Personal Reflection

From your responses to the preceding questions, identify a long-range goal you could pursue that's compatible with your personal values. In the space that follows, write down the goal and your values that are compatible with it.

Recognition. This will happen starting with the people around me. I have to become fully myself. That includes physically, spiritually, & mentally. Put myself out there.

Step 2. Awareness of Your Options

The second critical step in the goal-setting process is to become aware of your options for long-range goals. For example, to effectively choose a career goal, you need to be aware of the career options available to you and have a realistic understanding of the types of work performance required by these careers. To gain this knowledge, you'll need to capitalize on available resources by doing the following:

1. Reading books about different careers

2. Taking career development courses

3. Interviewing people in different career fields

4. Observing (shadowing) people working in different careers

Joe Super

"If all you're getting out of the class is academic knowledge, you're missing out. As you go through the course, and as your education becomes a part of your life for a time, I hope you grow spirituality by learning more about perseverance."

Step 3. Awareness of Options That Best "Fit" You

A third key step in the goal-setting process is becoming aware of the full range of options available to you as potential goals. For instance, in college you have multiple courses and majors from which to choose. To deepen your awareness of whether a field may be a good fit for you, take a course in that field to test out how well it matches your interests, values, talents, and learning style. Ideally, you want to select a field that closely taps into, or builds on, your strongest skills and talents. Choosing a field that's compatible with your strongest abilities will enable you to master the skills required by that field more deeply and efficiently. You are also more likely to succeed or excel in a field that draws on your talents, and the success you experience will, in turn, strengthen your self-esteem, self-confidence, and drive to continue with it. You've probably heard of the proverb "If there's a will, there's a way"—when you're motivated, you're more likely to succeed. It's also true that "If there's a way, there's a will"—when you know how to do something well, you're more motivated to do it.

Step 4. Awareness of the Key Steps Needed to Reach Your Goal

This is the fourth and final step in an effective goal-setting process. For example, if you've set the goal of achieving a college degree in a particular major, you need to be aware of the courses you need to complete to reach that major. Similarly, with a career goal, you need to know what major or majors lead to that career; some careers may require a specific major, but many careers may be reached through a variety of different majors.

Personal Reflection

Think about a major you've chosen or are considering and answer the following questions:

1. Why are you considering this major? What led or caused you to become interested in this choice?

   Psychology: Crisis Counseling. Why? This is an area I can relate to personally. Led? I'm a great listener and what to share my story with those seeking help.

Terry

Share a realistic goal.

"I believe a realistic goal is moving up in my company."

Share an unrealistic goal.

"Owning that company, but I could certainly own my own company."

2. Would you say that your interest in this major is motivated primarily by intrinsic factors—i.e., factors "inside" of you, such as your personal abilities, interests, needs, and values? Or is your interest in the career motivated more heavily by extrinsic factors—i.e., factors "outside" of you, such as starting salary or meeting the expectations of parents?

Most definitely by intrinsic factors. I want to help and listen to people. People need each other and I can be there.

Cheryl

Q: *How did your goals change throughout your experience?*

A: "As I met goals, I would reevaluate myself, and create NEW goals, to constantly keep moving forward. That has been so VERY important to me throughout my educational path . . . to keep moving forward. I have often had large gaps of time when I struggled to keep moving forward, and not GIVE UP, because of circumstances. Instead, God taught me the amazing concept of His timing. Adaptation is also integral to my philosophy of moving forward. For example: looking at an obstacle, and not being able to go over it . . . so going around it, under it, or THROUGH it, instead."

The word motivation derives from the Latin word *movere*, meaning "to move." Success comes to those who overcome inertia—they first initiate momentum to start moving them toward their goal; then they maintain motivation until their goal is reached. Goal setting only creates the potential for success; it takes motivation to turn this potential into reality by converting intention into action. You can have the best-planned goals and all the knowledge, strategies, and skills to be successful, but if you don't have the will to succeed, there's no way you will succeed. Studies show that without a strong personal commitment to achieve a goal, that goal will be not be achieved, no matter how well designed the plan is to reach it (Locke, 2000; Locke & Latham, 1990).

Personal Reflection

The process of effective goal setting applies to more than just educational goals. It's a strategic process that can and should be applied to any goal you set for yourself in life, at any stage of your life. Take a few minutes to set some educational goals. What strategies can you use to achieve those goals?

Strategies: Study time, length of study time, getting rid of distractions, time on each assignment, knowing when assignment is due, planning assignment time, creating a calendar.

A SMART Method of Goal Setting

A popular mnemonic device for remembering the key components of a well-designed goal is the acronym "SMART" (Doran, 1981; Meyer, 2003).

A **SMART** goal is one that is:

Specific: States exactly what the goal is and what will be done to achieve it.

Example: I'll achieve at least a "B" average this term by spending 25 hours per week on my course work outside of class and by using the effective learning strategies described in this book. (As opposed to the non-specific goal, "I'm really going to work hard.")

Meaningful (and **M**easurable): A goal that really matters to the individual, for which progress can be steadily measured or tracked.

Example: I will achieve at least a "B" average this term because it will enable to me to get into a field that I really want to pursue as a career, and I will measure my progress toward this goal by keeping track of the grades I'm earning in all my courses throughout the term.

Actionable: Identifies the concrete actions or behaviors that will be engaged in to reach the goal.

Example: I will achieve at least a "B" average this term by (1) attending all classes, (2) taking detailed notes in all my classes, (3) completing all reading assignments before their due dates, and (4) avoiding cramming by studying in advance of all my major exams.

Realistic: A goal capable of being achieved or attained.

Example: Achieving a "B" average this term will be a realistic goal for me because my course load is manageable and I will not be working at my part-time job for more than 15 hours per week.

Timed: A goal that is broken down into a timeline that includes short-range, mid-range, and long-range steps.

Example: To achieve at least a "B" average this term, first I'll acquire the information I need to learn by taking complete notes in class and on my assigned readings (short-range step). Second, I'll study the information I've acquired from my notes and readings in short study sessions held in advance of major exams (mid-range step). Third, I'll hold a final review session for all information previously studied on the day before my exams, and after exams I'll review my test results as feedback to determine what I did well and what I need to do better in order to maintain at least a "B" average (long-range step).

Note: The strategy for setting SMART goals is a transferable process that can be applied to reaching goals in any aspect or dimension of your life, including health-related goals such as losing weight, social goals such as meeting new people, and fiscal goals such as saving money.

Strategize Motivation Maintenance

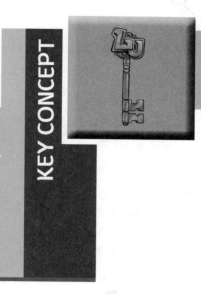

I Thessalonians 1:2–4,
"We always thank God for all of you and continually mention you in our prayers. We remember before our God and Father your work produced by faith, your labor prompted by love, and your endurance inspired by hope in our Lord Jesus Christ. For we know, brothers and sisters loved by God, that he has chosen you" (NIV).

Strategies for Maintaining Motivation and Progress toward Your Goals

Reaching your goals requires will and energy; it also requires skill and strategy. Listed here are strategies for maintaining your motivation and commitment to reaching your goals.

Visualize Reaching Your Long-Range Goal

Create mental images of being successful. For example, if your goal is to achieve a college degree, imagine a crowd of cheering family, friends, and faculty at your graduation. Visualize how you'll be able to cherish and carry this proud memory with you for the rest of your life, and how the benefits of a college degree will last your entire lifetime. Imagine yourself in the career that your college degree enabled you to enter. Visualize your typical workday going something like this: You wake up in the morning and hop out of bed enthusiastically, looking forward to your day at work. When you're at work, time flies by, and before you know it, the day's over. When you return to bed that night and look back on your day, you feel good about what you did and how well you did it.

Cheryl

Q: What is a favorite Bible verse that has kept you focused on your goals?

A: Romans 8:28, "And we know that in all things God works for the good of those who love him, who[a] have been called according to his purpose," (NIV). I have claimed this verse and the promises within, just about every single day. I often CLING to it . . . especially when things get REALLY rough in my life. This verse gives me hope for how things will work out.

Put Your Goals in Writing

When you put your goals in writing, you remain aware of them and remember them. This can stimulate your motivation to pursue your plan into action by serving almost like a written contract that holds you accountable to following through on your commitment. Place your written goals where

Alexandra Barnett

"Explain to your family your educational goals, expectations for study time, and how your education will benefit them. Let them know that you obtaining your degree is a team effort and you are counting on them to support you. Develop a plan that allows your family to celebrate your accomplishments with you."

Terry

Q: *Have you achieved the specific goals (educational, career, other) that you set in college?*

A: "Most of them, not all of them can happen at this point. I've completed my degree and while completing my degree was able to apply some of the information I learned directly to my job. This has helped me progress towards my other goal of achieving an upper level position."

Alexandra Barnett

"Continue to remind yourself that the next four years will pass either way. At the end of those four years you can either have the same level of education you have today, or you can have earned your Bachelor's degree!"

you see them regularly. Consider writing them on sticky notes and posting them in multiple places that you encounter on a daily basis (e.g., your laptop, refrigerator, and bathroom mirror). If you keep them constantly in sight, you'll keep them constantly in mind.

Map Out Your Goals

Lay out your goals in the form of a flowchart to show the steps you'll be taking to move from your short-range to mid-range to long-range goals. Visual diagrams can help you "see" where you want to go, enabling you to connect where you are now and where you want to be. Diagramming can also be energizing because it gives you a sneak preview of the finish line and a map-like overview of how to get there.

Keep a Record of Your Progress

Research indicates that the act of monitoring and recording progress toward goals can increase motivation to continue pursuing them (Locke & Latham, 2005; Matsui, Okada, & Inoshita, 1983). The act of keeping records of your progress probably increases your motivation by giving you frequent feedback on your progress and positive reinforcement for staying on track and moving toward your target (long-range goal) (Bandura & Cervone, 1983; Schunk, 1995). For example, mark your accomplishments in red on your calendar, or keep a journal of the goals you've reached; your entries will keep you motivated by supplying you with concrete evidence of your progress and commitment. You can also chart or graph your progress, which provides a powerful visual display of your upward trends and patterns. Keep the chart where you can see it on a daily basis so you can use it as an ongoing source of inspiration and motivation. You can add musical inspiration by playing a motivational song in your head to keep you going.

Develop a Skeletal Resume of Your Career Goals

Include your goals as separate sections or categories that will be fleshed out as you complete them. Your to-be-completed resume can provide a framework or blueprint for organizing, building, and tracking progress toward your goals. It can also serve as a visual reminder of the things you plan to accomplish and eventually showcase to potential employers. Furthermore, every time you look at your growing resume, you'll be reminded of your past accomplishments, which can energize and motivate you to reach your goals. As you fill in and build up your resume, you will see (literally) how much you have achieved, which boosts your self-confidence and motivation to continue achieving.

Reward Yourself for Making Steady Progress Toward Your Long-Range Goal

Reward is already built into reaching your long-range goal because it represents the end of your trip: it lands you at your desired destination. However, short- and mid-range goals may not be desirable ends in themselves; often, they are merely the means to a desirable end (your long-range goal). Consequently, you need to intentionally reward yourself for landing on these smaller stepping stones up the path to your long-range goal. When you complete these short- and mid-range goals, record and reward your accomplishments (e.g., celebrate your successful completion of midterms or finals by treating yourself to something you enjoy).

Like any other habit, the habit of perseverance and persistence through all intermediate steps needed to reach a long-range goal is more likely to continue if it's followed by a reward (positive reinforcement). The process of setting small goals, moving steadily toward them, and rewarding yourself for reaching them is a simple but powerful strategy. It helps you maintain motivation over the extended period needed to reach your long-range goal.

Capitalize on Available Resources That Can Help You Stay on Track and Moving Toward Your Goal

Research indicates that college success results from a combination of what students do for themselves (personal responsibility) and what students do to capitalize on resources available to them—i.e., their resourcefulness (Pascarella & Terenzini, 1991, 2005). Successful college students are resourceful students; they seek out and take advantage of college resources to help them reach their goals.

For example, a resourceful student who is having trouble deciding what field of study to pursue for a degree will seek assistance from an academic advisor. A resourceful student who is interested in a particular career but is unclear about the best educational path to take toward that career will use the Career Center as a resource.

Use Your Social Resources

Ask yourself, "Who can help me stick to my plan and complete the steps needed to reach my goal?" The power of social support groups for helping people achieve personal goals is well documented by research in various fields (Brissette, Cohen, & Seeman, 2000; Ewell, 1997). You can use the power of people by surrounding yourself with peers who are committed to successfully achieving their educational goals and by avoiding toxic people who are likely to poison your plans or dampen your dreams.

Terry

Q: *What is a favorite Bible verse that has kept you focused on your goals?*

A: Psalm 91

Whoever dwells in the shelter of the Most High will rest in the shadow of the Almighty.

[2] I will say of the LORD, "He is my refuge and my fortress, my God, in whom I trust."

[3] Surely he will save you from the fowler's snare and from the deadly pestilence.

[4] He will cover you with his feathers, and under his wings you will find refuge; his faithfulness will be your shield and rampart.

[5] You will not fear the terror of night, nor the arrow that flies by day,

[6] nor the pestilence that stalks in the darkness, nor the plague that destroys at midday.

[7] A thousand may fall at your side, ten thousand at your right hand, but it will not come near you.

[8] You will only observe with your eyes and see the punishment of the wicked.

[9] If you say, "The LORD is my refuge," and you make the Most High your dwelling,

[10] no harm will overtake you, no disaster will come near your tent.

[11] For he will command his angels concerning you to guard you in all your ways;

[12] they will lift you up in their hands, so that you will not strike your foot against a stone.

[13] You will tread on the lion and the cobra; you will trample the great lion and the serpent.

[14] "Because he loves me," says the LORD, "I will rescue him; I will protect him, for he acknowledges my name.

[15] He will call on me, and I will answer him; I will be with him in trouble, I will deliver him and honor him.

[16] With long life I will satisfy him and show him my salvation" (NIV).

Find Supportive, Motivated Friends and Make a Mutual Pact to Help Each Other Reach Your Respective Goals

This step could be taken to a more formal level by drawing up a "social contract" whereby you and your partner are "co-witnesses" or designated social-support agents, whose role is to help each other stay on track and moving toward long-range goals. Studies show that making a public commitment to a goal increases your commitment to it, probably because it becomes a matter of personal pride and integrity that's seen not only through your own eyes but also through the eyes of others (Hollenbeck, Williams, & Klein, 1989; Locke, 2000).

Convert Setbacks into Comebacks

The type of thoughts you have after experiencing a setback can affect your emotional reaction to the setback and the action you take in response to it. What you think about a poor performance (e.g., a poor test grade) can affect your emotional reaction to that grade and what action, or lack of action, you take to improve it. You can react to the poor grade by knocking yourself down with a putdown ("I'm a loser") or by building yourself back up with a positive pep talk ("I'm going to learn from my mistakes on this test and rebound with a stronger performance on the next one").

It's noteworthy that the root of the word failure is *fallere,* which means to "trip or fall," while the root word for success is *successus,* which means "to follow or come after." Thus, when we fail at something, it doesn't mean we've been defeated: it just means we've stumbled and fallen. Success can still be achieved after the fall by getting up, not giving up, and continuing to take the succession of steps, need to successfully reach our goal.

Personal Reflection

What would you say is the biggest setback or obstacle you've overcome in your life thus far? How did you overcome it? (What enabled you to get past it or prevented you from being blocked by it?)

Quiting school. I returned to school to continue my dreams. Motivation from my main squeeze

If a poor past performance is seen not as a personal failure, but as a learning opportunity, the setback may be turned into a comeback. Here are some notable people who turned early setbacks into successful comebacks:

- Louis Pasteur, famous bacteriologist, who failed his admission test to the University of Paris;

- Albert Einstein, Nobel Prize–winning physicist, who failed math in elementary school;

- Thomas Edison, prolific inventor, who was once expelled from school as "uneducable";

- Johnny Unitas, Hall of Fame football player, who was cut twice from professional football teams early in his career.

In response to their early setbacks, these successful professionals didn't become discouraged. Getting mad or sad about a setback is likely to make you stressed or depressed and leave you focused on a past event that you can no longer control. By reacting optimistically to a poor performance and using the results as feedback to improve your future performance, you can gain control of it. You can put yourself in the position to bounce back from the setback and turn a liability into an opportunity.

Maintain Positive Expectations

Just as your thoughts in reaction to something that's already taken place can affect your motivation, thoughts about what you expect to happen next can affect what will occur. Your expectations of things to come can be either positive or negative. For example, before a test you could think, "I'm poised, confident, and ready to do it." Or you could think, "I know I'm going to fail this test; I just know it."

Expectations can lead to what sociologists and psychologists have called a self-fulfilling prophecy—a positive or negative expectation leads you to act in a way that is consistent with your expectation, which, in turn, makes your expectation come true. For instance, if you expect to fail an exam ("What's the use? I'm going to fail anyway."), you're less likely to put as much effort into studying for the test. During the test, your negative expectation is likely to reduce your test confidence and elevate you test anxiety; for example, if you experience difficulty with the first item on a test, you may get anxious and begin to think you're going to have difficulty with all remaining items and flunk the entire exam. All of this negative thinking is likely to increase the probability that your expectation of doing poorly on the exam will become a reality.

Ruth

Q: *How did you determine your goals for college study?*

A: "Since it was later in life when I began to work on my college degree, it was for my personal satisfaction to earn the degree. Because of my past years as a Sunday school teacher, for my cognates, I chose Religion and Business because of my position at LU."

Cheryl

Q: *Did you begin with your goals set, or did they take shape as you made progress?*

A: "They definitely became clearer, as I progressed."

Q: *Have you achieved the specific goals (educational, career, and other) that you set in college?*

A: "Yes, and no. I have met some, then made new ones. Others, I have not quite completed as yet, and I continue to work towards them."

Personal Reflection

Would you consider yourself to be an optimist or a pessimist? In what situations are you more likely to think optimistically and pessimistically? Why?

Optimist. Usually I see the positive in most situations. I've always had a positive input and output in life. See the best in all situations. I am, however, beginning to be a pessimist towards people.

In contrast, positive expectations can lead to a positive self-fulfilling prophecy: If you expect to do well on an exam, you're more likely to demonstrate higher levels of effort, confidence, and concentration, all of which combine to increase the likelihood that you'll earn a higher test grade. Research shows that learning and practicing positive self-talk serves to promote hope—belief in one's ability to reach goals and the ability to actually reach them (Snyder, 1994).

Keep Your Eye on the Prize

Don't lose sight of the long-term consequences of your short-term choices and decisions. Long-range thinking is the key to reaching long-range goals. Unfortunately, humans are often more motivated by short-range thinking because it produces quicker results and more immediate gratification. It's more convenient and tempting to think in the short term ("I like it. I want it. I want it now."). Many years of research reveal that the later consequences follow a decision, the less likely people are to consider those consequences of their decisions (Ainslie, 1975; Elster & Lowenstein, 1992; Goldstein & Hogarth, 1997). For example, choosing to do what you feel like doing instead of doing work that needs to be done is why so many people procrastinate, and choosing to use a credit card to get something now instead of saving money to buy it later is why so many people pile up credit-card debt.

To be successful in the long run, you need to keep your focus on the big picture—your dream. At the same time, you need to focus on the details— the due dates, to-do lists, and day-to-day duties that require perspiration but keep you on track and going in the right direction.

Setting Meaningful Life Goals and Steadily Progressing Toward Them Require Two Focus Points

Tim, Active Duty Marine

One involves a narrow-focus lens that allows you to focus in on the details immediately in front of you. The other is a wide-angle lens that gives you a big-picture view of what's further ahead of you (your long-range goal). Success involves your ability to see and make connections between small, short-term chores and challenges (e.g., completing an assignment that's due next week) and the large, long-range picture (e.g., college graduation and a successful future). Thus, you need to switch back and forth from the wide-angle lens that gives you a vision of the bigger, more distant picture (your dream) to a narrow-focus lens that shifts your attention to completing the smaller tasks immediately ahead of you and keeping on the path to your dream.

From *Thriving in College and Beyond*, 3/e by Joseph B. Cuseo, Aaron Thompson, Michele Campagna and Viki S. Fecas. Copyright © 2013 by Kendall Hunt Publishing Company. Reprinted by permission.

Q: *How did you determine your goals for college study? Did you begin with your goals set, or did they take shape as you made progress? How did you refine your goals? Have you achieved the specific goals (educational, career, other) that you set in college? What goals did you set up for yourself when entering college? How did your goals change throughout your experience?*

A: "My personal goals for college study did not really take shape until I had actually participated in a few classes. My study habits are not necessarily the best simply because my schedule fluctuates so much. Therefore, I study whenever I get a chance and typically on a lot of weekends. My specific goal was to graduate quickly; however, because of work it has taken much longer than I expected. Therefore, my goal went from graduating quickly to simply completing one class each sub term or term. This has helped me to be able to complete my goal and I am now on track to graduate sooner than I expected."

Cari Smith: "Setting goals is important in all aspects of life. As you set your educational goals, think about the following questions: Why are you in school? What do you want to accomplish once you obtain your degree?

When do you plan to graduate? Write the goal down, share it with family and friends, and post it somewhere prominent as a reminder of your purpose.

Example: I am going to school to earn a business degree. This will afford me the opportunity to obtain a job in a major corporation. Having a good job will allow me to provide for my family's needs and even some of their wants. I plan to graduate in May 2015.

Example: I am returning to school to obtain my degree in nursing. This will give me the opportunity to have a career, once my children begin school fulltime. I think it will help me be a better role model to my children. I plan to graduate in December 2016.

Now that you have a target date, look at the courses you have yet to complete. How many classes will you need to take each term to graduate in May 2015? Is this still a feasible goal? If not, adjust your target graduation date. It is important to ensure that the goal you are setting is attainable. You want to set yourself up for success, not failure."

Determine Valuable, Goal-Setting Character Traits

Proverbs 1:5,
"Let the wise listen and add to their learning,
and let the discerning get guidance" (NIV).

The Importance of Personal Character

Reaching your goals depends on acquiring and using effective strategies, but it takes something more. Ultimately, success emerges from the inside out; it flows from positive qualities or attributes found within you, which, collectively, form your personal character.

Photo courtesy of Thomas Road Baptist Church.

"Nothing of eternal importance is ever accomplished apart from prayer."—Dr. Jerry Falwell

We become effective and successful human beings when our actions and deeds become a natural extension of who we are and how we live. At first, developing the habits associated with achieving success and leading a productive life may require substantial effort and intense concentration because these behaviors may be new to us. However, if these actions occur consistently enough, they're transformed into natural habits.

When you engage in effective habits regularly, they become virtues. A virtue may be defined as a characteristic or trait that is valued as good or admirable, and someone who possesses a collection of important virtues is said to be a person of character (Peterson & Seligman, 2004). There are three key character traits or virtues that typify highly motivated people:

1. Drive

2. Discipline

3. Determination

Drive

Drive is the force within you that supplies you with the energy needed to initiate action. Much like shifting into the drive gear is necessary to move your car forward, it takes personal drive to move forward and toward your goals. People with drive are not just dreamers: they are also doers. They take the action needed to convert their dreams into reality; they hustle—they go all out and give it their all, all of the time, to achieve their goals. College students with drive approach college with passion and enthusiasm. They don't hold back or work half-heartedly; they give 100 percent by putting their whole heart and soul into it. Studies show that individuals with dedication—who are deeply committed to what they do—are more likely to report that they are healthy and happy (Csikszentmihalyi, 1990; Maddi, 2002; Myers, 1993).

Discipline

Discipline includes such positive qualities as commitment, devotion, and dedication. These personal qualities enable us to keep going and continue moving toward our long-range goals over an extended period of time. Successful people think big but start small; they take all the small steps and diligently do all the little things that need to be done, which, in the long run, adds up to a big accomplishment—achievement of their long-range goal.

People who are self-disciplined accept the day-to-day sweat, toil, and perspiration needed to attain their long-term aspirations. They're willing to tolerate short-term strain or pain for long-term gain. They have the self-control and self-restraint needed to resist the impulse for instant gratification or the temptation to do what they feel like doing instead of what they need to do. They're willing to sacrifice their immediate needs and desires in the short run to do what is necessary to put them where they want to be in the long run.

Personal Reflection

Think about something that you do with drive, effort, and intensity. What thoughts, attitudes, and behaviors do you display when you do it? Do you see ways in which you could apply the same approach to achieving your goals in college?

Working out. Determination, persistence, Consitency, motivation, vision
All of these are needed for School.

Determination

People who are determined pursue their goals with a relentless tenacity. They have the fortitude to persist in the face of frustration and the resiliency to bounce back after setbacks. If they encounter something on the road to their goal that's hard to do, they work harder and longer to do it. When they encounter a major bump or barrier, they don't let it stand in their way by giving up or giving in; instead, they dig deeper and keep going.

People with determination are also more likely to seek out challenges. Research indicates that people who continue to pursue opportunities for personal growth and self-development throughout life are more likely to report feeling happy and healthy (Maddi, 2002; Myers, 1993). Rather than remaining stagnant and simply doing what's safe, secure, or easy, they stay hungry and display an ongoing commitment to personal growth and development; they keep striving and driving to be the best they can possibly be in all aspects of life.

Studies of highly successful people, whether they are scientists, musicians, writers, chess masters, or basketball stars, consistently show that achieving high levels of skill and success requires dedicated practice (Levitin, 2006). This is true even of people whose success is thought to be due to natural gifts or talents. For example, during the Beatles' first four years as a band and before they burst into musical stardom, they performed live an estimated 1,200 times, and many of these performances lasted five or more hours a night. They performed (practiced) for more hours during those first four years than most bands perform during their entire careers. Similarly, before Bill Gates became a computer software giant and creator of Microsoft, he logged almost 1,600 hours of computer time during one seven-month period alone, averaging eight hours a day, seven days a week (Gladwell, 2008). What these extraordinary success stories show is that success takes dedication to putting in the time and practice to be successful. Reaching long-range goals means making small steps; they aren't achieved in one quick, quantum leap; it requires patience, persistence, and practice.

In addition to drive, discipline, and determination, three other character traits or virtues typify successful people:

1. Wisdom

2. Integrity

3. Civility

President Jerry Falwell, Jr.

"The key is perseverance. Your ultimate success will be determined not by what it takes to knock you down, but by what it takes to keep you down" (Falwell, 2014).

Wisdom

You demonstrate wisdom when you use the knowledge you acquire to guide you toward becoming an effective and successful human being (Staudinger & Baltes, 1994). For instance, if you apply the knowledge you've acquired in this chapter about goal setting and motivation to guide your behavior in college and beyond, you are exhibiting wisdom.

Integrity

The word integrity comes from the same root as the word integrate, which captures a key characteristic of people with integrity: their outer selves are integrated or in harmony with their inner selves. "Outer-directed" people decide on their personal standards of conduct by looking outward to see what others are doing (Riesman, Glazer, & Denney, 2001). In contrast, individuals with integrity are "inner-directed"—their actions reflect their inner qualities and are guided by their consciences.

Dr. Jerry Falwell

"Faith is believing what God says in spite of the circumstances. Faith is simply taking God at His Word" (Falwell, 1997, p. 126).

People of character are not only wise, they're ethical. They don't pursue success at any ethical cost. They have a strong set of personal values that steer them in the right moral direction. Besides doing things effectively and successfully, they do what's good and right. For instance, college students with integrity don't cheat and then rationalize that their cheating is acceptable because "others are doing it." They don't look to other people to determine their goals and values, and they don't conform to the norm if the norm is wrong; instead, they look inward, use their consciences as their guides, and self-determine their goals.

Civility

People of character are personally and socially responsible. They model what it means to live in a civilized community by demonstrating civility— they respect the rights of other members of their community, including members of their college community. In exercising their own rights and freedoms, they don't step (or stomp) on the rights and freedoms of others. They treat other members of their community in a sensitive and courteous manner and are willing to confront others who violate the rights of their fellow citizens. They are model citizens whose actions visibly demonstrate to others that they oppose any attempt to disrespect or interfere with the rights of fellow members of their community.

BUILDING BLOCKS

Now that you know what to consider in setting goals, let's get to work! You will need to set both long-term goals, which will take many steps to accomplish, as well as short-term goals, which can contribute in small steps to achieving your long-term goals. First, though, think about this continuum:

wishes

dreams

goals

plans

actions

accomplishments

What dreams do you have for your future? How do you define the difference between a dream and a plan? What does the Bible have to say about making plans for the future? In Jeremiah 29:11, we read, "For I know the plans I have for you, plans to prosper and not to harm you, plan to give you a hope and a future." That is a pretty exciting verse, because God promises that He has a plan for each of us! Where do your thoughts for your life fall now? If you have made the commitment to online college education, you have at least wished for a college degree. You may have dreamed of walking across the stage to receive your diploma, along with a handshake, from a college official. Perhaps you have gone a step further in that continuum identified above . . . and you have set some goals. Do you notice, as you look from left to right on the continuum, the change from unrealistic and unsupported wishing and dreaming to possible goals, then on to realistic and supported accomplishments? You need to move from the wishing/dream state of "wouldn't it be magical if . . ." to "I am going to . . ." to "I am doing . . ." to "see my completed work." The steps of goal setting can help you set concrete plans to move forward to achieve them. The good news is you have already begun taking steps to achieve your dreams-to-goals of a college education.

Goal-setting can be divided into short-term and long-term goals. Your short-term goals, when achieved, can contribute to achievement of long-term goals. For example, you may set a goal to complete two core courses

Jerry Falwell

"What would you do for God, if you were sure you couldn't fail" (Miller, 2007).

Jerry Falwell

"If God's people will see nothing but the goal line, will accept nothing but victory, will pay any price, will suffer any hurt and hardship, will refuse to be discouraged or disheartened, we cannot help but win; because we are charged with the power of God's Holy Spirit" (Falwell, 1997, p. 236).

Jerry Falwell

"God has a vision for you. Don't settle for second best. Don't ever retire. Don't ever quit. Let your vision become an obsessive reality" (Falwell, 1997, p. 479).

in the fall for your major program. When you accomplish this goal, you are creating a building block toward a long-term goal of completing your degree. Sometimes, short-term goals can be accomplished quite quickly. (I intend to purchase a new computer this weekend, for example.)

What goals will you set for your educational career? Take a few minutes to flesh out some SMART goals on the next page.

Roger

Q: *Have you achieved the specific goals (educational, career, other) that you set in college?*

What goals did you set up for yourself when entering college?

How did your goals change throughout your experience?

A: "I have enjoyed the foresight of two college experiences, first as a 19 year-old in New York, and second as an experienced middle-aged adult. In the first college experience, I had no clear vision of what I wanted to do with my life. I felt that I would figure it out as I went along. As a result, I wasted a lot of time, effort, and money. The administration was less than helpful in describing what I needed for my major in order to graduate. In my last semester, the registrar told me that I still needed 15 liberal arts credits in order to finish my courses. I had enough credit hours but I didn't realize that music courses did not qualify for liberal arts credits. That resulted in spending more time and money in order to receive a diploma.

But here at Liberty University, I kept closely in touch with my academic advisors. Every course taken was purposeful and was in accordance to the degree plan. Every course was available every semester, so I didn't have to do any course juggling."

Goal #1: A Average this semester

S Maintain 'A' Average by dedicating 20 hours per week

M Better Chances for higher level of knowledge (lets me know I understand what I learn)

A 1) Reading, turning in assignments 2) Taking notes studying

R I only work part-time, Dedication

T 3) study to Achieve 'A' 4) Review Day of Exam 5) Re-examine what I missed (Better understand) Exams (3 days)

Goal #2: Graduate with Degree

S Walk across Stage with a degree in December 2017

M Early gradution. Continue to my Masters

A Take Summer courses (Take more courses throughout the year)

R Applying. Maintain Part time Job

T Ask an Academic Advisor. Prioritize my studies.

Goal #3: Job hunt for Psychology position

S Find a job that fits my values & look to open

M I want to work for myself, on my time My private practice.

A Learn what it looks like to have own Practice. Legally Finically

R Determination. Wisdom. Counsel

T 5) work for a practice 4) Build clientel 1) open own practice

You can repeat this process for your work life, your family life, and your spiritual/prayer life. Evaluate the goals you have made in the past in light of what you know about creating SMART goals, both long- and short-term. Does accomplishment of a goal in one area of your life contribute to accomplishments in other areas? Why or why not? How might you coordinate your goals for maximum effect?

Personal Reflection

What biblical guidance do you have for setting your goals? In the book of Genesis in the Bible, we read the account of God's creation of the Earth and all that live in it. The first chapter begins, "In the beginning, God created the heavens and the earth" (Genesis 1:1). On each of the six days of creation, God adds to what He has created, extending and developing the Earth from its initial formlessness and void. On closer examination, we can see that God goes about the process of creation in a very orderly way. Orderliness is one of God's characteristics. In the Bible, we learn to model ourselves on God's character. What do you see in yourself that can mirror God's orderliness? How can you apply that characteristic to your work as you attempt to begin well in online education?

Proverbs 3:15-16

Acknowledging all my ways unto God
Seeking His guidance and understanding
that it is for Him. Seeking the
bigger plan God has for my life
and knowing that His plan is
greatness.

TOOL BOX

Attaining Self-Awareness

Focus 2—The Liberty University Career Center has adopted the Focus 2 software to assist you in the process of assessing your interests, options, talents, and values. Liberty University students may register and use the tool for free. Once registered, you will work your way through a series of self-assessments, each designed to explore and expose different aspects of your interests, talents, and values. Upon completing the assessments, you will be able to explore a large database of degree and career options, each cross-referenced against your results in order to show you which are most compatible with your goals.

Establishing Goals

Programs at Liberty—Having explored which degrees may be best suited for your interests and talents, you can jump on the Liberty University website to review the different degree options available to you. With over 160 programs, you are sure to find something that piques your interest.

www.liberty.edu/admissions

Degree Completion Plan Audit—Once you have chosen a specific degree program, Liberty's Degree Completion Plan (DCP) Audit can help keep you on track. Your personal degree audit is located within your Liberty University account. Here you will be able to see where your transfer credits fit into your existing program, the courses you are currently enrolled in, as well as a listing of the courses you need to take in order to complete your program.

Course Guides—After you use the DCP Audit to determine which classes you need to take, you can use the Liberty University Course Guides to help you narrow down your exact choices for the next term. Each course guide offers you a look at the course syllabus, as well as the schedule of readings and assignments. This information is extremely valuable when you are trying to determine what your workload will be for the next term.

www.liberty.edu/online/course-guides

Course Sequencing—Each degree completion plan lists a suggested course sequence. Following this suggested order of classes will ensure that you are fully prepared for the next level of courses in your program.

Academic Advising—While Liberty University does everything possible to provide a comprehensive list of tools for the completely independent learner, there are always those who would prefer to speak with a live person when planning their next courses or making decisions that will affect their degree program. If you are that type of person, Liberty has a dedicated team of Academic Advisors to assist you. Advising is available by email, online chat, and by phone.

www.liberty.edu/online/academic-advisors

Staying Motivated

Aside from the plethora of tools that Liberty University has made available to help you set your goals, there are an even larger number of tools to help you stay motivated and achieve your goals.

Degree Completion Plan (DCP) Audit—Mentioned earlier, this tool will plug each course you take into your own custom degree plan. Watching your plan fill up as you near completion acts as a huge motivational tool.

Calendars—As calendars are available in both paper and electronic formats, these are a wonderful tool that any student can use to plot out short-term, mid-range, and long-term goals. Most electronic calendars will even sync across your devices, enabling you to keep close tabs on your progress.

Applications and Sites—Beyond the basic calendar, there are a vast array of goal-setting and motivational tools. Some of these are easily accessible checklists enabling you to map out the short-term steps toward a larger goal. As you check off the smaller items on your list, you see a nice visual representation of your progress. More aggressive applications will allow you to sign up for an account, set a series of goals, and then have your bank account charged a small fee if you happen to wander off course. You can review the Breaking Ground website for a listing of various applications and sites, along with brief descriptions.

Additional resources, and links to specific sites, worksheets, and apps can be located by accessing the Breaking Ground website:

www.breakinggroundlu.com

References

Ainslie, G. (1975). Specious reward: A behavioral theory of impulsiveness and impulse control. *Psychological Bulletin, 82,* 463–496.

Bandura, A. (1986). *Social foundations of thought and action: A social cognitive theory.* Englewood Cliffs, NJ: Prentice Hall.

Bandura, A. (1994). Self-efficacy. In V. S. Ramachaudran (Ed.), *Encyclopedia of human behavior* (vol. 4, pp. 71–81). New York, NY: Academic Press.

Bandura, A. (1997). *Self-efficacy: The exercise of control.* New York, NY: Freeman.

Bandura, A., & Cervone, D. (1983). Self-evaluative and self-efficacy mechanisms governing the motivational effects of goal systems. *Journal of Personality and Social Psychology, 45*(5), 1017–1028.

Boekaerts, M., Pintrich, P. R., & Zeidner, M. (2000). *Handbook of self-regulation.* San Diego, CA: Academic Press.

Brown, S. D., & Krane, N. E. R. (2000). Four (or five) sessions and a cloud of dust: Old assumptions and new observations about career counseling. In S. D. Brown & R. W. Lent (Eds.), *Handbook of counseling psychology* (3rd ed., pp. 740–766). New York, NY: Wiley.

Brooks, K. (2009). *You majored in what? Mapping your path from chaos to career.* New York, NY: Penguin.

Bargdill, R. W. (2000). A phenomenological investigation of being bored with life. *Psychological Reports, 86,* 493–494.

Brissette, I., Cohen, S., & Seeman, T. E. (2000). Measuring social integration and social networks. In S. Cohen, L. G. Underwood, & B. H. Gottlieb (Eds.), *Social support measurement and intervention* (pp. 53–85). New York, NY: Oxford University Press.

Carlson, N. R., Buskist, W., Heth, D. H., & Schmaltz, G. (2007). *Psychology: The science of behaviour* (4th ed.). Toronto, Canada: Pearson Education Canada.

Csikszentmihalyi, M. (1990). *Flow: The psychology of optimal experience.* New York, NY: Harper and Row.

Doran, G. T. (1981). There's a S.M.A.R.T. way to write management's goals and objectives. *Management Review, 70*(11), 35–36.

Elster, J., & Loewenstein, G. (Eds.). (1992). *Choice over time.* New York, NY: Russell Sage.

Ewell, P. T. (1997). Organizing for learning. *AAHE Bulletin, 50*(4), 3–6.

Falwell, J. (1997). *Falwell: An autobiography.* Lynchburg, VA: Liberty House Publishers.

Falwell, J. (2014). *Press quotes.* Retrieved from http://www.liberty.edu/about liberty/index.cfm?PID = 26726.

Falwell, M. (2008). *Jerry Falwell: His life and legacy.* New York, NY: Howard Books.

Jernigan, C. G. (2004). What do students expect to learn? The role of learner expectancies, beliefs, and attributions for success and failure in student motivation.

Current Issues in Education, 7(4). Retrieved January 16, 2012, from http://cie. ed.asu.edu/volume7/number4

Gladwell, M. (2008). *Outliers: The story of success.* New York, NY: Little, Brown.

Goldstein, W. M. & Hogarth, R. M. (Eds.). (1997). *Research on judgment and decision making.* Cambridge, UK: Cambridge University Press.

Hashaw, R. M., Hammond, C. J., & Rogers, P. H. (1990). Academic locus of control and the collegiate experience. *Research & Teaching in Developmental Education, 7*(1), 45–54.

Hollenbeck, J. R., Williams, C. R., & Klein, H. J. (1989). An empirical examination of the antecedents of commitment to difficult goals. *Journal of Applied Psychology, 74*(1), 18–23.

Levitin, D. J. (2006). *This is your brain on music: The science of a human obsession.* New York, NY: Dutton.

Locke, E. A. (2000). Motivation, cognition, and action: An analysis of studies of task goals and knowledge. *Applied Psychology: An International Review, 49,* 408–429.

Locke, E. A., & Latham, G. P. (1990). *A theory of goal setting and task performance.* Englewood Cliffs, NJ: Prentice Hall.

Locke, E.A., & Latham, G. P. (2005). Goal setting theory: Theory building by induction. In K. G. Smith & M. A. Mitt (Eds.), *Great minds in management: The process of theory development.* New York, NY: Oxford.

Maddi, S. R. (2002). The story of hardiness: Twenty years of theorizing, research, and practice. *Consulting Psychology Journal: Practice and Research, 54*(3), 175–185.

Matsui, T., Okada, A., & Inoshita, O. (1983). Mechanism of feedback affecting task performance. *Organizational Behavior and Human Performance, 31,* 114–122.

McKay, Dominique. (2009). *Dr. Elmer Towns speaks at convocation.* Retrieved from http://www.liberty.edu/news/index.cfm?PID = 18495&MID = 5840.

Meyer, P. J. (2003). *Attitude is everything: If you want to succeed above and beyond.* Waco, TX: Meyer Resource Group.

Miller, R. L. (2007). Farewell to my boss and friend, Dr. Jerry Falwell. *The Biblical evangelist, 38*(4). Retrieved from http://www.biblicalevangelist.org/index.php ?id = 539&issue = Volume + 38%2C + Number + 4

Multon, K. D., Brown, S. D., & Lent, R. W. (1991). Relation of self-efficacy beliefs to academic outcomes: A meta-analytic investigation. *Journal of Counseling Psychology, 38*(1), 30–38.

Myers, D. G. (1993). *The pursuit of happiness: Who is happy—and why?* New York, NY: Morrow.

Newell, A., & Simon, H. A. (1959). *The simulation of human thought.* Santa Monica, CA: Rand Corporation.

Pascarella, E. T., & Terenzini, P. (1991). *How college affects students: Findings and insights from twenty years of research.* San Francisco, CA: Jossey-Bass.

Pascarella, E. T., & Terenzini, P. (2005). *How college affects students: A third decade of research* (Vol. 2). San Francisco, CA: Jossey-Bass.

Peterson, C., & Seligman, M. E. P. (2004). *Character strengths and virtues: A handbook and classification*. New York, NY: Oxford University Press.

Riesman, D., Glazer, N., & Denney, R. (2001). *The lonely crowd: A study of the changing American character* (Rev. ed.). New Haven, CT: Yale University Press.

Rotter, J. (1966). Generalized expectancies for internal versus external controls of reinforcement. *Psychological Monographs: General and Applied, 80*(609), 1–28.

Schunk, D. H. (1995). Self-efficacy and education and instruction. In J. E. Maddux (Ed.), *Self-efficacy, adaptation, and adjustment: Theory, research, and application* (pp. 281–303). New York, NY: Plenum Press.

Seligman, M. E. P. (1991). *Learned optimism*. New York, NY: Knopf.

Snyder, C. R. (1994). *Psychology of hope: You can get from here to there*. New York, NY: Free Press.

Staudinger, U. M. (2008). A psychology of wisdom: History and recent developments. *Research in Human Development, 5*, 107–120.

Van Overwalle, F. I., Mervielde, I., & De Schuyer, J. (1995). Structural modeling of the relationships between attributional dimensions, emotions, and performance of college freshmen. *Cognition and Emotion, 9*(1), 59–85.

Wilhite, S. (1990). Self-efficacy, locus of control, self-assessment of memory ability, and student activities as predictors of college course achievement. *Journal of Educational Psychology, 82*(4), 696–700.

Zimmerman, B. J. (1995). Self-efficacy and educational development. In A. Bandura (Ed.), *Self-efficacy in changing societies*. New York, NY: Cambridge University Press.

Zimmerman, B. J. (2000). Self-efficacy: An essential motive to earn. *Contemporary Educational Psychology, 25*, 82–91.

Chapter 3

Time Management: The Blueprint

In this chapter, you will:

- Determine the necessity of time management.
- Set priorities and plan your use of time.
- Defeat distractions and procrastination.

THE BLUEPRINTS

Psalm 90:12, Teach us to number our days, that we may gain a heart of wisdom (NIV).

Blueprints are the guiding documents for any construction job. They provide a visible representation of the culmination of dreams, thoughts, and plans for a project. They are the springboard from which the work process can begin. Imagine trying to build a home with no plans . . . the result would not be very pleasing! Just as blueprints provide a guide for construction, time management is a careful plan for how to use time to build the life you have dreamed about and planned. Your work in college depends on committing a certain amount of your time to completing your assignments and then following through with that commitment to create your success.

© 2013 by STILLFX. Used under license of Shutterstock, Inc.

Jeremiah 29:11,
"For I know the plans I have for you," declares the Lord, "plans to prosper you and not to harm you, plans to give you hope and a future" (NIV).

THE CORNERSTONE

Ecclesiastes 3:1, "There is a time for everything, and a season for every activity under the heavens" (NIV).

As a teenager, I made many poor choices and saw my share of ridiculously scary movies. One such choice was the movie *Fallen*, starring Denzel Washington. It brought practicality and relevance to the Sunday school song, "Oh, be careful little eyes what you see! Oh, be careful little ears what you hear!" As the title suggests, the movie told the story of a demonic spirit, who took possession of humans and used them as vessels to carry out his serial killing agenda. The demon would pass from vessel to vessel, and the audience knew that the transfer had taken place, because the vessel would begin singing "Time is on my Side" by the Rolling Stones. This movie left me bug-eyed and sleepless with goose bumps and chills down my spine anytime I heard the haunting lyrics, "Time is on my side; yes, it is!" To this day, I still think of that movie whenever that Rolling Stones' song comes on the radio, but I celebrate in the truth that God holds every moment of time in His hand. Time is on *His* side, and He is on mine.

In Psalm 90, verses 1–4, it states,

> "Lord, you have been our dwelling place throughout all generations. Before the mountains were born or you brought forth the whole world, from everlasting to everlasting you are God. You turn people back to dust, saying, 'Return to dust, you mortals.' A thousand years in your sight are like a day that has just gone by, or like a watch in the night" (NIV).

Photo courtesy of Faith Perry

Time management puts you in the starting position to accomplish your goals and plans.

The Psalmist goes on to say in verse 12, ". . . Teach us to number our days, that we may gain a heart of wisdom" (NIV). In Ecclesiastes 3:1, we are told that "There is a time for everything, and a season for every activity under the heavens" (NIV). Since our days are numbered, and every purpose in our lives has an assigned time, managing our time wisely is crucial!

One day recently, I had my day planned down to the minute. I would leave my house one hour before I had to be at work, giving me enough time to drop my 9-month-old daughter off at the babysitter's house, drive to work, find a parking space, and walk to my meeting that afternoon. Right before I left my house, I received a call from the babysitter informing me that she could not watch my daughter because her children were sick. I called my mom, who eagerly volunteered to take on some grandbaby time. On my way to Mom's house, I got behind the *slowest* driver Amherst, VA, has ever seen and then encountered traffic due to construction. I waved and smiled at the construction workers holding signs telling me "Stop" and "Slow," but inside I just wanted to scream. I was going to be late to my meeting. I just knew it.

Finally, I made it to Mom's house. I practically threw the baby into Mom's arms, along with bags of baby food, changes of clothes, diapers, wipes, and toys. I quickly said my thanks and goodbyes and jumped in the car. Mom shouted, "Be careful," and I sped away, only to be stalled by construction—again.

I took a deep breath of relief as I merged into the lane of traffic, which meant I was only a mile away from work. Lo and behold, there was a wreck; no one was hurt, praise God! . . . but here I was facing another delay, police cars, glass on the pavement, and detours. Realizing I had little control over the matter, I prayed, "Lord, I know this is an unrealistic prayer, but please help me to be on time to this meeting. I budgeted down to the minute to make it, and every imaginable obstacle has come up! Looking at the clock, I know it is impossible, but nothing is impossible for You. Could you slow time down or something?" It was a selfish prayer, and I knew it.

When I got to work, I pulled into the first available parking spot I spied, ran into the building, up three flights of stairs, and entered the meeting room, breathless with *three minutes to spare*. It was a miracle. I mean it . . . God answered my prayer, my selfish, ridiculous, unrealistic prayer.

I budgeted my time wisely, but even with my time management efforts, hurdles came out of nowhere to interfere. Ecclesiastes 3:9–12 says,

> "What do workers gain from their toil? I have seen the burden God has laid on the human race. He has made everything beautiful in its time. He has also set eternity in the human heart; yet no one can fathom what God has done from beginning to end" (NIV).

God gave me a special gift that day by answering my prayer and rewarding my time management efforts, even though everything else seemed to rise up against me. Once again, He reminded me that He is on my side.

As you manage your time and plot out your daily activities and responsibilities, remember Galatians 6:9, "Let us not become weary in doing good, for at the proper time we will reap a harvest if we do not give up" (NIV). Even when it seems like everything is against you and causing interference, remember that God is on your side, and He will make "all things beautiful in its time" Ecc. 3:11 (NIV).

Determine the Necessity of Time Management

Ecc. 8:6,
"For there is a proper time and procedure for every matter" (NIV).

The Importance of Time Management

Reaching goals requires managing time because it takes time to successfully complete the series of steps that lead to accomplishing those goals. For **first-year**, new online college students, time management is especially essential for achieving goals because the beginning of college brings with it the challenge of adding college study to an already busy life. Many new online learners have full-time jobs, families, and a full life before registering to take college courses. The responsibilities of church, family, and work all require a commitment of time for success, and the same is true of college study. Some new college students impulsively respond to a desire for a college education, without first considering how college coursework will fit into an already busy life. **We take up the subject of time management here because this is a critical skill for college success.** This is particularly true for online learners, who must work with greater independence outside the traditional brick-and-mortar (residential) classroom. Students who opt for online learning can avoid the time spent in commuting, parking, and actually attending class in a lecture hall, but most agree that online learners must commit a nearly equivalent time for reading and study. Sometimes, it is easy to overlook this when considering an online program of study. Even for first-year students who have lived on their own for some time, managing time remains a crucial skill because they will be juggling multiple responsibilities, including school, family, and work.

In addition, the academic calendar and class scheduling patterns in college differ radically from high school. There's less "seat time" in class each week and more "free time" outside of class, which leaves you with a lot more personal time to manage. Your time is not as closely monitored by school authorities or family members, and you are expected to do more academic work on your own outside of class. Personal time-management skills grow in importance when one's time is less structured

Alissa Keith

"Everyone has time for the things that are important to them."

Cari Smith

"Each person has 24 hours in a day. It is what you do with your time that determines your success."

Dr. Jerry Falwell, founder

"God is always right on time. There are no panic buttons near the throne. The Holy Trinity has never gone into emergency session. Everything is under control and going according to plan" (Falwell, 1997, p. 408).

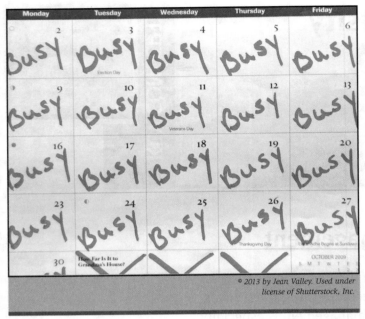

Monday	Tuesday	Wednesday	Thursday	Friday
2 Busy	3 Busy Election Day	4 Busy	5 Busy	6 Busy
9 Busy	10 Busy	11 Busy Veterans Day	12 Busy	13 Busy
16 Busy	17 Busy	18 Busy	19 Busy	20 Busy
23 Busy	24 Busy	25 Busy	26 Busy Thanksgiving Day	27 Busy
30	How Far Is It to Grandma's House?			OCTOBER 2009

Alexandra Barnett

"Are you a morning person or a night owl? Complete your schoolwork during the time of day when you are at your best. You can often complete as much work in 30 minutes during your "prime time," as you can in two hours when you are tired or unable to concentrate well."

Photo courtesy of Joel Coleman (Liberty University).

Liberty University prayer chapel seen in winter beauty.

and controlled by others, leaving the individual with more decision-making power about how to spend personal time. Thus, it's not surprising that research shows the ability to manage time effectively plays a crucial role in college success (Erickson, Peters, & Strommer, 2006).

Simply stated, college students who have difficulty managing their time have difficulty managing college. In one study, college sophomores who had an outstanding first year (both academically and personally) were compared to another group of sophomores who struggled during the prior year. Interviews conducted with these students revealed one key difference between the two groups. The sophomores who experienced a successful first year repeatedly brought up the topic of time during the interviews. The successful students said they had to think carefully about how they spent their time and that they needed to budget their time because it was a scarce resource. In contrast, the sophomores who experienced difficulty in their first year of college hardly talked about the topic of time during their interviews, even when they were specifically asked about it (Light, 2001).

Studies also indicate that managing time plays a pivotal role in the lives of working adults. Setting priorities and balancing multiple responsibilities (e.g., work and family) that compete for limited time and energy can be a stressful juggling act for people of all ages (Harriott & Ferrari, 1996). Thus, good time management serves as good stress management.

For these reasons, time management should be viewed not only as a college-success strategy, but also as a life-management and life-success skill. Studies show that people who manage their time well report they are more in control of their lives and are happier (Myers, 1993; 2000). In short, when you gain greater control of your time, you become more satisfied with your life.

Strategies for Managing Time

Effective time management involves three key mental processes:

1. **Analysis.** Breaking down time into specific segments and work into smaller tasks;

2. **Itemizing.** Identifying all key tasks that need to be done and by what dates;

3. **Prioritizing.** Organizing and attacking tasks in order of their importance.

The following steps can help you apply these skills to find more time in your schedule and use this time more productively.

1. **Break time down into smaller units to become more aware of how your time is being spent.** Have you ever asked yourself, "Where did all the time go?" or told yourself, "I just can't seem to find the time"? One way to find out where your time went is by taking a time inventory. Conduct a time analysis by tracking your time and recording what you do and when you do it. By mapping out how you spend time, you become more aware of how much total time you actually have and where it goes, including patches of wasted time during which you get little or nothing accomplished. You just need to do this time analysis for more than a week or two to see where your time is going and to get started on strategies for using your time more productively.

2. **Identify the key tasks you need to accomplish and when you need to accomplish them.** People make lists to be sure they don't forget items they need from the grocery store or people they want to be sure are invited to a party. You can use the same list-making strategy for work tasks, so that you don't forget to do them or forget to do them on time. Studies of effective people show that they are list makers; they write out lists not only for grocery items and wedding invitations, but also for things they want to accomplish each day (Covey, 2004).

Roger

Q: *Are you a good manager of time?*

A: "Time management is a learned skill. A person is not born managing time. I have never seen a baby wear a watch. One must continually work at managing time wisely. I can spend hours working on a paper while watching television or I can spend half that time completing my paper at the library desk. It's important to get away from distractions to complete work in a timely fashion. In the end, I will have more time to do what I want to do. I also like to reward myself for productive behavior. If I work diligently for one hour, I will give myself a ten minute break doing something fun and relaxing."

© 2013 by razihusin. Used under license of Shutterstock, Inc.

Emily

Q: *What prompted you to consider time management a necessary skill (if you do)?*

A: "When I wasn't doing very well in classes and I just felt like I didn't have a good balance of anything."

Terry

You can itemize the tasks on your lists by using the following time-management tools:

- **Personal digital assistant (PDA) Smartphone or cell phone.** You can use these to do a lot more than check social networking sites and send and receive text messages. Use the calendar tools in these devices to record due dates and set up the alert functions to remind you of these deadlines. Many PDAs and smartphones will also allow you to set up task or "to-do" lists and to set priorities for each item you enter.

- **Small, portable planner.** List all your major assignments and exams for the term, along with their due dates. Putting all work tasks from different courses into one place makes it easier to keep track of what you have to do and when you have to do it.

- **Large, stable calendar.** In the calendar's date boxes, record your major assignments for the academic term and when they are due. Place the calendar in a position or location where it's in full view and you can't help but see it every day (e.g., on your bedroom or refrigerator door). If you regularly and literally "look" at the things you have to do, you're less likely to "overlook" them, forget about them, or subconsciously push them out of your mind because you don't really want to do them.

3. **Rank your tasks in order of their importance.** Once you've itemized your work by listing all tasks you need to do, prioritize them—determine the order in which you will do them. Prioritizing basically involves ranking your tasks in terms of their importance, with the highest-ranked tasks appearing at the top of your list to ensure that they are tackled first. How do you determine which tasks are most important and should be ranked highest? Two criteria or standards of judgment can be used to help determine which tasks should be your highest priorities:

- **Urgency.** Tasks that are closest to their deadlines or due dates should receive high priority. For example, finishing an assignment that's due tomorrow should receive higher priority than starting an assignment that's due next month.

- **Gravity.** Tasks that carry the heaviest weight (count the most) should receive highest priority. For example, if an assignment worth 100 points and another worth 10 points are due at the same time, the 100-point task should receive higher priority. Just like investing money, you want to invest your time in tasks that yield the greatest dividends or payoff. One strategy for prioritizing your tasks is to divide them into A, B, and C lists (Lakein, 1973; Morgenstern, 2004). The A list is for _essential_ tasks—what you _must_ do now. The B list is for _important_ tasks—what you _should_ do soon. Finally, the C list is for _optional_ tasks—what you _could_ or _might_ do if there is time remaining after you've completed the tasks on the A and B lists. Organizing your tasks in this fashion can help you decide how to divide your labor in a way that ensures you put first things first. Don't waste time doing unimportant things to deceive yourself into thinking that you're keeping busy and getting things done; in reality, all you're doing is taking time (and your mind) away from the more important things you should be doing.

At first glance, itemizing and prioritizing may appear to be rather boring chores. However, if you look at these mental tasks carefully, they require higher-level thinking skills, such as:

1. **Analysis.** Dividing time into component elements or segments and breaking down work into specific tasks;

2. **Evaluation.** Critically evaluating the relative importance or value of tasks; and

3. **Synthesis.** Organizing individual tasks into classes or categories based on their level of priority.

Cheryl

Q: _Are you a good manager of time?_

A: "When I need to be . . . yes."

Q: _Do you believe that time management is a natural gift, or do you have to work at it?_

A: "Not for me. I definitely have to work at it. Taking the (optional) Study Skills class at Liberty U was so incredibly helpful. I remember telling my Professor at the time how I wish it had been my FIRST class at LU, as the class taught me HOW to study. I learned tools in that class that I utilize, whenever I do ANY kind of work at my desk. My favorite tools for studying are my to-do-list, and my BRIGHT highlighters, BRIGHT post-its, and BRIGHT colored index cards. They work for my individual learning style."

© 2013 by Pincasso. Used under license of Shutterstock, Inc.

Set Priorities and Plan Your Use of Time

I Samuel 12:23,
"I will teach you the way that is good and right" (NIV).

Develop a Time-Management Plan

Kristy Motte

"Don't forget to schedule in personal time each week of the term. Even just an hour or two each week gives you something to look forward to, motivation to get other tasks completed on time, and the ability to refresh/refocus in the midst of a busy week."

Sherry Dickerson

"Use the calendar tool in your Outlook school email to schedule due dates for all of your assignments at the beginning of the term. Avoid missing deadlines by setting up reminders and checking them off as you complete your assignments."

Hanna Bruce

"Begin studying and completing assignments early in the week. It seems that those unexpected life events always seem to "pop up" near the end of the week. If you have spaced out your work, starting on the first day of the module, when something goes awry on Saturday, you won't feel behind in your studies."

Humans are creatures of habit. Routines help you organize and gain control of your life. Doing things by design, rather than leaving them to chance or accident, is the first step toward making things happen for you rather than allowing them to happen. By developing an intentional plan for how you're going to spend your time, you're developing a plan to gain greater control of your life.

Don't buy into the myth that you don't have time to plan because it takes too much time that could be spent getting started and getting things done. Time-management experts estimate that the amount of time you spend planning your work reduces your total work time by a factor of three (Goldsmith, 2010; Lakein, 1973). In other words, for every one unit of time you spend planning, you save three units of work time. Thus, five minutes of planning time will typically save you 15 minutes of total work time, and 10 minutes of planning time will save you 30 minutes of work time. You save work time by engaging in planning time because you end up with a clearer understanding of what needs to be done and the order of steps you need to take to get it done. This clearer sense of direction reduces the likelihood of losing time to "false starts"—having to restart your work because you started off in the wrong direction. If you have no plan of attack, you're more likely to go off track; when you discover this at some point after you've started, you're then forced to retreat and start all over again.

As the proverb goes, "A stitch in time saves nine." Planning your time represents the "stitch" (unit of time) that saves you nine additional stitches (units of time). Similar to successful chess players, successful time managers plan ahead and anticipate their next moves.

Elements of a Comprehensive Time-Management Plan

Once you've accepted the notion that taking the time to plan your time saves you time in the long run, you're ready to design a time-management plan. The following are elements of a comprehensive, well-designed plan for managing time.

1. **A good time-management plan includes short, mid- and long-range time frames.** For instance, a good academic time-management plan for the term should include:

- A *long-range* plan for the entire term that identifies deadline dates for reports and papers that are due toward the end of the term;

- A *mid-range* plan for the upcoming month and week; and

- A *short-range* plan for the following day.

Here's how you can put this three-stage plan into action this term:

- Review the *course syllabus and course chart* for each class you are enrolled in this term, and highlight all major exams, tests, quizzes, assignments and papers and the dates on which they are due.

- Obtain a *large calendar* for the academic term and record all your exams, assignments, and so on, for all your courses in the calendar boxes that represent their due dates. To fit this information within the calendar boxes, use creative abbreviations to represent different tasks, such as E for exam and TP for term paper (not toilet paper). When you're done, you'll have a centralized chart or map of deadline dates and a potential master plan for the entire term. Get in the habit of not only doing short-range academic planning and calendaring for the upcoming day or week, but also long-range planning for the academic semester or term.

- Activate the calendar and task lists functions on your Smartphone or cell phone. Enter your schedule, important dates, deadlines, and set alert reminders. Since you carry your PDA or cell phone with you regularly, you will always have this information at your fingertips.

Work backward from this long-range plan to:

- Plan your week.

   a. Make a map of your *weekly schedule* that includes times during the week when you are in class working, when you typically

Michael Marrano

"Use an 'organizer' such as the MS Outlook features in your LU Webmail account. Set up task and calendar reminders to help keep yourself organized and on schedule."

Debra Magnuson

"You can always work ahead in each week. That way if an emergency arises the day of the deadline, you won't be stressed out about turning in an assignment late."

Mark Heideman

"If you need to eliminate any item, begin with the lowest priority."

Sherrie Welfel

Get a weekly/monthly planner when opened to a page, a full week is visible. Utilize erasable colored pencils to color code your individual course assignments and personal events!

Mark Heideman

"Plan your time by writing down everything you want to do or accomplish."

To Do List:

1._____
2._____
3._____
4._____
5._____
6._____
7._____

© 2013 by mexrix. Used under license of Shutterstock, Inc.

© 2013 by Aquir. Used under license of Shutterstock, Inc.

eat and sleep, as well as anything you do on a regular basis, such as church attendance, clubs or group meetings, and exercise, and if you are employed, when you work.

b. As an online student, you will need to dedicate at least two hours of work each week for each credit hour you are enrolled in. Taking two three-credit courses would require you to dedicate at least 12 hours per week, for example.

c. Make good use of your *free time* by working on assignments and studying in advance for upcoming exams.

■ Plan your day.

a. Make a *daily to-do list*. This can be done each evening before bed to plan the next day, or first thing each morning.

b. Attack daily tasks in *priority order*. Not all items on your list will have the same urgency for completion. Understand that some less-urgent tasks may appear on your daily list for a few days until there is time to accomplish them. Picking up the dry cleaning or getting the car washed are examples of daily tasks that might move from day to day until you complete them.

■ Carry a *small calendar, planner, or appointment book* at all times. This will enable you to record appointments that you may make on the run during the day and will allow you to jot down creative ideas or memories of things you need to do—which can sometimes pop into your mind at the most unexpected times.

- Take *portable work* with you during the day that you can carry with you and do in any place at any time. This will enable you to take advantage of "dead time" during the day. For example, carry material with you that you can read while sitting and waiting for appointments or transportation, allowing you to resurrect this dead time and convert it to "live" work time. (Not only is this a good time management strategy, it's a good stress-management strategy because it puts you in control of "wait time," enabling you use it to save time later and reducing the likelihood that you'll feel frustrated, anxious, or bored.)

- Wear a watch or carry a cell phone that can accurately and instantly tell you what time it is and what date it is. You can't even begin to manage time if you don't know what time it is, and you can't plan a schedule if you don't know what date it is. (Try setting the time on your watch or cell phone slightly ahead of the actual time to help ensure that you arrive to class, work, or meetings on time.)

© 2013 by Sergey Karpov. Used under license of Shutterstock, Inc.

(2.) **A good time-management plan includes planning reserve time to take care of the unexpected.** Always hope for the best, but always be prepared for the worst. Your time-management plan should include a buffer zone or safety net of extra time in case you encounter unforeseen developments or unexpected emergencies. Just as you should plan to have extra funds in your account to pay for unexpected costs (e.g., an auto repair), you should plan to have extra time in your schedule for unexpected events (e.g., a random emergency).

Mark Heideman

"Assign amounts of time to each item by projecting the amount of time you 'think' each will take. It's always a good idea to add 10% or 20% to the time as we often underestimate our time."

Alexandra Barnett

"Plan out your week by determining what you need to study when and what assignments you will complete when to avoid last minute, less than stellar assignment submissions."

Making Productive Use of Free Time Outside the Classroom

Unlike in high school, homework in college often does not involve turning things in to your instructor daily or weekly. The academic work you do outside the classroom may not even be collected and graded. Instead, it is done for your own benefit to help prepare yourself for upcoming exams

Mark Heideman

"Prioritize each item."

Photo courtesy of Kevin Manguiob.

Liberty students are served by several pedestrian tunnels. Time management can provide the light at the end of the tunnel when you are a busy student!

and major assignments (e.g., term papers or research reports). Rather than formally assigning work to you as homework, your professors expect that you will do this work on your own and without supervision. Listed below are strategies for working independently and in advance of college exams and assignments. These strategies will increase the quality of your time management in college and the quality of your academic performance.

Working Independently in Advance of Exams

Use the following strategies to use time wisely to prepare for exams:

Mark Heideman

"Allow for reward time. Everyone needs to relax, so reward time is beneficial."

Mark Heideman

"When setting out to complete each task, think 'baby steps.' Thinking about completing a task can often be overwhelming; however, once you begin a task it often becomes less overwhelming as it's put into perspective. Therefore, break each task into smaller, doable tasks and schedule several small windows of time to complete each task. The goal is to simply get started rather than trying to complete the entire task at once."

- **Complete reading assignments** relating to presentations before reviewing the video or Pointecast presentation. This will make lectures easier to understand and will prepare you to participate intelligently in class discussion board work.

- **Review your class notes** from previous sessions or modules so that you can construct a mental bridge from one class module or presentation to the next and make each upcoming lecture video easier to follow. When reviewing your notes, rewrite any that may be sloppily written the first time. If you find notes related to the same point all over the place, reorganize them by combining them into one set of notes. Lastly, if you find any information gaps or confusing points in your notes, seek out the course instructor or a trusted classmate to clear them up.

- **Review information** you highlighted in your reading assignments to improve your retention of the information. If certain points are confusing to you, discuss them with your course instructor or with a fellow classmate by email. Your instructor is always happy to help you understand the topics covered in the course and wants to help you be successful.

- **Integrate key ideas** in your class notes with information that you have highlighted in your assigned reading, which relates to the same major point or general category. In other words, put related information from your lecture notes and your reading in the same place (e.g., on the same index card).

■ **Use a part-to-whole study method**, whereby you study material from your class notes and assigned reading in small pieces during short, separate study sessions that take place well in advance of the exam; then make your last study session before the exam a longer review session during which you restudy all the small parts together as a whole. It's a myth that studying in advance is a waste of time because you'll forget it all anyway by test time. Even if you cannot recall the previously studied information when you first start reviewing it, you will relearn it faster than you did the first time, thus proving that some memory of it was retained from your earlier study sessions.

Work Independently Well in Advance of Due Dates for Term Papers and Research Reports

Work on large, long-range assignments by breaking them into the following smaller, short-term tasks:

1. Search for and select a topic.

2. Locate sources of information on the topic.

3. Organize the information obtained from these sources into categories.

4. Develop an outline of the report's major points and the order or sequence in which you plan to discuss them.

5. Construct a first draft of the paper (and, if necessary, a second draft).

6. Write a final draft of the paper.

7. Proofread the final draft of your paper for minor mechanical mistakes, such as spelling and grammatical errors, before submitting it to your instructor.

8. A good time-management plan should balance work and recreation. Don't only plan work time: plan time to relax, refuel, and recharge. Your overall time management plan shouldn't turn you into an obsessive-compulsive workaholic. Instead, it should represent a balanced blend of work and play, including activities that promote your mental and physical wellness, such as relaxation, recreation, and reflection. If your schedule makes room for the things you like to do, you're more likely to do the things you have to do. You could also arrange your schedule of work and play as a self-motivation strategy by using your play time

Tim

Q: *What prompted you to consider time management a necessary skill (if you do)?*

A: "Time management is something that everyone must work at. Time management is not a natural gift that everyone receives; it is something that requires discipline. The best way to balance your personal life, school, and work is with what I call a 'tasker.' First, you need to get a dry-erase board and dry-erase markers. Next, you need to get your course syllabus and schedule along with your work schedule. Mark out your course schedule into sectors and then add your work schedule to that schedule. With each input, you will draw a box beside it. Finally, hang the dry erase board beside, above, under, or in front of your television. As your course work moves along, you can add in personal task or events. Yes, this is the same thing as a day planner. However, with a dry erase board beside your television nagging you to do your course work- it is much more effective. Once you complete a specific task, put a check in the box. This will help to keep you motivated as you complete your course work and will be a constant reminder to do your course work."

Emily

Q: *Do you believe that time management is a natural gift, or do you have to work at it?*

A: "I think it varies. Some people are naturally better at it but I think everyone has to work at it."

Maddy

Q: *Are you a good manager of time? Do you believe that time management is a natural gift, or do you have to work at it? How do you balance competing demands in your life?*

A: "I am a good manager of time when I have a specific motivation to do so. The general idea of 'free time' never seems like a good enough reason, but having a particular event to go to does motivate me to get work done. I believe that there is some natural ability in time management, but like all gifts and abilities, it must be nurtured and developed or it will go to waste. As someone who isn't very good at managing my time, I sometimes stay up late to make sure I get things done, simply because I didn't do what I needed to in the normal daytime hours."

Ruth

Q: *Are you a good manager of time?*
A: "Yes."

Q: *Do you believe that time management is a natural gift, or do you have to work at it?*
A: "You have to work at it."

Q: *How do you balance competing demands in your life?*
A: "Family is always first, then plan ahead for all things necessary, even the smallest things."

Q: *What prompted you to consider time management a necessary skill (if you do)?*
A: "Raising three children as a single Mom."

Q: *What is non-negotiable in your schedule?*
A: "Putting family first in case of emergency. It's my responsibility."

to reward completion of your work time. A good time-management plan includes a balanced blend of time planned for both work and recreation. Remember that online learning for college is much more like a marathon than a sprint and plan times to relax and celebrate the accomplishments you have made so far.

9. A good time-management plan has some flexibility. Some students are immediately turned off by the idea of developing a schedule and planning their time because they feel it over-structures their lives and limits their freedom. It's only natural for you to prize your personal freedom and resist anything that appears to restrict your freedom in any way. However, a good time-management plan doesn't limit freedom: it preserves freedom by helping you get done what you must do and reserves free time to do what you want and like to do. A good time-management plan shouldn't enslave you to a rigid work schedule. The plan should be flexible enough to allow you to occasionally bend it without breaking it. Just as work commitments and family responsibilities can crop up unexpectedly, so, too, can opportunities for fun and enjoyable activities. Your plan should allow you the freedom to modify your schedule so that you can take advantage of these enjoyable opportunities and experiences. However, you should plan to make up the work time you lost. In other words, you can borrow or trade work time for play time, but don't "steal" it; plan to pay back the work time you borrowed by substituting it for play time that was planned for another time. If you can't do something you planned to do, the next best thing is to re-plan when you'll do it.

Converting a Time-Management Plan into an Action Plan

Once you've planned the work, the next step is to work the plan. A good action plan is one that enables you to (1) preview what you intend to accomplish and (2) review what you actually accomplished. You can begin to implement an action plan by constructing a daily to-do list, bringing that list with you as the day begins, and checking off items on the list as you get them done throughout the day. At the end of the day, review your list and identify what was completed and what still needs to be done. The uncompleted tasks should become high priorities for the next day. At the end of the day, if you find many unchecked items remain on your daily to-do list, this may mean that you're spreading yourself too thin by trying to do too many things in a day. You may need to be more realistic about the number of items you can accomplish per day by shortening your daily to-do list. Being unable to complete many of your intended daily tasks may also mean that you need to modify your time-management plan by adding more work time or subtracting activities that are drawing time and attention away from your work (e.g., responding to phone calls and text messages during your planned work times).

From *Thriving in College and Beyond,* 3/e by Joseph B. Cuseo, Aaron Thompson, Michele Campagna and Viki S. Fecas. Copyright © 2013 by Kendall Hunt Publishing Company. Reprinted by permission.

Roger

Q: *Do you believe that time management is a natural gift, or do you have to work at it? How do you balance competing demands in your life?*

A: "One strategy I have developed is to prioritize my responsibilities into categories: urgent, important, can wait. I also have maintained a list of those things which I need to do on a regular basis and devote a portion of time for that. For example, I teach Sunday school so I have devoted a time slot in my week for that. And if there is any reading involved, I will reserve a few minutes at the start and end of the day for reading."

Cheryl

Q: *How do you balance competing demands in your life?*

A: "Prioritization and my to-do-list (with check marks, so I can see progress, and visually diagram what is left to do, each day)."

Q: *What is non-negotiable in your schedule? Why?*

A: "My family's medical situations.

It is amazing the stress that a single parent has, to get everything 'done.' I know scheduling and time-management is challenging for all adult learners. However, I have to give extra props to single parents, as there are huge sacrifices made, in order to take care of the needs of children and school. I cannot even estimate the number of days that I had (and still do) familial medical and emergency situations. This has been the second biggest challenge with my education (first being finances).

Assignment deadlines are a nightmare when the medical needs of the family and educational 'deadlines' have a conflict. Time management is the ONLY tool I used, that helped me to be successful with my incredibly hectic schedule. I very simply could NOT have done well, if I left all of my assignments until the last minute."

Q: *What did you have to give up for college success?*

A: "Free time . . . and reading for pleasure."

Defeat Distractions and Deal with Procrastination

Psalm 119:66
"Teach me knowledge and good judgment, for I trust your commands" (NIV).

Debra Magnuson

"You can always work ahead in each week. That way if an emergency arises the day of the deadline, you won't be stressed out about turning in an assignment late."

Cari Smith

"Obtaining a degree includes sacrifice. You have to make a conscious decision to put aside some of your extra-curricular activity and you have to be willing to say 'no.'"

Dr. Jerry Falwell, founder

"It always costs you something to do a work for the Lord. If it does not cost you anything, it is not worth doing" (Falwell, 1997, p. 206).

Emily

Q: *Are you a good manager of time?*

A: "Not really. I am when it comes to scheduling plans but not when it comes to school work."

Often, students struggle to complete their work not because they are not interested, but because there are just too many good options for how to spend time. Are you familiar with the story related in Luke 10:38–42?

> As Jesus and his disciples were on their way, he came to a village where a woman named Martha opened her home to him. She had a sister called Mary, who sat at the Lord's feet listening to what he said. But Martha was distracted by all the preparations that had to be made. She came to him and asked, "Lord, don't you care that my sister has left me to do the work by myself? Tell her to help me!"

> "Martha, Martha," the Lord answered, "You are worried and upset about many things, but few things are needed—or indeed only one. Mary has chosen what is better, and it will not be taken away from her" (NIV).

In the Bible story above, Martha was not uninterested in what her Lord was teaching, but she was distracted by other tasks. She had not correctly prioritized what she should be doing and had chosen poorly. Too often, students do the same thing. There are a dizzying number of options for how to spend time, and many of them are good choices. Good time management requires making the **best** use of time and avoiding anything that will distract from that choice. Sometimes it is necessary to limit the number of activities you agree to or the number of organizations to which you promise your time. For example, while you may really enjoy being a leader in a scouting organization, that may be a commitment you will have to forego while you are pursuing a college degree. Take a careful look at the commitments you give your time to now. Are there any responsibilities that you can share with others, cease temporarily, or even abandon for the long term?

Do not feel that you must give up family responsibilities and time together, but consider how you might give time to your family in a different way. Does your family spend several hours in front of the television each night as "family time"? That may not fit your schedule as an online learner, as you may need to spend time reading or viewing course presentations online. Think of ways to spend meaningful time with family while still maintaining your commitment to your course work. Consider things like working together to make simple meals, time spent around the table at mealtime (not in front of the television!), and other similar ways to give time to your family in a meaningful way.

Distractions may come in the form of activities, but can also be a bit more insidious. While you are working, are you often distracted? Distractions might crop up such as a ringing phone (or a text message arriving), the lure of Facebook, or internet or phone games. What can you do to limit the intrusion of these sorts of distractors? Consider adopting the following practices when you are doing your course work in order to be prepared for success:

- Turn off your phone or leave it in another room. There is nothing so urgent that it cannot wait until you have completed your planned study time.

- Use restraint in opening additional tabs on your computer. Do not be available to your email, or Facebook, or . . . anything that might distract you.

- Set a timer for your work. Once you have worked for the planned period of time, take a break. You may allow yourself some time with one of the distractors mentioned above (phone, Facebook, etc.), but again, set yourself a time limit and use the timer to let you know when the time is up.

- Let family and friends know your work plans, and ask that they help you stick to your plan. For family, set some clear signals, such as a closed door, note on the door, or something similar to remind others to respect your study time.

- Use headphones. This can help you avoid hearing any auditory distractors and also can be a visual clue for family that you are "in the zone" for classwork.

- Avoid distractions by family by arising early in the morning to do your course work. This can help you finish the tasks you want to accomplish before the day officially begins.

- Do not attempt marathon study sessions. What we refer to as "spaced practice" is much more effective for your learning and less likely to cause you to fall to distractions than "massed practice," otherwise known as cramming.

- Do not begin a work/study session when you are hungry or thirsty. Take care of those needs first so you will not be distracted by thinking about foods or beverages.

Roger

Q: *What did you have to give up for college success? What is non-negotiable in your schedule?*

A: "Managing a family, work, church, and school is tricky, like learning to juggle. It doesn't pay to be successful at school or work while being a failure at home. I must devote some time for family things. When I'm not in school I will take my wife and kids out shopping or bowling. If I have an errand to perform, I will bring one of the children with me. If I have to go to the library to study, I might take a child with the promise that after an hour, I will do something he likes to do for fun. I will reserve time to date my wife. That's a bit trickier these days since we our built in babysitter moved out(our adult daughter).

There is no excuse for failing to work hard. Since I paid for my education (and am still paying for LU with student loans) I refused to waste my time by not putting in the effort. It costs too much to redo a class. So I completed my work on time and studied hard for exams. In the end, I was rewarded with a 4.0 GPA and a good job."

Dealing With Procrastination

Procrastination Defined

Tim

Q: *What is non-negotiable in your schedule? Why? What did you have to give up for college success?*

A: "Something that is non-negotiable in my schedule is my work schedule and field duty. I personally have had to give up sleep, set meal times, and many fun events so that I could complete my course work."

The word *procrastination* derives from two roots: *pro* (meaning "forward") plus crastinus (meaning "tomorrow"). As these roots suggest, procrastinators don't abide by the proverb "Why put off to tomorrow what can be done today?" Their philosophy is just the opposite: "Why do today what can be put off until tomorrow?" Adopting this philosophy promotes a perpetual pattern of postponing what needs to be done until the last possible moment, forcing a frantic rush to finish the job in time, which results in a product of poorer quality (or not finishing the product at all). Research shows that 80–95 percent of college students procrastinate (Steel, 2007) and almost 50 percent report that they procrastinate consistently (Onwuegbuzie, 2000). Furthermore, the percentage of people reporting that they procrastinate is on the rise (Kachgal, Hansen, & Nutter, 2001).

Procrastination is such a serious issue for college students that some colleges and universities have opened "procrastination centers" to provide help exclusively for students who are experiencing problems with procrastination (Burka & Yuen, 2008).

Myths That Promote Procrastination

Before there can be any hope of putting a stop to procrastination, procrastinators need to let go of two popular myths (misconceptions) about time and performance.

Myth 1. "I work better under pressure" (e.g., on the day or night before something is due). Procrastinators often confuse desperation with motivation. Their belief that they work better under pressure is often just a rationalization to justify or deny the reality that they *only* work when they're under pressure—that is, when they've run out of time and have no choice but to do it under the gun of the final deadline.

It's true that some people will only start to work and will work really fast when they're under pressure, but that does not mean they're working more *effectively* and producing work of better quality. Because they're playing "beat the clock," the procrastinator's focus is no longer is on doing the job *well* but is on doing the job *fast* so that it gets done before they run out of time. This typically results in a work product that turns out to be incomplete or inferior to what could have been produced if the work process began earlier.

Myth 2. "**Studying in advance is a waste of time because you will forget it all by test time.**" The misconception that information learned early will be forgotten is commonly used to justify procrastinating with respect to preparing for upcoming exams. As will be discussed in Chapter 5, studying that is distributed (spread out) over time is more effective than massed (crammed) studying. Furthermore, last minute studying that takes place the night before exams often results in lost sleep time resulting from pulling "late-nighters" or "all-nighters." This fly-by-night strategy interferes with retention of information that has been studied and elevates test anxiety because of lost dream sleep (a.k.a. rapid eye movement, or REM) that the brain needs to store memories and manage stress (Hobson, 1988; Voelker, 2004). Research indicates that procrastinators experience higher rates of stress-related physical disorders, such as insomnia, stomach problems, colds, and flu (McCance & Pychyl, 2003).

Working under time pressure adds to performance pressure because procrastinators are left with no margin of error to correct mistakes, no time to seek help on their work, and no chance to handle random catastrophes that may arise at the last minute (e.g., an attack of the flu or a family emergency).

Psychological Causes of Procrastination

Sometimes, procrastination has deeper psychological roots. People may procrastinate for reasons that do not relate directly to poor time-management habits but to emotional issues. For instance, studies show that procrastination is sometimes used as a psychological strategy to protect self-esteem. Referred to as *self-handicapping* (Rhodewalt & Vohs, 2005), this strategy is used, either consciously or unconsciously, by some procrastinators to give themselves a "handicap" or disadvantage. Thus, if their performance turns out to be less than spectacular, they can conclude (rationalize) that it was because they were performing under a handicap—lack of time rather than lack of ability (Chu & Cho, 2005). For example, if they receive a low grade on a test or paper, they can "save face" (self-esteem) by concluding that it was because they waited until the last minute and didn't put much time or effort into it. In other words, they had enough ability or intelligence to earn a high grade; they just didn't have enough time. Better yet, if they happened to luck out and get a good grade—despite doing it at the last minute—they can think it proves just how smart they are because they were able to get that good grade without putting in much time at all! Thus, self-handicapping creates a fail-safe or win-win scenario that's guaranteed to protect the procrastinator's self-image. If the work performance or product is less than excellent, it can be blamed on external factors (e.g., lack of time); if it happens to earn them a high grade, they can attribute the result to themselves—their extraordinary ability enabled them to do so well despite working at the last minute.

In addition to self-handicapping, other psychological factors have been found to contribute to procrastination, including the following:

- **Fear of failure.** The procrastinator feels better about not completing the work on time than doing it and experiencing failure (Burka & Yuen, 2008; Solomon & Rothblum, 1984);

- **Perfectionism.** Having unrealistically high personal standards or expectations, which leads to the procrastinator's belief that it's better to postpone work or not do it than to risk doing it less than perfectly (Kachgal et al., 2001);

- **Fear of success.** Fearing that doing well will show others that the procrastinator has the ability to achieve success and will lead others to expect the procrastinator to maintain those high standards in the future (Beck, Koons, & Milgram, 2000; Ellis & Knaus, 2002)

- **Indecisiveness.** The procrastinator has difficulty making decisions, including decisions about what to do first, when to do it, or whether to do it (Anderson, 2003; Steel, 2007);

- **Thrill seeking.** The procrastinator enjoys the adrenaline rush triggered by hurrying to get things done just before a deadline (Szalavitz, 2003). If these underlying psychological issues are at the root of procrastination, they must be dealt with before procrastination can be overcome. Because they have deeper roots, it may take some time and professional assistance to uproot them.

Self-Help Strategies for Beating the Procrastination Habit

Once inaccurate beliefs or emotional issues underlying procrastination have been identified and dealt with, the next step is to take direct action on the procrastination habit itself. What follows are seven key strategies for minimizing or eliminating the procrastination habit.

1. **Continually practice effective time-management strategies.** If effective time management practices, such as those previously cited in this chapter, are implemented consistently, they can turn into a habit. When people repeatedly practice effective time-management strategies, these practices gradually become part of their routine and develop into habits. For instance, when procrastinators repeatedly practice

effective time-management strategies with respect to tasks that they procrastinate on, their procrastination tendencies begin to fade and are gradually replaced by good habits of time management (Ainslie, 1992; Baumeister, Heatherton, & Tice, 1994).

2. **Make the start of work as inviting or appealing as possible.** Getting started can be a stumbling block for many procrastinators. They experience what's called "start-up stress"—when they're about to begin a task, they start to experience negative feelings about the task being unpleasant, difficult, or boring (Burka & Yuen, 2008). If you have trouble starting your work, one way to give yourself a jump-start is to arrange your work tasks in an order that allows you to start with tasks that you're likely to find most interesting or to succeed in. Once you overcome the initial inertia and get going, you can ride the momentum you've created to attack other tasks that you find less appealing or more daunting. You're also likely to discover that the dreaded work wasn't as difficult, boring, or time-consuming as it appeared to be. When you sense that you're making some progress toward getting work done, your anxiety begins to decline. As with many experiences in life that are feared and avoided, the anticipation of the event turns out to be worse than the event itself. Research on students who hadn't started a project until it was about to be due indicates that they experienced anxiety and guilt about delaying their work, but once they began working, these negative emotions subsided and were replaced by more positive feelings of progress and accomplishment (McCance & Pychyl, 2003).

3. **Make the work manageable.** Work becomes less overwhelming and less stressful when it's handled in small chunks or pieces. You can conquer procrastination for large tasks by using a "divide and conquer" strategy: divide the large task into smaller, more manageable units, and then attack and complete them one at a time. Don't underestimate the power of short work sessions. They can be more effective than longer sessions because it's easier to maintain momentum and concentration for shorter periods of time. If you're working on a large project or preparing for a major exam, dividing your work into short sessions will enable you to take quick jabs and poke small holes in it, reducing its overall size with each successive punch. This approach will also give you the sense of satisfaction that comes with knowing that you're making steady progress toward completing a big task—by continually jabbing at it in short strokes and gradually reducing the pressure associated with having to go for a big knockout punch right before the final bell (deadline).

4. **Organization matters.** Research indicates that disorganization is a factor that contributes to procrastination (Steel, 2007). How well you organize your workplace and manage your work materials can reduce your risk of procrastination. Ask yourself, "Can I just go in and do it?" Having the right materials in the right place at the right time can make it easier to get to your work and get going on your work. Once you've made a decision to start working, you don't want to delay acting on that decision by looking for the tools you need to get started. For procrastinators, this time delay may be just the amount of time they need to change their minds and decide not to start working! One simple but effective way to organize your college work materials is to develop your own file system. You can begin to create an effective academic file system by filing (storing) materials from different courses in different-colored folders or notebooks. This will allow you to keep all materials related to the same course in the same place, giving you direct and immediate access to the materials you need as soon as you need them. Such a system helps you get organized, reduces stress associated with having things all over the place, and reduces the risk of procrastination by reducing the time it takes for you to start working.

5. **Location matters.** Where you choose to work can influence whether you work. Research on procrastinators demonstrates that distraction is a factor that can contribute to procrastination (Steel, 2007). Thus, you can reduce your risk of procrastinating by working in an environment whose location and arrangement prevent distraction and promote concentration. Remember that distractions tend to come in two major forms: social distractions, e.g., people nearby who are not working, and media distractions, e.g., cell phones, e-mails, text messages, music, and TV. Research on college students indicates that the number of hours per week they spend watching TV is *negatively* associated with success: more TV leads to lower grade point averages, less likelihood of graduating with honors, and lower levels of personal development (Astin, 1993).

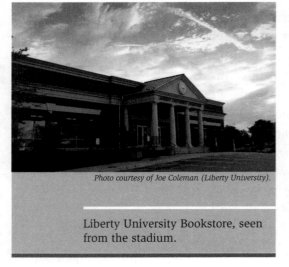

Photo courtesy of Joe Coleman (Liberty University).

Liberty University Bookstore, seen from the stadium.

You can arrange your work environment in a way that not only disables distraction but also enables concentration. Your concentration is easier to maintain when you work in an environment that allows you easy access to (1) work support materials, e.g., class notes, textbooks, and a dictionary, and (2) social support networks, e.g., a group of motivated students who will help you stay focused, on task, and on track toward completing your work.

6. **Arrange the order or sequence of work tasks to intercept procrastination at times when you're most likely to experience it.** While procrastination often involves difficulty starting work, it can also involve difficulty continuing and completing work (Lay & Silverman, 1996). As previously mentioned, if you have trouble starting work, it might be best to first do the tasks that you find most interesting or easiest. However, if you have difficulty maintaining or sustaining your work until it's finished, you might try to schedule work tasks that you find easier and more interesting *in the middle or toward the end* of your planned work time. If you perform tasks of greater interest and ease at a time when you typically lose interest or energy, you may be able to restore or revive your interest and energy. Also, doing your most enjoyable and easiest tasks later can provide an incentive or reward for completing your less enjoyable tasks first.

7. **If you're close to completing a task, don't stop until you complete it.** It's often harder to restart a task than it is to finish a task that you've already started, because you've overcome the initial inertia needed to get started and can ride the momentum you've created until you finish. Furthermore, finishing a task can give you a sense of *closure*—the feeling of personal accomplishment and self-satisfaction that comes from knowing that you "closed the deal." Placing a checkmark next to a completed task can serve as a source of positive self-reinforcement that increases your motivation to complete other tasks on your to-do list.

From *Thriving in College and Beyond*, 3/e by Joseph B. Cuseo, Aaron Thompson, Michele Campagna and Viki S. Fecas. Copyright © 2013 by Kendall Hunt Publishing Company. Reprinted by permission.

Photo courtesy of David Duncan (Liberty University).

Construction on the new library continues.

BUILDING BLOCKS

Remember, to manage time effectively, you need to:

- **Analyze.** Break down time and become aware of how you spend it;
- **Itemize.** Identify the tasks you need to accomplish and their due dates; and
- **Prioritize.** Tackle your tasks in their order of importance.

Developing a comprehensive time-management plan for academic work involves:

- Planning the total term (long-range);
- Planning your week (mid-range); and
- Planning your day (short-range).

A good time-management plan also has the following features:

- It sets aside time to take care of unexpected developments;
- It takes advantage of your natural peak periods and down times;
- It balances work and recreation; and
- It gives you the flexibility to accommodate unforeseen opportunities.

The enemy of effective time management is procrastination, which is often rooted in the following myths:

- Better work occurs on the day or night before something is due.
- Studying in advance is a waste of time, because everything you study will be forgotten by test time.

Effective strategies for beating the procrastination habit include the following:

- Start with the work that is the most inviting or appealing.
- Divide large tasks into smaller, more manageable units.
- Organize your work materials to make it easy and convenient for you to start working.
- Organize your work place or space so that you work in a location that minimizes distractions and temptations not to work.

- Intentionally arrange your work tasks so that you're working on more enjoyable or stimulating tasks at times when you're vulnerable to procrastination.

- If you're close to finishing a task, finish it, because it's often harder to restart a task than to complete one you've already started.

Personal Reflection

Mastering the skill of managing time is critical for success in college and beyond. Time is one of our most powerful personal resources; the better we manage it, the more likely we are to achieve our goals and gain control of our lives.

Ponder Galatians 6:7 and 6:9: "Do not be deceived: God cannot be mocked. A man reaps what he sows" (NIV). "Let us not become weary in doing good, for at the proper time, we will reap a harvest if we do not give up" (NIV).

Do you see the relationship between these two verses as they relate to your use of time? Consider the implications of procrastination versus timeliness in light of these verses. What do they have to say about your stewardship of the time God has given you? Think about what your responsibilities are in regard to your use of time. Do you need to make any changes? Make some notes here about what you think needs to change:

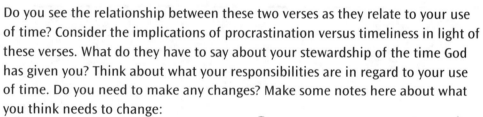

Things will not just fall in my lap but I have to dedicate time into what I am doing. I need to manage my schedule and run my time and not let time manage me.

We began this chapter with Psalm 90:12, which says, in the King James Version, "Teach us to number our days aright, that we may gain a heart of wisdom." What do you think wisdom has to do with "numbering our days aright," or using time well?

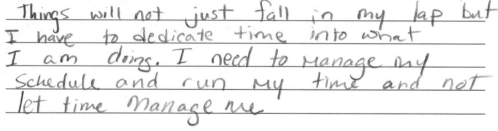

Making the most of each moment. Learning to prioritize what we plan our lives to be.

Personal Reflection

In Luke 2:53, it says that "Jesus grew in wisdom and stature and favor with God and men" (NIV). What does that verse indicate to you about the balance we should try to achieve in our lives? How does this balance look when you evaluate your use of time?

There is a healthy balance in what we do. That includes how we spend our time.

If we procrastinate then we will learn to make excuses and not be wise what has been given to us: time.

WORSHEET

Setting Priorities Exercise

The life of the online learner is certainly a *full* life: Each day presents challenges to your plans for completing your college work in a timely, thoughtful way. The following exercise will help you think about how you manage your time with a focus on prioritizing your time to achieve the tasks that are important to you.

Given the many tasks, responsibilities, and activities that are demanding your time, how will you spend the time from now until bedtime? Using the tasks below, prioritize them from 1 (do this first) through 12 (do this last). You need not include every choice, but you may not leave out, for example, the children's activities (even if you do not have children) to make thetime work out before bedtime (midnight).

It's Thursday, 4:30 P.M. Here are the many tasks that lie ahead for you:

_1_ Pick up the children from daycare.

_3_ Prepare dinner, serve it, and clean up.

_7_ Work on your history paper, which requires a number of drafts over a few weeks.

_2_ Your Discussion Board thread is due tonight.

_4_ There are two presentations for this week's work that you have not viewed.

_6_ An assignment is due on Monday for your other course. You first will need to read the two chapters of the textbook for that course.

_5_ The children have homework.

_8_ Bath time/bedtime for the children should be completed by 9:00 P.M. Don't forget to read a bedtime story and pray with them!

_12_ Your favorite show is on television tonight at 10:00 P.M.

_10_ You teach a weekly Sunday school class but haven't yet read this week's lesson.

_9_ You did your Bible study this morning, but slept in a bit, so you didn't have time to exercise yet today.

_11_ Two weeks ago, you had agreed to meet with friends for coffee to celebrate a birthday. You don't see these friends very often and have been looking forward to this time.

Once you have completed this exercise, turn to the end of this chapter to find additional information about the Setting Priorities Exercise.

WORKSHEET

Time Management: Lists

Time is a wonderful gift from God. While we do not know how many years we will be granted here on Earth, we do know that everyone has the same 24 hours each day, with 168 hours each week. The busiest person utilizes the same amount of time each day as the least accomplished person who only manages to spend the day on the couch, watching TV or playing computer games! What does your current use of time indicate about you? This activity will help you see how much time you truly have left to "manage" once you determine what time you currently have committed to your daily activities and tasks. Complete the chart provided below to see where you stand now. Simply write in the hours spent on each activity and total up each column.

	MON.	TUES.	WED.	THURS.	FRI.	SAT.	SUN.	WEEKLY TOTAL
Commuting	30	30	30	30	30	30	30	3.50
Work	—	6	6	6	6	6	—	30
Eating	30	30	30	30	30	30	30	3.50
Exercise	1.5	1.5	1.5	1.5	1.5	1.5	—	9
Home chores	5	5	5	5	5	5	5	35 min
Family time	10	10	10	10	10	10	1	2
Social time								
Volunteering	—	—	—	—	—	—	—	0
Worship	—	—	—	—	—	—	45	.45 min
Prayer/Bible study	10	10	10	10	10	10	10	1.10
Personal grooming/ hygiene	45	30	30	45	30	30	45	6.25
Entertainment (TV, movies, games, etc.)	—	—	—	—	—	2	—	2
Shopping	—	—	—	—	—	—	—	0
Sleeping	8	8	8	8	8	8	8	56
Other								
Daily Total	11.40	17.35	17.35	11.40	17.38	19.38	11.50	107.20
Time Left (24-daily total) (168-weekly total)	13.20	7.25	7.25	13.20	7.25	5.25	13.10	61.40

118　　40　　35

Once you complete the chart, answer the following questions thoroughly.

1. How much time do you have available on a daily basis? Take the total hours committed for each day and subtract it from 24.

   M _13.20_ T _7.25_ W _7.25_ R _13.20_ F _7.25_ S _5.25_ S _13.10_

2. How much time do you have available on a weekly basis? Take your weekly total and subtract it from 168. _61 hr 40 min_

3. Do you think there is enough time "left" to accomplish what you need to do each week when you are doing online college work? Explain. _Yes. I am dedicating 4hrs per day to homework_

4. Are there areas that you think may need some changes in the weeks ahead? If so, how will you implement those changes? If you do not see the need for changes, explain why. _Yes. Schedule my homework in advance_

   The Bible says, in Psalm 90:12, "So teach us to number our days, that we may apply our hearts unto wisdom" (NIV). If we ask God to help us manage our time wisely, He will!

TOOL BOX

Analyze Time

Spreadsheets—The most basic way to track and analyze your time is to create a simple spreadsheet and enter information manually. You can break your analysis down any way you like, which allows you to track your time in a way that makes sense to you. If you want to track your day as you move through it, you can create an hour-by-hour list and enter your activities. You could also make an activity listing and then enter the chunks of time you spend on those activities. The possibilities are endless, and if you are savvy with the program you are using, there is an almost limitless number of ways to analyze your data. There are several different examples and templates on the Breaking Ground website.

Mobile Apps—Since most people carry their mobile devices with them nearly every second of the day, it is likely that you do, too. If that is the case, then using a mobile app to track and analyze your time may be the way to go. While many of the best time-tracking apps are designed with professionals in mind, it is very easy to alter their purpose to your own needs. There are also a plethora of free apps designed just for personal time tracking. Most of these apps will allow you to enter the amount of time you spend on various activities, along with dates and times, then offer visual reports where you can see just how much time you are really spending on each activity. Check out the website for an updated list of apps.

Itemize and Prioritize Time

Planners—There are still a large number of people who have not made the transition to a "mobile life." If this is you, then a physical planner could be a good way to plot out your time. Most planners come with yearly, monthly, and daily calendars, which allow you to plan everything from a large project to a coffee date with friends. Most even have a daily to-do list that allows you to write out your specific tasks for the day in order of priority. These types of planners can be purchased at a local office supply store or online and range in price.

Mobile Apps—There are to-do apps for nearly every device on the market, and each has its own strengths and weaknesses. The primary benefit of these applications is that they travel with you everywhere you go since they are located on your phone. Most of these apps will allow you to categorize, prioritize, and rearrange your tasks with ease. The biggest drawback to these types of to-do applications is that they tend to be operating system specific, which limits the ability to sync your information across your devices.

Calendar Programs—Calendar programs tend to be developed on a much larger scale than your average to-do application. Companies who create these programs tend to design them to be all-in-one solutions to your time management needs. By entering a specific activity, you can assign a date, time, duration, category, and priority all at once. Your information is simultaneously entered into your calendar and task list, which simplifies things since you only enter the information one time. Calendar programs will often include other advanced tasks that allow you to invite other attendees to your activities, share your calendar information with others, and to check items off your task list as you complete them. Most of these programs can be expensive or are only included with the purchase of a hardware device, but there are free alternatives, which are every bit as powerful.

Additional resources and links to specific sites, worksheets, and apps can be located by accessing the Breaking Ground website:

www.breakinggroundlu.com

WORKSHEET

Setting Priorities Exercise, a Second Look

Did you have difficulty fitting everything from the Setting Priorities Exercise into the time available? If so, what does that indicate to you? You may be surprised to learn that you were not *expected* to be able to find a way to fit everything shown there into the evening hours allowed. Those tasks were simply too time consuming to be able to do them all and certainly do them well! Many students find themselves in a similar situation with more to do than will fit into the time allowed. If this situation is uncomfortably close to home, it is time to rethink priorities. During your time as an online college student, you may have to relinquish some responsibilities. This may involve handing off some duties you do not enjoy, but it also may mean deferring, for a time, tasks you find fulfilling. Perhaps it is time for someone else to step up to teach the Sunday school class, or lead the scouting group, or some other task you are enjoying now. These changes do not have to be permanent but can free you to commit time to school tasks. Think carefully about how you can arrange your time and commitments so that you can be successful in the long run. You will want to put your priorities in order: God, family, work/school. Notice that even though school is critical in this time of your life, it is not the primary task in your life. Nevertheless, ensure that you plan sufficient time to complete your work well. This is a balancing act and may require a few revisions before you get it just right for yourself and your commitments. Take heart, as the Bible assures us that "the wise in heart will know the proper time and procedure" Ecc. 8:5 (NIV). Pray that God will grant you wisdom to plan your time well.

References

Ainslie, G. (1992). *Picoeconomics: The strategic interaction of successive motivational states within the person.* New York, NY: Cambridge University Press.

Anderson, C. J. (2003). The psychology of doing nothing: Forms of decision avoidance result from reason and emotion. *Psychological Bulletin, 129,* 139–167.

Astin, A. W. (1993). *What matters in college?* San Francisco, CA: Jossey-Bass.

Baumeister, R. F., Heatherton, T. F., & Tice, D. M. (1994). *Losing control: How and why people fail at self-regulation.* San Diego, CA: Academic Press.

Beck, B. L., Koons, S. R., & Milgram, D. L. (2000). Correlates and consequences of behavioral procrastination: the effects of academic procrastination, self-consciousness, self-esteem, and self-handicapping. *Journal of Social Behavior and Personality, 15,* 3–13.

Burka, J. B., & Yuen, L. M. (2008). *Procrastination: Why you do it, what to do about it now.* Cambridge, MA: De Capo Press.

Chu, A. H. C., & Cho, J. N. (2005). Rethinking procrastination: Positive effects of "active" procrastination behavior on attitudes and performance. *The Journal of Social Psychology, 145*(3), 245–264.

Covey, S. R. (2004). *The seven habits of highly effective people* (3rd ed.). New York, NY: Fireside.

Ellis, A., & Knaus, W. J. (2002). *Overcoming procrastination* (Rev. ed.). New York, NY: New American Library.

Erickson, B. L., Peters, C. B., & Strommer, D. W. (2006). *Teaching first-year college students.* San Francisco, CA: Jossey-Bass.

Falwell, J. (1997). *Falwell: An autobiography.* Lynchburg, VA: Liberty House Publishers.

Goldsmith, E. B. (2010). *Resource management for individuals and families* (4th ed.). Upper Saddle River, NJ: Prentice Hall.

Harriott, J., & Ferrari, J. R. (1996). Prevalence of chronic procrastination among samples of adults. *Psychological Reports, 73,* 873–877.

Hobson, J. A. (1988). *The dreaming brain.* New York, NY: Basic Books.

Kachgal, M. M., Hansen, L. S., & Nutter, K. T. (2001). Academic procrastination prevention/intervention: Strategies and recommendations. *Journal of Developmental Education, 25*(1), 2–12.

Lakein, A. (1973). *How to get control of your time and your life.* New York, NY: New American Library.

Lay, C. H., & Silverman, S. (1996). Trait procrastination, time management, and dilatory behavior. *Personality & Individual Differences, 21,* 61–67.

Light, R. J. (2001). *Making the most of college: Students speak their minds.* Cambridge, MA: Harvard University Press.

McCance, N., & Pychyl, T. A. (2003, August). *From task avoidance to action: An experience sampling study of undergraduate students' thoughts, feelings and coping strategies in relation to academic procrastination.* Paper presented at the Third Annual Conference for Counseling Procrastinators in the Academic Context, University of Ohio, Columbus, OH.

Morgenstern, J. (2004). *Time management from the inside out: The foolproof system for taking control of your schedule—and your life* (2nd ed.). New York, NY: Henry Holt.

Myers, D. G. (1993). *The pursuit of happiness: Who is happy—and why?* New York, NY: Morrow.

Myers, D. G. (2000). The funds, friends, and faith of happy people. *American Psychologist, 55*, 56–67.

Onwuegbuzie, A. J. (2000). Academic procrastinators and perfectionistic tendencies among graduate students. *Journal of Social Behavior and Personality, 15*, 103–109.

Rhodewalt, F., & Vohs, K. D. (2005). Defensive strategies, motivation, and the self. In A. Elliot & C. Dweck (Eds.), *Handbook of competence and motivation* (pp. 548–565). New York, NY: Guilford Press.

Solomon, L. J., & Rothblum, E. D. (1984). Academic procrastination: Frequency and cognitive-behavioral correlates. *Journal of Counseling Psychology, 31*(4), 503–509.

Steel, P. (2007). The nature of procrastination: A meta-analytic and theoretical review of quintessential self-regulatory failure. *Psychological Bulletin, 133*(1), 65–94.

Voelker, R. (2004). Stress, sleep loss, and substance abuse create potent recipe for college depression. *Journal of the American Medical Association, 291*, 2177–2179.

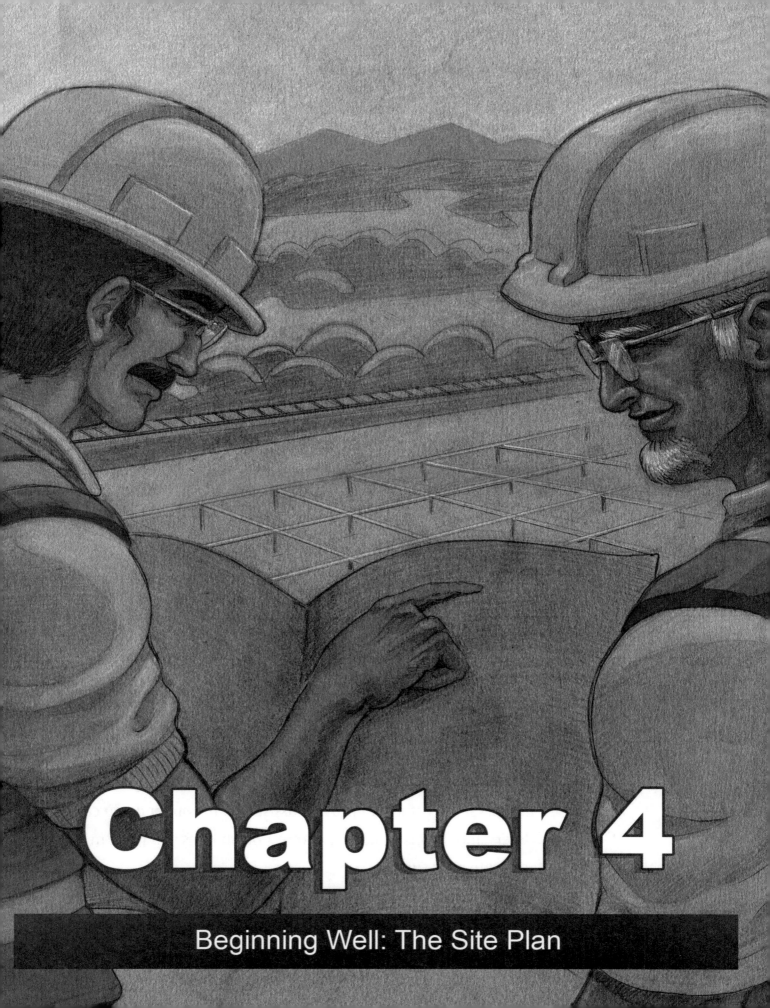

Chapter 4

Beginning Well: The Site Plan

In this chapter you will:

- Understand what is expected of you as an online college student.
- Determine to be actively engaged with your courses.
- Explore the Liberty University resources available to help you.
- Practice self-reflection to fuel personal academic growth.

SITE PLAN

When you first dream of building a new building, there are many tasks to complete to ensure that the building will go from concept to reality as planned. One of the crucial steps is to understand how your proposed building fits into the existing landscape and infrastructure. In order to see that, a site plan is carefully developed. According to Dictionary of Construction.com, the definition of _site plan_ is: "A plan of the area of a proposed construction operation, including the building outline, parking, work areas, and/or property lines." In developing a site plan for your college education and the degree you are pursuing, you must understand the parameters under which you are working. This would include the guiding documents, policies, and student expectations that Liberty University holds. Once you understand the "lay of the land," so to speak, you can identify the offices and personnel who can provide assistance to you, and you can determine the tasks, habits, and responsibilities you must meet to create your success.

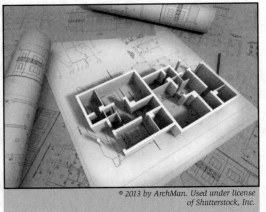

© 2013 by ArchMan. Used under license of Shutterstock, Inc.

Proverbs 15:22, "Plans fail for lack of counsel, but with many advisers they succeed" (NIV).

CORNERSTONE

Proverbs 6:6–8, "Go to the ant, you sluggard; consider its ways and be wise! It has no commander, no overseer or ruler, yet it stores its provisions in summer and gathers its food at harvest" (NIV).

I love the fall in Virginia. In the early days of Virginia's autumn, the temperature settles in between 60 and 75 degrees. The cooler temperatures produce a freshness to the air that compels Virginians, and visitors alike, to draw in a deep breath and exhale, releasing the stresses of the day. Later in the fall comes the change in the leaves. Our mountains transform from a lovely blanket of green to a patchwork quilt with hues of orange, red, and gold—until at last, the leaves of the trees fall to the ground ushering in the early days of winter. In the fall, my husband's grandparents, Nanny and PaPa Tomlin, faithfully remind me, "You can always tell what kind of winter you are going to have, depending on the amount of nuts that fall from the trees onto the ground." PaPa will go on to explain, "God is going to take care of His animals, so if there are a lot of nuts, you know it's gonna be a hard winter."

Photo courtesy of Les Schofer (Liberty University).

Jerry Falwell wore a Jesus First lapel pin every day. This is a constant reminder of how our university began, and how it continues to this day.

On a beautiful day this fall, I decided to hike up our hill at the foot of Bear Mountain for exercise. While drawing in my favorite breaths of the cool autumn air, I noticed the squirrels busying about our house underneath a grand hickory tree. They darted up and down the tree, crossed over our yard from one forest of trees to the next, skipped, jumped, and swiveled about in mid-air. Their acrobatics were really quite impressive. As they'd run up our hickory tree, I'd hear clickety-clacking noises and see the shells of hickory nuts fall onto our sidewalk. Below the grand old tree, I noticed a generous covering of hickory nuts and realized that this winter was going to be a bear.

The Lord brought Proverbs 6:6–8 to mind as I watched the industrious squirrels, "Go to the ant, you sluggard; consider its ways and be wise! It has no commander, no overseer or ruler, yet it stores its provisions in summer and gathers its food at harvest" (NIV). Humbly, I realized that I had better prepare our home and family for the cold days ahead, for though that crisp, clean, and cool air cleanses my lungs, it also signifies the beginning of harsh weather. In order to begin the winter well, I need to gather food, blankets, candles, kerosene for lanterns, batteries for flashlights, and bottles of water. I must be as industrious as the squirrel.

In your college career, the same is true; you must be as industrious as the squirrel to begin well. God is going to take care of you; He's dropped little nuts of information throughout this textbook and throughout your course to prepare you. These nuts come in the form of facts relating to navigation of your online course and campus, the student honor code and code of conduct, student expectations, and proper communication. By collecting this information, you will store up a healthy supply of information to help you survive and thrive in the days ahead, "May the favor of the Lord our God rest on us; establish the work of our hands for us—yes, establish the work of our hands" (Psalms 90:17, ESV).

Understand What Is Expected of You

KEY CONCEPT

Psalm 51:10,
"Create in me a clean heart, O God; and renew a right spirit within me" (KJV).

At the beginning of a new student's experiences with Liberty University in the first term, there are many things to learn that are not necessarily related to course content. Students learn how to meet basic expectations for course behavior, communication, submission of work, and much more. Once you understand the basic expectations, it is easy to create your academic success. Let's look at some of the early nonacademic lessons that new online students must master.

Course Requirements Checklist

The first task of each term is to complete what we call the Course Requirements Checklist (CRC). This brief checklist ensures that students are aware of some basic expectations and is the tool we use to record attendance. For federal financial aid reporting, it is our roll-taking tool. Students may access this first "assignment" no sooner than midnight on the first Monday morning of the course. Those who fail to complete the CRC risk being dropped from the course for non-participation.

Course Documents

Each course has a syllabus and course schedule, which are the blueprints for expectations and how they will play out during the course. The **course schedule** specifies what reading and study assignments are to be done for each module/week of the term. The assignment expectations are detailed

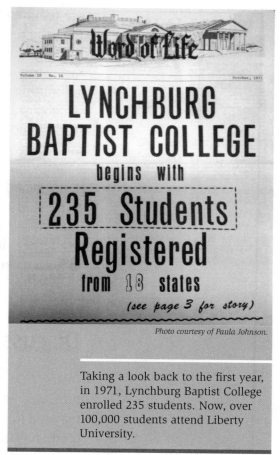

Photo courtesy of Paula Johnson.

Taking a look back to the first year, in 1971, Lynchburg Baptist College enrolled 235 students. Now, over 100,000 students attend Liberty University.

by week, as well. The **course syllabus** includes a description of the course content, rationale, prerequisite courses, required course materials, and expected learning outcomes. Details of expectations for required assignments, evaluation and grading, and late work policies are included. Each course syllabus includes information for those students who have a disability that may require academic accommodations. The course syllabus is the guiding policy document, while the course schedule lays out how assignment expectations will be met over the weeks of the course term.

Timely Work

Terri Washer

"Be sure to request extensions at least 24 hours ahead of time since faculty members are not always online."

Lucy LeRose

"Review the rubric for each assignment before completing it. This can assist you when you do not understand the instructions thoroughly. Also, this way you know exactly what is requested from to obtain a perfect score. After submitting your assignment and you've noticed it has been graded make sure to review the graded rubric and the instructor feedback."

While the beauty of online education is that students may complete their assignments online at their leisure, there are routine deadlines to be met in each course each week. Some students are surprised to learn that we expect regular "attendance" in our online program through work on various assignments. In other words, we mark your routine weekly attendance by noting the assignments that you complete in each module/week. You are required to keep up with weekly assignments, submitting each no later than the required due date in order to earn credit for the work. Just checking in to the course, looking at assignments, or viewing a presentation does not count as "attendance." Students who do not engage in the course (by submitting assignments) for 21 consecutive days receive a final grade of FN, which means "failure, nonattendance." The FN grade is a blow not only to the student's academic standing and transcript, but can also limit the availability of federal financial aid in future terms. Regular attendance and submission of work is critical, particularly in courses (such as math) where concepts build on each other. Getting behind in reading, viewing presentations, and doing regular assignments can lead to very poor outcomes, as students struggle to catch up and complete work quickly that should have been done previously. There are penalties for late work in each course. For these reasons, timely work that complies with the attendance policy and course deadlines is essential!

Discussion Boards

In the first week, students can begin to get to know each other and the professor as they engage in the discussion board. This is a form of online, ongoing (over a few days) conversation that allows students to "meet" each other. Students learn from the experiences and ideas shared in the forum, with a topic specified by the instructor, which highlights the instruction for the module. Generally speaking, undergraduate students post their "thread" (introductory post) in the discussion board no later than midnight on the specified day of the module/week. Students answer the prompt question(s) in paragraph format, expounding on what they have learned from the study material, which might include textbook reading, course presentations, and website links. They share their ideas and interpretations of what they have learned so far. Then, students reply to a few of their peers' threads, responding to ideas presented. Sharing your thinking, in response to others in the discussion board, can help develop and extend your ideas as you consider points provided by others that may not previously have occurred to you. This conversation goes on for a few days and usually closes, when the module/week ends.

Netiquette

Students who make their posts and replies in the discussion board forums must adhere to a code of ethical behavior that permits the free flow of ideas while respecting the thoughts and words of other posters. Students must be careful to observe the rules of "netiquette" or network etiquette, which require that responses be respectful, using polite language to agree or disagree with the thoughts shared by others. Students are free to disagree without being disagreeable! Carefully responding with evidence to refute a claim with which you disagree is a skill that students learn and develop in their discussion board work. While it is important to be polite when disagreeing, it is also important to avoid simply agreeing with each post to which you respond. The point of the discussion board is to share ideas and develop your thinking. Agreeing with everyone you respond to does not allow you to demonstrate your understanding of deeper meaning in the topic. Try to ask a question to extend the discussion or bring up a different aspect of the topic, or disagree politely, but be sure to post in such a way as to carry the conversation forward.

Careful, Respectful Communication

The respectful tone required in the discussion board is to be observed in all Liberty University communication. It is important to frame communication, by email or phone, in polite speech, using correct grammar, punctuation, and proper terminology. Students should begin each message by identifying themselves fully, which means giving their full name (Jane T. Doe) and student identification number (L00######). Letting the recipient know the name, number, and section of your course helps give context to what will follow. Only after identifying yourself and the course should you launch into what you are writing about. Choosing your words carefully, after gathering all appropriate facts for the inquiry you wish to pose, is critical for a quick response and resolution of the concern you are attempting to express. If you are writing to ask about a certain quiz item, it is best to identify the quiz, the topic, and the content of the question, rather than just asking "Why did I get #7 wrong?," especially since most quiz questions are randomized (meaning that the #7 for your quiz may be #3 for someone else's quiz). Providing as much information as possible is the key to having your inquiry answered quickly and correctly the first time. While most professors are very responsive to student emails, remember that Liberty University expects faculty to respond to email messages within 48 hours of receiving them. In other words, if you have a question on Monday night at 10:00 P.M. and you write an email to your professor to ask for clarification, you should expect to have an answer no later than Wednesday night at 10:00 P.M. Again, many professors respond more quickly than that, but try to temper your expectations with the turnaround time in mind. Consider that questions asked just minutes before an assignment deadline will probably NOT receive a reply in time for you to submit your work on time.

Weekly Deadlines

It is a wise student who consistently works ahead of routine deadlines. Balancing the life you already have before you decide to become a student with course work in college can be a challenge for many students. With work, church, family, and community commitments, many students are already fully engaged before trying to factor in college coursework. As mentioned earlier, while the beauty of online college work is that you have flexibility in how you complete your work, you still must meet regular deadlines. No one expects the unexpected events that happen, such as lost power, a balky computer, sudden illness, or any of the other "dog ate my homework" events in life that just happen! The way to avoid difficulties of this sort is to work a bit ahead of deadlines. Completing the module/week's work on the weekend can help avoid the stress of frantic late-night Monday work . . . particularly when something goes wrong or assignments simply take longer to complete than you expect. Emailing the professor just minutes before the submission deadline to request an extension is **not** an acceptable way to end the week's work!

Katie Stewart

"The best thing you can do for yourself as a student and employee is to learn how to write a professional and courteous email. If you introduce yourself politely, state your concern as specifically as possible, and end with a courteous salutation, you will find that your instructor, boss, co-worker, etc. will take you more seriously and treat you with more respect."

Michael Marrano

"Take each set of assignment instructions and break down its requirements into its component pieces in bullet point fashion. Review the grading rubric also for possible additional details to include on your list. This way you do not miss the finer details of an assignment and lose points when it is graded."

Ethical Behavior

Liberty University was founded in 1971 as a Christian university. Consequently, there is a basic expectation of ethical behavior in all work done for courses. Here is the Preamble to the Code of Honor:

> Liberty University students, faculty, administrators, and staff together form a Christian community based upon the values and goals of the Bible. These are defined in our foundational statements, including our Doctrinal Statement, our Philosophy of Education and Mission Statement, the Statement of Professional Ethics for the Faculty, and our Student Code. Together, these statements situate Liberty University within the long tradition of university culture, which in its beginnings was distinctively Christian, designed to preserve and advance truth.

> Anyone, whether Christian or non-Christian, who shares our values and goals, is both welcome and valued in our community. We want all students to feel comfortable in our community of learning, and we extend to all of our students our spiritual and academic resources, with the goal of fostering spiritual growth, character development, and academic maturity.

> Communities are based upon shared values and practices. This Code of Honor, an expression of the values inherent in our Doctrinal Statement, defines the rules and principles by which our community functions. At the core of this Code are two key concepts: a belief in the dignity of all persons and an insistence on the existence of objective truth.

> While we understand that everyone will not agree with the statements that follow, we do expect that our students respect and uphold these standards while registered at Liberty University. Abiding by the principles and behaviors established in this Code of Honor makes possible the success of our students and the strengthening of the Liberty community.

> Students who violate the Code of Honor, with either academic or personal offenses, are subject to sanctions as administered through the Graduate and Online Student Affairs Office. The Liberty University Code of Honor is a guiding document, which describes expectations for appropriate/acceptable student conduct, both on campus and online.

This preamble is followed by a detailed description of the academic code of honor, which identifies academic misconduct in three forms: plagiarism, cheating, and falsification. Definitions, consequences, and appeal procedures are described in full.

The personal code of honor for Liberty University Online is described, along with consequences and appeal procedures. The full Code of Honor for Liberty University Online students can be found on the Liberty University website (Liberty University Student Affairs, 2014).

Lucy LeRose

"Consider the following when addressing your instructor for an extension:

1. Proactive steps consist of giving your instructor a time plan/goal allowing the instructor to see the intentions you have of completing the assignment you are requesting an extension for.

2. Properly identifying yourself by including your full name followed by the course and section. This is necessary for when an instructor has several classes."

Determine to Be Actively Engaged with Your Courses

Micah 6:8,

"He has shown you, O mortal, what is good. And what does the Lord require of you? To act justly and to love mercy and to walk humbly with your God" (NIV).

Research indicates that active involvement may be the most powerful principle of human learning and college success (Astin, 1993; Kuh et al., 2005). The bottom line is this: To maximize your success in college, you cannot be a passive spectator; you need to be an active player.

The principle of active involvement includes the following key components:

- The amount of personal time devoted to learning in college.

- The degree of personal effort or energy (mental and physical) put into the learning process.

Think of something you do with intensity, passion, and commitment. If you were to approach academic work in the same way, you would be faithfully implementing the principle of active involvement.

One way to ensure that you're actively involved in the learning process and putting forth high levels of energy or effort is to take action on what you're learning. You can engage in any of the following actions to ensure that you are investing a high level of effort and energy:

- **Writing.** Write in response to what you're trying to learn. *Example:* Write notes when reading rather than passively underlining sentences.

- **Speaking.** Say aloud what you're trying to learn. *Example:* Explain course concepts to a study-group partner rather than studying them silently.

- **Organizing.** Connect or integrate the ideas you're trying to learn. *Example:* Create an outline, diagram, or concept map to visually connect ideas.

The following section explains how you can apply both key components of active involvement—spending time and expending energy—to the major learning challenges that you will encounter in college.

Time Spent on Coursework

In college, you will be expected to spend more of your own time on academic work outside of class presentations and videos. Studies clearly show that when college students spend more time on academic work outside of class, it results in better learning and higher grades (National Survey of Student Engagement, 2009). For example, one study of more than 25,000 college students found that the percentage of students receiving mostly "A" grades was almost three times higher for students who spent 40 or more hours per week on academic work than it was for students who spent between 20 and 40 hours. Among students who spent 20 or fewer hours per week on academic work, the percentage receiving grades of mostly "C" or below was almost twice as high as it was for students who spent 40 or more hours on academic work (Pace, 1990; 1995).

Unfortunately, less than 40 percent of beginning college students report having studied for six or more hours per week during their final year in high school (Pryor, De Angelo, Palucki-Blake, Hurtado, & Tran, 2012), and only one-third expect to spend more than 20 hours per week preparing for class in college (National Survey of Student Engagement, 2009). Just as successful athletes need to put in time and often work hard to improve their physical performance, successful students need to do the same to improve their academic performance.

Alexandra Barnett

"Use the discussion boards to complete assignments, but also to connect with your classmates. Build connections by reading your peers responses to your discussion board posts and respond to those peers!"

If you need further motivation to achieve good grades, keep in mind that higher grades earned in college are related to higher prospects for career success after college. Research on college graduates indicates that the higher their grades were in college, the higher: (1) their annual salary, (2) the status (prestige) of their first job, (3) their career mobility (ability to change jobs or move into different positions). This relationship between college grades and career advantages exists for students at all types of colleges and universities, regardless of the reputation or prestige of the institution that the students are attending (Pascarella & Terenzini, 1991; 2005). In other words, how well you do academically in college matters more to your career success than where you went to college.

Active Listening and Note Taking

You'll find that college professors rely heavily on the lecture method—they profess their knowledge by speaking for long stretches of time, and the students' job is to listen and take notes on the knowledge they dispense. This method of instruction places great demands on your ability to listen carefully and take notes that are both accurate and complete. Online learners do not attend lengthy lectures, as content is delivered in shorter presentations. The reading load, however, matches that of the regular semester, though the term is only half as long. In other words, the reading load for online students is roughly double that of the residential students working over an entire semester.

The best way to apply the principle of active involvement during a class lecture is to engage in the physical action of writing notes. Writing down what your instructor is saying in class "forces" you to pay closer attention to what is being said and reinforces your retention of what was said. By taking notes, you not only hear the information (auditory memory), you also see it on paper (visual memory) and feel it in the muscles of your hand as you write it (motor memory). The best thing about attending lectures online is that you can pause the presentation if you need to finish something in your notes and then resume when you are ready to continue.

From *Thriving in College and Beyond*, 3/e by Joseph B. Cuseo, Aaron Thompson, Michele Campagna and Viki S. Fecas. Copyright © 2013 by Kendall Hunt Publishing Company. Reprinted by permission.

Preparing for Listening and Notetaking From Your Course Materials

Before you begin a course learning session, make sure you have prepared yourself for success by setting the stage for success.

1. Do your work in an area that is free of distractions. This can be an office, a corner of your bedroom, or even the dining table, as long as you are able to limit distractions while you are there for a learning session.

2. Organize your materials. Get what you need for note taking, whether that means pen or pencil, notepaper or 3 × 5 cards, or your favorite note-taking app.

3. Consider using headphones to enable you to both hear well for an audio presentation, and avoid distracting sounds in your environment.

4. Put away other distractors. Turn off the television. Turn your phone to "silent" or, better yet, leave it in another room while you are working. Teach your family that unless the house is on fire while you are studying, you are not to be disturbed. Do NOT be tempted to have Facebook or chat features open while you are doing your schoolwork.

5. Quickly review your notes from the reading material, your previous study/learning session, or the previous module. See if you can activate your thinking for the concepts you will be learning in this session.

6. Say a brief prayer, asking God to open your mind to the material you are about to encounter and to bless you with clear thought and easy understanding.

   Now you're ready to begin!

Active Reading

Writing not only promotes active listening in class, but also can promote active reading out of class. Taking notes on information that you're reading (or on information you've highlighted while reading) keeps you actively involved in the reading process because it requires more mental and physical energy than merely reading the material or passively highlighting sentences.

Top Strategies: Improving Textbook Reading Comprehension and Retention

If you haven't already acquired textbooks for your courses, get them immediately and get ahead on your reading assignments. Information from reading assignments ranks right behind lecture notes as a source of test questions on college exams. Your professors are likely to deliver class lectures with the expectation that you have done the assigned reading and can build on that knowledge when they're lecturing. If you haven't done the reading, you'll have more difficulty following and taking notes on what your instructor is saying. Thus, by not doing the reading you pay a double penalty: You miss information that will appear directly on course exams, and you miss information delivered by your instructor, because you don't have the background knowledge to make sense of it. College professors also expect you to relate or connect what they talk about to the reading they have assigned. Thus, it's important to start developing good reading habits now. You can do so by using the following strategies to improve your reading comprehension and retention.

1. **Read with the right equipment.**
   - Bring tools to record and store information. Always bring a writing tool (pen or pencil) to record important information and a storage space (notebook or laptop) in which you can save and retrieve information acquired from your reading for later use on tests and assignments.

- Have a dictionary nearby to quickly find the meaning of unfamiliar words that may interfere with your ability to comprehend what you're reading. Looking up definitions of unfamiliar words does more than help you understand what you're reading: it's also an effective way to build your vocabulary. A strong vocabulary will improve your reading comprehension in all college courses, as well as your performance on standardized tests, such as those required for admission to graduate and professional schools.

- Check the back of your textbook for a list of key terms included in the book. Each academic subject or discipline has its own vocabulary, and knowing the meaning of these terms is often the key to understanding the concepts covered in the text. Don't ignore the glossary; it's more than an ancillary or afterthought to the textbook. Use it regularly to increase your comprehension of course concepts. Consider making a photocopy of the glossary of terms at the back of your textbook so that you can have a copy of it in front of you while you're reading, rather than having to repeatedly stop, hold your place, and go to the back of the text to find the glossary.

2. **Get in the right position.** Sit upright and have light coming from behind you, over opposite your writing hand. This will reduce the distracting and fatiguing effects of glare shadows.

3. **Get a sneak preview.** Approach the chapter by first reading its boldface headings and any chapter outline, summary, or end-of-chapter questions that may be provided. This will supply you with a mental map of the chapter's important ideas before you start your reading trip and provide an overview that will help you keep track of the chapter's major ideas (the "big picture"), reducing the risk that you'll get lost among the smaller details you encounter along the way.

4. **Use boldface headings and subheadings.** Headings are cues for important information. Turn them into questions, and then read to find their answers. This will launch you on an answer-finding mission that will keep you mentally active while reading and enable you to read with a purpose. Turning headings into questions is also a good way to prepare for tests because you're practicing exactly what you'll be expected to do on tests—answer questions.

5. **Pay attention to the first and last sentences.** Absorb opening and closing sentences in sections beneath the chapter's major headings and subheadings. These sentences often contain an important introduction and conclusion to the material covered in that section of the text.

6. **Finish each of your reading sessions with a short review.** Recall what you have highlighted or noted as important information (rather than trying to cover a few more pages). It's best to use the last few minutes of reading time to "lock in" the most important information you've just read because most forgetting takes place immediately after you stop processing (taking in) information and start doing something else.

From *Thriving in College and Beyond*, 3/e by Joseph B. Cuseo, Aaron Thompson, Michele Campagna and Viki S. Fecas. Copyright © 2013 by Kendall Hunt Publishing Company. Reprinted by permission.

Interpersonal Interaction

Learning is strengthened when it takes place in a social context that involves interpersonal interaction. As some scholars put it, human knowledge is "socially constructed" or built up through interpersonal interaction and dialogue. According to these scholars, your conversations with others become internalized as ideas in your mind and influence your way of thinking (Bruffee, 1993; Johnson, Johnson, & Smith, 1998). Thus, by having frequent, intelligent conversations with others, you broaden your knowledge and deepen your thinking.

Four particular forms of interpersonal interaction have been found to be strongly associated with student learning and motivation in college:

1. Student-faculty interaction

2. Student-advisor interaction

3. Student-mentor interaction

4. Student-student (peer) interaction

Interacting with Faculty Members

Studies repeatedly show that college success is strongly influenced by the quality and quantity of student-faculty interaction *outside the classroom.* Such contact is associated with the following positive outcomes for college students:

- Improved academic performance;

- Increased critical thinking skills;

- Greater satisfaction with the college experience;

- Increased likelihood of completing a college degree; and

- Stronger desire to seek education beyond college (Astin, 1993; Pascarella & Terenzini, 1991; 2005).

Alexandra Barnett

"Introduce yourself to your instructor via email during the first week of class and let him/her know about any challenges you may be facing during the course term."

These positive outcomes are so strong and widespread that we encourage you to immediately begin seeking interaction with college faculty outside of class time. Connect with your instructors through e-mail, which can be accomplished from within your course. Find the professor's contact information by looking under Faculty Information, on the top left side when you sign in to Blackboard. Your professor's email address will be there, as well as any phone number the professor may use for student contacts. Because of the variety of time zones/work schedules for students and faculty at Liberty University Online, email may well be the most efficient way to make contact with your professor at a time that is convenient for him or her.

In one national survey, almost half of college students reported that e-mail has allowed them to communicate their ideas with professors on subjects that they would not have discussed in person (Pew Internet & American Life Project, 2002).

Interaction with Academic Advisors

An academic advisor may serve as a very effective referral agent who can direct you to, and connect you with, campus support services that can promote your success. An advisor can also help you understand college procedures and navigate the bureaucratic maze of college policies and politics. You will read more about Academic Advising later in this chapter.

Interaction with a Mentor

A mentor may be described as an experienced guide who takes personal interest in you and the progress you're making toward your goals. (For example, in the movie *Star Wars,* Yoda served as a mentor for Luke Skywalker.) Research in higher education demonstrates that a mentor can make first-time students feel significant and enable them to stay on track until they complete their college degree (Campbell & Campbell, 1997; Knox, 2004). A mentor can assist you in troubleshooting difficult or complicated issues that you may not be able to resolve on your own and is someone with whom you can share good news, such as your success stories and personal accomplishments.

Look for someone with whom you can develop this type of trusting relationship. Many people on campus have the potential to be outstanding mentors, including the following:

- Your academic advisor

- Your instructor in a first-year seminar or experience course

- Faculty in your intended major

- Juniors, seniors, or graduate students in your intended field of study

- Working professionals in careers that interest you

- Academic support professionals (e.g., professional tutors in the Learning Center)

- Career counselors

- Campus minister or chaplain

- Financial aid counselors

Interaction with Peers (Student-Student Interaction)

Studies repeatedly point to the power of the peer group as a source of social and academic support during the college years (Pascarella, 2005). One study of more than 25,000 college students revealed that when peers interact with one another while learning they achieve higher levels of academic performance and are more likely to persist to degree completion (Astin, 1993). In another study that involved in-depth interviews with more than 1,600 college students, it was discovered that almost all students who struggled academically had one particular study habit in common: They always studied alone (Light, 2001).

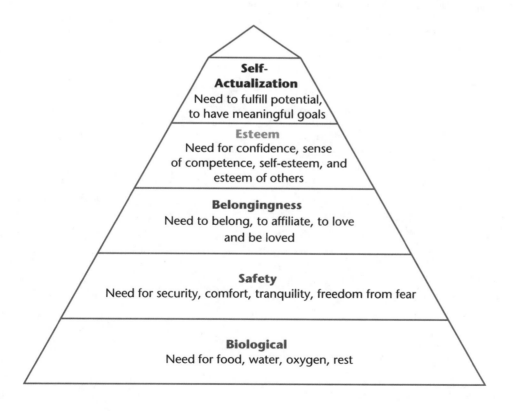

Alexandra Barnett

"Ask your instructor questions if you don't understand the material or assignments. Your professor will welcome your proactive attitude towards school and will be happy to answer any questions you may have!"

Peer interaction is especially important during the first term of college. At this stage of the college experience, new students have a strong need for belonging and social acceptance because many of them have just left the lifelong security of family and hometown friends. As a new student, it may be useful to view the early stage of your college experience through the lens of psychologist Abraham Maslow's hierarchy of human needs. According to Maslow's hierarchy of needs, humans cannot reach their full potential and achieve peak performance until their more basic emotional and social needs have been met (e.g., their needs for personal safety, social acceptance, and self-esteem). Making early connections with your peers helps you meet these basic human needs, provides you with a base of social support to ease your integration into the college community, and prepares you to move up to higher levels of the need hierarchy (e.g., achieving educational excellence and fulfilling your potential). In online education, these first contacts with student peers come through the course Discussion Board. Note that each course offers not only the required Discussion Board threads and replies, in which you discuss with classmates pre-selected topics, but also a Course Community Center. This area of the Discussion Board is where you may interact with peers to share prayer requests and praises, ask questions of the group, and share what you are learning.

From *Thriving in College and Beyond*, 3/e by Joseph B. Cuseo, Aaron Thompson, Michele Campagna and Viki S. Fecas. Copyright © 2013 by Kendall Hunt Publishing Company. Reprinted by permission.

Explore the Liberty University Resources Available to Help You

Jeremiah 3:15,
"Then I will give you shepherds after my own heart, who will lead you with knowledge and understanding" (NIV).

Your time in college learning can bring a bewildering array of information, choices, and tasks. Make sure you understand the opportunities that you have to ask for and receive guidance and support. Liberty University provides online students a wealth of campus-based online resources to smooth the path to online learning success. Studies show that students who take advantage of campus resources report higher levels of satisfaction with college and get more out of the college experience (Pascarella & Terenzini, 1991, 2005). Using your campus resources is an important, research-backed principle of college success, and it is a natural extension of the principle of active involvement. Active involvement includes making use of campus resources.

An essential first step in making effective use of campus resources is to become aware of what they are and what they're designed to do. Read the following to learn about opportunities for assistance from the offices and services designed to help you create your successful college learning experiences. The offices and resources are given in alphabetical order for easy future reference.

Photo by Kevin Manguiob, courtesy of Liberty University.

President Jerry Falwell Jr., reviewing plans for future developments on campus.

Academic Advising Office

The Academic Advising professionals provide a campus resource for help with course selection, educational planning, and choosing or changing a major. Studies show that college students who have developed clear educational and career goals are more likely to persist in college until they complete their college degree (Willingham, 1985; Wyckoff, 1999). Research indicates that beginning college students need help clarifying their educational goals, selecting an academic major, and exploring careers (Cuseo, 2005; Frost, 1991). As a first-year college student, being undecided or uncertain about your educational and career goals is nothing to be embarrassed about. However, you should start thinking about your future now. Connect early and often with an academic advisor to help you clarify your educational goals and find a field of study that best complements your interests, talents, and values. Online learners may have a firm idea of the courses that are interesting, but the academic advisors can help you understand the correct course sequence to help you complete your program well and in the time frame you have in mind. Because online academic advising is done by major, you can be assured that the individual helping you is fully aware of the details of the degree that you are seeking.

Atomic Learning

This resource is not an office but is a resource you can access when you need quick information on software and related learning tools. Atomic Learning is a nearly boundless resource available to students and is as close as Blackboard. The Atomic learning resources provide brief (30 seconds to a few minutes) tutorials on every topic imaginable from Facebook to YouTube to all sorts of software tools. Access Atomic Learning to find exactly what you need, when you need it. Software and technology learning resources are available around the clock on demand with this free service provided to all online learners.

Financial Aid Office

This campus resource is designed to help you finance your college education. If you have questions concerning how to obtain assistance in paying for college, the staff of this office is there to guide you through the application process. The paperwork needed to apply for and secure financial aid can sometimes be confusing or overwhelming.

Don't let this intimidate you enough to prevent you from seeking financial aid; assistance is available to you from the knowledgeable staff in the Financial Aid Office. You can also seek help from this office to find:

- Low-interest student loans;
- Grants; and
- Scholarships.

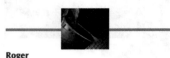

Roger

"Online students must realize that they are responsible for their online education. They are the best advocates for a good education. But they don't have to figure it all out on their own. There are resources such as degree completion plans. The school has invested heavily in training academic advisors.

"Students must realize that they are expected to produce college level work. They need to learn how to write in Turabian, APA, and other formats. The school has entered into partnership with the Online Writing Center and Tutor. com to assist students with writing assignments.

"Students do not have to feel that they are carrying heavy burdens alone. There is an entire online community to come alongside and bring encouragement and assistance. The LU Online Ministries department has advocates trained to provide prayerful support in time of need. Many classrooms have a community center (in the discussion board forums) where students can fellowship and pray with one another."

If you have any doubt about whether you are using the most effective plan for financing your college education, speak to a professional in the Financial Aid Office.

IT Help Desk/IT Marketplace

Did you know that students can purchase computer software at a discounted rate through the IT Marketplace? All the software required for courses is available for students at a specially arranged student price when purchased through the University's IT Marketplace.

Betsey Caballero

"When in doubt . . . ASK!"

Another service that nearly every student will eventually become familiar with is the IT Help Desk. This is the resource to consult when you are having technical difficulty. Problems with Blackboard? Can't get the presentation to open? Your test "freezes" while you are in the middle of taking it? These issues, and others, can all be handled by submitting a HelpTicket to the IT HelpDesk. The professionals at the IT HelpDesk can assist you remotely or by phone to quickly resolve whatever technical issue is preventing your smooth progress.

Virus protection is essential for keeping your computer safe online. Liberty University provides antivirus protection to students, faculty, and staff at no cost.

Even before you need to seek help to resolve a problem, you may find that if you consult Ask LUKE, you can solve your own problem. (Ask LUKE stands for "Ask Liberty University Knowledge Experts.") There are quick tutorials that describe steps to set up your iPhone or Android smartphone, and answer questions on applications, Blackboard, our webmail program etc.

Liberty University Jerry Falwell Library

The library is your campus resource for finding information and completing research assignments (e.g., term papers and group projects). Librarians are professional educators who provide instruction outside the classroom. You can learn from them just as you can learn from faculty inside the classroom. Furthermore, the library is a place where you can acquire skills for locating, retrieving, and evaluating

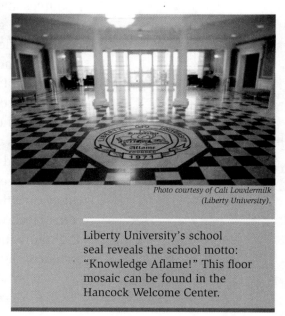

Photo courtesy of Cali Lowdermilk (Liberty University).

Liberty University's school seal reveals the school motto: "Knowledge Aflame!" This floor mosaic can be found in the Hancock Welcome Center.

information that you may apply to any course you are taking or will ever take. Your college library is your campus resource for developing research skills that let you access, retrieve, and evaluate information, which are skills for achieving both educational and occupational success. Online learners have access to the full range of scholarly materials available through the Jerry Falwell Library.

Liberty Online Communities

Liberty University Online students can keep abreast of all that is happening on campus with the link to LU Communities. This site provides many ways for distant students to engage Liberty University through live streaming events, social media options, and links to the events and services of the university community. Requests for prayer can also be submitted through LU Communities, which is then shared with campus pastors as prayer partners.

Office of Military Affairs

Excerpt provided by Emily Foutz, Director, Office of Military Affairs

Liberty University greatly appreciates the dedication and sacrifices made by our nation's Armed Forces, and we understand the needs of our service members, veterans, and military spouses and dependents. There are several resources and provisions provided for military students as they pursue their educational goals.

The Office of Military Affairs exists to support our service members, veterans, and military families with specific needs related to their education, including military and veteran benefit counseling to help students navigate through the process for military Tuition Assistance and the GI Bill, and assistance when military duty occasionally impedes progress toward educational goals. Military Affairs acts as a liaison among the student, the military, and the Department of Veterans Affairs to assist students with their financial needs so that they may focus on their educational pursuits. The Office of Online Disability Academic Support offers assistance for those veterans faced with challenges related to posttraumatic stress disorder (PTSD) and traumatic brain injury (TBI). Students who are facing these challenges are encouraged to contact this office for support.

Online Office of Disability Academic Support

The Liberty University Online Office of Disability Academic Support (LU ODAS) works with students and faculty to coordinate support services for online students with a documented disability. Under Section 504 of the Rehabilitation Act of 1973, this office provides "reasonable" accommodations and creates equal program access for all students. The online ODAS office works in conjunction with students and faculty to ensure that reasonable accommodations are made for students with documented disabilities. Once a student's disability is verified, this office notifies faculty members of the appropriate accommodations to make for students. These accommodations might include extended time on testing or other reasonable adjustments to ensure the student receives appropriate support despite a disability.

Katie Stewart

"Reach out to your instructor! When you are confused about an assignment or unsure of your ability to write a college level summary, let your instructor know your concern as soon as possible. Instructors want to help their students succeed but they can't offer the extra help you need unless they know how you are struggling specifically."

Online Writing Center

Liberty University Online offers specialized support for students who would like to improve their writing skills. The Online Writing Center is the place where you can receive assistance at any stage of the writing process, whether it be collecting and organizing your ideas, composing your first draft, or proofreading your final draft. Since writing is an academic skill that you will use in many of your courses, if you improve your writing, you're likely to improve your overall academic performance. Thus, we strongly encourage you to capitalize on this resource. To use the resources of the Online Writing Center, you will need to make an appointment. The service is free of charge, but the Online Writing Center will only review each writing assignment one time. Be sure to choose what stage of the work you wish to have help with and make your appointment for help with that in mind. An alternative that is available around the clock is a service called Tutor.com. Students can access tutors on-demand and gain assistance with a host of topics, not limited just to writing.

© 2013 by Andresr. Used under license of Shutterstock, Inc.

Registrar's Office

The Registrar's Office is the official custodian of all your academic records for the university. When you need to check your transcript or have a copy of it mailed to a potential employer or scholarship granter, the Registrar's Office is your contact point.

Student Accounts

The Student Accounts Office keeps track of your financial obligations and payments to the university. The Student Accounts Office and the Financial Aid Office work together to manage and disburse your financial aid funds, whether from scholarships, military/veterans benefits, or outside sources.

Student Advocate Office

Alexandra Barnett

"Do not be afraid to let your instructor and ODAS (Office of Disability Academic Support) know if you have challenges that we can help you overcome by offering accommodations—we all have challenges in one area or another!"

The Student Advocate Office is available to help online students dealing with obstacles to their academic progress. In order to accomplish this, the office acts as a liaison between a student and other university departments and helps students who face difficulties that affect their progress, such as emergencies or situations such as course problems, medical difficulties, or any situation involving academic warning or probation, and so on. The Student Advocate Office also assists in resolution of student appeals. In an effort to be proactive, the Student Advocate Office regularly polls students in order to discover ways to improve the experiences of online learners at Liberty University.

Tutor.com

Cari Smith

"When you are unsure of something or find yourself confused—ASK THE PROFESSOR. We are here to help you succeed."

The individual tutoring provided by this service can help you master difficult course concepts and assignments, and the people working here are professionally trained to help you learn how to learn. While your professors may have expert knowledge of the subject matter they teach, learning resource specialists are experts on the process of learning. Studies show that college students who become actively involved with academic support services outside the classroom are more likely to attain higher grades and complete their college degree, particularly if they begin their involvement with these support services during the first year of college (Cuseo, 2003). Also, students who seek and receive assistance from their college learning center show significant improvement in academic self-efficacy—that is, they develop a stronger sense of personal control over their academic performance and higher expectations for academic success (Smith, Walter, & Hoey, 1992).

Despite the powerful advantages of using academic support services, these services are typically underused by college students, especially by those students who need them the most (Cuseo, 2003; Knapp & Karabenick, 1988; Walter & Smith, 1990). Some students believe that seeking academic help is admitting they are not smart, self-sufficient, or unable to succeed on their own. Do not buy into this belief system. Using academic support services doesn't mean you're helpless or clueless; instead, it indicates that you're a motivated and resourceful student who is striving to achieve academic excellence.

Virtual Career Center

Research on college students indicates that they are more likely to stay in school and graduate when they have some sense of how their present academic experience relates to their future career goals (Levitz & Noel, 1989; Tinto, 1993; Wyckoff, 1999).

Studies also show that most new students are uncertain about what career they would like to pursue (Gordon & Steele, 2003). So, if you are uncertain about your future career, welcome to the club that includes a very large number of other first-year students. The Career Center is the place to contact for help in finding a meaningful answer to the important question of how to connect your current college experience with your ongoing or future career goals. This campus resource typically provides such services as personal career counseling, workshops on career exploration and development, and career fairs where you are able to meet professionals working in different fields. Your process of exploring, planning, and preparing for career success can start as soon as you begin college.

Cari Smith

"When emailing your professor, ask specific questions and provide lots of detail."

From *Thriving in College and Beyond,* 3/e by Joseph B. Cuseo, Aaron Thompson, Michele Campagna and Viki S. Fecas. Copyright © 2013 by Kendall Hunt Publishing Company. Reprinted by permission.

Practice Self-Reflection to Fuel Personal Academic Growth

Job 34:4, "Let us discern for ourselves what is right; let us learn together what is good" (NLT).

2 Cor. 12:9a, "My grace is sufficient for you, for my power is made perfect in weakness" (ESV).

For many online learners, juggling responsibilities of family, work, and church can be nearly consuming. Adding in college coursework brings another layer of responsibility, but it does not really stop there, as there is more to be considered. Students need to be introspective, making a conscious effort to reflect on the choices made, the lessons learned, and how everything fits together to complete a cohesive plan of academic growth. Your times of introspection can be guided by God's Holy Spirit if you ask for wisdom and guidance.

Personal Reflection and Self-Awareness

Dr. Jerry Falwell, founder

"In the life of a believer, nothing happens by chance, fate or fortune" (Falwell, 1997, p. 428).

The final step in the learning process, whether it be learning in the course or learning from experience, is to step back from the process, thoughtfully review it, and connect it to what you already know. Reflection may be defined as the flip side of active involvement; both processes are necessary for learning to be complete. Learning requires not only effortful action but also thoughtful reflection. Active involvement gets and holds your focus of *attention,* which enables information to reach your brain, and personal reflection promotes *consolidation,* which locks that information into your brain's long-term memory (Bligh, 2000; Roediger, Dudai, & Fitzpatrick, 2007).

Personal reflection also involves introspection—turning inward and inspecting yourself to gain deeper *self-awareness* of what you've done, what you're doing, or what you intend to do. Two forms of self-awareness are particularly important for success in college:

 1. Self-assessment

2. Self-monitoring

Self-Assessment

Simply defined, self-assessment is the process of reflecting on and evaluating characteristics of your "self," such as your personality traits, learning habits, personal strengths, and personal weaknesses that need improvement. Self-assessment is the critical first step in the process of self-improvement, personal planning, and effective decision making. The following are important target areas for self-assessment because they reflect personal characteristics that play a pivotal role in promoting success in college and beyond:

- Personal interests. What you like to do or enjoy doing.

- Personal values. What is important to you and what you care about doing.

- Personal abilities or aptitudes. What you do well or have the potential to do well.

- Learning habits. How you go about learning and the usual approaches, methods, or techniques you use to learn.

- Learning styles. How you prefer to learn—the way you like to:

  - Receive information—the learning format you prefer (e.g., learning by reading, listening, or experiencing);

  - Perceive information—what sensory modality you prefer to use (e.g., vision, sound, or touch);

  - Process information—how you prefer to deal with or think about information you've taken in (e.g., whether you like to think about it on your own or discuss it with others).

- Personality traits. Your temperament, emotional characteristics, and social tendencies (e.g., whether you lean toward being outgoing or reserved).

- Academic self-concept. What kind of student you think you are and how you perceive yourself as a learner (e.g., your level of self-confidence and whether you believe academic success is within your control or depends on factors beyond your control).

Roger

"I can honestly say that I was not surprised by Liberty's expectations. I had experienced a rigorous education in both college and seminary. So I knew the level of work that I had to perform. I had forgotten the amount of reading required and at first was overwhelmed. Yet, I expected to be overwhelmed at first. But I knew the best thing to do is keep moving forward to accomplish projects a little at a time."

Photo courtesy of David Duncan (Liberty University).

Carving out a roadway on campus requires lots of planning and moving of mountains of dirt!

Self-Monitoring

Research indicates that one characteristic of successful learners is that they monitor or watch themselves and maintain self-awareness of:

- Whether they're using effective learning strategies (e.g., they are aware of their level of attention or concentration in class);

- Whether they're comprehending what they are attempting to learn (e.g., if they're understanding it at a deep level or merely memorizing it at a surface level); and

- How to regulate or adjust their learning strategies to meet the demands of different academic tasks and subjects (e.g., they read technical material in a science textbook more slowly and stop to test their understanding more often than when they're reading a novel; Pintrich, 1995; Pintrich & Schunk, 2002; Weinstein, 1994; Weinstein & Meyer, 1991).

You can begin to establish good self-monitoring habits by creating a routine of periodically pausing to reflect on the strategies you're using to learn and "do" college. For instance, you can ask yourself the following questions:

- Am I listening attentively to what my instructor is saying in class presentations?

- Do I comprehend what I am reading in my textbook?

- Am I effectively using campus resources that are designed to support my success?

- Am I interacting with campus professionals who can contribute to my current success and future development?

- Am I interacting with peers who can contribute to my learning and increase my level of involvement in the college experience?

- Am I effectively implementing the success strategies identified in this book? Why?

BUILDING BLOCKS

Summary and Conclusion

Research reviewed in this chapter points to the conclusion that successful students are:

1. **Engaged.** They seek to understand and meet basic Liberty University expectations of students in the online community.

2. **Involved.** They invest time and effort in the college experience and are careful to understand what is expected of them in the way of participation, communication, and timeliness of work.

3. **Resourceful.** They capitalize on their surrounding resources, knowing who or which office can provide assistance in each situation encountered on the path to completing a college degree online.

4. **Reflective.** They are self-aware learners who assess and monitor their own performance in order to turn academic potential into positive outcomes.

Personal Reflection

Now that you have seen what it takes to begin well, consider areas that you think will require additional effort on your part. What surprises you in the expectations of students? Are there areas that you think will be difficult for you? Describe below the difficulty and how you plan to mitigate it.

A difficulty will be self-monitoring. Pausing to reflect on what is being taught. I have to comprehend what I am reading and not just read to read.

• I am going to understand everything I am reading or ask for help.

Personal Reflection

Now, as you consider the helpers in place on campus, determine which ones you think will be necessary for you to contact. List below the contacts that you may need to make and jot down what you will need to have ready when you make the contact:

Academic Advising - Degree Goals
Online Writing Center - Proof Read my papers
Tutor.com - Seeking help in bettering my academics
Virtual Career Center - Direction of my career

Word Study

Using Biblegateway.com or Blueletterbible.com, do a word study on "plan" or "plans" to determine what God's Word has to say about making and carrying out plans.

Personal Reflection

How does God's plan for you include education here at Liberty University Online? Have you followed His guidance in your educational pursuits? Here is a verse to get you started. It is our wish for you as you begin well:

Psalm 20:4, "May he give you the desire of your heart and make all your plans succeed" (ESV).

I believe that God has directed me here. Whatever I plan I plan to do for the goodness of God. We have a choice to do evil or good with our lives. I choose to make the evil into good. I am pursuing what He has put in my heart.

TOOL BOX

- **Course Requirements Checklist (CRC):** As indicated in the chapter, the CRC is a crucial tool for taking attendance and for financial aid reporting. You can locate a tutorial on how to complete the CRC on the Breaking Ground website.

- **Syllabus and Course Schedule:** While the official syllabus and course schedule will not be available until your courses are available for the term, you may review the samples provided in the Course Guides section of the website (www.liberty.edu/online/course-guides).

- **Discussion Boards:** You will interact with faculty and students through Discussion Board forums in most of your courses. Review the tutorial on the Breaking Ground website to be sure you know how to use this critical tool.

- **Deadlines:** Deadlines for each course are unique; use the calendar feature on your smartphone or computer to track upcoming due dates and to stay on track.

- **Ethical Behavior:** As an online student with Liberty University, you are expected to uphold the online honor code. You can access a copy of the Liberty Online Honor Code through the Liberty University website or by navigating to the Breaking Ground website.

- **Interpersonal Communication**

  - *Student to Faculty*—To communicate with faculty you will typically use your Liberty University email address. You can email your professor through the webmail tool or directly through the Blackboard Learning Management System. Some faculty may even offer optional live sessions or interaction through social media sites.

  - *Student to Advisor*—Advisors can be reached by phone, email, and even by live chat.

  - *Student to Student*—You can communicate with other students using the Discussion Boards in your courses, but you might also consider connecting through the Liberty University social media sites or even by creating your own cohort of students in a social media group.

- **Student Support Offices:** For a full listing of links to the support offices referenced in the chapter, please navigate to the Breaking Ground website.

Additional resources and links to specific sites, worksheets, and apps can be located by accessing the Breaking Ground website:

www.breakinggroundlu.com

References

Astin, A. W. (1993). *What matters in college?* San Francisco, CA: Jossey-Bass.

Bligh, D. A. (2000). *What's the use of lectures?* San Francisco, CA: Jossey-Bass.

Bruffee, K. A. (1993). *Collaborative learning: Higher education, interdependence, and the authority of knowledge.* Baltimore, MD: Johns Hopkins University Press.

Campbell, T. A., & Campbell, D. E. (1997, December). Faculty/student mentor program: Effects on academic performance and retention. *Research in Higher Education, 38,* 727–742.

Cuseo, J. B. (2003). Comprehensive academic support for students during the first year of college. In G. L. Kramer et al. (Eds.), *Student academic services: An integrated approach* (pp. 271–310). San Francisco, CA: Jossey-Bass.

Cuseo, J. B. (2005). "Decided," "undecided," and "in transition": Implications for academic advisement, career counseling, and student retention. In R. S. Feldman (Ed.), *Improving the first year of college: Research and practice* (pp. 27–50). Mahwah, NJ: Lawrence Erlbaum.

Falwell, J. (1997). *Falwell: An autobiography.* Lynchburg, VA: Liberty House Publishers.

Frost, S. H. (1991). *Academic advising for student success: A system of shared responsibility* (ASHE-ERIC Higher Education Report No. 3). Washington, DC: School of Education and Human Development, George Washington University.

Gordon, V. N., & Steele, G. E. (2003). Undecided first-year students: A 25-year longitudinal study. *Journal of the First-Year Experience and Students in Transition, 15*(1), 19–38.

Johnson, D., Johnson, R., & Smith, K. (1998). Cooperative learning returns to college: What evidence is there that it works? *Change, 30,* 26–35.

Knapp, J. R., & Karabenick, S. A. (1988). Incidence of formal and informal academic help-seeking in higher education. *Journal of College Student Development, 29*(3), 223–227.

Knox, S. (2004). *Financial basics: A money management guide for students.* Columbus, OH: Ohio State University Press.

Kuh, G. D., Kinzie, J., Schuh, J. H., Whitt, E. J., et al. (2005). *Student success in college: Creating conditions that matter.* San Francisco, CA: Jossey-Bass.

Levitz, R., & Noel, L. (1989). Connecting student to the institution: Keys to retention and success. In M. L. Upcraft, J. N. Gardner, et al. (Eds.), *The freshman year experience* (pp. 65–81). San Francisco, CA: Jossey-Bass.

Liberty University Student Affairs. (2014). *Liberty University Online honor code: Preamble.* Retrieved from https://www.liberty.edu/index.cfm?PID = 19155.

Light, R. J. (2001). *Making the most of college: Students speak their minds.* Cambridge, MA: Harvard University Press.

National Survey of Student Engagement. (2009). *NSSE Annual Results 2009. Assessment for improvement: Tracking student engagement over time.*

Pace, C. (1990). *The undergraduates: A report of their activities.* Los Angeles, CA: University of California, Center for the Study of Evaluation.

Pace, C. (1995, May). *From good processes to good products: Relating good practices in undergraduate education to student achievement.* Paper presented at the meeting of the Association for Institutional Research, Boston, MA.

Pascarella, E. T., & Terenzini, P. (1991). *How college affects students: Findings and insights from twenty years of research.* San Francisco, CA: Jossey-Bass.

Pascarella, E. T., & Terenzini, P. (2005). *How college affects students: A third decade of research* (Vol. 2). San Francisco, CA: Jossey-Bass.

Pew Internet & American Life Project. (2002). *The Internet goes to college: How students are living in the future with today's technology.* Retrieved January 30, 2005, from http://www. perinternet.org/reports/pdfs/Report1.pdf

Pintrich, P. R. (Ed.). (1995). *Understanding self-regulated learning* (New Directions for Teaching and Learning, No. 63). San Francisco, CA: Jossey-Bass.

Pintrich, P. R., & Schunk, D. H. (2002). *Motivation in education: Theory, research, and applications.* Upper Saddle River, NJ: Merrill-Prentice Hall.

Pryor, J. H., De Angelo, L., Palucki-Blake, B., Hurtado, S., & Tran, S. (2012). *The American freshman: National norms fall 2011.* Los Angeles, CA: Higher Education Research Institute, UCLA.

Roediger, H. L., Dudai, Y., & Fitzpatrick, S. M. (2007). *Science of memory: concepts.* New York, NY: Oxford University Press.

Smith, J. B., Walter, T. L., & Hoey, G. (1992). Support programs and student self-efficacy: Do first-year students know when they need help? *Journal of the Freshman Year Experience, 4*(2), 41–67.

Tinto, V. (1993). *Leaving college: Rethinking the causes and cures of student attrition* (2nd ed.). Chicago, IL: University of Chicago Press.

Walter, T. L., & Smith, J. (1990, April). *Self-assessment and academic support: Do students know they need help?* Paper presented at the annual Freshman Year Experience Conference, Austin, TX.

Weinstein, C. F. (1994). Students at risk for academic failure. In K. W. Prichard & R.M. Sawyer (Eds.), *Handbook of college teaching: Theory and applications* (pp. 375–385). Westport, CT: Greenwood Press.

Weinstein, C. F., & Meyer, D. K. (1991). Cognitive learning strategies. In R. J. Menges & M. D. Svinicki (Eds.), *College teaching: From theory to practice* (New Directions for Teaching and Learning, No. 45, pp. 15–26). San Francisco, CA: Jossey-Bass.

Willingham, W. W. (1985). *Success in college: The role of personal qualities and academic ability.* New York, NY: College Entrance Examination Board.

Wyckoff, S. C. (1999). The academic advising process in higher education: History, research, and improvement. *Recruitment & Retention in Higher Education, 13*(1), 1–3.

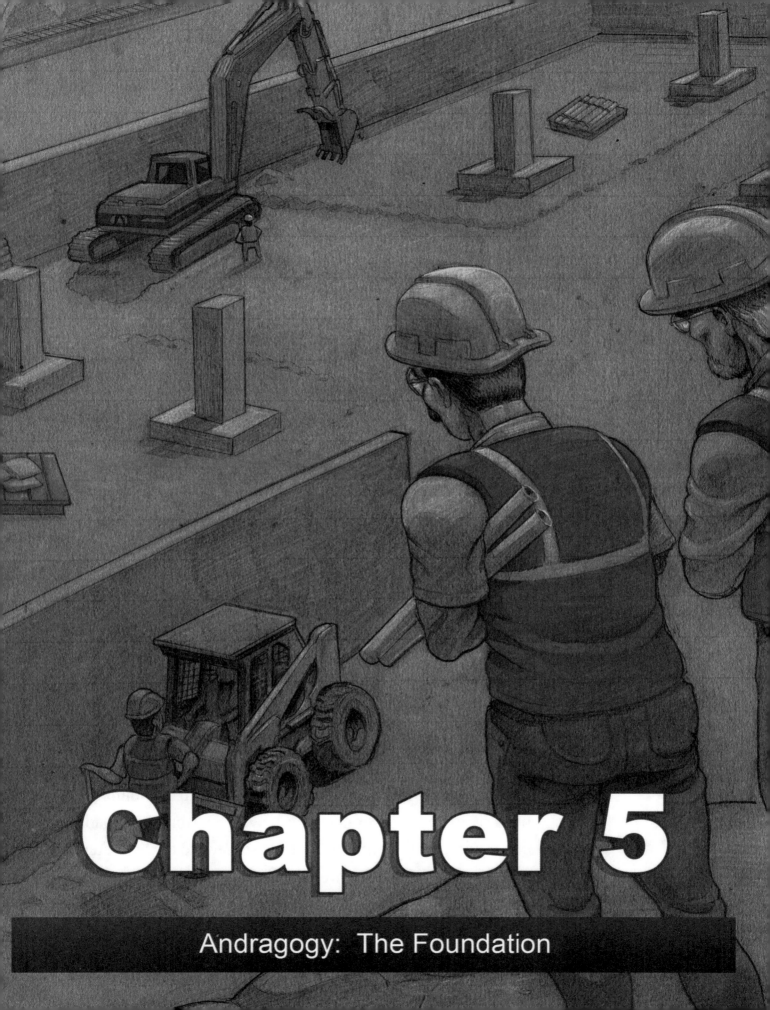

Chapter 5

Andragogy: The Foundation

In this chapter, you will:

- Define pedagogy and andragogy.
- Explore what makes you an adult learner.
- Examine the six assumptions of andragogy.

THE FOUNDATION

The task of establishing a firm foundation is pivotal to the success of any building project. If the appropriate calculations are not done, your foundation may not support the load that will eventually bear down on it. If the wrong material is chosen, then the foundation may develop cracks, leaks, or even cave in from the pressure of the surrounding dirt. Establishing a foundation for your educational journey is every bit as important and every bit as technical. There are considerations you must make in order to ensure that you will hold up under the pressure, and you need to know what material you are working with in order to avoid cracks and leaks. Coming to understand who you are as an adult learner will help you to establish the firm foundation you need by helping you understand how to distribute the load you are about to endure and to become self-aware of the material you are made of as a learner.

© 2013 by iQoncept. Used under license of Shutterstock, Inc.

I Cor. 3:11,
"For no one can lay any foundation other than what is being laid, which is Jesus Christ" (NET).

THE CORNERSTONE

John 14:1-2, "Let not your heart be troubled: ye believe in God, believe also in me. In my Father's house are many mansions: if it were not so, I would have told you. I go to prepare a place for you" (KJV).

"Imagine yourself as a living house. God comes in to rebuild that house. At first, perhaps, you can understand what He is doing. He is getting the drains right and stopping the leaks in the roof and so on; you knew that those jobs needed doing and so you are not surprised. But presently He starts knocking the house about in a way that hurts abominably and does not seem to make any sense. What on earth is He up to? The explanation is that He is building quite a different house from the one you thought of—throwing out a new wing here, putting on an extra floor there, running up towers, making courtyards. You thought you were being made into a decent little cottage: but He is building a palace. He intends to come and live in it Himself" (Lewis, 1996, p. 176).

When I finally decided to complete my master's degree, the decision was a long time coming. I put it off for many years and for a variety of reasons, but the three primary ones were insecurity, time investment, and convenience. Through it all, the Lord was at work, and I wondered "What on earth is He up to?"

Photo courtesy of David Duncan (Liberty University).

Build a strong foundation by understanding how you learn.

As I considered pursuing my master's degree, I was terribly insecure. I honestly didn't think I was smart enough to earn a master's degree; all of the people I knew with a master's were intellectual and interesting. When I compared myself to them, I just didn't measure up. Additionally, the degree I wanted required that I take the Graduate Record Exam (GRE) in order to complete the application process. Realizing this, test anxiety immediately set in fueling my insecurity, so I decided to wait until I thought I was smarter or until I had the time to study to prepare for it.

Additionally, I did not feel that I had the time to invest in the degree because I taught English at our local high school; my day was long and filled with preparing lessons, helping students, and grading papers. When I got home, the last thing I wanted to do was to study for a class of my own. I simply had no time if I wanted to have a life outside of the classroom.

Finally, I feared the inconvenience of attending a physical campus. I was an adult now, and the fun of attending courses with younger students just didn't inspire like it did when I was working on my undergraduate degree. Also, when I explored my degree options, I would have to travel to campus to attend courses. Though campus was only 30 minutes away, this would be an hour of my day that would be erased as a result of travel time. This would not do!

My fears, however, began to subside a little when I discovered that Liberty University was offering my degree in the online format. Finally, a school had established a program meant for the busy adult with responsibilities and a fast-paced life. I would be able to work from home for all of my coursework, and even though I still had to take the dreaded GRE, I recognized that this new opportunity was worth setting aside some fun time to prepare for the test. My husband, Terry, decided to take the GRE, too, so he and I spent quality time together at restaurants and coffee shops with flash cards of Latin roots and a GRE study book. Finally, Terry and I passed the test, applied for our programs, and began working toward degree completion.

Many years later, I recognized that God was at work in my life, as C. S. Lewis' quote suggests. He was breaking down the walls that I had built up with my fears of being inconvenienced, of missing valuable relaxing time, and my feelings of insecurity; He wanted to build me up with the truth of His Word that "I can do all things through Christ who strengthens me" (Philippians 4:13, NKJV). He wanted to make me palatial, and I was almost willing to settle on the cottage.

As you learn what it means to be an adult learner, with all of your responsibilities and people in your care, remember Philippians 4:6–7, "Be anxious for nothing, but in everything by prayer and supplication, with thanksgiving, let your requests be made known to God; and the peace of God, which surpasses all understanding, will guard your hearts and minds through Christ Jesus" (NKJV). Don't let your fears get in the way of God's big, palatial plans for you! Let Jesus' words reassure you that though the growing pains may "hurt abominably and don't seem to make any sense," (Lewis, 1996, p. 176). He has big plans for you, "Let not your heart be troubled: ye believe in God, believe also in me. In my Father's house are many mansions: if it were not so, I would have told you. I go to prepare a place for you" (John 14:1–2, KJV).

Define Pedagogy and Andragogy

Hebrews 5:12-14,

"For though you should in fact be teachers by this time, you need someone to teach you the beginning elements of God's utterances. You have gone back to needing milk, not solid food. For everyone who lives on milk is inexperienced in the message of righteousness, because he is an infant. But solid food is for the mature, whose perceptions are trained by practice to discern both good and evil" (NET).

Hebrews 5:12–14 acts as an excellent illustration of the differences between pedagogy (ped-uh-goh-jee) and andragogy (an-druh-goh-jee), which are educational theories that seek to describe the different ways that children and adults learn. The two theories are commonly seen as competing perspectives on learning, separated by a distinct line-in-the-sand, with children on one side and adults on the other (Holton & Swanson, 2012).

Terry Conner

"In childhood you are establishing the foundation for your education, and in adulthood, you are adding on or enhancing the building by applying theories to your education and your career."

Pedagogy

The term pedagogy comes from the Greek words, *paid,* meaning "child" and *agogus,* meaning "leader of." Put the two together, and it is easy to see how the term pedagogy has come to be defined as "the art and science of teaching children" (Holton & Swanson, 2012, loc. 1160). The concept of teaching children has existed since Cain and Abel but was developed into a more formal structure during the seventh century in Europe. Over time, the concept evolved from a framework for educating children into a much broader theory of educating in general, coming to be defined as "the art and science of teaching" (Wurm, 2005, p. 159). However, the original concept of pedagogy as a theory for educating children seems to be making a comeback as theories of adult learning emerge.

Pedagogy is broadly defined by the following assumptions of the learner:

© 2013 by hxdbzxy. Used under license of Shutterstock, Inc.

- **Need to know**—An understanding of "why" the individual needs to learn is not necessary.

- **Self-concept**—The learner is conditioned to be dependent on the instructor.

- **Experience**—Students learn from the instructor's experiences.

- **Readiness to learn**—Must be ready to learn at the will of the instructor.

- **Orientation to learning**—Learning is centered on the content and aimed at future use.

- **Motivation to learn**—Motivated by primarily external factors.

(Holton & Swanson, 2012)

Andragogy

The term andragogy comes from the Greek words, *aner,* meaning "man" and *agogus,* meaning "leader of." So, andragogy is defined as "the art and science of teaching adults" (Knowles as cited in Merriam & Bierema, 2013, loc. 1326). The concept of andragogy, or adult learning, has existed as a formal inquiry since the early 1800s, when Alexander Kapp first published a study regarding the matter. Between 1833 and the mid 1900s, bits and pieces were added to the idea of how adults learn, but no formal, cohesive theory had been established. Through the early 1900s, the concept of andragogy began to take shape, and in the 1960s, Malcolm Knowles popularized the concept as a single, cohesive way of understanding how adults learn (Chan, 2010).

Andragogy is broadly defined by the following assumptions of the learner:

- **Need to know**—The learner needs to understand "why" something is important before he or she will be ready to learn.

- **Self-concept**—The learner is independent and self-directed.

- **Experience**—The learner possesses a vast set of experiences, which act as the foundation for learning.

- **Readiness to learn**—Learning must be relevant and is often best conducted when the learner is in a transitional stage regarding his or her social role.

- **Orientation to learning**—The learner is a problem solver who learns best in the context of real-world situations that are immediately applicable.

Cheryl

"Going to school as an adult learner is dramatically different, than as a younger 'college' student."

- **Motivation to learn**—The learner is motivated by primarily internal factors.

(Holton & Swanson, 2012; Taylor & Kroth, 2009; Wurm, 2005)

While pedagogy and andragogy tend to be viewed as competing theories—one describing the way that children learn, and the other describing how adults learn—this does not have to be the case. People develop varying levels of self-directedness and independence as they gain experience in life. Some people will become more independent very early on, while others may remain more dependent until later in life. This means that there may be plenty of room for these two theories to overlap with one another; we simply view them from the distinct perspective in which they predominantly describe the group for which they are intended (Holton & Swanson, 2012; Wurm, 2005).

Tim

"There is definitely a major difference between when I was learning at a younger age and how I learn now. I have found 'shortcuts' that have helped me more than I ever imagined. Some of these shortcuts have allowed me to learn at a faster pace and help me complete my course work on time."

Personal Reflection

Fill in the chart below with the primary tenets of pedagogy and andragogy. This chart will help you to answer the next reflection question.

PEDAGOGY		ANDRAGOGY
'why' is not necessary	Need to Know	'why' is important
Dependent on the instructor	Self-Concept	Independent and self-directed
Instructor's experiences	Experience	Personal experience acts as a foundation for learning
Will of the instructor	Readiness to Learn	Relevant
Content and future use	Orientation to Learn	Problem solving and immediate application
External factors	Motivation to Learn	Internal factors

Roger

"As an adult returning to the classroom after many years, I lacked confidence. I wondered if I could really do the work and complete with other, brighter, younger students. After the first class, I realized that I had the tools of perseverance, a strong internal drive to achieve, proven time management experience, greater organizational skills, and maturity. I didn't have these things as a young college student."

Think about the definitions above, then make a list of learning experiences in your life that have fallen into each of these two categories. Try to list at least five in each column.

PEDAGOGY

For example:

High school class, U.S. History

College @ BCOM

Living of the parents

Dressing me

ANDRAGOGY

Learning new software on YouTube

College online @ LVO

Learning to be self-efficient

Dressing to my taste

BREAKING GROUND

Explore What Makes You an Adult Learner

I Cor. 13:11,
"When I was a child, I talked like a child, I thought like a child, I reasoned like a child. But when I became an adult, I set aside childish ways" (NET).

Where do you fall in the scheme of things? If you have a little bit of age on you, then you may be pretty quick to jump on the adult learning band wagon, but what about those of you who are just coming out of high school? Where you do fit? Many of you might not consider yourselves to be "adults" yet. At the same time, there are a few of you who have felt as if you have been an adult for quite some time now. The question you need to ask yourself is, what is the definition of an adult?

The role of an adult could be based on any of the following definitions.

- **Biological**—Based on the ability of the individual to reproduce.

- **Legal**—As the laws of a given jurisdiction dictate that an individual has the rights of an adult.

- **Social**—As an individual takes on roles that would typically be associated with being an adult.

- **Psychological**—Once an individual comes to see him- or herself as independent.

(Holton & Swanson, 2012; Taylor & Kroth, 2009)

It would be hard to argue that you suddenly became an adult in an instant, at least as it relates to your willingness or ability to learn. So, it would be safe to say that the physical or legal definitions may not be the best definitions to help us in understanding where you fall in the spectrum of learning. For our purposes it might be best to consider the implications of combining the social and psychological definitions as we explore the assumptions of how adults learn (Holton & Swanson, 2012).

Cheryl

"As a young college student (living on campus), the only things I had to focus on were my education and my social life. As an adult learner, I am responsible for more than just me. My 'time' no longer belongs to 'me.' I must insert here, that I would have it no other way."

© 2013 by Gelpi JM. Used under license of Shutterstock, Inc.

Ruth

Q: *What challenges have you faced/ overcome/still working on as an adult learner?*

A: [My] Parent's health and their needs.

Examine the Six Assumptions of Andragogy

Matthew 16:5–12,

"When the disciples went to the other side, they forgot to take bread. 'Watch out,' Jesus said to them, 'Beware of the yeast of the Pharisees and Sadducees.' So they began to discuss this among themselves, saying, 'It is because we brought no bread.' When Jesus learned of this, he said, 'You who have such little faith! Why are you arguing among yourselves about having no bread? Do you still not understand? Don't you remember the five loaves for the five thousand, and how many baskets you took up? Or the seven loaves for the four thousand and how many baskets you took up? How could you not understand that I was not speaking to you about bread? But beware of the yeast of the Pharisees and Sadducees!' Then they understood that he had not told them to be on guard against the yeast in bread, but against the teaching of the Pharisees and Sadducees" (NET).

✗ 1. Need to Know *Why is this important?*

The disciples didn't really get it; they figured that Jesus' warning had to mean something important, but what was it? They were struggling to grasp what Jesus was saying to them about the yeast. This was an important warning, but they lacked the appropriate understanding to appreciate it. They didn't know *why* it was important. So Jesus addressed them again; this time He was very clear about why this statement was so important. Only then did the disciples come to understand what Jesus was trying to tell them. They came to understand *why* Jesus' statement was so profound, and suddenly, His words were no longer lost on them.

The concept of "need to know" describes the adult learners' need to understand *why* a particular topic is valuable to them before they invest the time and effort into learning about it (Holton & Swanson, 2012; Merriam & Bierema, 2013; Taylor & Kroth, 2009). Adult learners are considered to be very practical and focused on real-world issues that exist in their lives (Wurm, 2005); before valuable time can be set aside to learn something new, they must be sure that the return is worth the investment. They are

T. Marcus Christian

"One of the best things to remember about Andragogy is that it describes the motivation for adult learning. This can be your motivation to be the first in your family to complete college or it can be the motivation to get a new job. Whatever motivates you to work hard is going to be the thing that gets you your degree."

simply not going to set aside an excessive amount of time to learn about something that that is not going to impact their lives (Holton & Swanson, 2012; Taylor & Kroth, 2009; Wurm, 2005).

What this means for you, as an online adult learner, is that you will need to spend some time before each term, class, week, or assignment assessing the impact that the information you are about to learn will have on your life. Some classes or assignments in your major could be easy to assess as they directly relate to your goals, but what about the classes or assignments that are difficult to connect with? Do they lack value for you? The most likely answer is no, but this doesn't mean that you won't need to dig a little to make a connection. A good place to start your inquiry is in the syllabus, as it typically contains a detailed description and rationale for the course. If you are still struggling to find the relevance, email your instructors; they care deeply about their disciplines, and would be more than excited to help.

Mary Dixon

"Adult learners can be wonderful leaders. Life experience has given them perspectives and opportunities that translate well into independent and creative thinking. Use those skills that you have developed and apply them to study and learning in the same way that you applied them to employment or negotiating life experience. Perseverance is a big asset and a great model for others to follow! You can show the less experienced learner a thing or two."

Personal Reflection

Describe an adult learning situation where your "need to know" *was not* satisfied. How did it impact your learning experience?

_____ ? _____

_____

_____

Describe an adult learning situation where your "need to know" *was* satisfied. How was this experience different from the one above?

Why is it important for me to take elective classes? This is done to complete general bases in a degree.

⚡2. Self-Concept

1 Peter 2:16, "Live as free people, not using your freedom as a pretext for evil, but as God's slaves" (NET).

According to I Peter 2:16, you are to live as a free person beholden only to God. You have a free mind and a free spirit, which leads you down paths of interest and discovery. You are naturally inclined to be self-directing and independent. Your natural state is to gravitate away from the direction of your parents and teachers and to head off into the world to live and learn.

The assumption of "self-concept" informs us that adult learners are independent and self-directed individuals (Holton & Swanson, 2012; Taylor & Kroth, 2009; Wurm, 2005). They are used to taking responsibility for themselves and making their own decisions, so they tend to struggle with situations where they feel that the ability to decide for themselves has been taken away. Adult learners desire to be viewed as independent and capable of making decisions on their own and tend to shut down when placed in a learning situation where their independence appears to be overlooked (Holton & Swanson, 2012; Merriam & Bierema, 2013; Taylor & Kroth, 2009). Adult learners are most invested when they are actively engaged in the learning process, meaning they are able to make choices and decisions regarding their learning (Wurm, 2005).

As an online college student and an adult learner, you have a significant amount of choice in deciding when, where, and how you will go about completing your work, but there are still some limits, which are to be expected. You have the benefit of being able to decide which program you would like to pursue and even the order in which you will take many of your classes. At the same time, there are a number of required courses that you may need to take in order to complete your degree. This can be a big sticking point for students. It is not infrequent to hear the question, "I'm studying to be a pastor. Why do I need to take a math class?" The resistance to the math class is based on the student feeling that his or her decision-making ability has been taken away. In this scenario it would be best to think back to the concept of "need to know" and try to find the value in the course that is being required. Understanding this need will help you address these issues when you encounter them.

Katie Robinson

"Adult learners bring something to learning that other students cannot: experience. Because of this advantage, adult learners have the unique opportunity to enrich their learning with past experience opposed to attempting to apply learning to future experience, which can be further disconnected."

Personal Reflection

Can you recall a situation that you faced as an adult, where you resisted a learning opportunity due to feeling that your decision-making ability was taken away?

Yes   No

Since awareness is the key to avoiding problems, jot down some of the issues related to self-concept you might face as you work to complete your degree. Then, take a minute to brainstorm a couple of strategies to keep these issues from becoming obstacles.

ISSUES	STRATEGIES
• Motivation • Distraction • Insecurity • Going against the grain	• Setting goals • Limiting distractions • Believing in myself and knowing what I am doing is important. • Asking 'why' but understanding the importance.

Alissa Keith

"Professors can lead students to knowledge, but they can't make them learn. As an adult learner, you must choose to learn that knowledge to reach your own personal goals."

✗ 3. Prior Experience

Hebrews 5:14, "But solid food is for the mature, whose perceptions are trained by practice to discern both good and evil" (NET).

As an adult believer you are able to analyze new spiritual teachings by testing them against what you already know about God based on biblical truth. You have the experience to know that each new teaching must be screened through Scripture. If it holds up with what you know to be true in the Bible, you may incorporate this concept into your knowledge base. At the same time, any new spiritual teaching that does not stand up to the test of Scripture is rejected.

© 2013 by donskarpo. Used under license of Shutterstock, Inc.

The concept of "prior experience" brings several different issues to the table. It reminds us that adult learners bring a number of unique experiences with them when they enter the classroom and that their store of experience continues to grow (Holton & Swanson, 2012; Taylor & Kroth, 2009). These experiences are the learners' best resource for learning and act as a foundation upon which to build understandings and through which they can test the validity of new information (Merriam & Bierema, 2013; Taylor & Kroth, 2009; Wurm, 2005). Adult learners are deeply connected to their experiences and see them as part of who they are as a person (Holton & Swanson, 2012; Merriam & Bierema, 2013).

Nathaniel Valle

"The best way to apply information from this course is by thinking not only about what you're learning, but how you interact with your professor to master whatever you're studying. Interacting with your instructor through andragogical instruction will help you realize that nearly every career utilizes some type of it. Whether in INFT 101 or your personal life, allow yourself to accept constructive criticism and never be afraid to ask any questions!"

Learning from a distance can be difficult, but you have the opportunity to make it an extremely personal endeavor. You have a storehouse of past experiences that you can use to help you connect with the information in your online classes. Taking a basic math course can be connected to your experiences paying the household bills or managing a small business. Studying a passage of Scripture on forgiveness can be connected to several past experiences where you struggled to forgive someone, and a lesson on how adults learn can be related back to previous learning experiences you have had at work or in other educational environments. The key is to use these experiences to connect with and remember the information you are learning. They will help you to internalize the concepts, which will increase the likelihood that you will store the information in your long-term memory.

Additionally, adult learners use their past experience to help them determine the validity of new information. As you listen to information in your classes, you are much more prone to accept or dismiss things based on your past experiences with similar situations or information. Information that does not pass the sniff test can be addressed with peers or the instructor. You might find that this new information needs to be considered in the light of experience you do not yet possess or that the specific concept is simply not as clear-cut as you thought. Either way, you have the potential to gain a deeper understanding by using your experiences as you consider what you are learning.

Personal Reflection

Take a moment to describe a situation where considering your past experience has helped you to understand new information.

_____

_____

_____

_____

List a couple of experiences from your life that you use to filter new information.

Scripture; Personal Belieys; Realistic situations; Common sense

_____

_____

_____

↲4. Readiness to Learn

Acts 3:19, "Therefore repent and turn back so that your sins may be wiped out" (NET).

One moment you are set in your life, and the next you experience a transition like no other. You have made a decision to become a follower of Christ, but you have so much to learn. Can you think of a time when you wanted to read or know more? You are voracious in your consumption of information regarding your newfound faith. You are completely open and ready to learn.

Adult learners' "readiness to learn" is heavily related to their social role, but they are most receptive to learning when they are transitioning into a new social role (Holton & Swanson, 2012; Merriam & Bierema, 2013; Taylor & Kroth, 2009). This period of transition creates what is referred to as a "teachable moment" where the learner is open to new information (Merriam & Bierema, 2013). Results of large-scale polling show that the vast majority of adults who were involved in some type of formal education cited their jobs as the reason (Merriam, Caffarella, & Baumgartner as cited in Merriam & Bierema, 2013).

Office personnel will maintain their job readiness, but are not typically open to learning about management tasks unless the possibility of moving into a management position exists. A mother of 20 years loves her children, but she most likely will not read through a stack of parenting books, while an expectant mother tends to read anything she can get her hands on that relates to parenting.

If you are among the vast majority of adults, you have returned to school for some transitional reason related to work. Some of you have been promoted or are seeking a promotion, some of you are transitioning to a new career field, and others of you are trying to transition from high school into your first career. You are in the middle of your "teachable moment" and eager to absorb the knowledge before you.

Emily

"In college you actually want to learn more and retain it all. In high school, you learn it and as long as you pass your test you don't really care if you remember it in the long run."

Personal Reflection

In the first column, make a list of the major transitional stages or life-tasks in which you were most open to learning new information. In the second column, describe what you were most open to learn about.

Transition/Life-Task	What did you want to learn?
Managing	Managing a business
Going back to School	Learning about Psychology

✳ 5. Orientation to Learn

2 Timothy 3:16–17, "Every scripture is inspired by God and useful for teaching, for reproof, for correction, and for training in righteousness, that the person dedicated to God may be capable and equipped for every good work" (NET).

As believers, we turn to the Scriptures on a daily basis for spiritual sustenance, but we also find ourselves searching the Bible or praying for answers when we encounter problems in life.

If a close friend does something to harm you, you might seek guidance and find an answer in Matt 18:15–17:

> "If your brother sins, go and show him his fault when the two of you are alone. If he listens to you, you have regained your brother. But if he does not listen, take one or two others with you, so that at the testimony of two or three witnesses every matter may be established. If he refuses to listen to them, tell it to the church. If he refuses to listen to the church, treat him like a Gentile or a tax collector" (NET).

If you are struggling with anger, you might seek advice in Ephesians 4:26:

> "Be angry and do not sin; do not let the sun go down on the cause of your anger" (NET).

If you were beginning a new marriage, you might spend time studying 1 Corinthians 13:4–7:

> "Love is patient, love is kind, it is not envious. Love does not brag, it is not puffed up. It is not rude, it is not self-serving, it is not easily angered or resentful. It is not glad about injustice, but rejoices in the truth. It bears all things, believes all things, hopes all things, endures all things" (NET).

The assumption of "orientation to learn" refers to the tendency of adult learners to be oriented towards learning when they feel it will assist them in solving a problem or performing a specific task (Holton & Swanson, 2012; Merriam & Bierema, 2013; Taylor & Kroth, 2009). Adult learners want to be able to utilize the new information they are learning immediately in order to solve real-world problems (Merriam & Bierema, 2013; Taylor & Kroth, 2009), so they desire learning situations that are practical in nature (Holton & Swanson, 2012; Wurm, 2005).

You have probably run into many situations where you needed to find the answer to a problem or needed to perform a task that you were unsure of, and you turned to the Internet. You may have searched for "how to tie a tie" or "How do I do _____ in Microsoft Excel?" or even something more serious such as "What are the treatment options

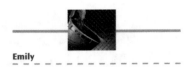

Emily

"You have to really spend time studying and apply [what you are learning] to life to retain it."

© 2013 by ALMAGAMI. Used under license of Shutterstock, Inc.

for _____ type of cancer?" A friend of mine even taught himself leatherworking, because he could not find a wallet to suit his needs. The point is that adult learners are problem solvers; they seek information that they can immediately apply to their real-life situations. Some of the topics that adults research are not topics that they would even be interested in if the topic were not presenting them with some kind of problem to solve.

As you enter the realm of online education, your problem might be bigger than "how to tie a tie." You are looking for knowledge and a degree so that you can change careers, obtain a promotion, or find employment that will allow you to support your family. You believe that learning about a particular field and earning a degree in that field will help you to solve your problem. This is a long-term goal though, so it will be easy to lose sight of the finish line. Use the assumption of "orientation" to your advantage and think about how your individual classes and lessons can help you to solve everyday problems in your life. This will keep things relevant and help you to stay motivated as you work toward your degree.

Maddy

Q: *Were you surprised in the difference in your learning as an adult, compared to what you remember when you were in school as a child? What differences were there?*

A: "The main difference I've noticed is that now I actually have to study. It wasn't really a surprise, because I had been told that college would be harder than any other schooling I had faced. It was more of a disappointment that adults were right."

Personal Reflection

Use this exercise to explore the application of this principle in your own life. In the space provided, describe a real-world problem that you needed to solve, then provide an explanation as to how you went about learning the information necessary to solve the problem.

For Example:

Problem: Needed to learn how to combine two cells into one in Excel 2010 for a project.

Solution: I searched the Internet for "Combine words from two cells into a single cell in Excel 2010." The results returned a YouTube video that I was able to watch. I learned how to use the "concat" formula to accomplish my goal.

Problem: Difficulty pronouncing words for Psyc

Solution: I looked up the word on dictionary.com and listened to the pronunciation. I also wrote in my text book the way it is pronounced.

Problem: Too many hours on Social Media

Solution: Limit Social media to Weekdays.

Terry

Q: *Were you surprised in the difference in your learning as an adult, compared to what you remember when you were in school as a child?*

A: "Not so much the difference between how I learned, but my investment in that learning. As a child, it was more passive, now as an adult I'm actively engaged in the material and applying it to my life as I go through the program, which is pretty cool."

✗6. Motivation to Learn

Matt 6:21, "For where your treasure is, there your heart will be also" (NET).

Roger

"When I first entered college at age 19, I was immature, inexperienced, trying to figure out what I wanted to do. I procrastinated and waited till the last minute to study or get my homework completed. I occasionally skipped classes and did not have the same passion and drive to achieve. By the time I graduated, I had developed better skills but it was not there at the beginning. I was satisfied with C's."

Money itself is not a horrible thing, but the love of money is warned against explicitly. Money is just an item, something that is external to your being. You might want it, or need it, so that you can pay bills or buy groceries, but the internal motivation might actually be that you need to support your family. When you love money, then money becomes the object or goal; you chase the money in the hopes that it will bring you satisfaction. In either situation it is the internal motivations that drive you toward your goal.

The assumption of "motivation to learn" informs us that adult learners are internally motivated to learn (Holton & Swanson, 2012; Merriam & Bierema, 2013; Taylor & Kroth, 2009) in order to achieve their goals and gain personal fulfillment (Merriam & Bierema, 2013; Taylor & Kroth, 2009). The driving forces behind adult learners' motivations are their "values, beliefs, and opinions" (Wurm, 2005, p. 160). When a learning situation is presented that was not initiated by an internal motivation, it is important that a connection be made to the adult learners' interests or needs (Merriam & Bierema, 2013).

As you begin your journey into online adult education, it will be crucial for you to understand the internal motivations that are driving you. As mentioned a little earlier in the chapter, earning a degree is a long-term goal, and losing your motivation is a real possibility. It is important to assess what brought you here and what is going to keep you working when you are ready to quit. Purposefully seeking to connect the information you are learning with your needs is an invaluable way to stay motivated. You might also try writing down a list of your motivators and keeping it near your computer, in your wallet, or as a note on your smartphone.

Personal Reflection

Think about the influences and motivational factors in your life right now. Categorize them below based on whether they are internal or external factors.

External	Internal
A degree	Achievement
Helping people	Wanting a healthier
Success	Generation

Now, take another look at the list above. Circle those influencers that are most significant and ask yourself why these are so important to you. You will often find that what seems like an external influence can often be tied to an internal motivation. Do you find this to be the case here?

Yes. My desire to help people is out of a selfless ambition. I want to see people be there 'full' Self. If I can invest my time into understanding the psychology of man and helping 10 people in my lifetime then I have touched a 1,000 generations to follow.

Ruth

Q: *Were you surprised in the difference in your learning as an adult, compared to what you remember when you were in school as a child?*

A: No, not surprised, I knew I would appreciate it more and wanted to learn.

BUILDING BLOCKS

Summary and Conclusion

This chapter compares the differences in learning orientation and focus of those who are pedagogical versus andragogical learners. You have had the opportunity to examine the features of each type of learner and the instruction that is geared to the needs of each. As you evaluate yourself, do you see yourself more as a pedagogical learner, or one who can benefit from the features of instruction for learners who are more self-directed, those we describe as andragogical learners?

Consider how each of the assumptions of learners (need to know; self-concept; experience; readiness to learn; orientation; motivation to learn) fits either those learning through the process of pedagogy or those who are ready for adult learning, or andragogy.

As you consider this, I'll use myself as an example for a particular topic, **learning physics**.

- For **need to know**, I would take this course because it is required for a program of study that I want, but I am not particularly interested in physics, per se. This would mean I am a pedagogical learner for physics.

- My **self-concept** and **experience** are both quite dependent on the teacher's instruction, as this is a course that I am not very familiar with and actually somewhat fearful of taking! I am planning to be led almost entirely by the instructor, rather than my own initiative.

- My **readiness to learn** is based on my need to learn this information to move forward with the program of study, but I am unable to move forward, I believe, without the instructor.

- While I am always motivated to do well, my **orientation** for this course is to master it so I can move on to other topics in the program,

- Thus, my **motivation** is based on the need to master this before moving on.

Can you see from this example that I am primarily a pedagogical learner with this topic?

In other instances, I may be an andragogical learner. Let's look at how this would play out if I decide to learn German for an upcoming family trip to our ancestral homeland, Germany.

- My drive to master the language is based on my desire to speak the language with distant family members. I understand the "why" (**need to know**).

- I am quite independent in learning the language, as it can benefit my trip, and is something I am choosing for myself, so it satisfies the **self-concept** component of andragogical learning.

- My background with travel assures me that my experiences will be heightened if I am able to speak the language of the country I am visiting, so I am eager to begin (**experience**).

- The relevance to my trip is obvious, so I am anxious to begin studying German as soon as possible (**readiness to learn**).

- Both my **orientation to learning** and **motivation to learn** are heightened by the prospect of being able to master a new skill that will be readily applicable on my family trip. I want to learn this new language to enrich my experience of another country and to enable me to speak with distant family members in their language.

Do you see that you might be an andragogical learner in one situation and yet a pedagogical one in another? In some instances, you may discover that you have a mixed collection of descriptors that fits your learning readiness and preferences.

Personal Reflection

Using the chart on the following page, choose an example from your own life, and keep in mind that you may not find yourself to be purely pedagogical or purely andragogical: Your responses may be a mix.

Assumptions	Example 1	Example 2	You 1	You 2
	Physics	Learning German	Psychology	History
Need to know	Pedagogy Required course; but low interest	Andragogy I want this skill to aid me in an upcoming trip	Required courses but high interest my major of Study	Required course but know my history
Self-concept	Pedagogy Dependent on teacher to calm my fears and lead me	Andragogy I see myself as a learner who is gaining a skill that will be beneficial to me	I have zero understanding on psych so I have to rely on my proffesors	Better understanding of U.S. history. No benefits for psychology?
Experience	Pedagogy No experience in my background; dependent on instructor	Andragogy My travel background helps me understand that speaking the language of the country is of benefit to me	No experience except being an excellent listener.	Took serveral classes in high School
Readiness to learn	Pedagogy Based on my need in my program, but dependent on my instructor	Andragogy Anxious to begin, because I have plans to use this soon	Eager to learn. I am relying on my professor.	I enjoy history so this should be an easier class
Orientation to learn	Pedagogy Determined to master this so I can move forward in my program	Andragogy Excitement for new skill development	Have to understand this topic in order to help people	Dependent on the instructors teaching
Motivation to learn	Pedagogy I need to master this before moving on to the next subject in my program of study	Andragogy My upcoming trip keeps me excited to learn more and speak with my distant family	Learning the basics to master psyc.	I will have a better understanding of history & the U.S.

Psalm 25:4, "Show me your ways, Lord, teach me your paths" (NIV).

Luke 2:52, "And Jesus grew in wisdom and stature, and in favor with God and man" (NIV).

Think about the two verses above. In the first one, the Psalmist is apparently eager to learn the lessons that God has to teach him. Do you suppose this is a godly student who is learning with andragogy? On the other hand, the verse from Luke describes Jesus' growth from a young boy to a young man. We could presume that as a young boy He learned as all young students do: with pedagogy. As He grew in stature and *wisdom,* this would change to a more mature learning, or andragogy. It is difficult for some people to think of the human Jesus, who came to earth as a baby, taking on human form, even as He remained fully God. As a human child, He learned and grew, as this verse tells us.

Personal Reflection

What parallels do you see in Jesus' growth and your own as a learner?

Jesus had to learn along the way. Even though He was God He did not obtain all knowledge. It was a learning process.

The same is true for me. I have to learn, knowledge does not pop into your midd. It is obtained through studying.

TOOL BOX

Career Center—If you are in that transitional period between careers, positions, or organizations, consider using the Liberty Career Center to explore your skills, marketability, and career options.

www.liberty.edu/careercenter

Course Guides—Since you won't be able to access the official syllabus until shortly before your classes begin, consider reviewing the Course Guides on the Liberty University Online website. These are samples of the syllabi for various courses. You will still be able to review the course description and rationale, but the official syllabus may contain slight differences.

www.liberty.edu/online/course-guides

Credit by Exam—Aside from job experience, you may possess enough knowledge or experience in a subject area to take a special exam and receive credit for courses without having to sit through them. While you have most likely heard of the CLEP exam that is available for this, you may not have heard of the Institutional Challenge Exam (ICE), which allows you to take the same type of tests for certain classes that are not available through the CLEP system.

Equivalency Credit—Liberty acknowledges the experience you have by awarding credit for many different job experiences, professional licenses, and military experience. Much of this credit can be earned by submitting the appropriate documentation to the Transfer Evaluation Office.

On-demand learning—While you are working your way through your degree, you may find yourself needing to acquire new skills that you don't necessarily want to take an additional class to learn. What are you going to do when you need to know how to use spreadsheet software for a business class, how to understand basic statistical information for a research class, or how to format a paper in APA for your INFT 101 class? Consider using some of the on-demand resources that Liberty has made available to you, like Atomic Learning, Tutor.com, or the Online Writing Center.

Portfolio Credit—If you possess life experience that is not accepted by automatic transfer, you might consider utilizing the portfolio process in order to earn credit for your experience. In order to earn portfolio credit, you will need to take GEED 205; in this course, you will be taught how to put together a portfolio and submit it for review. From there, you will be able to submit additional portfolios on your own. Submitted portfolios are reviewed by the appropriate academic departments in order to determine if credit will be awarded or not.

Syllabi—The syllabus for each class contains a course description and course rationale. These will assist you in establishing the "why" behind each course. The official syllabus will be available to you as soon as you gain access to your courses; typically, access is granted the week before classes begin.

Additional resources and links to specific sites, worksheets, and apps can be located by accessing the Breaking Ground website:

www.breakinggroundlu.com

References

Chan, S. (2010). Applications of andragogy in multi-disciplined teaching and learning. *Journal of Adult Education, 39*(2), 25–35. Retrieved from http://search.proquest.com/docview/871911642.

Holton, E. F., & Swanson, R. A. (2012). *The Adult Learner: The Definitive Classic in Adult Education and Human Resource Development* (7th ed.). [Kindle Edition]. Retrieved from Amazon.com.

Lewis, C.S. (1996). *Mere Christianity.* New York, NY: Simon & Schuster.

Merriam, S. B., & Bierema, L. L. (2013). *Adult Learning: Linking Theory and Practice.* [Kindle Edition]. Retrieved from Amazon.com.

Taylor, B., & Kroth, M. (2009). Andragogy's Transition Into the Future: Meta-Analysis of Andragogy and Its Search for a Measurable Instrument. *Journal of Adult Education, 38*(1), 1–11. Retrieved from http://search.proquest.com/docview/204494009.

Wurm, K. B. (2005). Andragogy in Survey Education. *Surveying and Land Information Science, 65*(3), 159–162. Retrieved from http://search.proquest.com/docview/202972619.

Chapter 6

Learning Styles: The Structure

In this chapter you will:

- Identify the elements of learning styles.
- Identify your personal learning style gifts.
- Determine learning strategies that align with your learning preferences for maximum effectiveness and learning efficiency.

STRUCTURE AND FRAMING

When constructing a building, the structure's framing provides a network of interconnected materials that serve a critical function. Though the framing is internal and not prominently visible when the building is completed, it determines the size, height, and overall design of the building by providing the form and dimensions of the completed structure. Just as in a construction project, the structure and framing of an individual's learning strength is his or her learning style. It is the frame, if you will, of the way each of us interacts with the world around us to best gain information. God has given each of us individual learning style gifts, and if we use these gifts to their best effect, the finished results can be strong and beautiful! This chapter will help you understand the concept of learning style and will guide you in maximizing the use of the learning gifts God has given you.

© 2013 by VLADGRIN. Used under license of Shutterstock, Inc.

Psalm 139:14,
"I praise you because I am **fearfully and wonderfully made**; your works are wonderful, I know that full well" (NLT).

THE CORNERSTONE

I Corinthians 12:5–6, "There are different kinds of gifts, but the same Spirit distributes them. There are different kinds of service, but the same Lord. There are different kinds of working, but in all of them and in everyone it is the same God at work" (NIV).

Renowned gospel singer, Doug Oldham, came to Thomas Road Baptist Church in the 1970s to help Dr. Jerry Falwell promote and raise funds for the college (Liberty University) he planned to establish. When describing Doug, Dr. Falwell wrote, "He has sung for presidents and royalty. Doug Oldham is as fine a singer as there is and he is a master communicator. But the important thing to me is that he has remained true to his Lord and his calling" (http://www.christianexaminer.com/Articles/Articles%20Aug10/Art_Aug10_01.html). In his lifetime, he recorded 66 albums, won two Dove Awards, sang many of the songs written by gospel songwriters Bill and Gloria Gaither, and performed for six United States Presidents and the Queen of England. While others knew him as a "master communicator," I knew him as "Grandpa."

Photo courtesy of David Duncan (Liberty University).

Liberty is always innovating. This vehicular tunnel beneath the railroad tracks will be cleared all at once, dragging the tunnel structure into place while simultaneously removing the materials beneath the train tracks.

My grandpa, Doug, was the only son of Dale and Polly Oldham. Dale served as the preacher of Park Place Church of God and hosted the Christian Brotherhood Hour radio show in Anderson, Indiana. Polly played the organ during church services. Dale and Polly raised Doug in the knowledge of Christ and encouraged his natural singing abilities, which later led to his profession as minister of music at various churches and ultimately, his own ministry of music that lasted until his death in 2010.

Being the only son of a preacher, Doug learned how to lead two lives . . . one for church and one for his own pleasure. When he married my grandmother, Laura Lee Makings, a simple yet beautiful girl from the Nebraska prairie, that double life continued. Together, they had three children: Paula, Karen, and Rebekah. Grandpa behaved badly in those early years of marriage and was unfaithful to my grandmother many times. Each time, he would apologize for his bad behavior and would find another minister of music position at a different church and repeat the pattern. It was not until my grandma left with the three little girls that my grandpa experienced a

Photo courtesy of Thomas Road Baptist Church.

In this picture, Dr. Falwell and Doug Oldham worship on the platform of Thomas Road Baptist Church together.

true conversion experience, committing his life to Christ. He then spent the next months winning back my grandma's heart and her trust and spent the rest of his life telling others the story of God's mercy and grace in his life.

After my grandpa passed away in 2010, a good friend and colleague of mine, Vangie Alban, came up to me at the family visitation and gave me a comforting hug. She then told me about a time when she was facing a terribly difficult, personal trial, and my grandpa comforted her with these words, "Ministries are born out of adversity." These words reflected the way he lived his life, and without that adversity in his own life, he would not have been able to touch so many other lives. While the enemy "intended to harm" him, "God intended it for good to accomplish what is now being done, the saving of many lives" (Genesis 50:20, NIV).

My great-grandpa, Dale, and grandpa Doug both impacted the lives of others for Christ; however, they both arrived at their ministries in different ways. PaPa Dale was faithful from the start, while PaPa Doug learned the hard way. Though they both learned differently, both were effective ministers of God's message of grace, love, and forgiveness, because both were willing. As you realize your own style of learning, consider ways that you can use your abilities, not only as you learn in your courses, but also as you live for the Lord, "There are different kinds of gifts, but the same Spirit distributes them. There are different kinds of service, but the same Lord. There are different kinds of working, but in all of them and in everyone it is the same God at work" (I Corinthians 12:5–6, NIV).

Identify the Elements of Learning Styles

Genesis 1:26, 31,
"Then God said, 'Let us make mankind in our image, in our likeness' God saw all that he had made, and it was very good" (NIV).

The Bible reassures us that while we have different gifts from God, we are all precious in His sight and perfect as He created us. In other words, no matter what our strengths and individual differences, we are all created by God to be like Him. The Bible confirms God's approval just a few verses later: All that God made was pleasing to Him! What a wonderful comfort to know that how we learn best is designed and approved by God!

Knowing about your learning style can help you to choose effective strategies for learning in school and on the job. Knowing about your preferred learning environment can help you increase productivity.

Silvia Graham

"Reduced to essentials, learning styles refer to the way we better channel information. For instance, some people take in information best through visual stimuli, some through auditory, and others through tactile processes. Knowing how we best cognitively approach the world might help us succeed academically."

What Is Learning Style?

Just as each individual has a unique personality, each individual has a unique learning style. It is important to remember that there are no good or bad learning styles. Your learning style is simply your preferred way of learning. It is how you like to learn and how you learn best. By understanding your learning style, you can maximize your potential by choosing the learning techniques that work best for you. Each individual also has a preferred learning environment. Knowing about your preferred learning environment and learning style helps you to be more productive, to increase achievement, to be more creative, to improve problem solving, to make good decisions, and to learn effectively. Knowing about how you learn best helps to reduce frustration and increase your confidence in learning.

Photo courtesy of David Duncan (Liberty University).

Students heading to Convocation. Liberty University hosts students from across the country and around the world!

Barbara Sherman

". . . learning styles are the ways we concentrate on, process, internalize and remember new and difficult information or skills. These styles often vary with age, achievement level, culture . . . and gender."

Katie Robinson

"We are all hard-wired oh so differently with various strengths and weaknesses, and this extends to how our minds work and how we learn. Research has shown that when a student is self-aware and understands how he or she learns, that student can use meta-cognition when approaching new material. Discovering one's learning style can greatly help when refining study skills. In this way, we can 'learn to learn.'"

Gary Price has developed the Productivity Environmental Preference Survey (PEPS), which identifies 20 different elements of learning style and environment, including the immediate environment, emotional factors, sociological needs, and physical needs. As you read the description of each of these elements, think about your preferences.

1. **Sound.** Some students need a quiet environment for study, whereas others find it distracting if it is too quiet.

   - If you prefer quiet, use the library or find another quiet place. If you cannot find a quiet place, sound-blocking earphones or earplugs may be helpful. Remember that not all people need a quiet environment for study.

   - If you study better with sound, play soft music or study in open areas. Use headphones for your music if you are studying with those who prefer quiet.

2. **Light.** Some students prefer bright light to see what they are studying, whereas others find bright light uncomfortable or irritating.

   - If you prefer bright light, study near a window with light shining over your shoulder or invest in a good study lamp.

   - If you prefer dim lights, sit away from direct sunlight or use a shaded light.

3. **Temperature.** Some students perform better in cool temperatures and others prefer warmer temperatures.

   - If you prefer a warm environment, remember to bring your sweater or jacket. Sit near a window or other source of heat.

   - If you prefer a cooler environment, study in a well-ventilated environment or even outside in the shade.

4. **Design.** Some students study best in a more formal environment or less formal environment.

   - If you prefer a formal environment, sit in a straight chair and use a desk.

   - If you prefer an informal environment, sit on the sofa or a soft chair or on some pillows on the floor.

5. **Motivation.** Some students are self-motivated to learn, and others lack motivation.

   - If you are self-motivated, you usually like school and enjoy learning on your own.

   - If you lack motivation, think about your reasons for attending college and review the material in the motivation chapter of this book.

6. **Persistence.** Some students finish what they start, whereas others have many things going on at once and may not finish what they have started.

- If you are persistent, you generally finish what you start.

- If you lack persistence, you may get bored or distracted easily. You may find it easier to break tasks into small steps and work steadily toward completing assignments on time. Think about your college and career goals to increase motivation and persistence.

7. **Responsibility (conforming).** This element has a unique meaning in the area of learning style.

- Some students like to please others by doing what is asked of them. They complete assignments to please the professor.

- Other students are less likely to conform. They prefer to complete assignments because they want to, rather than because someone else wants the assignment done. These students may need to look for something interesting and personally meaningful in school assignments.

8. **Structure.** Students prefer more or less structure.

- Students who prefer structure want the teacher to give details about how to complete the assignment. They need clear directions before completing an assignment.

- Students who prefer less structure want the teacher to give assignments in which the students can choose the topic and organize the material on their own.

9. **Alone/peer.** Some students prefer to study alone, and others prefer to study with others.

- You may find other people distracting and prefer to study alone. You need to study in a private area.

- You may enjoy working in a group because talking with others helps you to learn.

10. **Authority figures present.** Some students are more or less independent learners.

- Some students prefer to have the professor available to guide learning. In the college environment, students may prefer traditional face-to-face classes.

- Others prefer to work on their own. In the college environment, students may prefer online classes or independent study.

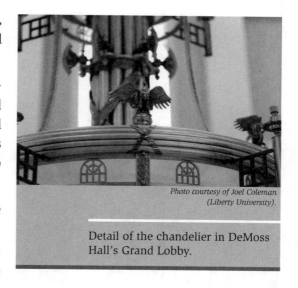

Photo courtesy of Joel Coleman (Liberty University).

Detail of the chandelier in DeMoss Hall's Grand Lobby.

Shaun D. Curran

"All too often students journey through our education with the belief that 'one size fits all' when it comes to studying and understanding the information they need to learn. This belief does little more than limit students and put their abilities in a box. Instead of the 'one size fits all' attitude towards learning, you should approach your education with the 'my size fits me' approach. This approach means understanding your learning style as much as you can, and using appropriate strategies that help make learning easier."

11. **Several ways.** Some students learn in several ways, and others have definite preferences.

- Some students like variety and can learn either on their own or with others.
- Some students definitely prefer learning on their own or prefer learning with others.

12. **Auditory.** Some students prefer to learn through listening and talking.

- Those who prefer auditory learning find it easier to learn through lectures, audio materials, discussion, and oral directions.
- Those who do not prefer auditory learning may find their minds wandering during lectures and become confused by oral directions. They do not learn through others talking about the topic. These students should read the material before the lecture and take notes during the lecture. Review the notes periodically to remember the material.

13. **Visual.** Some students learn through reading or seeing things.

- Those who prefer visual learning benefit from pictures and reading.
- Those who are not visual learners may dislike reading. If auditory learning is preferred, attend the lecture first to hear the lecturer talk about the subject and then do the reading. It is important to do the reading because not all the material is covered in the lecture.

14. **Tactile.** Some students prefer to touch the material as they learn.

- Students who prefer tactile learning prefer manipulative and three-dimensional materials. They learn from working with models and writing. Taking notes is one of the best tactile learning strategies.
- Students who are not tactile learners can focus on visual or auditory strategies for learning.

15. **Kinesthetic.** Kinesthetic learning is related to tactile learning. Students learn best by acting out material to be learned or moving around while learning.

- Students who prefer kinesthetic learning enjoy field trips, drama, and becoming physically involved with learning. For example, they can learn fractions by slicing an apple into parts or manipulating blocks. It is important to be actively involved in learning.

- Students who are not kinesthetic learners will use another preferred method of learning such as auditory or visual.

16. **Intake.** Some students need to chew or drink something while learning.

  - If you prefer intake while learning, drink water and have nutritious snacks such as fruits and vegetables.

  - Some students do not need intake to study and find food items distracting.

© 2013 by suphakit73. Used under license of Shutterstock, Inc.

17. **Evening/morning.** Some students are more awake in the morning and prefer to go to bed early at night. If this is your preference, schedule your most challenging studying in the morning and do your routine tasks later.

18. **Late morning.** Some students are more awake from 10:00 A.M. until noon. If this is your preference, use this time for studying. Use other times for more routine tasks.

19. **Afternoon.** Some students are more productive in the afternoon. If this is your preference, schedule your study time in the afternoon. Do your routine tasks at other times.

20. **Mobility.** Some students like to move around while studying.

  - If you prefer mobility, you may find it difficult to sit still for a long time. Take a break every 15 or 20 minutes to move around. When choosing an occupation, consider one that requires you to move around.

  - If you don't need to move around while studying, a stationary desk and chair are sufficient to help you concentrate on learning.

From *College and Career Success*, 5/e by Marsha Fralick. Copyright © 2011 by Kendall Hunt Publishing Company. Reprinted by permission.

Shaun D. Curran

"The purpose of learning styles is not to generate frustration, but to show you that what strategies work for one student may not work for you, and that simply staring at a computer screen in hopes that somehow you 'get' what is being taught may not be the most effective way to learn. Auditory learners may benefit from reading texts aloud and recording themselves, while kinesthetic learners may benefit from using flashcards to best master the material. Visual learners may be at a benefit in online classrooms, but this does not mean people with other types of learning styles cannot enjoy the rewarding freedom of an online education."

Identify Your Personal Learning Style Gifts

Proverbs 20:12,
"Ears that hear and eyes that see—the Lord has made them both" (NIV).

Jenny Walter

"Finding out the style that best suits you can help you throughout college. Have some fun learning more about yourself."

T. Marcus Christian

"You learn differently than any other student. There are special ways you can focus your attention depending on your learning style. Once you find the learning style that works best for you, the world of learning will open wide."

Mary Dixon

"God has made us unique and gifted us in a variety of ways. The way we process information and learn is one of those. Get to know yourself; get acquainted with God's gifts in you. Experiment until you know what works best for you because God has a plan that he will bring to completion as you cooperate with him. You are God's work of art, so show it in all that you do."

We know that individuals are different. I love the expression, "You're unique . . . just like everyone else!" Break that down, and here is what it means: God created each of us in His image, but we are all special and precious to Him. Even if you are an identical twin, you and your sibling are different. Your appearance may make it very difficult for others to tell you apart, but you may yet be very different when it comes to your learning style preferences. You are unique, so celebrate what God has given you as learning style gifts. Take this quiz to discover who you are as a learner.

Learning Style

Read the following questions and circle the letter of the best answer for each in your opinion. There are no right or wrong answers in this quiz. Just circle what you usually prefer.

1. When learning how to use my computer, I prefer to
   a. read the manual first.
   b. have someone explain how to do it first.
   c. just start using the computer and get help if I need it.

2. When getting directions to a new location, it is easier to
   a. look at a map.
   b. have someone tell me how to get there.
   c. follow someone or have him or her take me there.

3. To remember a phone number, I
   a. look at the number and dial it several times.
   b. repeat it silently or out loud to myself several times.
   c. remember the number by the pattern pressed on the keypad, the tones of each number, or writing it down.

4. For relaxation, I prefer to
   a. read a book or magazine.
   b. listen to or play music.
   c. go for a walk or do something physical.

5. I am better at
   a. reading.
   b. talking.
   c. physical activities.

6. In school, I learn best by
   a. reading.
   b. listening.
   c. hands-on activities.

7. I tend to be a
   a. thinker.
   b. talker.
   c. doer.

8. When I study for a test, it works best when I
   a. read and picture the information in my head.
   b. read and say the ideas out loud or silently.
   c. highlight, write notes, and outline.

9. It is easier for me to remember
   a. faces.
   b. names.
   c. events.

10. On a Saturday, I would prefer to
    a. see a movie.
    b. go to a concert.
    c. participate in athletics or be outside.

11. In a college class, it is most important to have
    a. a good textbook with pictures, graphs, and diagrams.
    b. a good teacher who gives interesting lectures.
    c. hands-on activities.

12. It is easier for me to study by

    a. reading and reviewing the material.

    b. discussing the subject with others.

    c. writing notes or outlines.

13. When I get lost, I prefer to

    a. look at the map.

    b. call or ask for directions.

    c. drive around the area until I recognize familiar landmarks.

14. When cooking, I often

    a. look for new recipes.

    b. talk to others to get new ideas.

    c. just put things together and it generally comes out okay.

15. When assembling a new toy or piece of furniture, I usually

    a. read the instructions first.

    b. talk myself through each step.

    c. start putting it together and read the directions if I get stuck.

16. When solving a problem, it is more useful to

    a. read a bestselling book on the topic.

    b. talk over the options with a trusted friend.

    c. do something about it.

17. Which statement do you like the best?

    a. A picture is worth a thousand words.

    b. Talk to me and I can understand.

    c. Just do it.

18. When I was a child, my mother said I

    a. spent a lot of time reading, taking photos, or drawing.

    b. had lots of friends and was always talking to someone on the phone.

    c. was always taking things apart to see how they worked.

Score your quiz:

Number of A answers ___3___ Visual Learner

Number of B answers ___7___ Auditory Learner

Number of C answers ___8___ Kinesthetic Learner

Personal Reflection

Were you surprised by what you found out about yourself, or were you easily able to predict your learning styles preference? Some students are very aware of their learning preferences, while others may be taken by surprise, having always just listened to lectures and taken notes, along with reading the textbook. Did your responses overwhelmingly fall into a single category, or did your answers range across the style choices? While some students are very heavily one type of learner, others may find strengths in a couple of categories. Still others discover that they score fairly evenly across the categories, with no clear preference. No matter what results you found from this exercise, you can be confident that you are perfectly set for learning just the way God made you!

Let's turn next to examine learning strategies that best match each of the three learning styles we have identified: visual, auditory, and kinesthetic learners. For those who find strengths in a pair of categories, you can be confident utilizing strategies from both of your learning styles. Experiment to find what suits you best. Did you find that you are a total mix of learning styles? Rejoice! This means that God has given you a host of learning strategies to work with: You can be successful with nearly every strategy outlined here. Praise Him for His generosity to you!

Roger

"As an online learner, I knew about different learning styles and was aware of how I learn best. I am not strongly kinesthetic or experiential. Nor am I strongly visual or acoustic. I am a wonderful blend of learning styles and can easily move from one mode of learning to another. I guess you can say, I love to learn about new things. I appreciate teachers who can present learning in a variety of styles, because they all appeal to me. So when I teach, I like to change my style and present information in several different ways by utilizing the senses, because people learn differently. They do not all process information the way I do. I have to show my wife how to perform certain computer applications. If I simply tell her how to do it, she will become confused and flustered, because that is not her learning style."

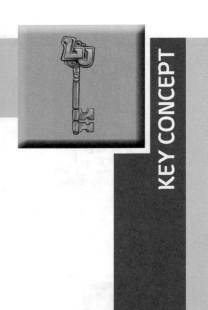

Determine Learning Strategies that Align with Your Learning Preferences for Maximum Effectiveness and Learning Efficiency

I Cor. 12:6,
"There are different kinds of working, but in all of them and in everyone it is the same God at work" (NIV).

Barbara Sherman

"Confucius stated: 'I hear and I forget; I see and I remember; I do and I understand.' Therefore, in studying, it is wise to first lean on your own preferences but, then, to also attempt to comprehend/process information in as many ways as you can."

It's a comfort to recall that no matter what learning techniques work for each of us, we are designed by God, and designed to be like Him. While some students find that there are many, many strategies that can help them learn easily, others have a more limited range of options to use. In any case, it is wise to try different strategies, rather than simply relying on what you have always done in the past. Your traditional strategies may be replaced when you discover new ones that are even more effective for you. Very few learners are all one way when it comes to learning style preference, so you may find that you are most efficient and effective when you apply a mix of strategies. Some learning tasks require a change of strategy, too. What works for you when you are learning a new concept may be different from what you do when you are trying to master a list of facts that must be memorized. No matter what you discover in terms of the strategies that work for you, know that you are unique, just as God designed you!

Learning Techniques

It is important to connect specific learning strategies to your preferred learning style. Even if you have definite preferences, you can experiment with other styles to improve your learning. If you become frustrated with a learning task, first try a familiar technique that you have used successfully in the past. If that does not work, experiment with different ways of learning. If one technique does not work, try another. It is powerful to combine techniques. For example, it is a good idea to make pictures of what you want to remember (visual), recite the ideas you want to remember (auditory), and take notes (kinesthetic).

The following are specific techniques for each type of learner. Underline or highlight techniques that are useful to you.

✱ Visual Learning Strategies —Seeing

(**Use as many visual resources as you can.**)

- In a classroom, sit at the front, away from distractions such as the door or window. At home, working by computer, position yourself with as few visual distractors as possible. Never work in front of the TV!

- Read textbooks to gain information when possible.

- Preview chapters, looking for main ideas, examining pictures, charts, graphics.

- In a presentation that is auditory (lecture or online course presentation), take notes to convert auditory stimuli to visual ones.

- Use colorful highlighters to mark main ideas, themes, and so on in your notes.

- Make flashcards of your noted information. Keep them with you and practice with them when you have a few moments to study: waiting in line, sitting in traffic, and so forth.

- When studying, review your notes or flashcards. Then put them away and see if you can rewrite them from memory. Rewriting is a powerful tool to build your memory of the visual stimulus.

- When selecting how to do course assignments, choose written work when possible, such as papers, PowerPoints, and so on.

- Visual learners usually work best alone, rather than with a study partner or group.

- Visual learners usually work best without auditory distractions, so no music, for example, in the background, except perhaps quiet classical music without vocals.

- Create a concept map of what you are trying to learn.

- Make a mental photograph or mental video of what you want to remember. Put action and color in the picture.

- Use different colors to highlight or underline your reading and lecture notes.

Dr. Jerry Falwell

"Life is filled with glorious opportunities brilliantly disguised as unsolvable problems" (Falwell, 1996, p. 97).

Alissa Keith

"Learn however you learn best, even if it means standing on your head to memorize math facts."

- Draw pictures to remember what you are learning.
- Use symbols or pictures in the margin to emphasize important points.
- Outline important points.

Auditory Learning Strategies ~ _Hearing_

Use as many auditory resources as possible. Create them if necessary!

- When reading course materials or PowerPoint presentations, read aloud.
- If you must read silently, try to "hear" the words as you are reading.
- Preview a textbook chapter by looking over the material in the chapter. Talk about what you see, so that you get an auditory stimulus of what you will be reading about. Talk your way through charts, pictograms, graphs, and so forth.
- Study with a buddy, so you can talk over what you are learning.
- Rehearse aloud what you are trying to learn. Add rhythm if possible.
- Join a study group to enable you to hear what others are saying about what you are studying. You can do this online with video conferencing software.
- Create flashcards for the material you want to learn. Practice with them repeatedly, aloud.
- Make a recording of the material on your flashcards and play it while you do other things (driving, etc.).
- Choose to make oral presentations for course assignments when possible. Record a video, make an audio clip, or something which employs your auditory learning strengths.
- Master what you are trying to learn by teaching it to someone else.
- If music is helpful to you, then use it while you are studying. Choose instrumental music to avoid being distracted by the lyrics of familiar music. (Use vocal music as your break-time entertainment.)
- Write a song or jingle filled with facts you want to remember, and sing it to a familiar tune.
- Turn your textbook into an auditory resource by reading it aloud. Record it so you can review it later.
- Use your computer's read-aloud function to have the e-textbook read to you.

Nathaniel Valle

"Knowing how you learn makes you a more equipped student as well as a holistic learner. If you struggle to understand a concept or information, think about how you're attempting to understand it; are you maximizing your natural style? Find ways to make your learning work for you."

✱ Kinesthetic Learning Strategies - "Hands-on"

(Use as much physical interaction with what you are learning as possible.)

- In a classroom, sit near the back of the room, so if you need to fidget (wiggle your foot, tap your pen, etc.), you will not be a distraction to others.

- For online work, have your computer where you can move your chair, wiggle, and so on. Be as comfortable as possible, but resist the urge to use your bed as a work area.

- You may consider abandoning the chair altogether and stretch out on the floor to do your work.

- Have a snack available while you are working.

- Try to work in briefer time frames, perhaps 20 to 25 minutes at a time. Take frequent breaks to stretch, move around, and refresh yourself. Quickly get back to your work, however.

- As you read from a textbook, follow along with your finger. Subvocalize (move your lips while reading silently) to make reading a kinesthetic activity.

- Make notes on what you are reading. Color-code them with highlighters.

- Make models to represent what you are learning.

- Create a card game so you can manipulate the information on each card as you are trying to master it.

- Create flashcards to use for study time. When you are using them, pace, rock, or otherwise be active as you work.

- Music is a good background for you, but use only music with no vocals. Keep it as a quiet background.

- Think ACTIVE learning. Use your body as much as possible to engage what you are trying to learn.

- If possible, choose hands-on activities for coursework presentations. Be creative with video, PowerPoint, or other presentation methods that take advantage of your kinesthetic learning style.

- Outdoor study can work well for you.

- Write summaries of the material to be learned.

- Think of practical applications for abstract material.

- Act out the material as in a play.

- Use puzzles, games, and computers.

Terry Conner

"The key to learning is not just understanding your learning style, but knowing how to apply it in the online environment. If you're a kinesthetic learner, find ways to bring the information out from the book and into your living room."

Michael Shenkle

"The topic of individual learning styles is one of my favorites, because it has such wide-ranging implications. Not only has it helped me understand my successes and failures in education, but it also has helped me better communicate with my family members by understanding how they receive and process information. By looking for ways to tailor my educational and relational interactions to a specific learning style, I have found greater success in both areas."

There are some strategies that are helpful for all learning styles. Flash cards can be useful for every learner, particularly if adapted to an individual's learning style. Auditory learners benefit from reading/quizzing the cards aloud, or by creating flash cards on a tablet, like the iPad. Record the information and quiz yourself. Visual learners benefit by seeing the information on the card, enhanced with colored ink or highlighting. Kinesthetic learners benefit most from the act of making the cards: writing the words and definitions/dates and so on helps in mastery. Reviewing the cards while moving (walking, pacing, or acting out) adds to the kinesthetic experience.

Photo courtesy of Dave Moquin.

Liberty Mountain boasts beautiful sunset views.

What other strategies do you think can be adapted for use by every learner? While it is important to understand and develop the particular strengths of your learning style, you should not ignore the strategies that can help other learners. Often, students have more than a single strong inclination for learning style, so you will want to practice strategies that will touch both/all of your learning strengths.

Multiple Intelligences

Tim

"Before starting my online courses, I did know a lot about my learning style. However, I did not know what strategies worked best with my learning style. The course offered by Liberty did help me learn more about my learning style and what I would need to do to complete my courses in a timely manner with high grades."

In 1904, the French psychologist Alfred Binet developed the IQ test, which provided a single score to measure intelligence. This once widely used and accepted test came into question because it measured the intelligence of individuals in schools in a particular culture. In different cultures and different situations, the test was less valid. As an alternative to traditional IQ tests, Harvard professor Howard Gardner developed the theory of multiple intelligences. He looked at intelligence in a broader and more inclusive way than people had done in the past.

Howard Gardner observed famous musicians, artists, athletes, scientists, inventors, naturalists, and others who were recognized contributors to society to formulate a more meaningful definition of intelligence. He defined intelligence as **the human ability to solve problems or design or compose something valued in at least one culture**. His definition broadens the scope of human potential. He identified eight different intelligences: musical, interpersonal, logical-mathematical, spatial, bodily-kinesthetic, linguistic, intrapersonal, and naturalist. He selected these intelligences because they are all represented by an area in the brain and are valued in different cultures. Howard Gardner has proposed adding existential intelligence to the list. He defines existential intelligence as the capacity to ask profound questions about the meaning of life and death. This intelligence is the cornerstone of art, religion, and philosophy. His theory can help us to understand and use many different kinds of talents.

Within the theory of multiple intelligences, learning style is defined as intelligences put to work. These intelligences are measured by looking at performance in activities associated with each intelligence. A key idea in this theory is that most people can develop all of their intelligences and become relatively competent in each area. Another key idea is that these intelligences work together in complex ways to make us unique. For example, an athlete uses bodily-kinesthetic intelligence to run, kick, or jump. They use spatial intelligence to keep their eye on the ball and hit it. They also need linguistic and interpersonal skills to be good members of a team.

Developing intelligences is a product of three factors:

1. Biological endowment based on heredity and genetics

2. Personal life history

3. Cultural and historical background

For example, Wolfgang Amadeus Mozart was born with musical talent (biological endowment). Members of his family were musicians who encouraged Mozart in music (personal life history). Mozart lived in Europe during a time when music flourished and wealthy patrons were willing to pay composers (cultural and historical background).

Each individual's life history contains crystallizers that promote the development of the intelligences and paralyzers that inhibit the development of the intelligences. These crystallizers and paralyzers often take place in early childhood. For example, Einstein was given a magnetic compass when he was four years old. He became so interested in the compass that he started on his journey of exploring the universe. An example of a paralyzer is being embarrassed or feeling humiliated about your math skills in elementary school so that you begin to lose confidence in your ability to do math. Paralyzers involve shame, guilt, fear, and anger and prevent intelligence from being developed.

Terry

Q: *When you began as an online learner, did you know anything about your learning style?*
A: "Yes"

Q: *What is your learning style?*
A: "I'm more of an auditory learner, but I'm equally versed in all three styles."

Q: *How did you learn about it?*
A: "A teacher in high school"

Q: *Were you able to take advantage of what you learned (or knew) about yourself?*
A: "Yes, it has helped me tremendously by informing me how best to study."

Q: *Why does choosing the correct strategies for learning matter, anyway?*
A: "If we choose a style that is outside of ours, we run the risk of becoming frustrated since the learning won't come easily."

WORKSHEET

Describing Your Multiple Intelligences

Below are some definitions and examples of the different intelligences. As you read each section, think positively about your intelligence in this area. Place a checkmark in front of each item that is true for you.

Musical

Musical intelligence involves hearing and remembering musical patterns and manipulating patterns in music. Some occupations connected with this intelligence include musician, performer, composer, and music critic. Place a checkmark next to each skill that you possess in this area.

- ☑ I enjoy singing, humming, or whistling.
- ☐ One of my interests is playing recorded music.
- ☐ I have collections of recorded music.
- ☑ I play or used to play a musical instrument.
- ☐ I can play the drums or tap out rhythms.
- ☑ I appreciate music.
- ☑ Music affects how I feel.

- ☑ I enjoy having music on while working or studying.
- ☑ I can clap my hands and keep time to music.
- ☑ I can tell when a musical note is off key.
- ☐ I remember melodies and the words to songs.
- ☐ I have participated in a band, chorus, or other musical group.

Interpersonal

Interpersonal intelligence is defined as understanding people. Occupations connected with this intelligence involve working with people and helping them, as in education or health care. Place a checkmark next to each skill that you possess in this area.

- ☑ I enjoy being around people.
- ☐ I am sensitive to other people's feelings.
- ☑ I am a good listener.
- ☐ I understand how others feel.
- ☐ I have many friends.
- ☐ I enjoy parties and social gatherings.
- ☐ I enjoy participating in groups.

- ☑ I can get people to cooperate and work together.
- ☐ I am involved in clubs or community activities.
- ☑ People come to me for advice.
- ☑ I am a peacemaker.
- ☑ I enjoy helping others.

Logical-Mathematical

Logical-mathematical intelligence involves understanding abstract principles and manipulating numbers, quantities, and operations. Some examples of occupations associated with logical-mathematical intelligence are mathematician, tax accountant, scientist, and computer programmer. Place a checkmark next to each skill that you possess. Keep an open mind. People usually either love or hate this area.

☑ I can do arithmetic problems quickly.

☑ I enjoy math.

❏ I enjoy doing puzzles.

❏ I enjoy working with computers.

❏ I am interested in computer programming.

❏ I enjoy science classes.

☑ I enjoy doing the experiments in lab science courses.

❏ I can look at information and outline it easily.

☑ I understand charts and diagrams.

☑ I enjoy playing chess or checkers.

☑ I use logic to solve problems.

❏ I can organize things and keep them in order.

Spatial

Spatial intelligence involves the ability to manipulate objects in space. For example, a baseball player uses spatial intelligence to hit a ball. Occupations associated with spatial intelligence include pilot, painter, sculptor, architect, inventor, and surgeon. This intelligence is often used in athletics, the arts, or the sciences. Place a checkmark next to each skill that you possess in this area.

☑ I can appreciate a good photograph or piece of art.

☑ I think in pictures and images.

☑ I can use visualization to remember.

☑ I can easily read maps, charts, and diagrams.

❏ I participate in artistic activities (art, drawing, painting, photography).

☑ I know which way is north, south, east, and west.

☑ I can put things together.

☑ I enjoy jigsaw puzzles or mazes.

☑ I enjoy seeing movies, slides, or photographs.

❏ I can appreciate good design.

❏ I enjoy using telescopes, microscopes, or binoculars.

❏ I understand color, line, shape, and form.

Bodily-Kinesthetic

Bodily-kinesthetic intelligence is defined as being able to use your body to solve problems. People with bodily-kinesthetic intelligence make or invent objects or perform. They learn by doing, touching, and handling. Occupations connected to this type of intelligence include athlete, performer (dancer, actor), craftsperson, sculptor, mechanic, and surgeon. Place a checkmark next to each skill that you possess in this area.

☑ I am good at using my hands.

☑ I have good coordination and balance.

☑ I learn best by moving around and touching things.

☑ I participate in physical activities or sports.

☑ I learn new sports easily.

☑ I enjoy watching sports events.

❏ I am skilled in a craft such as woodworking, sewing, art, or fixing machines.

☑ I have good manual dexterity.

☑ I find it difficult to sit still for a long time.

☑ I prefer to be up and moving.

❏ I am good at dancing and remember dance steps easily.

❏ It was easy for me to learn to ride a bike or skateboard.

Linguistic

People with linguistic intelligence are good with language and words. They have good reading, writing, and speaking skills. Linguistic intelligence is an asset in any occupation. Specific related careers include writing, education, and politics. Place a checkmark next to each skill that you possess in this area.

❏ I am a good writer.

❏ I am a good reader.

☑ I enjoy word games and crossword puzzles.

❏ I can tell jokes and stories.

☑ I am good at explaining.

☑ I can remember names, places, facts, and trivia.

❏ I'm generally good at spelling.

❏ I have a good vocabulary.

☑ I read for fun and relaxation.

☑ I am good at memorizing.

❏ I enjoy group discussions.

☑ I have a journal or diary.

Intrapersonal

Intrapersonal intelligence is the ability to understand yourself and how to best use your natural talents and abilities. Examples of careers associated with this intelligence include novelist, psychologist, or being self-employed. Place a checkmark next to each skill that you possess in this area.

- ☑ I understand and accept my strengths and weaknesses.
- ☑ I am very independent.
- ☑ I am self-motivated.
- ☑ I have definite opinions on controversial issues.
- ☑ I enjoy quiet time alone to pursue a hobby or work on a project.

- ☑ I am self-confident.
- ☑ I can work independently.
- ☑ I can help others with self-understanding.
- ☑ I appreciate quiet time for concentration.
- ☐ I am aware of my own feelings and sensitive to others.
- ☑ I am self-directed.
- ☐ I enjoy reflecting on ideas and concepts.

Naturalist

The naturalist is able to recognize, classify, and analyze plants, animals, and cultural artifacts. Occupations associated with this intelligence include botanist, horticulturist, biologist, archeologist, and environmental occupations. Place a checkmark next to each skill you possess in this area.

- ☐ I know the names of minerals, plants, trees, and animals.
- ☑ I think it is important to preserve our natural environment.
- ☐ I enjoy taking classes in the natural sciences such as biology.
- ☑ I enjoy the outdoors.
- ☐ I take care of flowers, plants, trees, or animals.
- ☐ I am interested in archeology or geology.

- ☐ I would enjoy a career involved in protecting the environment.
- ☐ I have or used to have a collection of rocks, shells, or insects.
- ☐ I belong to organizations interested in protecting the environment.
- ☐ I think it is important to protect endangered species.
- ☑ I enjoy camping or hiking.
- ☑ I appreciate natural beauty.

Personal Reflection

According to Gardner's theory, what are your most developed intelligences? Are there any you need to improve?

Logical - Mathematics & Naturalist
were my two lowest scores.

Multiple Intelligences

Test what you have learned by selecting the correct answers to the following questions.

1. Multiple intelligences are defined as
   a. the many parts of intelligence as measured by an IQ test.
   b. the ability to design something valued in at least one culture.
   c. the ability to read, write, and do mathematical computations.

2. The concept of multiple intelligences is significant because
   a. it measures the intelligence of students in schools.
   b. it does not use culture in measuring intelligence.
   c. it broadens the scope of human potential and includes all cultures.

3. Intelligences are measured by
   a. IQ tests.
   b. performance in activities related to the intelligence.
   c. performance in the classroom.

4. Each individual's life history contains crystallizers that
   a. promote the development of the intelligences.
   b. inhibit the development of the intelligences.
   c. cause the individual to be set in their ways.

5. Multiple intelligences include
   a. getting good grades in college.
   b. bodily kinesthetic skills.
   c. good test-taking skills.

How did you do on the quiz? Check your answers: **1.** b, **2.** c, **3.** b, **4.** a, **5.** b

Developing Your E-Learning Style

Students who are independent learners or introverts who enjoy individual learning in a quiet place may prefer online learning. Students who prefer having a professor to guide learning with immediate feedback and extraverts who are energized by social interaction may prefer traditional classroom education.

Because of work, family, and time constraints, online learning might be a convenient way to access education. No matter what your learning style, you are able to take advantage of online learning.

If you have never taken an online course, be aware of some of the myths of online learning. One of the most popular myths is than online courses are easier than traditional courses. Online courses cover the same content and are just as rigorous as traditional face-to-face courses. It is likely that your online course will require more writing; instead of responding verbally in discussions, you will have to write your answer. Online courses generally require the same amount of time as traditional courses. However, you will save time in commuting to class and have the added convenience of working on your class at any time or place where you can access the internet.

Here are some suggestions for a successful e-learning experience.

- The most important factor in online learning is to **log in regularly** and complete the work in a systematic way. Set goals for what you need to accomplish each week and do the work a step at a time. Get in the habit of regularly doing your online study, just as you would attend a traditional course each week.

- It is important to **carefully read the instructions** for the assignments and **ask for help** if you need it. Your online professor will not know when you need help.

- Begin your online work by getting familiar with the requirements and components of the course. Generally, online courses have reading material, quizzes, discussion boards, assignments, and multimedia presentations. Make sure that you **understand all the resources, components, and requirements** of the course.

- **Have a backup plan** if your computer crashes or your internet connection is interrupted. Public libraries offer computers with internet, free for their patrons' use, where you can do your work if you have technical problems at home. Do you have a library card? If not, be sure to sign up for one before you need it!

- Remember to **participate** in the online discussion boards. This is part of your grade and a good way to learn from other students and apply what you have learned. The advantage of online communication is that you have time to think about your responses.

- **Check your grades** online to make sure you are completing all the requirements. Make sure to look for comments from your professor to guide you in future similar assignments.

Celebrate your success as you complete your online studies. Online learning becomes easier with experience.

Keys to Success

We are responsible for what happens in our lives. We make decisions and choices that create the future. Our behavior leads to success or failure. Too often, we believe that we are victims of circumstance. When looking at our lives, we often look for others to blame for how our lives are going:

- My grandparents did it to me. I inherited these genes.

- My parents did it to me. My childhood experiences shaped who I am.

- My teacher did it to me. He gave me a poor grade.

- My boss did it to me. She gave me a poor evaluation.

- The government did it to me. All my money goes to taxes.

- Society did it to me. I have no opportunity.

These factors are powerful influences in our lives, but we are still left with choices. Concentration camp survivor Viktor Frankl wrote a book, *Man's Search for Meaning,* in which he describes his experiences and how he survived his ordeal. His parents, brother, and wife died in the camps. He suffered starvation and torture. Through all of his sufferings and imprisonment, he still maintained that he was a free man because he could make choices.

> We who lived in concentration camps can remember the men who walked through the huts comforting others, giving away their last piece of bread. They may have been few in number, but they offer sufficient proof that everything can be taken from a man but one thing: the last of the human freedoms—to choose one's attitude in any given set of circumstances, to choose one's own way. . . .
>
> Fundamentally, therefore, any man can, even under such circumstances, decide what shall become of him—mentally and spiritually. He may retain his human dignity even in a concentration camp.*
>
> *Viktor Frankl, *Man's Search for Meaning* (New York: Pocket Books, 1963), 104–5.

Viktor Frankl could not choose his circumstances at that time, but he did choose his attitude. He decided how he would respond to the situation. He realized that he still had the freedom to make choices. He used his memory and imagination to exercise his freedom. When times were the most difficult, he would imagine that he was in the classroom lecturing to his students about psychology. He eventually did get out of the concentration camp and became a famous psychiatrist.

Christopher Reeve is another example of a person who maintained his freedom to make choices in difficult circumstances. Reeve, who once played the character Superman, was paralyzed from the neck down as the result of an accident he suffered when he was thrown from his horse. When he first awoke after the accident, he saw little reason for living. With the help of his family, he made the decision to keep fighting and do as much as he could to promote research on spinal cord injuries.

He succeeded in raising awareness and money for this cause. As a result, there have been many advancements in the study and treatment of spinal cord injuries. Reeve believed that he and others in similar circumstances would walk again some day. Sadly, Reeve passed away in 2004. However, his advocacy for the cause of finding a cure for spinal injuries has led to research that will help others in the future.

Hopefully, none of you will ever have to experience the circumstances faced by Viktor Frankl or Christopher Reeve, but we all face challenging situations. It is empowering to think that our behavior is more a function of our decisions than of our circumstances. It is not productive to look around and find someone to blame for your problems. Psychologist Abraham Maslow says that instead of blaming, we should see how we can make the best of the situation.

One can spend a lifetime assigning blame, finding a cause, "out there" for all the troubles that exist. Contrast this with the responsible attitude of confronting the situation, bad or good, and instead of asking, "What caused the trouble? Who was to blame?" asking, "How can I handle the present situation to make the best of it?"

Author Stephen Covey suggests that we look at the word responsibility as "response-ability." It is the ability to choose responses and make decisions about the future. When you are dealing with a problem, it is useful to ask yourself what decisions **you** made that led to the problem. How did **you** create the situation? If you created the problem, **you** can create a solution.

At times, you may ask, "How did I create this?" and find that the answer is that you did not create the situation. We certainly do not create earthquakes or hurricanes, for example. But we do create or at least contribute to many of the things that happen to us. Even if you did not create your circumstances, you can create your reaction to the situation. In the case of an earthquake, you can decide to panic or find the best course of action at the moment.

Stephen Covey believes that we can use our resourcefulness and initiative in dealing with most problems. When his children were growing up and they asked him how to solve a certain problem, he would say, "Use your R and I!" He meant resourcefulness and initiative. He notes that adults can use this R and I to get good jobs.

But the people who end up with the good jobs are the proactive ones who are solutions to problems, not problems themselves, who seize the initiative to do whatever is necessary, consistent with correct principles, to get the job done.

Use your resourcefulness and initiative to create the future that you want.

From *College and Career Success*, 5/e by Marsha Fralick. Copyright © 2011 by Kendall Hunt Publishing Company. Reprinted by permission.

Photo courtesy of Joel Coleman (Liberty University).

Light-covered trees line the sidewalks in preparation for Christmas.

BUILDING BLOCKS

In the Bible, we read about the Israelites, God's chosen people, who left Egypt and wandered in the desert for 40 years, finally coming to the land that God had promised to give them. As their leader Moses was about to send the Israelites across the Jordan River into their new land, he spoke to them, giving farewell instructions that would carry them forward to success. Here is a bit of what he told them:

Deuteronomy 6:1-12

[1] These are the commands, decrees and laws the LORD your **God directed me to teach you** to observe in the land that you are crossing the Jordan to possess, [2] so that you, your children and their children after them may fear the LORD your God as long as you live by keeping all his decrees and commands that I give you, and so that you may enjoy long life.

[4] Hear, O Israel: The LORD our God, the LORD is one. Love the LORD your God with all your heart and with all your soul and with all your strength. [6] These commandments that I give you today are to be on your hearts. [7] Impress them on your children. **Talk about them when you sit** at home and **when you walk** along the road, **when you lie down and when you get up**.[8] Tie them as **symbols on your hands** and bind them **on your foreheads**. [9] **Write them** on the **doorframes of your houses** and **on your gates** . . .[12] be careful that you do not forget the LORD, who brought you out of Egypt, out of the land of slavery (NIV).

Notice the highlighted words in the passage. Do you see that God was using a variety of methods to help His chosen people remember what He was having Moses teach them? He encouraged them to use auditory methods (by talking about the commands, decrees, and laws). He gave them kinesthetic ways to remember, too (referring to walking, lying down, and getting up). He used visual methods as well, when he told them to put the symbols where they would see it: on their hands, foreheads, doorframes, and gates. God wanted to be sure that His people could learn in any of their preferred methods. Just as the Israelites could learn best by using the methods that they individually preferred, you can, too! Choose strategies that play to your strengths and use them frequently as you try to learn and do so efficiently. Do not simply rely on whatever methods you have used in the past, such as note-taking, but also, try to develop your learning skills by selecting new strategies within your preferred learning style. This can help you learn more in less time, which is an important consideration for a busy online learner.

Be careful to choose a learning environment that suits you best. While some students seek absolute quiet in a room far from friends or family, others will be able to thrive in a more active, busy environment. You may determine that you are best served in a cool room, spread out on the floor to learn, or you may prefer the structure of a desk in the library. Whatever your learning style preferences, choose strategies that match them, in order to gain maximum benefit from your time committed to study.

TOOL BOX

Visual

- **In Your Online Classroom**—Lessons in the online classroom are delivered through varying media in order to address the different ways that students learn. As a visual learner you want to look for charts, diagrams, and video presentations.

- **Mind Mapping**—Visual learners tend to do better when they can view a concept, so the use of mind mapping as a study tool can be very helpful. You can use presentation software like PowerPoint or you can utilize mind mapping websites/software to help you develop your visual aids.

- **Note Taking**—Take your own notes, using a text or word processing program, while you watch videos or listen to lectures. For lessons that are already written out, you might consider using the highlighting or underlining feature in your word processing program.

Auditory

- **In Your Online Classroom**—Lessons in the online classroom are delivered through varying media in order to address the different ways that students learn. As an auditory learner, you may want to pay particular attention to narrated slide presentations, basic audio lectures, or even consider downloading audio lectures from iTunes U, if available.

- **Podcasts**—These are online audio broadcasts that typically have subscriptions. There are several programs and apps that you can use to help you locate and subscribe to podcasts on a range of topics. One of the big benefits of podcasts is the ability to have them automatically downloaded to your mobile device and then listen to them as you commute to and from work.

- **Discussions**—While much of the discussion in online classrooms is done through email or the Discussion Board forum, you can communicate with others about what you are learning. Consider discussing relevant course topics with friends or family. This will afford you the opportunity to review the information verbally.

- **Text-to-Speech Software**—Auditory learners often find themselves struggling when they are in a course that requires an extensive amount of reading. In these circumstances you could consider using a text-to-speech program that will read the text to you. This creates a sort of audio book and enhances the auditory learner's ability to absorb the material.

Kinesthetic

- **In Your Online Classroom**—Lessons in the online classroom are delivered through varying media in order to address the different ways that students learn. As a kinesthetic learner, you will want to be on the lookout for interactive tutorials and assignments that ask you to create or develop things on your own.

- **Demonstrations/Labs**—Many courses, especially in the math and science areas, will offer online labs. These labs offer you the opportunity to interact with materials in the same way you might in a residential classroom. A classic example is the online dissection labs in biology that allow you to virtually dissect a frog.

- **Building or Designing on Your Own**—While taking basic tests and quizzes may not be a favorite for kinesthetic learners, creating them can be a huge help. Consider writing your own tests/quizzes in a word processing program or use an online quiz-making site.

Additional resources and links to specific sites, worksheets, and apps can be located by accessing the Breaking Ground website:

www.breakinggroundlu.com

References

Falwell, J. (1997). *Falwell: An autobiography.* Lynchburg, VA: Liberty House Publishers.

Fralik, M. (2011). *College and career success.* Dubuque, IA: Kendall Hunt Publishing Company.

Price, G. E., "Productivity Environmental Preference Survey," Price Systems, Inc., Box 1818, Lawrence, KS 66044-8818.

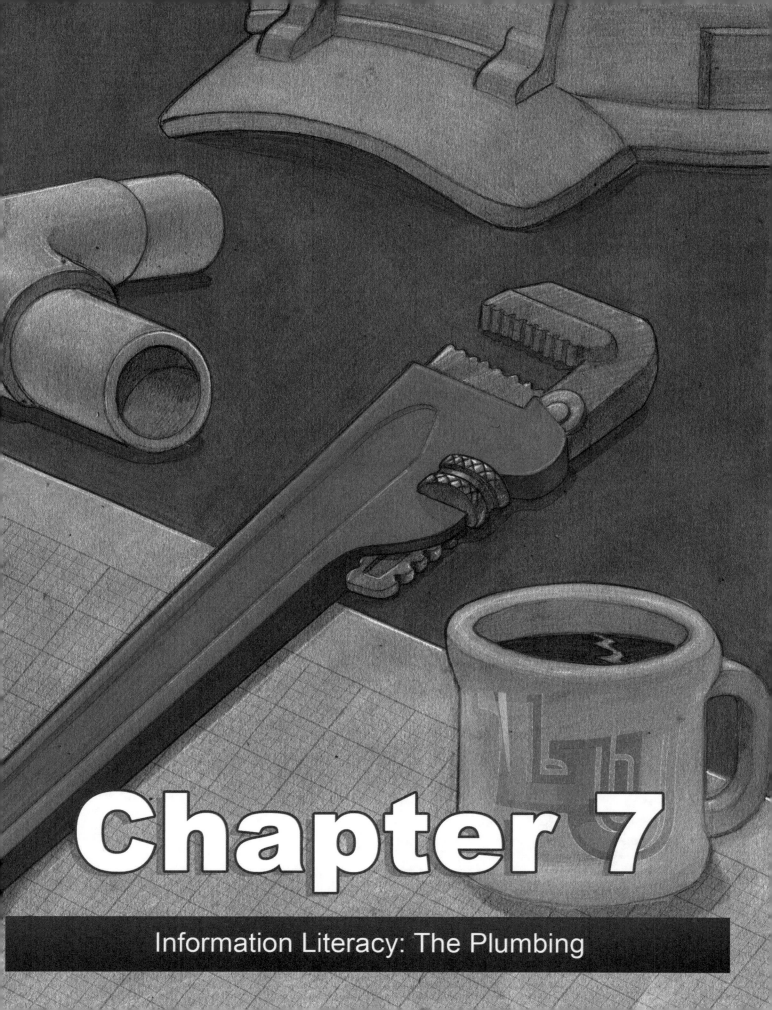

Chapter 7

Information Literacy: The Plumbing

In this chapter, you will:

- Explore the definition and importance of information literacy.
- Develop a strategy for research.
- Identify and avoid plagiarism.

THE PLUMBING

When tasked to plumb a new building, the inexperienced or unskilled plumber might accidentally use the wrong type of pipe or incorrectly fuse the pieces together, leading to contaminants in the water or a breach in the integrity of the system. This is not unlike the inexperienced or unskilled student choosing to use the wrong resources or inadvertently plagiarizing while patching together the first research paper. On the other hand, a master plumber would analyze and plan the job so as to protect the purity of the water and the integrity of the system. In the same way, a student who is information literate will be more than capable of selecting appropriate resources and skillfully citing his or her work.

© 2013 by Paul Fleet. Used under license of Shutterstock, Inc.

Acts 17:11,
"These Jews were more open-minded than those in Thessalonica, for they eagerly received the message, examining the scriptures carefully every day to see if these things were so" (NET).

THE CORNERSTONE

Philippians 1:9–10, "And this is my prayer: that your love may abound more and more in knowledge and depth of insight, so that you may be able to discern what is best and may be pure and blameless for the day of Christ" (NIV).

After visiting "A Bug's Life: It's Tough to Be a Bug," a 4-D experience found in the Tree of Life at Disney's Animal Kingdom, my daughter, Laura Grace, peppered me with questions, specifically about one character in the show, the Termitator. In the program, the Termitator is a termite that spews acid (water) at its predators (the audience). The Termitator fascinated Laura Grace, so she begged to know more about termites on our way to our home-away-from-home that evening. She asked me, hoping that I would be the authority on the topic, since I know everything else (or at least that's what she thinks).

My basic knowledge of termites was limited to two facts: termites live in mounds, and they like to eat wood. That simply did not satisfy my curious 6-year-old's brain. She wanted to know if the acid was poisonous. I explained that the acid in the show was just water, but she still wanted to know if the real acid was poisonous. In a moment of information desperation, I grabbed my smart phone and did a quick search for termites. I quickly scrolled past Wikipedia and landed on an entomology site for children. My, oh, my! Information overload! This led to many more questions and answers about termite behaviors, habitats, diet, and more.

Laura and I had a great time engaging each other in conversation and learning about termites, of all things. I felt like I became the informed hero to her inquisitive brain, until she said the words that humbled me instantly, "Mommy, would you please ask the phone . . . ?" I don't even remember the rest of her question. With those words, Laura put me in my place. I didn't know everything. I had to go to another source to track down information, and she knew it. However, her meaning was not judgmental; she just recognized the source of information (not her mommy, sadly) and longed to know more.

Much like my termite conversation with Laura Grace, research in any area of life—be it academic or spiritual—requires seeking out correct answers to our questions and relying on the best authoritative sources available to us. Research requires checking and double-checking the facts to be sure that they are correct, choosing the best resource rather than the most convenient. In our spiritual walk, our authoritative resource is God's Word; in academics, we also must be selective, actively searching out the information and not relying only on what we already know. I was not the authority on the subject of termites; I knew it, and because of that, I sought out assistance. The beautiful thing is, I didn't have to know it all, because I knew where to go to find the reliable information. In your academic pursuits, remember that you do not have to know the answers to everything; just select the best resource(s) and remember Paul's words in Philippians 1:9–10, "And this is my prayer: that your love may abound more and more in knowledge and depth of insight, so that you may be able to discern what is best and may be pure and blameless for the day of Christ" (NIV).

Explore the Definition and Importance of Information Literacy

KEY CONCEPT

> Ecc, 1:13,
> "I applied my mind to study and to explore by wisdom all that is done under the heavens. What a heavy burden God has laid on mankind!" (KJV).

We're now living in an era commonly referred to as the "information and communication" age, because more information is being produced and communicated in today's world than at any other time in history (Breivik, 1998; Cairncross, 2001; Thornburg, 1994). Since information is being generated and disseminated at such a rapid rate, "**information literacy**"—the ability to search for, locate, and evaluate information for relevance and accuracy—is now an essential 21st-century skill for managing and making sense of the overload of information that's currently available to us. If you dedicate yourself to improving your information literacy skills, you'll improve not only your academic performance in college, but also your career performance beyond college. This chapter is designed to strengthen your skills in this key area.

In addition to assignments relating to material covered in course readings and class lectures, you are likely to be assigned research projects that involve writing in response to information you locate and evaluate on your own. One of the key outcomes of a college education is for students to become self-reliant, lifelong learners. One key characteristic of a self-reliant, lifelong learner is information literacy. When you're information literate, you become a critical consumer of information: you know where and how to find credible information whenever you need it (National Forum on Information Literacy, 2005).

Terry

"I learned research skills initially in my high school courses, but more thoroughly in my English classes in college."

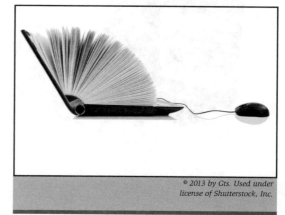

© 2013 by Gts. Used under license of Shutterstock, Inc.

Develop a Strategy for Research

Hebrews 4:12,
"For the word of God is quick, and powerful, and sharper than any two-edged sword, piercing even to the dividing asunder of soul and spirit, and of the joints and marrow, and is a discerner of the thoughts and intents of the heart" (KJV).

Following, is a six-step process for locating, evaluating, and using information to write research papers and reports in college (and beyond). This process can also be used to research information for oral presentations and group projects.

Terry

Q: *What is information literacy?*

A: "Information Literacy is the ability to know how to get information and determining the validity of that information."

1. Define a Research Topic/Question

Be sure that your research topic is relevant to the assignment and that its scope is neither too narrow, leaving you with too little available information on the topic, nor too broad, leaving you with too much information to cover within the maximum number of pages allowed for your paper or report.

If you have any doubts about your topic's relevance or scope, before going any further, seek feedback from your instructor or from a professional in your college library.

2. Locate Potential Sources of Information

You have two major types of resources you can use to search for and locate information:

- **Print resources**—e.g., card catalogs, published indexes, and guidebooks; and

- **Online resources**—e.g., online card catalogs, Internet search engines, and electronic databases.

Since different information-search tools are likely to generate different types of information, it's best not to rely exclusively on just one research tool. See Snapshot Summary 7.1 for a summary of key information-search tools and terms.

© 2013 by koya979. Used under license of Shutterstock, Inc.

As an online student, the bulk of your research will be done using online resources. As an active student at Liberty University, you can search through thousands of full-text scholarly articles by accessing the online library. If you can't locate what you are looking for there, the library also offers interlibrary loan services and will actually mail material to your home or scan copies of some articles that are not currently available online.

However, the first question to ask yourself about potential sources is whether they are acceptable to the instructor who assigned your research paper. Before you even begin the information-search process, be sure to read the assignment instructions carefully so that you know what sources your instructor requires or prefers.

Roger

"This is a skill that continues to change over time. I picked up some of these skills while asking questions at the library. As technology continues to advance, there are more and more tools available to research topics. The best thing that helped me was when I had to take a class that taught me how to perform searches to find the best sources. With online tools at the student's disposal, researching topics should not be as time consuming."

7.1 Snapshot Summary—Key Information Search Tools and Terms

Abstract. A concise summary of the source's content, usually appearing at the beginning of an article, which can help you to decide quickly whether the source is relevant to your research topic.

Catalog. A library database containing information about what information sources the library owns and where they are located. Libraries may still have some or all parts of their catalogs available on cards (i.e., in a card catalog); however, most catalogs are now in electronic form and can be searched by typing in a topic heading, author, topic, or keyword.

Citation. A reference to an information source (e.g., book, article, Web page) that provides enough information to allow the reader to retrieve the source. Citations used in a college research paper must be given in a standard format, such as APA or MLA format.

Database. A collection of data (information) that has been organized to make the information easily accessible and retrievable. A database may include:

1. Reference citations—e.g., author, date, and publication source,
2. Abstracts—summaries of the contents of scholarly articles,
3. Full-length documents, or
4. A combination of 1, 2, and 3.

Descriptor (a.k.a. subject heading). A keyword or key phrase in the index of a database (card or catalog) that describes the subjects or content areas found within it, enabling you to quickly locate sources relevant to your research topic. For example, emotional disorders may be a descriptor for a psychology database to help researchers find information related to anxiety and depression. (Some descriptors or subject headings will be accompanied by suggestions for different words or phrases that you can use in your search.)

Index. An alphabetical listing of topics contained in a database.

Keyword. A word used to search multiple databases by matching the search word to items found in different databases. Keywords are very specific, so if the exact word is not found in the database, any information related to the topic you're researching that doesn't exactly match the keyword will be missed. For example, if the keyword is college, it will not pick up relevant sources that may have university instead of college in their titles.

Search engine. A computer-run program that allows you to search for information across the entire Internet or at a particular Web site. For regularly updated summaries of different electronic search engines, how they work, and the types of information they generate, check the Web sites searchenginewatch.com/reports and researchbuzz.com.

Search thesaurus. A list of words or phrases with similar meaning, allowing you to identify which of these words or phrases could be used as keywords, descriptors, or subject headings in the database. This feature enables you to choose the best search terms before beginning the search process.

Subscription database. A database that can only be accessed through a paid subscription. You may be able to access through your college or university library because most electronic databases available in libraries are paid for through subscriptions.

Roger

"Not all research evidence is the same. For example, using Wikipedia is not a valid academic source because the imbedded information is not based upon scholarly research. One must examine the abstract, author, supporting documents, the data gathered to determine if it is appropriate academic material for citation in a paper."

URL (Uniform Resource Locator). An Internet address consisting of a series of letters and/or numbers that pinpoints the exact location of an information resource (e.g., www.breakinggroundlu.com)

Wildcard. A symbol, such as an asterisk (*), question mark (?), or exclamation point (!), that may be used to substitute different letters into a search word or phrase, so that an electronic search will be performed on all variations of the word represented by the symbol. For example, an asterisk at the end of the keyword econom* may be used to search for all information sources containing the words economy, economical, or economist.

Source: Hacker, D., & Fister, B. (2010). *Research and documentation in the electronic age* (5th ed.). Boston, MA: Bedford/St. Martin's.

For a more extensive glossary of Internet terms, see "Matisse's Glossary of Internet Terms" at www.matisse.net/files/glossary. html.

Personal Reflection

Look back at the terms listed in Snapshot Summary 7.1 and make note of any terms or definitions which were unfamiliar to you.

Wildcard ; Subscription database ;
Descriptor ; Catalog ; abstract

When you locate a source, your first step is to evaluate its relevance to your paper's topic. One strategy for efficiently determining the relevance of a source is to ask if it will help you answer one or more of the following questions about your topic: Who? What? When? Where? Why? How?

3. Evaluate the Credibility and Quality of Your Sources

The primary purpose of your sources is to provide documentation—references that support or confirm your conclusions. Since sources of information can vary widely in terms of their accuracy and quality, you'll need to think critically and make sound judgments about what are solid sources to select and use as documentation. The Internet has made this selection process more challenging, because most of its posted information is self-published and not subjected to the same quality control measures as information published in journals and books—which go to press only after they are reviewed for acceptance by a neutral panel of experts and are carefully edited by a professional editor. Listed below are some criteria to help you critically evaluate the quality of the sources you locate:

Terry

"In today's information age, anyone who wants to can put information out for public consumption. Just as I would verify that my mechanic can work on cars, I need to evaluate whether the author behind a source is knowledgeable in the area they claim they are."

CREDIBLE. Is the source written by an authority or expert in the field, such as someone with an advanced educational degree or professional experience relating to the topic? For example, if your topic relates to an international issue, a highly credible source would be an author who has an advanced degree in international relations or professional experience in international affairs.

SCHOLARLY. Is the source a scholarly publication that has been reviewed by a panel or board of impartial experts in the field before being published? If the source is written in formal style and includes references to other published sources, this is a good indication that it's a scholarly reference. Journal articles that have been "peer-reviewed" or "peer-refereed" have been reviewed, evaluated, and approved for publication by other experts in the field. This is a good indication that the source is a scholarly publication. Professional journals (e.g., the *New England Journal of Medicine*) are peer-reviewed, but popular magazines (e.g., *Newsweek*) and popular Web sites (e.g., Wikipedia) are not. Liberty University offers current students free access to several subscription databases, which are more likely to contain scholarly, peer-reviewed sources that are more closely monitored for quality than free databases available to you on the Internet.

CURRENT. Is it a recent or current source of information? In certain fields of study, such as the natural and social sciences, recent references may be strongly preferred because new data is generated rapidly in these fields and information can become quickly outdated. In other fields, such as history and philosophy, older references may be viewed as classics, and citing them is perfectly acceptable. If you're not sure whether current references are strongly preferred, check the specific assignment instructions and then email your instructor if you are still unsure.

OBJECTIVE. Is the author likely to be impartial or unbiased toward the subject? One way to answer this question is to consider how the professional positions or personal backgrounds of the authors may influence their ideas or their interpretation of evidence. Scholars should be impartial pursuers of truth who attempt to maximize their objectivity and minimize their level of emotional and political involvement with the topic. They should also not be in a position to gain personally or fiscally from favoring a certain conclusion about the topic. To assess the objectivity of a website, always ask yourself why the site was created, what its objective or purpose is, and who sponsors it.

Mary Dixon

"Education is a process in which we must develop ideas and execute them. It is not harvesting information."

Research articles you locate may also demonstrate a lack of objectivity. Suppose your topic relates to a controversial political issue such as global warming and you find an article written by a researcher who works for or consults with an industry that would incur significant costs to switch to more ecologically efficient sources of energy. It would be reasonable to suspect that this researcher has a conflict of interest and may be biased toward reaching a conclusion that financially benefits his employer (and himself). In this case, the objectivity of the article may be questionable, and you may not want to use it as a source in your paper. If scholars are not neutral, it increases the risk that they will find what they want to find. In scientific research, this risk is referred to as experimenter bias, and it stems from the natural tendency for people to see what they expect to see, or what they hope to see (King, 2010; Rosenthal, 1966). When evaluating an article, ask yourself the following questions to check for bias:

1. Is the author a member of a special-interest group or political or religious organization that could affect the article's objectivity?

2. Does the author consider alternative and opposing viewpoints and deal with those viewpoints fairly?

3. Does the author use words that convey a sense of rationality and objectivity, or are they characterized by emotionality and an inflammatory tone?

If you think an article may lack complete objectivity, but still find that it's well written and contains good information and arguments, you can cite it in your paper; however, be sure you demonstrate critical thinking by noting that its conclusions may have been biased by the author's background or position.

4. Evaluate the Quantity and Variety of Your Sources

Your research will be judged not only in terms of the quality of your individual sources, but also in terms of the overall set or total collection of references you used throughout your paper. Your total set of references is likely to be judged in terms of the following two criteria:

QUANTITY OF REFERENCES. Have you cited a sufficient number of references? As a general rule, it is better to use a larger rather than smaller number of references because it will provide your paper with a stronger research foundation and a greater number of perspectives. In addition, using multiple sources allows more opportunity to demonstrate the higher-level thinking skill of synthesis because you can demonstrate your ability to integrate information from different sources. Keep in mind that this is a general rule, and that some assignments may require you to use a specific number of references. Be sure you know what is required for each assignment before you begin.

VARIETY OF REFERENCES. Have you used different types of sources? For some research papers and some professors, the variety of references you use matters as much as (or more than) the sheer quantity. You can intentionally vary your sources by drawing on different types of references, such as:

- Books,

- Scholarly journal articles written by professionals and research scholars in the field,

- Magazine or newspaper articles written by journalists,

- Course readings or class notes, and

- Personal interviews or personal experiences.

You can also vary your references in terms of using **primary sources**—firsthand information or original documents (e.g., research experiments or novels)—and **secondary sources**—publications that rely on or respond to primary sources (e.g., a textbook or a newspaper article that critically reviews a novel or movie). Lastly, varying your references by including a balanced blend of older, classic sources and newer, cutting-edge references may also be desirable. This combination will enable you to demonstrate how certain ideas have changed or evolved over time, or how certain ideas have withstood the test of time and continue to remain important.

In the end, the individual assignment instructions and the purpose of your writing should be the major factor in the variety of references you use.

Mary Dixon

"We can access so much information that it is tempting to circumvent our own thought process by borrowing the thought processes of others. This does not help us to learn, nor does it help us to develop characteristics that will honor God."

5. Use Your Sources as Stepping Stones to Your Own Ideas and Conclusions

Your paper should represent something more than an accumulation of ideas gathered from other people. Simply collecting and compiling the ideas of others will result in a final product that reads more like a high school book report than a college research paper. It's your name that appears on the front cover of the paper. Your sources just provide the raw material for your paper; it's your job to shape that raw material into a finished product that's uniquely your own. Do not just report or describe information you've drawn from your sources: instead, react to them, draw conclusions from them, and use them as evidence to support your reactions and conclusions.

Personal Reflection

Prior to college, did you write papers in which you had to cite references? If so, do you remember the reference style you were required to use?

Yes, books, internet, articles. We use MLA Style.

Identify and Avoid Plagiarism

I Timothy 2:1-3,
"I exhort therefore, that, first of all, supplications, prayers, intercessions, and giving of thanks, be made for all men; For kings, and for all that are in authority; that we may lead a quiet and peaceable life in all godliness and honesty. For this is good and acceptable in the sight of God our Saviour" (KJV).

Before you can move on to the sixth step in the research process, properly citing your sources, you need to become familiar with the concepts of academic integrity and plagiarism.

Jenny Walter

"Plagiarism is defined as using anyone's words or ideas as your own. Whether you include the exact words from another, summarize or paraphrase another's thoughts, always give that person the credit."

What Is Academic Integrity?

Academic integrity involves avoiding the unethical practice of stealing the ideas of others, whether they are the ideas of peers (e.g., cheating on exams) or the words and ideas of authorities that have been used in a written paper (plagiarism). When writing papers and reports, students with academic integrity give credit where credit is due: they carefully cite and reference their sources.

What Exactly Is Plagiarism?

Plagiarism is a violation of academic integrity that involves intentional or unintentional use of someone else's work without acknowledging it, giving the reader the impression that it's the writer's original work.

Common Forms of Plagiarism

1. Paying someone, or paying for a service, for a paper and turning it in as your own work

2. Submitting an entire paper, or portion thereof, that was written by someone else.

Photo courtesy of Sielan University.

3. Copying sections of someone else's work and inserting it into your own work.

4. Cutting paragraphs from separate sources and pasting them into the body of your own paper.

5. Paraphrasing (rewording) someone else's words or ideas without citing that person as a source.

6. Not placing quotation marks around someone else's exact words that appear in the body of your paper.

7. Failing to cite the source of factual information in your paper that's not common knowledge.

Note: If the source for information included in your paper is listed at the end of your paper in your reference (works cited) section but is not cited in the body of your paper, this still qualifies as plagiarism.

Final Note: Only include sources in your reference section that you actually used and cited in the body of your paper. Including sources in your reference section that aren't cited in your paper isn't technically a form of plagiarism; however, it can be perceived as being deceitful because you're "padding" your reference section, giving the reader the impression that you incorporated more sources of information into your paper than you actually did.

Sources: Academic Integrity at Princeton (2011); Purdue University Online Writing Lab (2012).

From *Thriving in College and Beyond*, 3/e by Joseph B. Cuseo, Aaron Thompson, Michele Campagna and Viki S. Fecas. Copyright © 2013 by Kendall Hunt Publishing Company. Reprinted by permission.

T. Marcus Christian

"One of the easiest ways to plagiarize is to wait until the last minute to complete an assignment. When you do that, it is easier to borrow from other sources. Save yourself from failure and plan to complete assignments long before they are due."

A Christian Worldview on Avoiding Plagiarism

While there are general rules that all academics follow regarding the avoidance of plagiarism, the Christian academic must also look at this issue using their biblical worldview. Dr. Emily Heady, Dean for the College of General Studies at Liberty University, shares how to apply a biblical worldview to this topic.

Almost anyone who has taught for any length of time has a story about a student who plagiarized in an unusually brazen (and sometimes laughable) way—the one, for instance, about the student who forgot to remove the hyperlinks when he cut and pasted a Wikipedia article, or the one about the student who plagiarized an article written by his professor, or the one about the student who denied that he could have plagiarized his paper because "[his] roommate wrote the essay for [him]." While students like these (thankfully) come along only rarely, they make a lasting impression—and not a good one. On the one hand, their instructors remember them because they made an extraordinarily poor decision that, more often than

(continues)

Alissa Keith

"If it doesn't come from your own brain, then cite it. It's better to over-cite than under-cite."

not, resulted in their failing the course they were taking. More than this, though, they are memorable for what their poor decision to plagiarize says about them as a person. Instead of using their God-given intellect, talents, and time to complete the requirements for the classes they were taking, these students chose to co-opt others' thoughts and labor, claiming them as their own without acknowledging it. In short, they chose to steal rather than to work.

As Christians striving to integrate faith and learning, we have an opportunity to develop further our Christian worldview every time we complete an assignment for a class or write something another will read. In part, this means that we avoid the behaviors of the sorts of students mentioned above—we can choose to work rather than to steal, and thus maintain high standards of academic honesty. At the same time, we can think about the way that practicing Christian virtues such as gratitude, generosity, humility, honesty, integrity, and industriousness gives us an opportunity to develop ourselves in ways that will allow us to bring God glory through all we do, whether in the classroom or anywhere else we may go.

The first two virtues that we can develop by maintaining a high standard of academic integrity—which both conveniently begin with the letter "g"—go hand-in-hand: **gratitude** and **generosity**. Grateful people are also generous people; when we recognize that what we have has been given to us as a gift rather than as an entitlement, we are more likely to share what we have with others.

When we write papers or complete academic assignments of any sort, we depend on the hard work of those who came before. In a broad sense, we operate within the confines of the discipline we study; if we are majoring in Psychology, for instance, we are indebted to Erickson, Freud, and many others who helped to shape the way we understand the rules and principles that govern the human mind. More specifically, if we are writing a paper or a discussion board post, we are building on the work of others who came before, including our instructors, the authors of our textbooks, and anyone whose work we consulted while we were formulating our own thoughts and ideas. The best way to express our gratitude to those whose work preceded us is to thank them with a correct citation that follows the formatting conventions of our fields of study.

In turn, our grateful acknowledgment of our debt to others' work helps us to give a generous gift to our own readers as well—the ability to enter into a productive scholarly conversation. If a student of mine is working on a project such as a thesis or a seminar paper, one of the first pieces of research advice I give is to find a great article, then read everything listed in

Mary Dixon

"Be true to yourself, and in turn, be true to others. Give credit where credit is due."

that article's bibliography or works cited page. The reason is not that I want my students to take a shortcut; rather, it is that I want them to benefit from the generosity of others who have invited them to share their scholarly conversation. What could be better than having Christians in the conversations that drive change in academic disciplines and workplaces across the world?

In addition to gratitude and generosity, writing a paper with a high degree of academic integrity requires another two related virtues, **humility** and **honesty**. While humility requires us to put others ahead of ourselves, it does NOT require us to think less of ourselves than is warranted; rather, it involves having a right view of ourselves and our own abilities, one which acknowledges that everything good in us comes from God. When we value ourselves rightly, we also find it easier to appreciate the giftedness and contributions of others, for we see their skills as evidence of God's goodness. Thus, the humble student feels no shame in giving credit where credit is due, via a proper citation or a cogent summary of another's work, because the student holds his or her own skills and talents loosely.

It follows, then, that humble students are also honest. They know what work they have done by themselves, and they are open and truthful about what they have gleaned from others. Sometimes, though, it takes hard, detailed work to be honest. During the research process, careful and correct note-taking allows you later on to give credit where credit is due—remember that it will be hard to cite a quotation properly if you can't remember where you found it!

Finally, students completing academic assignments have the opportunity to develop two virtues that begin with the letter "i": **integrity** and **industriousness**. Of all the virtues discussed here, these are perhaps the most obviously applicable to an academic context. Integrity means that we are the same people in private as we are in public; it means we have nothing to hide. Imagine that your course instructor watched you through all phases of your writing process—research, reading, note taking, drafting, and editing. Would your instructor find that you were operating with integrity as you note others' ideas and then develop your own, or would your instructor discover that you are taking shortcuts to make your work look more impressive than it really was?

The best way to operate with integrity is to make sure that you have worked hard. Of course, we all spend a little bit of time fighting distraction when we are working (I know that my house is never cleaner than on days when I have a major project to complete!), and we all struggle to keep our eyes open when we are reading a pile of articles on a less-than-interesting topic. Yet working industriously is a choice we make. If we research diligently—not

(continues)

Mary Dixon

"Honor God's work in yourself and his work in others by citing information and ideas that you use to become truly educated."

Mark Heideman

"Do not minimize the importance of adhering to Academic Writing Standards such as APA, Turabian, etc. Students often say 'I won't use this after college,' which is sometimes true but writing standards hone in on other writing skills such as spelling/grammar, formatting, professional looking documents, etc."

Katie Robinson

"Information literacy and avoiding plagiarism isn't just about avoiding the trespass of taking credit for someone else's work. Instead, writing a body of work that includes thorough research and support from other sources (documented correctly, of course) serves to demonstrate that the writer has done his or her job well in presenting good, solid information that is backed up by other researchers."

reading everything we could, but reading enough to have a thorough understanding of our topic—take careful notes, draft conscientiously, and edit in such a way as to produce a finished project of which we can be proud, then we have put ourselves in a position to demonstrate all these virtues to their fullest. We will find it easy to be humbly grateful for the work others have done because we will have a thorough knowledge of what everyone has contributed, and in turn, we will be able to operate with honesty and integrity because we will have nothing to hide. This will have the final benefit of giving us an opportunity to contribute generously to our field of study.

Of course, schools across the country have strict policies against plagiarism and other types of academic misconduct (cheating, falsification, etc.). Liberty University (like its secular peers) values academic integrity and holds its students to high standards. We have set rules about what is allowed and not allowed, and we publish them in obvious places such as the academic catalog and even some course syllabi. Should students violate these rules, there are consequences, ranging from minor grade deductions to failure in a class to expulsion from the university. Liberty is unlike its secular peers, though, in the reason it has these rules: the intimate connection between Christian worldview and academic ethics. We publish and enforce policies about academic ethics not only to protect the academic reputation of Liberty University, but also because the best way to learn about the Christian worldview is to put it into practice. Like driving a car, being an effective Christian requires not just knowing but doing—studying the driver's manual AND getting out on the road.

As you journey to your degree, we hope and pray that you'll not only stay out of trouble by maintaining the highest academic standards, but also that you'll think of your assignments as opportunities to put your worldview into practice.

 ## Cite Your Sources with Integrity—The Sixth Step in the Research Process

Now that you are familiar with the concepts of academic integrity and plagiarism, it's time to discuss the primary technique you can employ to practice academic integrity and avoid plagiarism. By citing and referencing your sources, you demonstrate intellectual honesty by giving credit where credit is due. You credit others whose ideas you've borrowed and you credit yourself for the careful research you've done.

When should sources be cited? You should cite the source of anything you include in your paper that does not represent your own work or thoughts. This includes other people's words, ideas, statistics, research findings, and visual work (e.g., diagrams, pictures, or drawings). There is only one exception to this rule: You don't need to cite sources for information that's common knowledge—i.e., information that most people already know. For example, common knowledge includes well-known facts (e.g., the earth is the third planet from the sun) and familiar dates (e.g., the Declaration of Independence was signed in 1776).

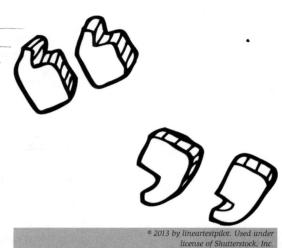

The Internet has allowed us to gain easy access to an extraordinary amount of information and has made research much easier—that's the good news. The bad news is that it has also made proper citation more challenging. Determining the true "owner" or original author of information posted online isn't as clear-cut as it is for published books and articles. If you have any doubt, print it out and check it out with your instructor or a professional librarian. If you don't have the time or opportunity to consult with either one of them, then play it safe and cite the source in your paper. If you cannot find the name of an author, at least cite the website, the date of the posted information (if available), and the date you accessed or downloaded it.

Remember: As a general rule, whenever you're unsure about the need to cite a source, it's better to cite it and risk being corrected for over-citing than it is to run the risk of being accused of plagiarism—a serious violation of academic integrity that can have grave consequences (e.g., probation, suspension, or expulsion).

Where and how should sources be cited? Sources should be cited in two places: (1) the body of your paper, and (2) the reference section at the end of your paper (also known as a "bibliography" or "works cited" section).

How you should cite your sources depends on the referencing style of the particular academic field or discipline in which you are writing your paper, so be sure that you know the citation style your instructor prefers. It's likely that you will be expected to use one of three referencing styles during your time at Liberty:

1. **MLA style**—standing for the Modern Language Association—the citation style commonly used in the humanities and fine arts (e.g., English and theatre arts); or

2. **APA style**—standing for the American Psychological Association—the citation style most commonly used in the social and natural sciences (e.g., sociology and anthropology).

Ramona Myers

"Rules to help avoid plagiarism (I call this the 'sandwich method'):

(1) Introduce the source with a signal phrase before providing the source information. Often, this signal phrase will include the name of the author (and in APA, the year in parenthesis). This is the 'top bun' of the sandwich.

(2) Source material may be written as a Direct Quote, a Summary, or a Paraphrase. This is the 'meat' and the 'condiments' of the sandwich.

(3) The 'bottom bun' of source material involves finalizing the source with an ending citation."

3. **Turabian Style**—named for the original author, Kate L. Turabian, and very similar to Chicago Style—the citation style commonly used in religion courses here at Liberty.

Be sure you're aware of the referencing style that is expected or preferred by your instructor before you begin to write your paper.

The key elements when citing another author's work in the body of your paper are the last name of the author, the date of publication, and, in situations where you are quoting, the page number from which the information was retrieved. When citing the same works in your references section you will need to include additional information. Refer to the specific writing manual for details, as the exact information and formatting required will vary by style.

Examples (in APA):

- When quoting—include the author's last name, publication date, and page number

- When paraphrasing—include the author's last name and publication date (a page number can be used here, but is not required)

- When summarizing—include the author's last name and publication date

If you paraphrase or summarize several ideas from the same source within the same paragraph, and if you are not mixing in the ideas of other authors, you do not need to cite the author after every single sentence; cite the source only once at the end of the paragraph. However, you do need to include a citation immediately following each quotation.

Personal Reflection

Take a look back at the definition and forms of plagiarism described in the early part of this chapter. List those forms of plagiarism that you were not aware of or weren't sure actually represented plagiarism.

_____

_____

_____

_____

_____

BUILDING BLOCKS

Summary and Conclusion

The key skill discussed in this chapter—research (information literacy)—is a powerful, transferable skill that can be applied across different academic subjects that you encounter in college and across different work situations you encounter beyond college.

Research, writing, and speaking are interrelated and complementary sets of success tools. Research skills are needed to acquire high-quality ideas from others, and both writing and speaking skills are needed to actively stimulate your own thinking about the ideas you acquire and as vehicles for communicating your ideas to others. Said in another way, research skills enable you to locate, evaluate, and integrate information, while writing and speaking skills enable you to comprehend, communicate, and demonstrate your mastery of that information to others.

These three key skills have always been relevant to the educational and professional success of college students and college alumni, but they are even more critical for success in today's information and communication age. Furthermore, as discussed earlier, they are valued highly by employers.

Is It or Is It Not Plagiarism?

The following four incidents were actually brought to a judicial review board to determine if plagiarism had occurred and, if so, what the penalty should be. After you read each case, answer the questions listed below it.

CASE 1. A student turned in an essay that included substantial material copied from a published source. The student admitted that he didn't cite the sources properly, but argued that it was because he misunderstood the directions, not because he was attempting to steal someone else's ideas.

1. Is this plagiarism?

   yes

2. How severe is it? (Rate it on a scale from 1 = low to 10 = high)

   7.8

3. What should the consequence or penalty be for the student?

   Probation

4. How could the suspicion of plagiarism have been avoided in this case?

   Citing the source, Even if it was over cited

CASE 2. A student turned in a paper that was identical to a paper submitted by another student for a different course.

1. Is this plagiarism?

   Yes

2. How severe is it? (Rate it on a scale from 1 = low to 10 = high)

   10

3. What should the consequence or penalty be for the student?

   Expolusion

4. How could the suspicion of plagiarism have been avoided in this case?

   If it wasn't identical to another individual's paper

CASE 3. A student submitted a paper he wrote in a previous course as an extra-credit paper for a course. Is this plagiarism?

1. Is this plagiarism?

   yes

2. How severe is it? (Rate it on a scale from 1 = low to 10 = high)

   10

3. What should the consequence or penalty be for the student?

   Expulsion

4. How could the suspicion of plagiarism have been avoided in this case?

   It is considered plagiarism. They needed a new paper with new ideas

CASE 4. A student submitted a paper in an art history course that contained some ideas from art critics that she read about and whose ideas she agreed with. The student claimed that not citing these critics' ideas wasn't plagiarism because their ideas were merely their own subjective judgments or opinions, not facts or findings, and, furthermore, they were opinions that she agreed with.

1. Is this plagiarism?

   yes

2. How severe is it? (Rate it on a scale from 1 = low to 10 = high)

   8

3. What should the consequence or penalty be for the student?

   Suspension

4. How could the suspicion of plagiarism have been avoided in this case?

   If it was written about and published then it needs to be cited. They weren't her thoughts.

EXERCISE

Crime and Punishment: Plagiarism and Its Consequences

Because of the ease with which internet sources can be copied and pasted, it is now common for college students to submit assignments using text that has been lifted off the Web. In response to this trend many universities now subscribe to Web sites that match the content of students' papers with content from books and online sources. To monitor plagiarism in their classes, faculty members require students to submit their papers through these Web sites. At Liberty University, we use a tool called SafeAssign. The SafeAssign tool compares students' work to find matches with previously-published work. The match may be to a work by a well-known source or to another student's work. The SafeAssign service can be described as a dumb tool, as it does not make judgments, it only finds matching words. It is the responsibility of faculty and students to carefully evaluate the matches to determine if matching words are common knowledge, properly cited paraphrases or quoted material, or at worst, plagiarism. If students are caught plagiarizing, for a first offense, they typically receive an F for the assignment or the course. A second offense can result in dismissal or expulsion from college.

Source: http://www.plagiarism.org/index.html

Personal Reflection

1. Why do you think students plagiarize? What do you suspect are the primary motives, reasons, or causes? (*Hint:* Remember what Dr. Heady had to say about this.) *It is easier to plagiarize because you don't have to work through your own thoughts and ideas*

2. What do you think is a fair or just penalty for those found guilty of a first plagiarism violation? What is fair for those who commit a second violation?
   Grace. 2nd: Expulsion

3. How do you think plagiarism could be most effectively reduced or prevented from happening in the first place?
   Better citations; more of one's own ideas

4. Do Christian students have any additional responsibilities when it comes to ethical behavior when producing written work? Why or why not?
   The responsibility of abiding by the requirements of their school)

Sources:

Information Literacy:
why? when? How to use different types of sources? How to pick the best sources for your needs?

Type of Sources:
- Magazines
  - periodicals
  - info/opinions
  - up-to-date info
  - general articles
    - not necessarily experts
- Journals
  - periodicals
  - scholarly research
  - studied on topic
  - bibliographies
- Newspapers
  - periodicals
  - Current info
  - about international, local, national
  - editorials, commentaries
  - expert or popular opinions
- Books
  - Any topic fact/fiction
  - Info on topic
  - Topic in context
  - Historical info
  - Summaries of research to support argument
- Library Catalog
  - books, journals, & audiovisual
  - find out books Library owns
  - where specific item is located
- Encyclopedias
  - factual items
  - general/subject
  - Background info
  - key ideas, dates or concepts
- Article Index
  - periodical index
  - Articles in magazines, journals or newspapers
  - Internet
    - Does it all

Library:
Quality over Quantity

The Web:
- Companies & organizations
- US. Government
- quick facts
- Current news
- Opinions of people
- Connecting to Library's Subscription resources

WEB:
http: hypertext transfer protocol
www: host computer/server name
liberty: second-level domain name
edu: top level domain; educational institution
informationservices/ilrc/library: directory/sub-directory names
.cfm: type of file, cold fusion mark-up, for active server pages
PID: Page Identification Number

America History and Life

~~Meta~~ Metacrawler: search several databases at once

(+) includes everything being searched
(−) excludes words not desired

LUCAS (Liberty University Catalog System)
- Books • Journal Titles • Electronic books • Newspapers & magazine titles
- microforms • Musical Scores • Sound recordings • DVDs

Keyword vs Subject Heading

- Quick way to do initial Search
- natural language
- Can be messy
- Risky; what you type is what you get

- uses "Controlled Vocabulary"; descriptor
- Organized list of subjects
  - more precise
- Subject headings are not flexible
- Requires thesaurus or index
- No guessing allowed

① Purpose
② Authorship/Source
③ Content
④ Design & usability

Visible Web: Obtain information about other cities.

Narrow   Broaden
AND/NOT   OR
"quotation Marks"   (?)
Advanced Search   Broader concept

(ILL)
InterLibrary Loan & ILLiad

Articles: Library Database: EBSCO
- Citation • Abstract • Full Text

① General Article Database   ② Subject Database

- Get It @ Liberty

TOOL BOX

Become Information Literate

InfoRM—Short for Information Research Modules, InfoRM is a six module, online tutorial designed by the skilled librarians in the Liberty University Library. In proceeding through this tutorial, students will examine the basics of information literacy, walking through the entire research process from choosing a topic to citing sources.

www.liberty.edu/index.cfm?PID = 19914

Search for Quality Sources

LibGuides—LibGuides is yet another invaluable resource provided to Liberty University students by the school's on-campus librarians. LibGuides are informational pages that explain the details of various resources or processes. You can locate information and tutorials on how to use the various, subject-specific databases, as well as gain direct access to thousands of media and web resources.

Liberty University Online Library—The Liberty University Online (LUO) Library is the primary means by which you will search for and locate scholarly journal articles, media, and web resources as you work to complete academic projects for your classes. Not only does the online library house thousands of full-text online resources, but the staff will also mail out physical media to online students.

www.liberty.edu/library

Cite Your Work

EndNote Citation Software—For help in citing your sources and building a reference page Liberty University offers a free download of EndNote Citation Software to active LUO students. The software can be used on both Mac and PC and allows you to fill out a brief survey of information regarding each of your sources; then, it formats your information based on the citation style you indicate. Be sure to check the results, as you are ultimately responsible for ensuring the accuracy of your work.

www.liberty.edu/informationservices/ilrc/library/index.cfm?PID = 15707

Citation: State where the info was found
Book: Author, Title of Book, Place of publication, Date of publication
Article: Author, Title of Article, Title of journal, volume/issue, page number, Date
Web: Author, Title of web page, Date viewed, URL

Writing aids from the LUO Writing Center—If you are looking for a check-list of a writing style's basic elements, this site is the place to go. You can quickly review all of the writing basics, as well as verify that you have met the required elements for standard citations types and even review samples of entire papers written in the various formats.

Additional resources and links to specific sites, worksheets, and apps can be located by accessing the Breaking Ground website:

www.breakinggroundlu.com/

6. Broadening your topic

Topic
CO2 pollution   Broader Subject

environmental pollution

7. To develop a Research Question, Ask...
   Why? What? How?

8: Game

9. Online index & Databases

10. Magic of Indexing
   · Author → Author
   · Title → Title
   · Subject → subject
   · Data → year

11. Keyword Searching ←
   · Included all of the above
   · Multiple Searches (ie. tobacco _and_ advertising)

12. Keyword Searching tools   (narrow)
   (Boolean) Connectors ; AND, OR, and NOT
                            (narrow)
   (2) LUCAS · Truncation; Wildcards
   (*) -EBSCO · Nesting; Organize search
   family Database   - using parentheses will
                      be searched first
                   (ie. alcohol AND (adolescents OR
                                     teenegers))

13. Types of Database
   · Library Catalogs
   · Article Databases

References

Academic Integrity at Princeton. (2011). *Examples of plagiarism.* Retrieved October 21, 2011, from http://www.princeton.edu/pr/pub/integrity.

Breivik, P. S. (1998). *Student learning in the information age.* Phoenix, AZ: The Oryx Press.

Cairncross, F. C. (2001). *The Death of Distance: How the Communication Revolution is Changing Our Lives.* Cambridge, MA: Harvard Business School Press.

Hacker, D., & Fister, B. (2010). *Research and Documentation in the Electronic Age* (5th ed.). Boston, MA: Bedford/St. Martin's.

King, G. (2010, April). A hard unsolved problem? Post-treatment bias in big social science questions. Presentation made at the Hard Problems in Social Science Symposium, Institute for Quantitative Social Science, Harvard University, Cambridge, MA.

National Forum on Information Literacy. (2005). *Forum overview.* Retrieved October 17, 2005, from http://www.infolit.org.

Purdue University Online Writing Lab. (2012). *Writing a research paper.* Retrieved May 18, 2012, from http://owl.english.purdue.edu.

Rosenthal, R. (1966). *Experimenter effects in behavioral research.* New York, NY: Appleton-Century-Crofts.

Thornburg, D. D. (1994). *Education in the communication age.* San Carlos, CA: Starsong.

inFORM — TOPIC

1. Get Curious ; Psychology
2. Narrowing your topic ; Behavior Psyc ; Behavior women Psyc ; Behavior abused women psyc
3. Narrowing your a topic ; sub topic
   · an age group
   · a location   Write out your topic as a
   · an additional topic   sentence or question.
   · a population
4. Brainstorm some keyword terms
   clothing (Products) Alternative words (women) — girls , mothers
   alcohol computers   ladies
5. Your Brainstorming Terms
   · Alternative words

Online Writing Center:

- online resource
- tutors written feedback
- students engage w/ tutors in live appointments
- offers writing & formatting resources

NOT:

- proofreading or editing service
- "prove my professor wrong" service
- system for checking for plagiarism

Tutor.com is a partner with LU

www. liberty.edu/library

Log-in to EZproxy

Summon Tool (Search bar)

If typing in multiple words the search will bring up every possible item with those words. If (" ") are added only those words will come up (ie. adult learning theory vs "adult learning theory")

Chapter 8

Academic Writing: The Lighting

In this chapter, you will:

- Determine the importance of writing.
- Select different writing strategies for active learning.
- Identify and use the essential stages of academic writing.

ELECTRICITY

In a construction project, every room requires electricity, just as in education, every class requires some sort of writing assignment. In a building, each room has different electrical needs, from wiring the lighting fixtures and the appliances to providing power to the air conditioning system. The builder must refer to the blueprints to determine where the wiring should go. The same is true for academic writing; each class will have different objectives that must be accomplished through writing. The author must refer to his or her writing blueprints (resources such as instructions, rubric, prewriting, etc.) to determine what to address when working on the assignment.

© 2013 by ??. Used under license of Shutterstock, Inc.

I Corinthians 14:40,
"Let all things be done decently and in order" (KJV).

THE CORNERSTONE

James 1:2–5, "Consider it pure joy, my brothers and sisters, whenever you face trials of many kinds, because you know that the testing of your faith produces perseverance. Let perseverance finish its work so that you may be mature and complete, not lacking anything. If any of you lacks wisdom, you should ask God, who gives generously to all without finding fault, and it will be given to you" (NIV) .

Fruitful Endeavors

© 2013 by Rock and Wasp. Used under license of Shutterstock, Inc.

Writing is hard work! The process itself takes diligence, patience, and perseverance. Like most worthwhile endeavors in life, the investment in these virtues yields a fruitful harvest. To illustrate, my little family learned the joys of diligence, patience, and perseverance in an outing that inspired a delicious blackberry cobbler.

One beautiful, sunny, Virginia morning in the early fall, our six-year-old daughter Laura Grace told us that she wanted to pick blackberries. My husband, Terry, looked online for a local orchard that offered the picking experience and found Morris' Orchard in Monroe, VA. Surrounded by luscious, green hills and Virginia's Blue Ridge Mountains, Morris' Orchard not only offers blackberry picking, but, depending on the season, also offers pink lemonade slushies, peaches, apples, apple donuts, pumpkins, and Christmas trees. We love any excuse to visit.

Terry and I loaded Laura Grace and her one-year-old sister, Marianna, into our blueberry blue 4 × 4 and headed to the orchard. Once we arrived at the orchard, friendly bunnies and goats greeted us, and our daughters giggled with excitement. Terry and I ushered the girls into the big, red barn that sells jams, jellies, salsas, and various peanut treats; we picked up our yellow bucket and headed toward the rows of blackberry bushes.

Terry selected a row that was a little off the beaten path; those rows tend to be less frequented by orchard visitors and yield more fruitful opportunities. Terry told Laura Grace that she should look for clusters of berries that had turned black and juicy. Laura Grace determined that she wanted to find the biggest and juiciest blackberry of the day and began her search. Marianna was more interested in the pretty pink and red berries that were not quite ripe. She picked one after another and handed them all to me, so proud of herself.

As we lifted up vines, picked clusters of berries, plopped them in our plastic yellow bucket, and moved toward the next bush, I noticed that our hands were all stained with a deep red berry juice. Marianna also had some convicting stains on her face and around her mouth—somebody had been sneaking a berry or two. We all worked so hard in the fall sunshine that our clothes stuck to our skin, sweat rolled down our faces, and our stomachs growled for lunch. We headed back to the big, red barn to pay for our bucket, brimming full of ripe blackberries. Terry treated us to pink lemonade slushies . . . yum! Then, we headed home for lunch, showers, and naps.

Having rinsed off the blackberries and pondering what to make, Terry decided to bake his Nanny's famous cobbler. We took the blackberry cobbler to Sunday lunch with our family. It was a hit! The combination of tart berry with the sweetness of the cobbler made our mouths long for more. People kept sneaking back into the kitchen and heaping another spoonful into their bowls. It was heavenly! Laura Grace told our family that the secret ingredient in the cobbler was the biggest, juiciest berry that she found. Marianna just smiled, said "Mmmm," and begged for more.

All of our perspiration and diligence paid off in that delicious, please-give-me-another-spoonful dessert and in the memory we shared with our two precious, hardworking daughters. The end product was truly amazing, but the journey itself helped us grow together as a family, toiling in the blackberry row with a united purpose.

Just like our blackberry adventure, writing is a chore and it is worth completing. When you commit to the process, invest yourself in the hard work, and see the final product, the trial itself will make you a better, stronger writer. Not only that, but just as it says in James 1:2–5, the efforts will produce perseverance and maturity in your character. So, approach opportunities to write with giggles and excitement, knowing that the Lord has delicious things in store for you.

Determine the Importance of Writing

Jeremiah 30:1–3 says,

"The word that came to Jeremiah from the Lord, saying,[2] Thus speaketh the Lord God of Israel, saying, Write thee all the words that I have spoken unto thee in a book.[3] For, lo, the days come, saith the Lord, that I will bring again the captivity of my people Israel and Judah, saith the Lord: and I will cause them to return to the land that I gave to their fathers, and they shall possess it" (NIV).

How do you feel about writing? Do you love it? Do you hate it? Is it something you approach with joy or with dread? Or are you indifferent? Regardless of how you approach writing, our Heavenly Father also has His own perspective. Writing is important to God. In Jeremiah 30:1–3, He tells Jeremiah to write a book to document the wondrous miracles that He would perform.

The Bible is God's love story for us. If we did not have the Bible, how else would we know that He sent His only Son, Jesus, as a Holy Sacrifice for our sins, so that we could be redeemed? It is no coincidence that God inspired men to write these words, so that we would know His redemption and love. Without these writings, without these willing hearts who wrote what the Lord asked of them, we would be lost.

Today, writing is important for a myriad of reasons. We communicate via letters, emails, social media, and texting. We develop resumes, portfolios, and cover letters for job hunting. We write essays and reports in academic settings. Writing should be important to us for practical reasons and also because writing is important to God. The Bible is an expression of His love for us through writing, through living words! He molded us in His image as creative beings, so embrace that creativity and start writing!

© 2013 by Dan Thornberg. Used under license of Shutterstock, Inc.

"If you can write, you can think; and if you can think, you can change the world."—Dr. Emily Heady

Katie Robinson

"While some students struggle with their writing process at first, developing the skills of communicating through written word presents a student with a source of empowerment. It is through writing that we can communicate with permanence."

Terry

Q: *Why is learning about writing important?*

A: "It is how we communicate; oftentimes, it's the first impression someone has of you in a work environment. Being able to communicate clearly is an essential skill."

T. Marcus Christian

"One of the best ways to insure you stay on the right path is to write well. Writing, along with any other skill, takes time and practice. When you write well, you will find your pathways opening."

Emily

Q: *Are you a good writer?*

A: "I'm a decent writer, and I became one by developing a wide vocabulary and learning how to use it properly. Plus, I use my imagination."

Michael Shenkle

"Fair or not, we are judged by the quality of our writing. Even the strongest of ideas can be lost in poor composition or less-than-ideal grammar. Regardless of your current level of expertise, I strongly encourage you to commit to improving this aspect of your academic and professional skill set. In the words of Dr. Emily Heady, 'If you can write, you can think; and if you can think, you can change the world.'"

Terry Conner

"Communication, in any form, but specifically in the written form, is imperative for your post-collegiate success. In a recent study of what employers look for in new employees, employers listed communication (both verbal and written) and problem solving skills as the most desirable qualities for new hires."

Writing Skills and Strategies

The Power of Writing

Writing is a powerful, transferable skill that you can use to promote your success across the curriculum, including both general education courses and courses in your academic major. Writing is a major route through which you can communicate your ideas, and it is a route of communication that your instructors will rely on to judge the extent of your knowledge and the quality of your thinking. You may have many great ideas in your head, but unless you can get them out of your head and onto paper, your instructors will never know you have them and you'll never receive full credit for them in your college courses. If you improve your writing skills, you will improve your ability to demonstrate your knowledge, communicate your ideas, and elevate your grades. Research indicates that writing is positively related to deep learning and student gains in personal development (National Survey of Student Engagement, 2008).

Your ability to write clearly, concisely, and persuasively is not only a skill that will help you succeed academically, it's also a skill that will help you succeed professionally. In a study of college alumni who were asked about the importance of different skills to their current work responsibilities up to 10 years after they graduated, more than 90 percent of them ranked "need to write effectively" as a skill they considered to be of "great importance" to their current work (Worth, as cited in Light, 2001). In fact, the first contact and first impression you will make on future employers is likely to be the letter of application or cover letter you write when applying for positions. Constructing a well-written letter of application may be your first step toward converting your college experience and college degree into a future career.

From *Thriving in College and Beyond,* 3/e by Joseph B. Cuseo, Aaron Thompson, Michele Campagna and Viki S. Fecas. Copyright © 2013 by Kendall Hunt Publishing Company. Reprinted by permission.

Select Different Writing Strategies for Active Learning

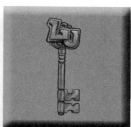

Proverbs 9:9,
"Instruct the wise and they will be wiser still; teach the righteous and they will add to their learning" (NIV).

Several different writing strategies exist that are designed to help you add to your learning; these include writing to learn, writing to listen, writing to read, writing to remember, writing to organize, writing to study, writing to understand, writing to create, writing to discuss, and writing to solve problems. Using these different writing strategies as you approach your academics will help you gain wisdom with each new learning experience. Determine which of these approaches will benefit you as you study the academic content of your online classes.

Photo courtesy of Aaron Traphagen

Writing to Learn

People learn most effectively from experience when they're actively involved in the learning experience and when they reflect on that experience after it has taken place. Writing can help you learn from any experience—either inside or outside the classroom—by increasing both active involvement and personal reflection. The phrase *writing to learn* has been coined by scholars to capture the idea that writing is not only a communication skill learned in English composition classes, but a learning skill that can deepen understanding of any academic subject or life experience (Ackerman, 1993; Applebee, 1984; Elbow, 1973; Zinsser, 1993). Just as you can learn to write better, you can write to learn better. Writing-to-learn activities differ from traditional writing assignments, such as essays or term papers, in two key ways:

1. They're shorter—requiring less amount of time to complete.

2. They're written primarily for the benefit of the writer—as an aid to thinking and learning (Tchudi, 1986).

Terry

Q: *Describe a great professor.*

A: "A great professor is one who is attentive and responds quickly with feedback on assignments and or responses to questions. They will also hold you accountable for the information they are supposed to teach. After all, they are the stewards of that discipline."

Mary Dixon

"Richard Reeves said, 'Writing energy is like anything else. The more you put in, the more you get out.' Treat writing like the work it is. Make a plan, focus on the task, start, and keep at it until the job is done."

Maddy

Q: *Are you a good writer? How did/do you become one? Describe your process of learning about good academic research/ writing.*

A: "I believe I am a good writer, and I am entirely certain it is due to the excellent English teachers I have had. Three in particular come to mind: one who taught me how to outline and write a good paper, one who taught me how to research, and one who taught me to love doing those things."

Writing-to-learn activities can be used for a wide variety of learning tasks and purposes in college, such as those listed below. As you read the following list of different writing activities and purposes, make a short note indicating whether you do each type of writing. If you don't do it, indicate whether you think it would be worth doing.

Writing to Listen

You can use writing to improve your attention and listening skills during *the videos and presentations in your online classroom.* For instance, immediately after each *video/presentation,* you could write a "one-minute paper" that only takes a minute or less to complete, yet enables you to assess whether you've actively listened to and grasped the most important message *communicated in the video/presentation* (e.g., "What was the most significant concept I learned?" or "What was the most confusing thing that I experienced that I should ask my instructor to clarify?")

Writing to Read

Just as writing can promote active listening, it can also promote active reading. Taking notes on what you're reading while you're reading implements the effective learning principle of active involvement because it requires more mental and physical energy than merely reading and highlighting sentences.

Writing to Remember

Writing lists of ideas generated at a group meeting, definitions, terms, or key concepts that you need to remember is an old-fashioned but surefire way not to forget them. When you've recorded an idea in print, you've created a permanent record of it that will enable you to access it and review it at any time. Furthermore, the act of writing itself creates motor (muscle) memory for the information you're writing, which enables you to better retain and retrieve the information you've written. Writing also improves memory by allowing you to see the information, which registers it in your brain as a visual memory trace.

Writing to Organize

Constructing summaries and outlines, or writing ideas on different index cards that relate to the same category or concept, are effective ways of organizing and learning information. This type of organizational writing deepens learning because it requires synthesis of different ideas and restatement of ideas in your own words, both of which are deep-learning strategies.

Writing to Study

Writing study guides or practice answers to potential test questions is an effective strategy that can be used when studying alone or when *studying with a friend*. This is particularly effective preparation for essay tests because it enables you to study in a way that closely matches what you will be expected to do on an essay test, which requires you to write out answers (not pick out answers as you would on a multiple-choice test).

Writing to Understand

Paraphrasing or restating what you're attempting to learn by writing it in your own words is an effective way to get feedback about whether you've truly understood it (not just memorized it) because you transform what you're learning into words that are meaningful to you.

Also, writing deepens learning because it requires physical action, which implements the effective learning principle of active involvement: writing essentially forces you to focus attention on your own thoughts and activate your thinking. In addition, writing slows down your thought process, allowing you to think in a more careful, systematic fashion that makes you more consciously aware of specific details. Lastly, the act of writing results in a visible product you can review and use as feedback to improve the quality of your thoughts (Applebee, 1984; Langer & Applebee, 1987). In other words, writing allows you to "think out loud on paper" (Bean, 2003, p. 102).

Writing to Create

Writing can also stimulate your discovery of ideas because new ideas are likely to emerge in your mind during the act or process of writing. Thus, writing is not just an end result or final product of your thinking: it is also a means or process of stimulating your thinking.

You can generate creative ideas through the process of *freewriting*, whereby you quickly jot down free-floating thoughts on paper without worrying about spelling and grammar. Freewriting can be used as a warm-up exercise to help you generate ideas for a research topic, to keep track of original ideas you happen to discover while brainstorming, or to record creative ideas that suddenly pop into your mind at unexpected times (before you forget them).

Writing to Discuss

Prior to participating in class *discussion boards or creating video projects or presentations*, you can gather your thoughts in writing to prepare to express them *verbally*. This will ensure that you've carefully reflected on your ideas, which, in turn, should improve the quality of ideas you contribute. Gathering your thoughts in writing before *posting or* speaking should also make you a less anxious, more confident *student* because you have a better idea about what you're going to say before you start to say it. *When creating video or audio presentations, your* written notes also give you a script to build on, or fall back on, in case you experience speech anxiety (or memory loss) while expressing your ideas.

Writing for Problem Solving

Writing can be used to capture your thought process while solving math and science problems. By writing down the thoughts going through your mind at each major step in the problem-solving process, you increase self-awareness of how your thinking progressed and you're left with a written record of your train of thought. You can review this written record later to help you retrieve the path of thought that led you to solve the problem successfully, allowing you to reuse the same path to solve similar problems in the future.

Personal Reflection

Which of the above-listed writing activities have you done? For those you haven't done, which would you strongly consider doing?

Writing to listen and writing to study are two of the things I am currently doing. I would like to be able to impliment more writing strategies but it seems boring to me.

Try to get into the habit of periodically stepping back to reflect on your thinking process. Ask yourself what type of thinking you are doing (such as analysis, synthesis, or evaluation) and record your personal reflections in writing. You could even keep a "thinking log" or "thinking journal" to increase self-awareness of the thinking strategies you develop across time, or how your thinking strategies may vary across different courses and academic fields.

From *Thriving in College and Beyond,* 3/e by Joseph B. Cuseo, Aaron Thompson, Michele Campagna and Viki S. Fecas. Copyright © 2013 by Kendall Hunt Publishing Company. Reprinted by permission.

Identify and Use the Essential Stages of Academic Writing

I Corinthians 14:40,
"Let all things be done decently and in order" (NIV).

Stephanie A. Hobson

"Writing well is hard work—even for your professors! But it is possible if you think of writing as a process. A good paper doesn't just happen by putting your fingers on the keyboard and hoping for inspiration. In fact, most of the work comes before you even start to draft your paper. Brainstorming, grouping together ideas, outlining, researching, drafting, revising, and proofreading are all important steps to producing a great paper. If you plan ahead so that you can work through all of these steps, you will see great improvement in your writing and grades!"

Terry

Q: *Describe your process of learning about good academic research/writing.*

A: "Practice, Practice, Practice."

Humble TIP (aka Jason Lewis), rapper and LU graduate

About brainstorming, "So I started writing lyrics—terrible, wack, just wack, you know what I'm saying—but you've got to crawl before you can walk" (Dunham, 2013).

In academic writing, it is essential that you follow the different steps of writing in order to create a polished final product. These organized steps are designed to help you achieve maximum success on each writing assignment you tackle. As you begin writing papers and reports for your college courses, be sure to follow each step carefully and completely.

Writing Papers and Reports

Studies show that a small percentage of high school students' class and homework time is spent on writing assignments that are as lengthy and demanding as those given in college. In high school, most writing assignments involve summaries or descriptive reports; in college, students are expected to engage in expository (persuasive) writing, which requires the writer to make or prove a case by supporting it with sound evidence (Applebee et al., 1990).

Completing papers and written reports almost always takes more time than you think it will. Writing is a multi-step process that cannot be completed in one night. Breaking down the writing process into smaller steps that are completed in advance of the paper's due date is an effective way to strengthen the quality of your final product. What follows is a sequence of steps that divides the writing process into different parts (planning, writing, revising, and editing), which should make your writing of papers and reports more manageable, less stressful, and more successful.

1. **Be sure you know the purpose or objective of the writing assignment.** You can't begin to take the right steps toward doing anything well until you know why you're doing it. Having a clear understanding of the purpose or goal of the writing assignment is the critical first step to completing it successfully. It helps you stay on track and moving in

the right direction. It also helps you to get going in the first place, because one major cause of writer's block is uncertainty about the goal or purpose of the writing task (Knaus, 2010; Rennie & Brewer, 1987). Before you begin to write anything, be sure you have a clear understanding of what your instructor expects you to accomplish. You can do this by asking yourself these three questions about the writing assignment:

- What is its objective or intended outcome?

- What type of thinking am I being asked to demonstrate?

- What criteria (standards) will my instructor use to evaluate and grade my performance?

2. **Generate ideas.** At this stage of the writing process, the only thing you're concerned about is getting the ideas you have in your head out of your head and onto paper. Don't worry about how good or bad the ideas may be. Writing scholars refer to this process as *focused freewriting*—you write freely for a certain period just to generate ideas—without worrying about writing complete or correct sentences (Bean, 2011). Remember that the act of writing itself can stimulate ideas, so if you're not sure what ideas you have, start writing because it will likely trigger ideas, which, in turn, will lead to additional ideas. One way to overcome writer's block is to start writing something (Zinsser, 1993). It could be anything, as long as it jump-starts the process. The creative thinking strategy of *brainstorming* can be an effective way to jump-start the freewriting process. Sometimes, even changing your working environment or format may stimulate new ideas, such as shifting from writing ideas in pen or pencil to typing them on your computer. Also, generating ideas with a friend, or testing your ideas with a classmate, can make the brainstorming stage more stimulating and productive. *(A brainstorming map example, also called a graphic organizer, is provided on page 245.)*

3. **Organize your ideas.** After all your ideas have been laid out, the next step is to sort them out and figure out how they can be pieced together. There are two key sub-steps in the process of organizing your ideas for a paper or written report.

Photos courtesy of Dave Moquin

Every sunset casts brilliant, vivid colors across the sky as it descends into the night; while it sets, the sun's positions and hues vary, revealing majestic stages of a beautiful process. Just as the stages of the sunset, everything in life requires a process of some kind, even the skill of writing; in order to write well, to achieve your purpose, and to write beautifully, you must complete strategic stages in a purposeful and beautiful process.

Josh Gerstner

"Consider your audience. The way you write for an undergraduate class should be different from how you write to a friend. Take note that writing for a class assignment should include a higher level of formality, which means proper attention should be given to capitalization, punctuation, and grammar."

Hanna Bruce

"A concise, yet informative thesis statement can make all the difference in a paper. Try to write one sentence that includes all the majors points of your paper. This will be your roadmap for writing and will help the reader know exactly what you plan to discuss."

Heather Patterson

"A good, strong thesis can help with logical flow issues, and act as a road map to whatever you are writing."

Betsey Caballero

"Follow directions carefully and ALWAYS proofread your assignments!"

First step: Connect separate pieces of information related to the same general idea by organizing them into categories. For instance, if your topic is terrorism and you find three ideas on your list referring to different causes of terrorism, group those ideas together under the category of "causes." Similarly, if you find ideas on your list that relate to possible solutions to the problem of terrorism, group those ideas under the category of "solutions." You could record your separate ideas on sticky notes and stick the notes with ideas pertaining to the same general category on index cards, with the category heading written at the top of the card.

Second step: Organize your categories of ideas into an order that flows smoothly or logically from start to finish. Arrange your different categories of ideas in an orderly sequence that has a meaningful beginning, middle, and end. Index cards come in handy when trying to find the best progression of your major ideas because the cards can be arranged and rearranged easily until you discover an order that produces the smoothest, most logical sequence. You can use your sequence of index cards to create an outline for your paper that lists the major categories of your ideas and the order in which they will appear in your paper.

Another effective way to organize and sequence your ideas is to map them out by creating a concept map that depicts your main categories of ideas in a visual-spatial format similar to a road map.

From *Thriving in College and Beyond*, 3/e by Joseph B. Cuseo, Aaron Thompson, Michele Campagna and Viki S. Fecas. Copyright © 2013 by Kendall Hunt Publishing Company. Reprinted by permission.

Susan Winebrenner, founder of Education Consulting Service and author of multiple learning resources for educators, developed a graphic organizer to assist with the prewriting process. See the example provided on the next page of how to organize your topics.

Once you have determined your topics, you can establish the order in which you wish to discuss them within your assignment (organize by Roman numerals, capital letters, numbers for more detail). Based on the order you assign the different categories, you can then design your assignment's outline, your thesis statement, and, ultimately, the order of the different paragraphs within your paper. (Notice the outline and the thesis statement that correspond with the graphic organizer.)

Writing Assignments: A Graphic Organizer

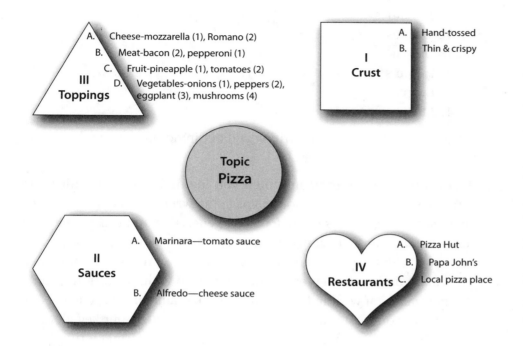

Topic
Pizza

III
Toppings
A. Cheese-mozzarella (1), Romano (2)
B. Meat-bacon (2), pepperoni (1)
C. Fruit-pineapple (1), tomatoes (2)
D. Vegetables-onions (1), peppers (2), eggplant (3), mushrooms (4)

I
Crust
A. Hand-tossed
B. Thin & crispy

II
Sauces
A. Marinara—tomato sauce
B. Alfredo—cheese sauce

IV
Restaurants
A. Pizza Hut
B. Papa John's
C. Local pizza place

David Hart

"Meet or exceed your target length. The assignment instructions give a minimum required length for written answers. If the required length is one paragraph, you should write at least three to five sentences. Therefore, you should not submit two sentences and expect to earn full credit for an answer. Also, remember that they should be substantive sentences. Rather than just assume your answer is sufficient, merely because you wrote three sentences, ask yourself if they sufficiently answer the question. An excellent answer is similar to an excellent sculpture or an excellent photograph: The strength of the finished work we see is determined by what is intentionally removed."

Thesis Statement: When craving a hot, cheesy pizza, there are many factors that must be considered; these include selecting the perfect crust, sauce, toppings, and restaurant to achieve maximum deliciousness.

Outline
I. Crust
   A. Hand-tossed
   B. Thin and crispy
II. Sauces
   A. Marinara
   B. Alfredo
III. Toppings
   A. Cheese
      1. Mozzarella
      2. Romano
   B. Meat
      1. Pepperoni
      2. Bacon

Terri Washer

"Make sure that you proofread closely before submitting assignments. One great way to identify errors is to read your papers aloud. It's amazing how many errors you hear, but don't see."

Josh Gerstner

"Avoid being a narrator in your writing. In other words, do not write, 'This paper is about . . .' or 'I have chosen Topic X as my subject, and the following . . .' Let your thesis statement do the work."

Dustin Williams

"After you finish writing a paragraph, reread that paragraph to make sure all of your sentences flow. Sometimes, it is beneficial to start with the last sentence in the paragraph and work backwards."

Kirsten Hoegh

"Give yourself plenty of time to work on your writing assignments. No first draft is perfect, and it is important to make sure that you double check your work for spelling, grammar, professional tone, formatting (APA, MLA, or Turabian), and of course to make sure that your ideas flow well. If you are new to the idea of formatting your essays in a specific style (APA, MLA, or Turabian), now is a good time to begin getting familiar with the style you will use for your major. Take advantage of the information available on Liberty's Online Writing Center webpage, and always feel free to ask your instructor for help with this. It is not as complicated as it may seem, but it is an important element in college writing."

Josh Gerstner

"A complete sentence has both a subject and a verb; a sentence fragment lacks one of the two. Note the difference, and write using only complete sentences."

C. Fruit
  1. Pineapple
  2. Tomatoes
D. Vegetables
  1. Onions
  2. Peppers
  3. Eggplant
  4. Mushrooms

After you complete your prewriting and outlining stage, you are ready to begin work on your rough draft!

4. **Write a first, *rough* draft in which you identify your main idea and supporting ideas.** The previous steps in the writing process are referred to as *prewriting* because they focus on generating and organizing your ideas before communicating them to anyone else (Murray, 2002). In a *first, rough draft,* you begin the formal writing process of converting your major ideas into sentences, but you do so without worrying about the mechanics of writing (e.g., punctuation, grammar, or spelling). The purpose of your first draft is to simply "talk through" your key ideas on paper. In your later drafts, you can convert your informal writing into more formal and polished prose.

At this stage in the process, you transform your major ideas into written paragraphs and arrange your paragraphs in a logical sequence. Here are some strategies for accomplishing each of these steps.

- Use your first paragraph to provide a meaningful introduction, overview, or preview of the major points you will make in the remainder (body) of the paper. Pay particular attention to your opening paragraph because it creates the all-important first impression and sets the stage for what will follow. Your introduction should include a *thesis statement*—a short summary (one sentence) of your key point or central idea—which you will follow up in the body of your paper with evidence to support it. Your thesis statement is the most important sentence in your introduction; it's the compass that will guide your thinking and keep you and your audience moving in the direction toward the same destination (conclusion). You may also phrase your thesis statement in the form of a question, and use the body of your paper as a quest or journey to reach an answer to that question.

- Keep different points (ideas) in different paragraphs. A paragraph should represent a chain of sentences that are linked to the same thought or idea. If you shift to a different idea, shift to a different paragraph.

- Whenever possible, start new paragraphs with a *topic sentence* that introduces the new point you're about to make and relates it to the major point being made in your paper—your thesis statement. Topic sentences help bring cohesion to your paper by organizing the points you make in separate paragraphs and by integrating your separate paragraphs into the body of the paper as a whole.

- Use your final paragraph to "tie it all together" and drive home your paper's major points. This will leave your paper with three distinctive parts:

  a. *Introduction.* An opening paragraph that includes a thesis statement;

  b. *Body.* A series of paragraphs that follows the introduction, each of which contains one of your paper's major points or ideas, and

  c. *Conclusion.* A final paragraph that summarizes your major points and relates them to the thesis statement in your introduction.

After you've completed your first draft, it's often a good idea to step away from it for a while and give your mind some time to cool off and incubate. When you return to it later, you're likely to think of new ideas and better ways to express the ideas you previously generated.

5. **Write more than one draft.** Don't expect to write a perfect draft of your paper on the first try. Even professional writers report that it takes them more than one draft (often three or four) before they produce their final draft. Although the final product of award-winning writers may look spectacular, what precedes it is a messy process that includes lots of revisions between the first try and the final product (Bean, 2011). Just as actors and actresses need multiple takes (take two, take three, etc.) to get their spoken lines right, writers need multiple takes (drafts) to get their written lines right.

It may be a particularly good idea to review your thesis statement because, in the process of rewriting, you're likely to discover new thoughts and better ideas. If this happens, you can modify your opening thesis statement so that it more closely matches your concluding statement (Bean, 2011). However, if you find yourself making radical changes to your thesis statement, this may indicate that you radically changed directions while writing the body of your paper, and you didn't accomplish what you said you were going to do in your introduction.

6. **Critique and edit your writing.** After completing each draft of your paper, take your mind off it for a while and come back to look it from a different perspective—as a reader and editor, rather than a writer. Read your own words as if they were written by someone else and critically

Lisa Eppard

"Once your paper is written, read each individual sentence aloud to check for clarity/fluency. Sometimes, it's easier to "hear" our mistakes, especially when we read each sentence one at a time. If a sentence doesn't sound "natural," it probably needs revising. This is a great way to catch spelling errors, as well."

Roger

Q: *Are you a good writer? How did/ do you become one? Why is learning about writing important? Describe your process of learning about good academic research/writing.*

A: "I was not born a good writer. I had to develop my writing skills. Years ago my college history teacher tried to tell me that my writing skills needed help. But I didn't know where to go to get the help. I learned to write over time and with experience. As computer spell-checking programs improved over time, so did the quality of my work. Today I grade the papers of students who do not proofread their work. They fail to properly reference and cite their sources. They rush through the assignments without really thinking about organizing their thoughts. They failed to answer all of the questions asked of them in the assignment and they have forgotten to examine the rubrics to determine how the paper will be graded. Quality writing takes time, energy, forethought and hard work. That is what is required of every college student."

Lisa Eppard

"If time permits, put your paper away overnight once it is written. Come back in a day or two and read it again with a fresh pair of eyes. It's amazing how easy it is to find errors when a little time has passed."

David Hart

"Finish well. Make sure that you follow the instructions for submitting the assignment. Sometimes students paste the text into Blackboard for something that should be attached as a Word document. Conversely, sometimes students attach a Word document for something that should be typed directly into Blackboard (such as a Discussion Board)."

evaluate the paper's ideas, organization, and writing style. If you find words and sentences that aren't clearly capturing or reflecting what you meant to say, this is the stage in the writing process when you make your major revisions. (At this stage, make sure your paper is double-spaced so that you have enough room for making changes and additions.)

When critiquing and editing your paper, critically evaluate each of the following features:

- **Documentation.** Are its major points and final conclusion well supported by evidence, such as:

  a. Direct quotes from authoritative sources,

  b. Specific examples,

  c. Statistical data,

  d. Scientific research findings, or

  e. Firsthand experiences? *(if appropriate for the assignment)*

- **Overall organization.** Take a *panoramic* or aerial view of your paper to see if you can clearly identify its three major parts: the beginning (introduction), the middle (body), and the end (conclusion). Do these three parts unite to form a connected whole? Also, check to see if there is *continuity* from one paragraph to the next throughout your paper: Does your train of thought stay on track from start to finish? If you find yourself getting off track at certain points in your paper, eliminate that information or rewrite it in a way that reroutes your thoughts back onto their main track (your thesis statement).

- **Sentence structure.** Do the sentences within each paragraph make sense and flow smoothly from one to another? Check for sentences that are too long—rambling sentences that go on and on without any punctuation or pauses that allow readers to catch their breath. You can correct rambling sentences by (1) punctuating them with a comma, signaling a short pause, (2) punctuating them with a semi-colon, signaling a longer pause than a comma (but not as long as a period), or (3) dividing them into two shorter sentences (separated by a period). Also, check for sentences that are too short—choppy sentences that "chop up" what you've written into such short statements that they interfere with the natural flow or rhythm of reading. Correct choppy sentences by joining them to form a larger sentence, punctuated by a comma or semicolon.

- A good strategy for helping you determine if your written sentences flow smoothly is to read them aloud. Note the places where you naturally tend to pause and where you tend to keep going. Your natural pauses may serve as cues for places where your sentences need punctuation, and your natural runs may indicate sentences that are flowing smoothly and should be left alone. Reading your writing out loud can help you find run-on sentences and choppy sentences.

- **Word selection.** Are certain words or phrases showing up so frequently in your paper that they sound repetitious? If so, try to add variety to your vocabulary by substituting words that have the same or similar meaning. This substitution process can be made easier by using a thesaurus, which may be conveniently available on your computer's word processing program.

7. **Get feedback on your writing from a trusted peer or writing professional.** You're always the first reader of your paper, but you don't have to be the only reader before you submit to your instructor and receive a grade. Sometimes, no matter how honest or objective we try to be about our own work, we may still be blind to its weaknesses. All of us may have a natural tendency to see what we hope or want to see in our work, rather than what's really there—especially after we've put a great deal of time, effort, and energy into the process of creating it. Consider getting a second opinion on your paper by asking a trusted friend or a tutor in the *Online Writing Center* or *Tutor.com* to read it.

You can seek feedback at any stage of the writing process—whether it be for help with understanding the assignment, brainstorming ideas, writing your first draft, or writing your final draft. Seeking help from the *the Online Writing Center* or *Tutor.com* is not limited to students experiencing writing problems or writer's block. Help may be sought by all students who want to push the quality of their writing to a higher level. Even if you consider yourself to be a good writer, your writing can get even better if you seek and receive feedback from others before submitting your final product. Consider pairing up with a partner to exchange and assess each other's papers, using a checklist of criteria that your instructor will use to evaluate and grade your papers. Studies show that when students with different levels of writing ability receive feedback from others prior to submitting a paper, it improves their quality of writing as well as their grade (Patchan, Charney, & Schunn, 2009; Thompson, 1981).

8. **In your final draft, be sure that your conclusion and introduction are connected or aligned.** The most important component of your conclusion involves revisiting or restating your original thesis and answering the question you originally posed in your introduction. Connecting

your thesis statement and concluding statement provides a pair of meaningful bookends to your paper, anchoring it at its two most pivotal points: beginning and end. This ensures you end up at the destination you intended to reach when you started, and enables you to maximize the power of the two most important impressions you can make: the first impression and the last impression.

9. **Carefully proofread your paper for structural and technical mistakes before submitting it.** Proofreading is a critical last step in the editorial process because small, technical errors are likely to have been overlooked during earlier stages of the writing process when your attention was focused on larger issues related to your paper's content and organizational structure. Proofreading may be viewed as a micro form of editing, during which you shift the focus of your editorial attention to the minute mechanics of your paper and detection of details related to referencing, grammar, punctuation, and spelling. For instance, check to be sure that none of your sentences are *sentence fragments*—missing either a noun or a verb—or *run-on sentences*—two sentences that are not separated by a period or conjunction word (e.g., *and* or *but*). Also, don't forget that your computer's spellchecker doesn't check whether words are correctly spelled in the context (sentence) in which you're using them. For instance, a spell-checker would not detect the three "correctly" spelled words that are actually misspelled words in the context of the following sentence: "*Ware* your high-*heal* sneakers because you're going out *two night.*"

Careful proofreading is the key, final step in the process of writing a high-quality paper. Earlier stages of the writing process involve generating, organizing, and expressing your ideas, which are more mentally demanding and time-consuming than proofreading. To overlook or underestimate this simple last step of proofreading and lose valuable points for a written product that you spent so much time creating would be a downright shame.

10. After the paper has been graded and returned to you, carefully review your instructor's written comments. Sometimes, no matter how hard you try to anticipate and demonstrate everything your instructor expects, particularly on the first major assignment, there are some things that can only be learned and corrected *after* you've received feedback from your instructor on your first performance. Review your paper closely when you get it back and pay special attention to any written comments provided by your instructor. If the grade you receive is lower than you expected, try not to get emotional or defensive. Instead, learn

from your mistakes and use your instructor's comments as constructive feedback to improve your performance on future assignments.

If your instructor's written feedback still leaves you unclear about what went wrong or what needs to be improved, make an appointment for an office visit. Receiving personalized feedback from the very person who has evaluated your work, and who will be evaluating your future work, may be the most powerful way to improve your future performance and final grade. If your instructor is willing to meet with you during office hours and review your paper with you, take full advantage of this opportunity. Besides receiving personalized performance-improving feedback, you will send a clear message to the instructor that you're a serious student who wants to learn from mistakes and achieve excellence.

From *Thriving in College and Beyond*, 3/e by Joseph B. Cuseo, Aaron Thompson, Michele Campagna and Viki S. Fecas. Copyright © 2013 by Kendall Hunt Publishing Company. Reprinted by permission.

BUILDING BLOCKS

How Does a Christian Student Look at the Task of Writing?

As always, we use the lens of scripture to inform our thinking. For writing, there are two ways to do this. First, we look at how the Holy Scriptures came to be. Did you know that the Bible is not written by a single author (other than God's Holy Spirit, of course)? There are literally *dozens* of writers of the Bible. These dozens of writers lived over *hundreds* of years. While none understood that he was working on a huge collaborative effort, that was essentially the result. The Bible, as we know it, was not completely compiled until more than 300 years after Jesus' death. As we look at the unity of the Bible message, it is an amazing piece of literature: dozens of authors, working over hundreds of years, and it is beautiful and complete as written.

God inspired men to write as He directed for the Bible. We do not know the actual process, but we do know that the writers were not merely scribes who took what might be described as "holy dictation" from God. Instead, God's Holy Spirit led men to write down their portion of scripture. Each man bent to the task to produce a written text as God directed. Each was faithful to his writing task. In some portions of scripture, we can see the same information given from a variety of perspectives. As we look at the gospel texts of Matthew, Mark, Luke, and John, we can see this clearly. Each of those books of the New Testament gives an account of Jesus' life on earth. We read stories of actual events: miracles, teaching moments, Jesus' crucifixion and resurrection. As we examine more closely, however, we see that each writer composed his portion of the text based on his own experience. Individual differences can be observed in the four versions of Jesus' life.

We can see the importance of the written word to God. We see in the New Testament's John 1:1,

> "In the beginning was the Word and the Word was with God, and the Word was God" (NIV).

Wow! In this verse, we see Jesus named as the Word. Many times, we have seen the Bible described variously as "God's love letter to us" or "God's guidebook for life" or even the acronym BIBLE: basic instructions before leaving earth. None of these adequately express the beauty and majesty of God's Word, given to us in love.

As you consider your academic writing task, it may seem overwhelming. In Isaiah 40:8 we read, "The grass withers, the flower fades, but the Word of our God will stand forever" (ESV). What you are writing for school will not need to be that long-lasting, but it is important to do your best. Take the writing process in step-by-step tasks, and you can produce a written piece that speaks well for you while meeting the demands of the assignment. Pray this verse as a prayer as you begin:

Psalm 19:14, "Let the words of my mouth, and the meditation of my heart, be acceptable in thy sight, O Lord, my strength, and my redeemer" (KJV).

Each time you have a writing assignment:

- Look carefully at your writing assignment. Determine the purpose and audience.

- Set a schedule for completing your work.

- Decide the steps that you should take in the writing process. Will you need to do research first?

- Determine sources to help you.

- Gather information, taking careful notes and determining citation information.

- Next, you must begin to organize your thoughts on how to present your ideas.

- Write a paragraph that conveys each idea you want to explore.

- Take a break when you have made a rough draft. When you come back, you will be refreshed.

- Revise your work to ensure that it is a succinct message that makes your points.

- Edit to eliminate grammar, spelling, punctuation, and capitalization mistakes that distract from what you are writing.

- Carefully check to ensure that you have properly cited each instance of "borrowing" the work, words, or ideas of others.

What Do You Do If You Are "Stuck"?

Sometimes, students find that once they have gathered information and made many notes, they have trouble continuing to the actual writing of the piece. You may face a period of difficulty with beginning the actual writing process, sometimes called "writer's block," just jump in and get going. Put pen to paper (or fingers to keyboard, as the case may be) and write what comes to mind. Do not judge what you are writing, just try to get your writing flowing. There will be opportunity to evaluate and revise later. At first, just try to capture your thoughts. As you proceed, you will organize your ideas into paragraphs, using one for each main idea you wish to convey. Make sure to keep careful notes as you work so you can properly cite any source material you are using. It is critical to avoid plagiarism, and keeping your notes organized by author or source will help you maintain your integrity as you "borrow" from the ideas of others.

Writing is a process, and by practicing, you will become better at it. Some students love to express their ideas in tweets, blogs, or texts but have difficulty writing for academic purposes. If that is your situation, take heart. Following the steps outlined in this chapter can help you create an organized, cogent, and meaningful written piece. The Bible tells us that "For the Spirit God gave us does not make us timid, but gives us power, love and self-discipline" (II Tim. 1:7, NIV). Take that message to heart, and let's get writing!

> Romans 5:1–5, "Therefore, since we have been justified through faith, we have peace with God through our Lord Jesus Christ, through whom we have gained access by faith into this grace in which we now stand. And we boast in the hope of the glory of God. Not only so, but we also glory in our sufferings, because we know that suffering produces perseverance; perseverance, character; and character, hope. And hope does not put us to shame, because God's love has been poured out into our hearts through the Holy Spirit, who has been given to us" (NIV).

TOOL BOX

Writing Tools

General Writing—For general paper writing, the most basic tool you will need is word processing software. Word processing software will allow you to write and edit anything from a paragraph to a novel and typically comes packaged with advanced editing and reference building tools. The most common programs for word processing are Microsoft Word (PC or Mac) and Pages (Mac). Both of these programs can be expensive, but as a Liberty University student, you are eligible to purchase these programs at a significantly reduced price through the IT Marketplace. A free alternative is Apache's Open Office (PC or Mac), available for download on the Internet.

Note Taking—For many writing strategies you do not need full-fledged word processing software. For these tasks you might enjoy using one of the many note-taking programs or applications available. These programs typically have much less sophisticated editing options, but are great for organizing your less formal thoughts. Most computers come with basic notepad or text editing software, but for the money, locating a program that will sync notes on your computer with notes on your mobile device may be the best bet. One of the premier note-taking programs on the market is Evernote, which offers versions for nearly any device you might have, and allows you to take and organize your notes while syncing them across all your devices.

Outlining—While you can create some great outlines in word processing or note software, there are several programs out there that specialize in this area. If you are a PC user, check out Microsoft's OneNote; it is a wonderful tool for organizing content. For Mac users, you might consider something along the lines of NoteBook. Both programs allow users to create and organize information in a variety of ways, and even allow you to import information from the web and insert pictures.

Mind Mapping—Mind mapping tools allow you to create visual representations of information that might otherwise be found in an outline. These tools work wonders for those of you who are visual learners. There are too many examples to mention here, but check the website for some great options.

Writing Helps and Tutoring

SafeAssign—This tool, provided by Liberty, allows professors and students to check text-based assignments for potential plagiarism. Students will only access this tool if it has been made available for a particular assignments in their course, but professors are able to submit papers directly to SafeAssign at any point. The tool works by checking documents against an existing database of writing, as well as against various web sources.

Liberty University Online Writing Center—The Online Writing Center is another wonderful resource available to you as a Liberty student. Using this tool, you may submit your work for review by trained graders and receive high quality feedback to improve your writing. Live sessions may also be scheduled using a request form on the Writing Center website.
www.liberty.edu/academics/graduate/writing

Additional Tools—While Liberty has spent an enormous amount of time and money developing in-house tools, they have also developed strategic partnerships with outside entities. These partnerships are designed to offer you, the student, the best tools available as you work toward your degree. To find out what tools are available to assist you with your writing, please visit the Breaking Ground website.

Websites—Aside from the multitude of tools available to you through Liberty University, there are an even greater number of websites that promise to do just about everything possible to assist you in improving your writing. While many sites make claims that they will check your spelling, grammar, and sources, the best sites are those that educate you in the writing process. Spend some time at places like Purdue's Owl and dailygrammar.com to get quick tips and build your long-term writing skills.

Additional resources and links to specific sites, worksheets, and apps can be located by accessing the Breaking Ground website:

www.breakinggroundlu.com

References

Ackerman, J. M. (1993). The promise of writing to learn. *Written Communication, 10*(3), 334–370.

Applebee, A. N. (1984). Writing and reasoning. *Review of Educational Research, 54*(4), 577–596.

Applebee, A. N., Langer, J. A., Jenkins, L. B., Mullis, I. V. S., & Foertsch, M. A. (1990). *Learning to write in our nation's schools: Instruction and achievement in 1988 at grades 4, 8, and 12.* Princeton, NJ: The National Assessment of Educational Progress.

Bean, J. C. (2003). *Engaging ideas: The professor's guide to integrating writing, critical thinking and active learning in the classroom.* San Francisco, CA: Jossey-Bass.

Bean, J. C. (2011). *Engaging ideas: The professor's guide to integrating writing, critical thinking and active learning in the classroom* (2nd ed.). San Francisco, CA: Jossey-Bass.

Dunham, Teresa. (2008). *Christian rapper Humble T.I.P. makes righteous rhymes.* Retrieved from http://www.liberty.edu/news/index.cfm?PID = 18495&MID = 97080.

Elbow, P. (1973). *Writing without teachers.* New York, NY: Oxford University Press.

Knaus, B. (2010, June 18). Ten top tips to end writer's block procrastination. *Psychology Today.* Retrieved March 7, 2012, from http://www.psychologytoday.com/blog/science-and-sensibility/201006ten-top-tips-end-writer-s-blockprocrastination.

Langer, J. A., & Applebee, A. N. (1987). *How writing shapes thinking* (NCTE Research Report No. 22). Urbana, IL: National Council of Teachers of English.

Light, R. J. (2001). *Making the most of college: Students speak their minds.* Cambridge, MA: Harvard University Press.

Murray, D. M. (2002). *Write to learn* (7th ed.). Fort Worth, TX: Harcourt Brace.

National Survey of Student Engagement. (2008). *NSSE Annual Results 2008. Promoting engagement for all students: The imperative to look within.* Bloomington, IN: Author.

Patchan, M. M., Charney, D., & Schunn, C. D. (2009). A validation study of students' end comments: Comparing comments by students, a writing instructor, and a content instructor. *Journal of Writing Research, 1*(2) 124–152.

Rennie, D., & Brewer, L. (1987). A grounded theory of thesis blocking. *Teaching of Psychology, 14*(1), 10–16.

Tchudi, S. N. (1986). *Teaching writing in the content areas: College level.* New York, NY: National Educational Association.

Thompson, R. F. (1981). Peer grading: some promising advantages for composition research and the classroom. *Research in the Teaching of English, 15*(2), 172–174.

Winebrenner, S. (2012). *Education Consulting Service, Inc.* Retrieved from http://susanwinebrenner.com/index.html.

Zinsser, W. (1993). *Writing to learn.* New York, NY: HarperCollins.

Inadvertent Plagiarism

- Poor time management
- Unfamiliar with material
- Tackling new & difficult writing assignments

Author's Idea & Language

- Quoting - enclose exact words with quotes " "
- Summarizing - main idea with your own language
- Paraphrasing - presenting your own idea

Note Taking

"Don't look at the original source when writing down notes."

Common Knowledge

- Appears in 3 different sources it is considered common knowledge and does not need to be cited
- Rule of thumb: if you are unsure; cite it

Createmypaper.com
Writemyessay2.com
Studymode.com

Chapter 9

Study Strategies: The Insulation

In this chapter, you will:

- Develop an effective strategy for careful reading and text mastery.
- Select techniques to gain maximum benefit from lecture presentations.
- Choose an effective note-taking strategy to document important information.
- Select study skills to make wise use of study time.

INSULATION

In order to keep a house cozy and warm, installing insulation before putting up the walls is a necessity. This insulation keeps the cold in and the heat out in the summer, and it keeps the heat in and the cold out during the winter. Without insulation, a house would be terribly uncomfortable and the heating and air conditioning bill would go through the roof (so to speak). In your academic experiences, learning skills and strategies are a lot like insulation; you have to develop these skills and strategies in order to keep in the information and to keep out the distractions. In doing this, you will learn "the way that is good and right."

© 2013 by doomu. Used under license of Shutterstock, Inc.

I Samuel 12:23,
"I will teach you the way that is good and right" (NIV).

THE CORNERSTONE

II Timothy 2:15, "Study to shew thyself approved unto God, a workman that needeth not to be ashamed, rightly dividing the word of truth" (KJV).

In life, there are many things that require careful study; while some of these things are academic in nature, many of them are not. Do you need to study to get better grades? Absolutely. However, you also need to study the cookbook to make sure that your dinner tastes delicious; for your plants, you need to study the elements that will make them thrive: partial sun or full sun, daily watering or occasional watering. Mark Tinsley, Army National Guard Chaplain and Department Chair for the College of General Studies, explains this further in this story from his childhood regarding the skill of studying.

"My father introduced me at a young age to the sport of shooting. Virtually every day during my childhood, I would grab the 12-gauge shotgun, the .38 caliber pistol, or one of the sundry hunting rifles my father owned, and I would shoot at cans, targets, bottles, trees, or whatever else I could find. Over the years, I became a pretty good shot and prided myself in taking out small targets at long distances. However, it didn't take me long in my shooting 'career' to realize that wind is the archenemy of any marksman, especially when firing at far-off targets. For instance, a swift breeze at a 100-meter target can be enough to blow a small caliber bullet slightly off course, resulting in a missed shot. As such, I learned early on to pay attention to the wind and adjust my point of aim. If the wind was blowing from the right, then I would aim a little bit to the right of my target. In this way, the bullet, as it was pushed left by the wind during flight, would ultimately impact the intended target. Those in the shooting 'business' will recognize this as the art of 'Kentucky windage.'

Our spiritual lives require a little bit of 'Kentucky windage' at times. Hebrews 2:1 states, "We must pay more careful attention . . . so that we do not drift away" (NIV). The winds of life—for example, stress, pride, loss, grief—can easily push us off course and cause us to drift away from God. Hitting the target—that is, maintaining a vibrant, fulfilling relationship with God—requires a precision shot that takes into account the complexities of the environment in which we find ourselves. Those Christians who believe the life of faith should be easy and simple are deluding themselves. God never promised us a windless shot. To the contrary, we are told to expect pain, hardship, and suffering. During all this, however, we are admonished to pay close attention to what we are doing and what God would have us do, adjust our aim according to the conditions presented, and take the shot that is most pleasing to God. Of course, like any marksman, we'll miss the target sometimes. However, the more we practice, the better our aim will become."

Mark's story urges us to study all of the elements that impact our relationship with the Lord and with others, aiming carefully at the things that matter most. In our relationships with the Lord and with others, as well as our academic, personal, and professional responsibilities, let us do as Chaplain Tinsley and II Timothy 2:15 urge us, "Study to shew thyself approved unto God, a workman that needeth not to be ashamed, rightly dividing the word of truth" (KJV).

Develop an Effective Strategy for Careful Reading and Text Mastery

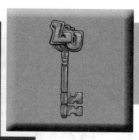
Acts 8:30–31,

"'Do you understand what you are reading?' 'How can I,' he said, 'unless someone explains it to me?' So he invited Philip to come up and sit with him" (NIV).

In the New Testament book of Acts, Chapter 8, we read the story of Philip and the Ethiopian man he met. Philip was walking on the road, and he met an important official in the Ethiopian kingdom. This man had been to Jerusalem to worship and was reading in the Old Testament book of Isaiah as he rode along in his chariot. Philip approached the man and asked, "'Do you understand what you are reading?' 'How can I,' he said, 'unless someone explains it to me?' So he invited Philip to come up and sit with him" (Acts 8:30–31, NIV). Philip was able to explain what the man was reading and was also able to tell him the good news of Jesus. Do you ever find that you have difficulty understanding what you are reading? What steps do you take to overcome this problem? Do you seek help, like the Ethiopian man did? Continue reading below to find strategies to help you understand and remember what you read.

© 2013 by michaeljung. Used under license of Shutterstock, Inc.

Reading Strategically to Comprehend and Retain Textbook Information

Second only to lecture notes as a source of test questions on college exams is information found in assigned readings (Brown, 1988). You're likely to find exam questions containing information that your professors didn't cover in class presentations, but that was contained in your assigned reading.

© 2013 by InesBazdar. Used under
license of Shutterstock, Inc.

Many students like to use sticky notes
to mark their textbooks, but don't get
carried away!

College professors often expect you to relate or connect what they lecture about with material that you've been assigned to read. Furthermore, they often deliver recorded class presentations with the assumption that you have done the assigned reading, so if you haven't done it, you're likely to have more difficulty following what your instructor is discussing.

When completing your reading assignments, use effective reading strategies that are based on sound principles of human learning and memory, such as those listed here. What follows is a series of research-based strategies for effective reading at three key stages in the learning process: before, during, and after reading.

Pre-Reading Strategies:
What to Do before Reading

Cari Smith

"Determine the number of pages for each week's reading and break that into days. Example, you have 70 pages to read for week two—that requires 10 pages of reading a day. Set aside a specific time each day for reading and when you are done, reward yourself with something fun."

Cari Smith

"Notecards can be used similar to the flashcards you had as a child; they are great for studying. Write the word or phrase on one side and on the other side, write out the definition."

1. **Before jumping into your assigned reading, look at how it fits into the overall organizational structure of the book and course.** You can do this efficiently by taking a quick look at the book's table of contents to see where the chapter you're about to read is placed in the overall sequence of chapters, especially its relation to chapters that immediately precede and follow it. Using this strategy will give you a sense of how the particular part you're focusing on connects with the bigger picture. Research shows that if learners gain access to advanced knowledge of how information they're about to learn is organized—if they see how its parts relate to the whole—*before* they attempt to start learning the specific parts, they're better able to comprehend and retain the material (Ausubel, Novak, & Hanesian, 1978; Mayer, 2003). Thus, the first step toward improving reading comprehension and retention of a book chapter is to see how it relates to the whole book before you begin to examine the chapter part by part.

2. **Preview the chapter you're about to read by reading its boldface headings and any chapter outline, objectives, summary, or end-of-chapter questions that may be included.** Before jumping right into the content, get in the habit of previewing what's in a chapter to gain an overall sense of its organization. If you dive into the specific details first, you lose sight of how the smaller details relate to the larger picture. The brain's natural tendency is to perceive and comprehend whole patterns rather than isolated bits of information. Start by seeing how the

parts of the chapter are integrated into the whole. This will enable you to better connect the separate pieces of information you encounter while you read, similar to seeing the whole picture of a completed jigsaw puzzle before you start assembling is pieces.

3. **Take a moment to think about what you already know that relates to the material in the chapter you're about to read.** By thinking about knowledge you possess about the topic you're about to read, you activate the areas of your brain where that knowledge is stored, thereby preparing it to make meaningful connections with the material you're about to read.

Photo courtesy of Aaron Traphagen.

Intensive student, Lynn Rabun, works diligently during her course.

Strategies to Use while Reading

1. **Read selectively to locate the most important information.** Rather than jumping into reading and randomly highlighting, effective reading begins with a plan or goal for identifying what should be noted and remembered. Here are three strategies to use while reading to help you determine what information should be noted and retained.

   - **Use boldface or dark-print headings and subheadings as cues for identifying important information.** These headings organize the chapter's major points; thus, you can use them as "traffic signs" to direct you to the most important information in the chapter. Better yet, turn the headings into questions and then read to find answers to these questions. This question-and answer strategy will ensure that you read actively and with a purpose. (You can set up this strategy when you preview the chapter by placing a question mark after each heading contained in the chapter.) Creating and answering questions while you read also keeps you motivated; the questions help stimulate your curiosity and finding answers to them serves to reward or reinforce your reading (Walter, Knudsbig, & Smith, 2003). Lastly, answering questions about what you're reading is an effective way to prepare for tests because you're practicing exactly what you'll be expected to do on exams—answering questions. You can quickly

© 2013 by Humannet Used under license of Shutterstock, Inc.

write the heading questions on separate index cards and use them as flash cards to review for exams. Use the question on the flash card as a way to flash back and trigger your recall of information from the text that answers the question.

- **Pay special attention to words that are** *italicized*, **underlined, or appear in boldface print.** These are usually signs for building-block terms that must be understood and built on before you can proceed to understand higher level concepts covered later in the reading. Don't simply highlight these words because their special appearance suggests they are important. Read these terms carefully and be sure you understand their meaning before you continue reading.

- **Pay special attention to the first and last sentences in each paragraph.** These sentences contain an important introduction and conclusion to the ideas covered in the paragraph. It's a good idea to reread the first and last sentences of each paragraph before you move on to the next paragraph, particularly when reading sequential or cumulative material (e.g., science or math) that requires full comprehension of what was previously covered to understand what will be covered next.

  Reread your chapter notes and highlights after you've listened to your course presentation on the material contained in the chapter. You can use your notes as a guide to help you focus on what information in the chapter your instructor feels is most important. If you adopt this strategy, your reading before lecture presentations will help you understand the lecture and take better notes, and your reading after lectures will help you locate and learn information in the textbook that your presentation is emphasizing—which is likely to be the information your instructor thinks is most important and is most likely to show up on your exams. Thus, it's a good idea to have your presentation notes nearby when you're completing your reading assignments to help you identify what you should pay special attention to while reading.

2. **Take written notes on what you're reading.** Just as you should take notes when listening to presentations, you should take notes in response to the author's words in the text. Writing requires more active thinking than highlighting because you're creating your own words rather than passively highlighting words written by somebody else. Don't get into the habit of using your textbook as a coloring book in which the artistic process of highlighting what you're reading with spectacular kaleidoscopic colors distracts you from the more important process of learning actively and thinking deeply.

If you can express what someone else has written in words that make sense to you, this means that you're relating it to what you already know—a sign of deep learning (Demmert & Towner, 2003). A good time to pause and summarize what you've read in your own words is when you encounter a boldface heading, because this indicates you've just completed reading about a major concept and are about to begin a new one.

3. **Use the visual aids included in your textbook.** Don't fall into the trap of thinking that visual aids can or should be skipped because they're merely secondary supplements to the written words in the body of the text. Visual aids, such as charts, graphs, diagrams, and concept maps, are powerful learning and memory tools for a couple of reasons: (1) they enable you to "see" the information in addition to reading (hearing) it, and (2) they organize and connect separate pieces of information into an integrated whole.

Furthermore, visual aids allow you to experience a form of information input other than repeatedly processing written words. This occasional change of sensory input brings variety to the reading process, which can recapture your attention and recharge your motivation.

Personal Reflection

When reading a textbook, do you usually have the following tools on hand?

Highlighter: YES   (NO)
Pen or pencil: (YES)   NO
Notebook: YES   (NO)
Class notes: YES   (NO)
Dictionary: (YES)   NO
Glossary: YES   (NO)

Post-Reading Strategies: What to Do after Reading

1. **End a reading session with a short review of the information you've noted or highlighted.** Most forgetting that takes place after you receive and process information occurs immediately after you stop focusing on the information and turn your attention to another task (Baddeley,

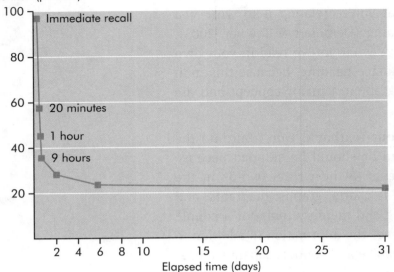

Retention (percent)

Immediate recall
20 minutes
1 hour
9 hours

Elapsed time (days)

1999; Underwood, 1983). Taking a few minutes at the end of your reading time to review the most important information works to lock that information into your memory before you turn your attention to something else and forget it.

The graph on the left represents the results of a classic experiment on how well information is recalled at various times after it was originally learned. As you can see on the far left of the graph, most forgetting occurs soon after information has been taken in (e.g., after 20 minutes, the participants in the study forgot more than 60 percent of it). The results of this classic study, which have been confirmed multiple times (Schacter, 2001), point to the importance of reviewing information you've acquired through reading immediately after you've read it. When you do so, your memory for that information will improve dramatically, because you're intercepting the forgetting curve at its steepest point of memory loss—immediately after information has been read.

2. **For difficult-to-understand concepts, seek out other information sources.** If you find you can't understand a concept explained in your text, even after rereading and repeatedly reflecting on it, try the following strategies:

- **Seek help from your instructor.** If you read carefully and made every effort to understand a particular concept but still can't grasp it, most instructors will be willing to assist you.

- **Consult with tutors available to you.** Students are able to seek help on a wide variety of topics from Tutor.com, which is available on demand (24/7). This paid service is available free to Liberty University students who sign in through Blackboard.

Photo courtesy of Faith Perry.

The Jerry Falwell Library has many books which students can consult for further information on any class topic. Online librarians can assist students with access to these resources.

From *Thriving in College and Beyond,* 3/e by Joseph B. Cuseo, Aaron Thompson, Michele Campagna and Viki S. Fecas. Copyright © 2013 by Kendall Hunt Publishing Company. Reprinted by permission.

Select Techniques to Gain Maximum Benefit from Lecture Presentations

Proverbs 1:5,
"Let the wise listen and add to their learning, and let the discerning get guidance" (NLT).

Much of the interaction you have with course materials in an online program of study is given to you in recorded presentations. Your professors have distilled critical information into presentations that last just a few minutes. Give yourself maximum benefit from the lecture presentations and PowerPoints by preparing ahead of time, taking good notes, and reviewing what you have heard and learned before moving on.

Studies show that information delivered during lecture presentations is the number one source of test questions (and answers) on college exams (Brown, 1988; Kuhn, 1988). When lecture information that hasn't been recorded in the student's notes appears on a test, it has only a five percent chance of being recalled (Kiewra et al., 2000). Students who write notes during lectures achieve higher course grades than students who just listen to lectures (Kiewra, 1985, 2005), and students with a more complete set of notes are more likely to demonstrate higher levels of overall academic achievement (Johnstone & Su, 1994; Kiewra & DuBois, 1998; Kiewra & Fletcher, 1984).

Contrary to popular belief that writing while listening interferes with the ability to listen, students report that taking notes actually increases their attention and concentration (Hartley, 1998; Hartley & Marshall, 1974). Studies also show that when students write down information that's presented to them, rather than just sitting and listening to it, they're more likely to remember the most important aspects of that information when tested later (Bligh, 2000; Kiewra et al., 1991). One study discovered that students with grade point averages (GPAs) of 2.53 or higher recorded more information in their notes and retained a larger percentage of the most important information than did students with GPAs of less than 2.53 (Einstein, Morris, & Smith, 1985). These findings are not surprising when you consider that

Alexandra Barnett

"The difference between success and failure in an online class is focus. Avoid multi-tasking; focus on one task at a time until the work is completed."

hearing information, *writing* it, and then *seeing* it after you've written it produces three different memory traces (tracks) in the brain, which combine to multiply your chances of remembering it. Furthermore, students with a good set of notes have a written record of that information, which can be reread and studied later.

These research findings suggest that you should view each lecture presentation as a test-review session during which your instructor is giving out test answers and you're given the opportunity to write all those answers in your notes. Open the presentation with the attitude that your instructors are dispensing answers to test questions as they speak, and your job is to pick out and pick up these answers.

The next sections give strategies for getting the most out of lectures at three stages in the learning process: *before, during,* and *after* lectures.

Previewing Strategies: What to Do before Lecture Presentations

1. **Check your syllabus to see where you are in the course and determine how the upcoming lesson fits into the total course picture.** Checking your syllabus before individual learning sessions strengthens learning, because you will see how each part relates to the whole. This strategy also capitalizes on the brain's natural tendency to seek larger patterns and see the "big picture." Rather than seeing things in separate parts, the brain is naturally inclined to connect parts into a meaningful whole (Caine & Caine, 1991). In other words, the brain looks for meaningful patterns and connections rather than isolated bits and pieces of information (Jensen, 2000).

2. **Review your notes from the previous presentation and from any reading assignment that relates to the lecture topic.** Research indicates that when students preview information related to an upcoming lecture topic, it improves their ability to take more accurate and complete lecture notes (Kiewra, 2005; Ladas, 1980). Thus, a good strategy to help you learn from lectures is to review your notes from the previous class presentation and read textbook information related to an upcoming lecture topic—before hearing the lecture. This strategy will help you better understand and take more detailed notes on the lecture. Reviewing previously learned information also activates your previous knowledge, enabling you to build a mental bridge from one learning session to the next, connecting new information to what you already know—a key to deep learning (Bruner, 1990; Piaget, 1978; Vygotsky,

1978). Acquiring knowledge isn't a matter of simply pouring information into the brain as if it were an empty jar. It's a matter of attaching or connecting new ideas to ideas that are already stored in the brain. When you learn deeply, a physical connection is actually made between nerve cells in your brain (Alkon, 1992).

3. **Choose a good time to listen to the lecture.** Some online learners prefer to arise early in the morning to review lectures before the rest of the family is up and active. Others prefer to wait until the children are in bed for the night, so they will be able to focus. Still others use breaks at work, such as lunchtime, to watch course presentations. Decide which window of time suits both your need for a distraction-free period, as well as what you know about your body's daily rhythm. Avoid listening to presentations when you are not yet fully awake or are drowsy before bedtime. Make sure you have chosen a time of day that allows you to be an effective listener and note taker.

4. **Choose a good place to listen to the presentation.** If you have a dedicated office or study room, this is the obvious place to be. For many online learners, that is not the case. Whatever your situation, ensure that you are in a location where you will be free of distractions. This may be a study carrel at the public library, at your desk at work after hours, or any other place you are able to be fully attentive as you listen and take notes.

5. **Adopt a seating posture that screams attention.** Sitting upright and leaning forward increases your attention because these bodily signals will reach your brain and increase mental alertness. If your body is in an alert and ready position, your mind tends to pick up these physical cues and follow your body's lead by also becoming alert and ready (to learn). Studies show that when humans are mentally alert and ready to learn, greater amounts of the brain chemical C-kinase are released at the connection points between brain cells, which increases the likelihood that a learning connection will form between them (Howard, 2000).

Listening and Note-Taking Strategies: What to Do during Audio Presentations

1. **Take notes as you listen.** Many students report that they take notes during audio presentations. Some are not able to get the full details they want to note in a first listening session and so prefer to listen all the way through the presentation before taking notes. A second session

will allow time to take good notes on important points. During recorded presentations, students can pause the presentation if they cannot keep pace with note taking.

2. **Focus full attention on the most important information.** Attention is the critical first step to successful learning and memory. Since the human attention span is limited, it's impossible to attend to and make note of (or take notes on) everything. Thus, you need to use your attention selectively to focus on, detect, and select information that matters most. Here are some strategies for attending to and recording the most important information delivered by professors in their presentations:

   - Pay attention to information your instructors put *in print* in a Powerpoint presentation. If your instructor takes the time and energy to display it in print, that's usually a good clue that the information is important and you're likely to see it again—on an exam.

   - Pay attention to information presented during the first and last few minutes of the presentation. Instructors are more likely to provide valuable reminders, reviews, and previews at these two points in time.

   - Use your instructor's *verbal and nonverbal cues* to detect important information.

   - Listen actively to receive and record important ideas in your notes that you *hear* your instructor saying.

3. **Take organized notes.** Keep taking notes in the same paragraph if the instructor is continuing on the same point or idea. When the instructor shifts to a new idea, skip a few lines and shift to a new paragraph. Be alert to phrases that your instructor may use to signal a shift to a new or different idea (e.g., "Let's turn to . . ." or "In addition to . . ."). Use these phrases as cues for taking notes in paragraph form. By recording different ideas in different paragraphs, you improve the organizational quality of your notes, which will improve your comprehension and retention of them. Also, be sure to leave extra space between paragraphs (ideas) to give yourself room to add information later that you may have initially missed, or to translate the professor's words into your own words that are more meaningful to you.

   Another popular strategy for taking organized notes, called the Cornell Note-Taking System, is shown later in this chapter.

4. **Keep taking notes even if you don't immediately understand what your instructor is saying.** If you are uncertain or confused about what your instructor is saying, don't stop taking notes, because your notes

will at least leave you with a record of the information to review later—when you have more time to think about and grasp their meaning. If you still don't understand the information after taking time to review it, check it out in your textbook, or email your instructor for clarification.

Post-Lecture Strategy:
What to Do after Lecture Presentations

1. **As soon as each presentation ends, quickly check your notes for missing information or incomplete thoughts.** Since the information is likely to be fresh in your mind, a quick check of your notes at this time will allow you to take advantage of your short-term memory. By reviewing and reflecting on it, you can help move the information into long-term memory before forgetting takes place. Don't rush to turn off your computer before you fully understand this lecture material. Reviewing may alert you to the fact that you missed something and need to view the presentation, or parts of it, again.

2. **Before viewing the next presentation, reflect on and review your notes to make sense of them.** Your presentations will often include information that you may have little prior knowledge about, so it is unrealistic to expect that you will understand everything that's being said the first time you hear it. Instead, you'll need to set aside time for making notes or taking notes on your own notes (i.e., rewriting them in your own words so that they make sense to you).

   During this reflect-and-rewrite process, we recommend that you take notes on your notes by:

   - Translating technical information into your own words to make it more meaningful to you; and

   - Reorganizing your notes to get ideas related to the same point in the same place. Studies show that when students organize lecture information into meaningful categories, they demonstrate greater recall for that information on a delayed memory test than do students who simply review their notes without organizing them into categories (Howe, 1970; Kiewra, 2005).

Choose an Effective Note-Taking Strategy to Document Important Information

Prov. 22:17,
"Pay attention and turn your ear to the sayings of the wise; apply your heart to what I teach" (NLT).

Cari Smith

"As you are reading, have a highlighter, pen, and paper or notecards nearby. Consider highlighting key words or phrases as you read through the material. Use your notebook to outline each chapter and reference important topics."

How good are you at taking notes? Do you have a strategy or method, or do you just try to pluck bits of information that you think may be important? Do you try to write down everything, capturing word-for-word what the professor shares in his or her presentation? Perhaps you write in sentences, making sure to use correct capitalization and punctuation. Do you often find that when you are finished taking notes, you have difficulty making sense of what you have written? Here is a popular note-taking strategy that can help you capture the essence of the important information, while creating a good study tool for later.

The Cornell Note-Taking System

1. On the page on which you're taking notes, draw a horizontal line about 2 inches from the bottom edge of the paper.

2. If there's no vertical line on the left side of the page, draw one line about 2½ inches from the left edge of the paper (as shown in the scaled-down illustration here).

3. When your instructor is lecturing, use the large space to the right of the vertical line (area A) to record your notes.

4. After a lecture, use the space at the bottom of the page (area B) to summarize the main points you recorded on that page.

5. Use the column of space on the left side of the page (area C) to write questions that are answered in the notes on the right.

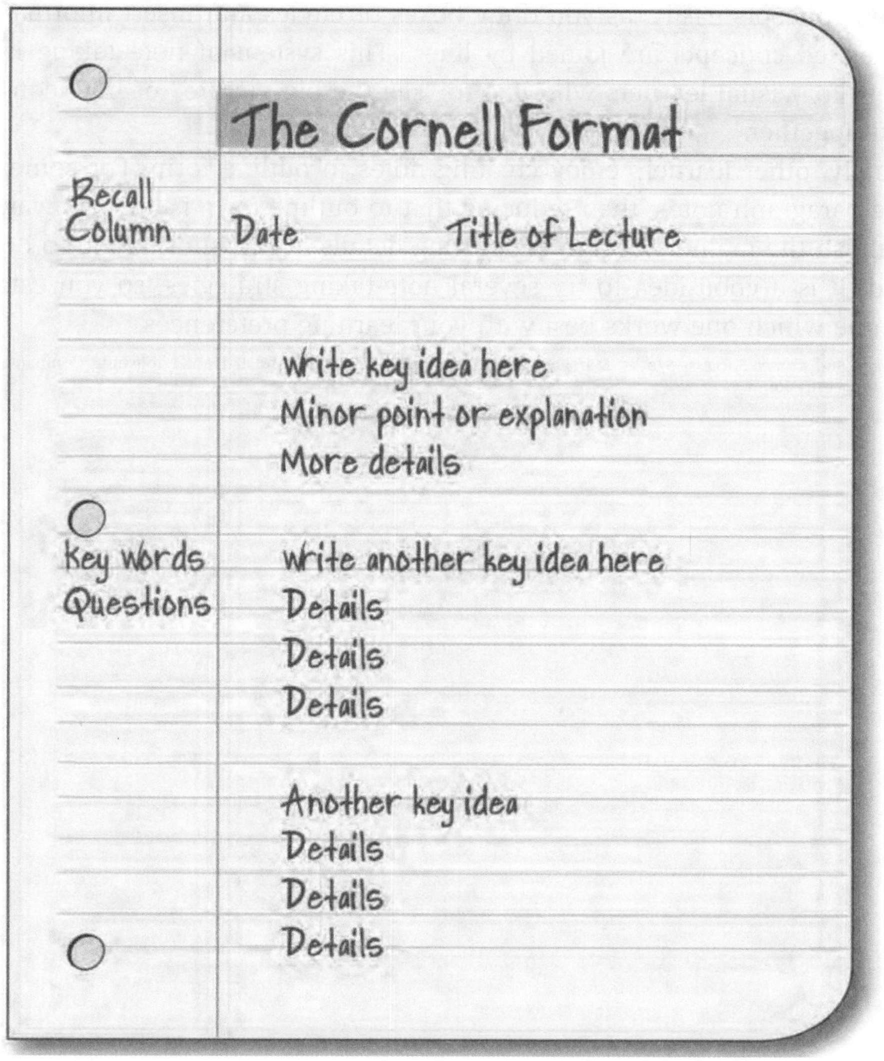

The Cornell Format

Recall Column	Date	Title of Lecture

Write key idea here
Minor point or explanation
More details

Key words
Questions

Write another key idea here
Details
Details
Details

Another key idea
Details
Details
Details

6. Quiz yourself by looking at the questions listed in the left margin while covering the answers to them that are found in your notes on the right.

   Note: You can use this note-taking and note-review method on your own, or you could ask a family member to quiz you by asking questions from one column to determine if you can provide the responses from the other. See if you can give a good summary of the page of noted information.

While the Cornell note-taking system is a powerful tool for some students, others prefer to take notes in paragraph form, while still others will create a concept map. Concept mapping allows you to see relationships between concepts easily, as you draw boxes or circles and insert information. Related concepts are joined by lines. This system of note taking is excellent for visual learners who like to "see the big picture" of how concepts fit together.

Finally, other learners enjoy creating notes in outline form. For some, writing paragraph notes, then reducing that to outline form is an easy way to establish the main ideas and supporting details of the information to be learned. It is a good idea to try several note-taking strategies, so you can determine which one works best with your learning preferences.

From *College and Career Success*, 5/e by Marsha Fralick. Copyright © 2011 by Kendall Hunt Publishing Company. Reprinted by permission.

Select Study Skills to Make Wise Use of Study Time

Prov. 9:9,
"Instruct the wise and they will be wiser still; teach the righteous and they will add to their learning" (NIV).

Reading course textbooks and viewing presentations and PowerPoints are important to your online college learning success . . . but these are foundations upon which to build your learning. There are other strategies that can enhance your learning beyond the initial reading of your textbook and review of presentations. Which of the following strategies are you using now? Which do you need to add to your study "tool kit"?

Cari Smith

"Choose a study place with no distractions—turn your phone off, turn off Facebook chat."

Study Strategies for Learning Deeply and Remembering Longer

The final step in the learning process is to save the information in your brain and bring it back to mind at the time you need it—e.g., test time. Described here is a series of effective study strategies for acquiring knowledge, keeping that knowledge in your brain (memory storage), and accessing that information when you need it (memory retrieval).

The Importance of Undivided Attention

The human attention span has limited capacity; we have only so much of it available to us at any point in time, and we can give all or part of it to whatever task we're working on. If study time is spent engaging in other activities besides studying (e.g., listening to music, watching TV, or text-messaging friends), the attention available for studying is subtracted and divided among the other activities. In other words, studying doesn't receive your undivided attention.

Studies show that when people multitask they don't pay equal attention to all tasks at the same time. Instead, they

Photo courtesy of David Duncan (Liberty University).

Liberty University Hancock Visitor's Center provides a gracious welcome to visitors.

divide their attention by shifting it back and forth between tasks (Howard, 2000) and their performance on the task that demands the most concentration or deepest thinking is what suffers the most (Crawford & Strapp, 1994). Furthermore, research shows that multitasking can increase boredom for the task that requires the most intense concentration.

When performing complex mental tasks that cannot be done automatically or mindlessly, other tasks and sources of external stimulation interfere with the quiet internal reflection needed for permanent connections to form between brain cells—which is what must happen if deep, long-lasting learning is to take place (Jensen, 2000).

Making Meaningful Associations

Connecting what you're trying to learn to something you already know is a powerful memory-improvement strategy because knowledge is stored in the form of a connected network of brain cells (Coward, 1990; Chaney, 2007).

The brain's natural tendency to seek meaningful, connected patterns applies to words as well as images. This is illustrated in the following passage that once appeared anonymously on the Internet. See whether you can read it and grasp its meaning.

> Aoccdrnig to rscheearch at Cmabridge Uinverstisy, it deos't mattaer in what order the ltteers in a word are, the only imp thing is that the frist and lsat ltteer be at the rghit pclae. The rset can be a total mses and you can still raed it wouthit a porbelm. This is bcusae the human mind deos not raed ervey lteter by istlef, but the word as a wlohe. Amzanig huh?

Notice how easily you found the meaning of the misspelled words by naturally transforming them into correctly spelled words—which you knew because the correctly spelled words were already stored in your brain. Thus, whenever you learn meaningfully, you do so by connecting what you're trying to understand to what you already know.

Learning by making meaningful connections is referred to as *deep learning* (Biggs & Tang, 2007; Entwistle & Ramsden, 1983). It involves moving beyond shallow memorization to deeper levels of understanding. This is a major a shift from the old view that learning occurs by passively absorbing information like a sponge—for example, by receiving it from the teacher or text and studying it in the same prepackaged form as you received it. Instead, you want to adopt an approach to learning that involves actively transforming the information you receive into a form that's meaningful to you (Feldman & Paulsen, 1994; Mayer, 2002). This transforms short-term, surface-level learning (memorization of information) into deep and meaningful long-term learning (acquisition of knowledge).

Cari Smith

"Let your family and friends know the days and times you have set aside to study. This gives them the opportunity to support you by helping protect your school time."

Alexandra Barnett

"Review all assignment information early in the week and email your instructor with questions as many days before the assignment due date as possible."

Cari Smith

"Read the directions. Read the directions again. Complete your assignment. Read the directions one last time to confirm your work is correct."

Alexandra Barnett

"Read the rubrics and use them as checklists to ensure all requirements are met prior to submitting assignments."

So, instead of immediately trying to learn something by repeatedly pounding it into your brain like a hammer, your first strategy should be to try hooking or hanging it onto something that's already stored in your brain—something you already know and is meaningful to you. It may take a little while and a little work to find the right hook, but once you've found it, you'll learn the information faster and retain it longer. For instance, here's a meaningful way to learn and remember how to correctly spell one of the most frequently misspelled words in the English language: *separate* (not *seperate*). If you remember that *par* means "to divide," as in the words *par*ts or *par*tition, it makes sense that *separate* should be spelled *separate* because its meaning is "to divide into parts."

Each of the academic subjects that comprise the college curriculum has a specialized vocabulary that can sound like a foreign language to someone who has no experience with the subject area. Before you start to brutally beat these terms into your brain through sheer repetition, try to find some meaning in them. One way you can make a term more meaningful to you is by looking up its word root in the dictionary or by identifying its prefix or suffix, which may give away the term's meaning.

For instance, suppose you're taking a biology course and studying the autonomic nervous system—the part of the nervous system that operates without your conscious awareness or voluntary control (e.g., your heart beating and lungs breathing). The meaning of the phrase is given away by the prefix *auto*, which means self-controlling, as in the word automatic (e.g., *automatic* transmission).

If looking up the term's root, prefix, or suffix doesn't give away its meaning, see if you can make it meaningful to you in some other way. For instance, suppose you looked up the root of the term *artery* and nothing about the origins of this term suggested its meaning or purpose. You could create your own meaning for this term by taking its first letter (a), and have it stand for "*a*way"—to help you remember that arteries carry blood away from the heart. Thus, you've taken a biological term and made it personally meaningful (and memorable).

Cari Smith

"Take frequent study breaks—give yourself 5–15 minutes before returning to your studies."

Lisa Eppard

"When tackling math, get a copy of *Forgotten Algebra*. This self-teaching workbook is a great resource that's user friendly and offers a step-by-step refresher for those who are a little rusty on their math skills. (*Forgotten Algebra*, Barbara Lee Bleau, Ph.D. Hauppauge: Barron's Educational Series, Inc., 2013. ISBN# 978-1-4380-0150-0). I am a firm believer in this book! I returned to college after a 17 year absence from the classroom, spent the summer months working through this workbook, and placed into pre-calculus (two levels higher than what I needed to place out of the math prerequisites)."

Cari Smith

"Use the assignment rubric as a guideline, as it shows EXACTLY what you will be graded on."

Personal Reflection

Think of a key term or concept you're learning in a course this term that you could form a meaningful association to remember. What is the information you're attempting to learn? What is the meaningful association you could use to help you remember it?

Memory retention, memory recall, & memory encoding I can associate with psychology.

_____

_____

_____

_____

Compare and Contrast

When you're studying something new, get in the habit of asking yourself the following questions:

1. Is this idea similar or comparable to something that I've already learned? (Compare)

2. How does this idea differ from what I already know? (Contrast)

Research indicates that this simple strategy is one of the most powerful ways to promote learning of academic information (Marzano, Pickering, & Pollock, 2001). Asking yourself the question "How is this similar to and different from concepts that I already know?" makes learning more personally meaningful because you are relating what you're trying to learn to what you already know.

Integration and Organization

Integrate or connect ideas from your class notes and assigned readings that relate to the same major point by organizing them into the same category. For example, get these related ideas in the same place by recording them on the same index card under the same category heading. Index cards are a good tool for such purposes; you can use each card as a miniature file cabinet for different categories of information. The category heading on each card functions like the hub of a wheel, around which individual pieces of related information are attached like spokes. Integrating information related to the same topic in the same place and studying it at the same time divides the total material you're learning into identifiable and manageable parts. In contrast, when ideas pertaining to the same point or concept are spread all over the place, they're more likely to take that form in your mind—leaving them mentally disconnected and leaving you confused (as well as feeling stressed and overwhelmed).

Divide and Conquer

Effective learning depends not only on _how_ you learn (your method), but on _when_ you learn (your timing). Although cramming just before exams is

Alexandra Barnett

"Complete small tasks and assignments first. The accomplishment you feel by completing these tasks will propel you forward to completing the bigger tasks."

Sue Ocealis

"I like to use yellow highlighter when I read to mark important words or facts. I also use 3 × 5 cards. I put an important term, name, or date on one side, and more information on the back. I go through the cards while riding in a car, waiting in line, etc. every day. I save all the ones I miss the first time and go through them again until there are none left. Then I do the same thing the next day. By the time the quiz comes, I know the information inside out."

better than not studying, it's far less effective than studying that's spread out across time. Rather than cramming all your studying into one long session, use the method of *distributed practice*: spread, or distribute, your study time over several shorter sessions. Research consistently shows that short, periodic practice sessions are more effective than a single marathon session.

Distributing study time over several shorter sessions improves your learning and memory by:

- Reducing loss of attention due to fatigue or boredom; and

- Reducing mental interference by giving your brain some downtime to cool down and lock in information it has received before it's interrupted by the need to deal with additional information (Malmberg & Murnane, 2002; Murnane & Shiffrin, 1991).

If the brain's downtime is interfered with by the arrival of additional information, it gets overloaded and its capacity for handling information becomes impaired. This is what cramming does—it overloads the brain with lots of information in a limited period of time. In contrast, distributed study does just the opposite—it uses shorter sessions with downtime between sessions, thereby giving the brain the time and opportunity to retain the information that it has received and processed (studied).

Another major advantage of distributed study is that it's less stressful and more motivating than cramming. Shorter sessions provide you with an incentive to start studying because you know that you're not going to be doing it for a long stretch of time or lose any sleep over it. It's easier to maintain your interest and motivation for any task that's done for a shorter rather than a longer period. Furthermore, distributing studying makes exam preparation easier because you know that if you run into difficulty understanding anything, you'll still have plenty of time to get help with it before you're tested and graded on it.

The "Part-to-Whole" Study Method

The part-to-whole method of studying is a natural extension of the distributed practice just discussed. With the part-to-whole method, you break up the material you need to learn into smaller parts and study those parts in separate sessions in advance of the exam; then you use your last study session just before the exam to review (restudy) all the parts you previously studied in separate sessions. Thus, your last session is not a cram session or even a study session: it's a review session.

Research shows that students of all ability levels learn material in college courses more effectively when it's studied in small units and when progression to the next unit takes place only after the previous unit has been

Emily

"Flash cards are really helpful for me when studying. It may seem like more work but having to write it all out then reading them over and over really helps."

Terry

Q: *What learning/test-taking strategies did you pick up in college that you did not use previously?*

A: "I always preferred the outline strategy. I would create an outline of the chapters that were being covered that included key topics/concepts as well as page numbers where I could find that information late."

Q: *Were you a "nervous Nellie" at test time?*

A: "No"

Q: *How can students overcome their test fears?*

A: "I believe most fear comes from lack of preparedness: prepare, prepare and prepare and you'll have nothing to fear."

mastered or understood (Pascarella & Terenzini, 1991, 2005). This strategy has two advantages: (1) it reinforces your memory for what you previously learned and (2) it builds on what you already know to help you learn new material. These advantages are particularly important in cumulative subjects that require memory for problem-solving procedures or steps, such as math and science. When you repeatedly practice these procedures, they become more automatic and you're able to retrieve them quicker (e.g., on a timed test). This enables you to use them efficiently without having to expend a lot of mental effort and energy (Samuels & Flor, 1997), freeing your working memory for more important tasks—such as critical thinking and creative problem solving (Schneider & Chein, 2003).

Don't buy into the myth that studying in advance is a waste of time because you'll forget it all by test time. As discussed in Chapter 3, this is a myth that procrastinators often use to rationalize their habit of putting off studying until the very last moment, which forces them to cram frantically the night before exams. Do not underestimate the power of breaking material to be learned into smaller parts and studying those parts some time before a major exam. Even if you cannot recall what you previously studied, when you start reviewing it you'll find that you will relearn it much faster than when you studied it the first time. This proves that studying in advance is not a waste of time, because it takes less time to relearn the material, indicating that information studied in the earlier sessions was still retained in your brain (Kintsch, 1994).

Build Variety into the Study Process

You can increase your concentration and motivation by using the following strategies to infuse variety and a change of pace into your study routine.

Periodically vary the type of academic work you do while studying. Changing the nature of your work activities or the type of mental tasks you're performing while studying increases your level of alertness and concentration by reducing *habituation*—attention loss that occurs after repeated engagement in the same type of mental task (McGuiness & Pribram, 1980). To combat attention loss due to habituation, occasionally vary the type of study task you're performing. For instance, shift periodically among tasks that involve reading, writing, studying, and problem-solving skills (e.g., math or science problems).

Study different subjects in different places. Studying in different locations provides different environmental contexts for learning, which reduces the amount of interference that normally builds up when all information is studied in the same place (Rankin et al., 2009). In addition to spreading out your studying at different times, it's also a good idea to spread it out in

Roger

"I have learned over the years to have a good night's sleep and a hearty breakfast before a taking a test. If I have studied for the exam, praying before taking the test has helped calm me down and prepare me. Through prayer I leave the results of the test to Him. I also understand that failing one test rarely results in a failed class. If I do poorly on one exam or a paper, usually the cumulative grades derived from good homework, essays, or discussion board grades will boost my score. So I try not to be too disappointed when I do not receive the grade I desire on one test."

different places. The great public speakers in ancient Greece and Rome used this method of changing places to remember long speeches by walking through different rooms while rehearsing their speech, learning each major part of their speech in a different room (Higbee, 1998).

Photo courtesy of Dave Moquin.

A simple cross overlooks the campus from atop Candlers Mountain.

Changing the nature of the learning task and place provides a change of pace that infuses variety into the learning process, which, in turn, stimulates your attention, concentration, and motivation. Although it's useful to have a set time and place to study for getting you into a regular work routine, this doesn't mean that learning occurs best by habitually performing all types of academic tasks in the same place.

Instead, research suggests that you should periodically change the learning tasks you perform and the environment in which you perform them to maximize attention and minimize interference (Druckman & Bjork, 1991).

Mix long study sessions with short study breaks that involve physical activity (e.g., a short jog or brisk walk). Study breaks that include physical activity not only refresh the mind by giving it a rest from studying, but also stimulate the mind by increasing blood flow to your brain, which will help you retain what you've already studied and regain concentration for what you'll study next.

Learn with all of your senses. When studying, try to use as many sensory channels as possible. Research shows that information perceived through multiple sensory modalities is remembered better because it creates multiple interconnections in long-term memory areas of the brain (Bjork, 1994; Shams & Seitz, 2011; Zull, 2002).

When a memory is formed in the brain, different sensory aspects of it are stored in different areas. For example, when your brain receives visual, auditory (hearing), and motor (movement) input while learning, each of these forms of sensory input is stored as memory trace in a different part of the brain. Different parts of the brain are specialized to receive input from different sensory modalities. When you use all of these sensory modalities while learning, multiple memory traces of what you're studying are recorded in different parts of your brain, which leads to deeper learning and stronger memory for what you have learned (Education Commission of the States, 1996).

Learn visually. The human brain consists of two hemispheres (half spheres): the left and the right. Each hemisphere of the brain specializes in a different type of learning. In most people, the left hemisphere specializes in verbal learning, dealing primarily with words. In contrast, the right hemisphere specializes in visual-spatial learning, dealing primarily with perceiving images and objects that occupy physical space. If you use both hemispheres while studying, you lay down two different memory traces in your brain: one in the left hemisphere where words are stored, and one in the right hemisphere where images are stored. This process of laying down a double memory trace (verbal and visual) is referred to as *dual coding* (Paivio, 1990). When this happens, memory for what you're learning is substantially strengthened, primarily because two memory traces are better than one.

To capitalize on the advantage of dual coding, be sure to use any visual aids that are available to you, including those provided in your textbook and by your instructor. You can also create your own visual aids by drawing pictures, symbols, and concept maps, such as flowcharts, Venn diagrams, spider webs, wheels with spokes, or branching tree diagrams.

Personal Reflection

Think of a course you're taking this term in which you're learning related pieces of information that could be joined together to form a concept map. In the space that follows, make a rough sketch of this map that includes the information you need to remember.

Learn by moving or using motor learning (a.k.a. muscle memory).
In addition to hearing and seeing, movement is a sensory channel. When you move, your brain receives kinesthetic stimulation—the sensations generated by your muscles. Research shows that memory traces for movement are commonly stored in an area of your brain that plays a major role for all types of learning (Middleton & Strick, 1994). Thus, associating movement with what you're learning can improve your ability to retain it because you add a muscle memory trace in the motor control area of your brain.

You can use movement to help you learn and retain academic information by using your body to act out what you're studying or to symbolize it with your hands (Kagan & Kagan, 1998). For example, if you're trying to remember five points about something (e.g., five consequences of the Civil War), when you're studying these points, count them on your fingers as you try to recall each of them. Also, remember that talking involves muscle movement of your lips and tongue. Thus, by speaking aloud when you're studying, either to a friend or to yourself, you can improve your memory of what you're studying by adding kinesthetic stimulation to the auditory or sound stimulation your brain receives from hearing what you're saying.

Learn with emotion. Information reaches the brain through your senses and is stored in the brain as a memory trace; the same is true of emotions. Numerous connections occur between brain cells in the emotional and memory centers (Zull, 1998). For instance, when you're experiencing emotional excitement about what you're learning, adrenaline is released and is carried through the bloodstream to the brain. Once adrenaline reaches the brain, it increases blood flow and glucose production, which stimulates learning and strengthens memory (LeDoux, 1998; Rosenfield, 1988). In fact, emotionally intense experiences can release such a substantial amount of adrenaline into the bloodstream that memories for them can be immediately stored in long-term memory and last an entire lifetime. For instance, most people remember exactly what they were doing at the time they experienced such emotionally intense events as the September 11 terrorist attack on the United States, their first kiss, or their favorite team winning a world championship.

What does this emotion-memory link have to do with helping you remember academic information while studying? Research indicates that emotional intensity, excitement, and enthusiasm strengthen memory of academic information just as they do for memory for life events and personal experiences. If you get psyched up about what you're learning, you have a much better chance of learning and remembering it. When you're passionate or intense about what you're learning

Photo courtesy of Dave Moquin.

Sharp Top and Flat Top, the Peaks of Otter, in nearby Bedford County, can be seen from the Liberty University campus.

and convince yourself that what you're learning is really important to know, you're more likely to remember it (Howard, 2000; Minninger, 1984). So, keep in mind the importance or significance of what you're learning. For instance, if you're learning about photosynthesis, remind yourself that you're not just learning about a chemical reaction, you're learning about the driving force that underlies all plant life on the planet! If you aren't aware of the importance or significance of a particular concept you're studying, ask your instructor. Enthusiasm can be contagious; you may catch it and become more passionate about learning the concept.

Self-Monitor Your Learning

Successful learners just don't put in study time; they reflect and check on themselves to see if they're putting in quality time and really understanding what they're attempting to learn. They monitor their comprehension as they go along by asking themselves questions such as "Am I following this?" "Do I really understand it?" and "Do I know it for sure?"

How do you know if you really know it? Probably the best answer to this question is "I find *meaning* in it—that is, I can relate to it personally or put it in terms that make sense to me" (Ramsden, 2003).

Following are some strategies for checking whether you truly understand what you're trying to learn. They help you answer the question "How do I know if I really know it?" These strategies can be used as indicators or checkpoints for determining whether you're just memorizing or learning at a deeper level.

- **Can you paraphrase (restate or translate) what you're learning into your own words?** When you can paraphrase what you're learning, you're able to complete the following sentence: "In other words . . ." If you can complete that sentence in your own words, this is a good indication that you've moved beyond memorization to comprehension because you've transformed what you're learning into words that are meaningful to you. You know you know it if you're not stating it the same way your instructor or textbook stated it, but restating it in words that are your own.

- **Can you explain what you're learning to someone who is unfamiliar with it?** Simply put, if you can't explain it to someone else, you probably don't really understand it yourself. If you can explain to a friend what you've learned, this is a good sign that you've moved beyond memorization to comprehension because you're able to translate it into language that's understandable to anyone. Studies show that students gain deeper levels of understanding for what they're learning when they're asked to explain it to someone else (Chi et al.,

1994). Sometimes, we only become aware of how well we know or don't know something until we have to explain it to someone who's never heard it before. If you cannot find someone else to explain it to, then explain it aloud as if you were talking to an imaginary friend.

- **Can you think of an example of what you've learned?** If you can come up with an instance or illustration of what you're learning that's your own—not one given by your instructor or textbook—this is a good sign that you truly understand it. It shows you're able to take a general, abstract concept and apply it to a specific real-life experience (Bligh, 2000). Furthermore, a personal example is a powerful memory tool. Studies show that when people retrieve a concept from memory, they first recall an example of it. The example then serves a memory-retrieval cue to trigger their memory of other details about the concept, such as its definition and relationship to other concepts (Norman, 1982; Okimoto & Norman, 2010; Park, 1984).

- **Can you represent or describe what you've learned in terms of an analogy or metaphor that compares it to something with similar meaning, or which works in a similar way?** Analogies and metaphors are basically ways of learning something new by understanding it in terms of its similarity to something you already understand. For instance, the computer can be used as a metaphor for the human brain to get a better understanding of learning and memory as a three-stage process in which information is (1) inputted—perceived or received (through lectures and readings), (2) stored or saved—by studying, and (3) retrieved—recalled from storage at test time. If you can use an analogy or metaphor to represent what you're learning, you're grasping it at a deep level because you're building a mental bridge that connects it to what you already know (Cameron, 2003).

- **Can you apply what you're learning to solve a new problem that you haven't previously seen?** The ability to use knowledge by applying it in a different situation is a good indicator of deep learning (Erickson & Strommer, 2005). Learning specialists refer to this mental process as *decontextualization*—taking what you learned in one context (situation) and applying it to another (Bransford, Brown, & Cocking, 1999). For instance, you know that you've learned a mathematical concept deeply when you can use that concept to solve math problems that are different from the ones used by your instructor or your textbook. This is why your math instructors rarely include on exams the exact problems that were solved in your textbook. They're not trying to trick you at test time: they're trying to see whether you've learned the concept or principle deeply.

Personal Reflection

Rate yourself in terms of how frequently you use these study strategies according to the following scale:

4 = always, 3 = sometimes, 2 = rarely, 1 = never

1. I block out all distracting sources of outside stimulation when I study. 4 ③ 2 1

2. I try to find meaning in technical terms by looking at their prefixes or suffixes or by looking up their word roots in the dictionary. 4 3 2 ①

3. I compare and contrast what I'm currently studying with what I've already learned. 4 3 ② 1

4. I organize the information I'm studying into categories or classes. 4 ③ 2 1

5. I integrate or pull together information from my notes and readings that relates to the same concept or general category. 4 3 ② 1

6. I distribute or spread out my study time over several short sessions in advance of the exam, and I use my last study session before the test to review the information I previously studied. 4 ③ 2 1

From *Thriving in College and Beyond*, 3/e by Joseph B. Cuseo, Aaron Thompson, Michele Campagna and Viki S. Fecas. Copyright © 2013 by Kendall Hunt Publishing Company. Reprinted by permission.

BUILDING BLOCKS

Information delivered during lectures is most likely to form questions and answers on college tests. Students who do not record information presented during lectures in their notes have a slim chance of recalling the information at test time. Thus, effective note-taking is critical to successful academic performance in college.

Information from reading assignments is the next most common source of test questions on college exams. Professors often don't discuss information contained in assigned reading during class presentations. Thus, doing the assigned reading, and doing it in a way that's most effective for promoting comprehension and retention, plays an important role in your academic success.

Active involvement is critical for learning from lecture presentations (e.g., actively taking notes while listening to lectures) and learning from reading (e.g., actively taking notes while reading). While active involvement is necessary for learning because it engages your attention and enables information to enter the brain, personal reflection is also necessary for deep learning because it keeps that information in the brain by locking it into long-term memory. Reflection also encourages deep learning by promoting self-awareness. By periodically pausing to reflect on whether you're truly understanding what you're studying, you become a more self-aware learner and a more successful student.

Learning is also deepened when it's a multisensory experience—when you engage as many senses as possible in the learning process.

Personal Reflection

How do you approach a learning session? Do you do anything to prepare for viewing a lecture presentation or PowerPoint? What strategies do you apply when it is time to read the textbook?

I approach learning sessions with favorable attention and time making sure to comprehend what is being taught and read.

Personal Reflection

Carefully review your reading and study habits, so you can incorporate wise practices. Record some strategies here that you are not currently using and that you plan to put into practice.

- Note taking
- Asking questions
- Investigating

In the Bible, we read about King Solomon, honored as the wisest man. The Old Testament book of I Kings, Chapter 2 relates that King David instructed his son Solomon to ". . . be strong, act like a man, and observe what the Lord your God requires: Walk in obedience to him, and keep his decrees and commands, his laws and regulations, as written in the Law of Moses. Do this so that you may prosper in all you do. . . ." (I Kings 2:2b–3a, NIV). Later, God told the young king to ask for whatever he wanted. Solomon answered, asking God to give him wisdom to rule His people. God was pleased by this request, and granted it and much more. God replied,

> ". . . I will do what you have asked. I will give you a wise and discerning heart, so that there will never have been anyone like you, nor will there ever be. Moreover, I will give you what you have not asked for—both wealth and honor—so that in your lifetime you will have no equal among kings. And if you walk in obedience to me and keep my decrees and commands as David your father did, I will give you a long life" (I Kings 3:11–14, NIV).

Have you asked God to grant you wisdom as you pursue your college education? You will need to be wise in determining how to use your time, as you learned in Chapter 3, and also how to devote yourself to careful reading, presentation review, and study practices. Pray with Solomon, that God will *"give me {you} wisdom and knowledge"* (II Chronicles 1:10, NIV).

TOOL BOX

Reading

Reading Speed and Comprehension—Since much of the material in the online classroom is written, good reading speed and comprehension are critical. If you are among the many who are less than happy with the speed at which they read while simultaneously absorbing information, you might consider taking a speed reading course. Liberty University offers a for-credit class that is designed to increase both reading speed and comprehension (CLST 301).

Studying

Flashcards—An old standby in the realm of study tools, but you may be happy to hear that the concept has been updated for the 21st century. Instead of walking around with a deck of cards in your pocket, consider downloading a flashcard app for your mobile device. These apps allow you to create digital flashcards in much the same way that you would create physical flashcards but also offer some additional features. Once you are through your stack of cards, the program will let you start again from the beginning, shuffle the deck, or even quiz you on just the items you got wrong the first time.

Note Taking—Programs like Evernote allow you to take notes, organize information, and perform detailed searches of your notes, all while syncing them across multiple devices. This means you can take notes on your laptop while listening to a lecture and then review them on your phone while you wait in line at the doctor's office. Best of all, most of these types of applications are low cost or free, work across multiple operating systems, and are fairly intuitive.

Additional resources and links to specific sites, worksheets, and apps can be located by accessing the Breaking Ground website:

www.breakinggroundlu.com

References

Alkon, D. L. (1992). *Memory's voice: Deciphering the brain-mind code.* New York, NY: HarperCollins.

Ausubel, D., Novak, J., & Hanesian, H. (1978). *Educational psychology: A cognitive view* (2nd ed.). New York, NY: Holt, Rinehart & Winston.

Baddeley, A. D. (1999). *Essentials of human memory.* Hove UK: Psychology.

Biggs, J., & Tang, C. (2007). *Teaching for quality learning at university* (3rd ed.) Buckingham England: SRHE and Open University Press.

Bjork, R. (1994). Memory and metamemory considerations in the training of human beings. In J. Metcalfe & A. P. Shimamura (Eds.), *Metacognition: Knowing about knowing* (pp. 185–206). Cambridge, MA: MIT Press.

Bligh, D. A. (2000). *What's the use of lectures?* San Francisco, CA: Jossey-Bass.

Bransford, J. D., Brown, A. L., & Cocking, R. R. (1999). *How people learn: Brain, mind, experience and school.* Washington, DC: National Academy Press.

Brown, R. D. (1988). Self-quiz on testing and grading issues. *Teaching at UNL (University of Nebraska–Lincoln), 10*(2), 1–3.

Bruner, J. (1990). *Acts of meaning.* Cambridge, MA: Harvard University Press.

Caine, R. N., & Caine, G. (1991). *Teaching and the human brain.* Alexandria, VA: Association for Supervision and Curriculum Development.

Cameron, L. (2003). *Metaphor in educational discourse.* London, England: Continuum.

Chaney, W. (2007). *Dynamic mind.* Las Vegas, NV: Houghton-Brace Publishing.

Chi, M., De Leeuw, N., Chiu, M. H., & LaVancher, C. (1994). Eliciting self-explanations improves understanding. *Cognitive Science, 18,* 439–477.

Coward, A. (1990). *Pattern thinking.* New York, NY: Praeger.

Crawford, H. J., & Strapp, C. H. (1994). Effects of vocal and instrumental music on visuospatial and verbal performance as moderated by studying preference and personality. *Personality and Individual Differences, 16*(2), 237–245.

Demmert, W. G., Jr., & Towner, J. C. (2003). *A review of the research literature on the influences of culturally based education on the academic performance of Native American students.* Retrieved from the Northwest Regional Educational Laboratory, Portland, Oregon, Web site: http://www.nrel.org/indianaed/cbe.pdf

Druckman, D., & Bjork, R. A. (Eds.). (1991). *In the mind's eye: Enhancing human performance.* Washington, DC: National Academy Press.

Education Commission of the States. (1996). *Bridging the gap between neuroscience and education.* Denver, CO: Author.

Einstein, G. O., Morris, J., & Smith, S. (1985). Note-taking, individual differences, and memory for lecture information. *Journal of Educational Psychology, 77*(5), 522–532.

Entwistle, N. J., & Ramsden, P. (1983). *Understanding student learning.* London, England: Croom Helm.

Erickson, B. L., & Strommer, D. W. (2005). Inside the first-year classroom: Challenges and constraints. In J. L. Upcraft, J. N. Gardner, & B. O. Barefoot

(Eds.), *Challenging and supporting the first-year student* (pp. 241–256). San Francisco, CA: Jossey-Bass.

Feldman, K. A., & Paulsen, M. B. (Eds.). (1994). *Teaching and learning in the college classroom.* Needham Heights, MA: Ginn Press.

Hartley, J. (1998). *Learning and studying: a research perspective.* London, England: Routledge.

Hartley, J., & Marshall, S. (1974). On notes and note taking. *Universities Quarterly, 28,* 225–235.

Howard, P. J. (2000). *The owner's manual for the brain: Everyday applications of mind-brain research* (2nd ed.). Atlanta, GA: Bard Press.

Howe, M. J. (1970). Note-taking strategy, review, and long-term retention of verbal information. *Journal of Educational Psychology, 63,* 285.

Jensen, E. (2000). *Brain-based learning.* San Diego, CA: The Brain Store.

Johnstone, A. H., & Su, W. Y. (1994). Lectures: A learning experience? *Education in Chemistry, 31*(1), 65–76, 79.

Kagan, S., & Kagan, M. (1998). *Multiple intelligences: The complete MI book.* San Clemente, CA: Kagan Cooperative Learning.

Kiewra, K. A. (1985). Students' note-taking behaviors and the efficacy of providing the instructor's notes for review. *Contemporary Educational Psychology, 10,* 378–386.

Kiewra, K. A. (2005). *Learn how to study and SOAR to success.* Upper Saddle River, NJ: Pearson Prentice Hall.

Kiewra, K. A., & DuBois, N. F. (1998). *Learning to learn: Making the transition from student to lifelong learner.* Needham Heights, MA: Allyn and Bacon.

Kiewra, K. A., DuBois, N., Christian, D., McShane, A., Meyerhoffer, M., & Roskelley, D. (1991). Note-taking functions and techniques. *Journal of Educational Psychology, 83*(2), 240–245.

Kiewra, K. A., & Fletcher, H. J. (1984). The relationship between notetaking variables and achievement measures. *Human Learning, 3,* 273–280.

Kiewra, K. A., Hart, K., Scoular, J., Stephen, M., Sterup, G., & Tyler, B. (2000). Fish giver or fishing teacher? The lure of strategy instruction. *Teaching at UNL (University of Nebraska–Lincoln), 22*(3).

Kintsch, W. (1994). Text comprehension, memory, and learning. *American Psychologist, 49,* 294–303.

Kuhn, L. (1988). What should we tell students about answer changing? *Research Serving Teaching, 1*(8).

Ladas, H. S. (1980). Note-taking on lectures: An information-processing approach. *Educational Psychologist, 15*(1), 44–53.

LeDoux, J. (1998). *The emotional brain: The mysterious underpinnings of emotional life.* New York, NY: Simon & Schuster.

Malmberg, K. J., & Murnane, K. (2002). List composition and the word-frequency effect for recognition memory. *Journal of Experimental Psychology: Learning, Memory, and Cognition, 28,* 616–630.

Marzano, R. J., Pickering, D. J., & Pollock, J. (2001). *Classroom instruction that works: Research-based strategies for increasing student achievement.* Alexandria, VA: Association for Supervision and Curriculum Development.

Mayer, R. E. (2002). Rote versus meaningful learning. *Theory Into Practice, 41*(4), 226–232.

Mayer, R. (2003). *Learning and instruction.* Upper Saddle River, NJ: Pearson Education.

McGuiness, D., & Pribram, K. (1980). The neurophysiology of attention: Emotional and motivational controls. In M. D. Wittrock (Ed.), *The brain and psychology* (pp. 95–139). New York, NY: Academic Press.

Middleton, F., & Strick, P. (1994). Anatomical evidence for cerebellar and basal ganglia involvement in higher brain function. *Science, 226*(51584), 458–461.

Minninger, J. (1984). *Total recall: How to boost your memory power.* Emmaus, PA: Rodale.

Murnane, K., & Shiffrin, R. M. (1991). Interference and the representation of events in memory. *Journal of Experimental Psychology: Learning, Memory, & Cognition, 17*, 855–874.

Norman, D. A. (1982). *Learning and memory.* San Francisco, CA: W. H. Freeman.

Okimoto, M., & Norman, D. A. (2010). *A comprehensive strategy for better reading, cognition and emotion.* Tokyo, Japan: Kaitakusha.

Paivio, A. (1990). *Mental representations: A dual coding approach.* New York, NY: Oxford University Press.

Park, O. (1984). Example comparison strategy versus attribute identification strategy in concept learning. *American Educational Research Journal, 21*(1), 145–162.

Pascarella, E. T., & Terenzini, P. (1991). *How college affects students: Findings and insights from twenty years of research.* San Francisco, CA: Jossey-Bass.

Pascarella, E. T., & Terenzini, P. (2005). *How college affects students: A third decade of research* (Vol. 2). San Francisco, CA: Jossey-Bass.

Piaget, J. (1978). *Success and understanding.* Cambridge, MA: Harvard University Press.

Ramsden, P. (2003). *Learning to teach in higher education* (2nd ed.). London, England: RoutledgeFalmer.

Rankin, H. A., Abrams, T., Barry, R. J., Bhatnagar, S., Clayton, D. F., Colombo, J., & Thompson, R. F. (2009). Habituation revisited: An updated and revised description of the behavioral characteristics of habituation. *Neurobiology of Learning and Memory, 92*(2), 135–138.

Rosenfield, I. (1988). *The invention of memory: A new view of the brain.* New York, NY: Basic Books.

Samuels, S. J., & Flor, R. F. (1997). The importance of automaticity for developing expertise in reading. *Reading & Writing Quarterly, 13*(2), 107–121.

Schacter, D. L. (2001). *The seven sins of memory: how the mind forgets and remembers.* Boston, MA: Houghton Mifflin.

Schneider, W., & Chein, J. M. (2003). Controlled and automatic processing: Behavior, theory, and biological mechanisms. *Cognitive Science, 27*, 525–559.

Shams, W., & Seitz, K. (2011). Influences of multisensory experience on subsequent unisensory processing. *Frontiers in Perception Science, 2*(264), 1–9.

Underwood, B. J. (1983). *Attributes of memory.* Glenview, IL: Scott, Foresman.

Vygotsky, L. S. (1978). Internalization of higher cognitive functions. In M. Cole, V. John-Steiner, S. Scribner, & E. Souberman (Eds. & Trans.), *Mind in society: The development of higher psychological processes* (pp. 52–57). Cambridge, MA: Harvard University Press.

Walter, T. W., Knudsbig, G. M., & Smith, D. E. P. (2003). *Critical thinking: Building the basics* (2nd ed.). Belmont, CA: Wadsworth.

Zull, J. E. (2002). *The art of changing the brain: Enriching the practice of teaching by exploring the biology of learning.* Sterling, VA: Stylus.

Chapter 10

Career Planning: The Finishings

In this chapter, you will:

- Examine strategies for career exploration, planning, and development.
- Review action steps to take for your future career growth.
- Create documents to use in your future job search.

FINISHING

When constructing a building, whether a home, an office building, or a college library, an important step in the process is to complete the structure with finishing details. The finishings and furnishing are planned from the beginning as the final step in making the building ready for occupancy and use. Just as a building must be finished with wall treatments, window trims, baseboards, and painting, a careful plan of finishing must be completed in an academic program. This finishing would consist of careful exploration, evaluation, and preparation for a career, which is the capstone of the educational endeavor.

© 2013 by irin-k. Used under license of Shutterstock, Inc.

Galatians 6:4,
"Make a careful exploration of who you are and the work you have been given, and then sink yourself into that"
(The Message).

THE CORNERSTONE

Philippians 1:6, "Being confident of this very thing, that he which hath begun a good work in you will perform it until the day of Jesus Christ" (KJV).

On May 15, 2007, Dr. Jerry Falwell went to be with the Lord. During his lifetime, he established Thomas Road Baptist Church and two schools, Liberty Christian Academy and Liberty University. He founded ministries, such as the Elim Home and the Liberty Godparent Home. He went on missions trips and encouraged his congregation and students to do the same. He generated political change and impacted his culture by using his pulpit and TV ministry as a platform to speak against sin and to share about salvation through Jesus Christ. Because of these ministries, he led multitudes to the Lord.

As a college student, Jerry originally chose to study journalism and engineering at Lynchburg College, but after his conversion, he felt called to the ministry and transferred to Bible Baptist College in Springfield, Missouri. This decision was not an easy one. Many family members and friends worried that Jerry's decision to attend the Baptist Bible College was not the best plan for a young man with so many talents and options for a career. However, Jerry felt that God was calling him to serve Him, and he followed the call. Imagine what would have happened if he hadn't been sensitive to God's guidance in his life?

We are not all meant to be pastors, but if you are a child of God, you do have a call to serve Him. In Ephesians 4:11–16, the Apostle Paul talks about the many different roles that God's children serve in ministry:

"So Christ himself gave the apostles, the prophets, the evangelists, the pastors and teachers, to equip his people for works of service, so that the body of Christ may be built up until we all reach unity in the faith and in the knowledge of the Son of God and become mature, attaining to the whole measure of the fullness of Christ. Then we will no longer be infants, tossed back and forth by the waves, and blown here and there by every wind of teaching and by the cunning and craftiness of people in their deceitful scheming. Instead, speaking the truth in love, we will grow to become in every respect the mature body of him who is the head, that is, Christ. From him the whole body, joined and held together by every supporting ligament, grows and builds itself up in love, as each part does its work" (NIV).

What role do you feel called to? What career plan is in store for you? Now's the time to think this through and to pray for God's guidance and discernment as you select courses and begin making decisions that will impact your career path.

Dr. Falwell's life verse was Philippians 1:6, "Being confident of this very thing, that he which hath begun a good work in you will perform it until the day of Jesus Christ" (KJV). Even though Dr. Falwell is in heaven with Jesus, his work continues now "until the day of Jesus Christ" in me and in you through the ministry of Liberty University. Today, I am thankful that Dr. Jerry was sensitive to God's calling in his life, and I pray that you will be sensitive to His calling in your life, knowing that God will use the "good work" He has begun in you to impact the lives of others for generations to come.

Photo courtesy of Cali Lowdermilk
(Liberty University).

From 1990 until his passing in 2007, Dr. Jerry Falwell's office was in the Montview Mansion on the campus of Liberty University. An historic home, the Mansion is now used as a guest house and museum. Dr. Falwell's office has been preserved just as it was the day he died. The lights in his office are never turned off, representing the fact that his work continues through the lives of those hundreds of thousands of students he helped train to become "Young Champions for Christ."

Examine Strategies for Career Exploration, Planning, and Development

Jeremiah 29:11,
"For I know the plans I have for you," declares the Lord, "plans to prosper you and not to harm you, plans to give you hope and a future" (NIV).

This verse is a continuing theme throughout this textbook and with good reason: God promises that He has a plan for each of us. We know that God is good and generous and that He loves us. He tells us in Romans 8:28, "And we know that in all things God works for the good of those who love him, who have been called according to his purpose" (NIV). This is not a blanket promise that we will have just what we desire in all situations, but rather that God works things out for our *ultimate* benefit. As you look ahead to career growth and development, plan steps that lead you to the calling that God has for your life. This will be your path to blessing and fulfillment.

President Jerry Falwell, Jr.

"Our Christian faculty and staff are so committed to the student body; they see their role here as a calling, not a job" (Falwell, 2014).

Career Exploration, Preparation, and Development

The Importance of Career Planning

College graduates in the 21st century are likely to continue working until age 75 (Herman, 2000). Once you enter the workforce full time, most of the remaining waking hours of your life will be spent working. The only other single activity you'll spend more time on in your entire life is sleeping. When you consider that such a sizable portion of life is spent working, it's understandable how your career can have such a strong influence on your personal identity and self-esteem. Given the importance of career choice, the process of career exploration and planning should begin now—during the first term of your college experience.

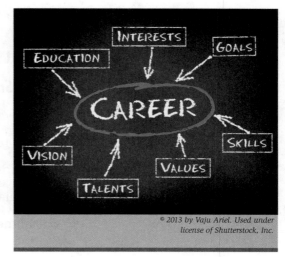

© 2013 by Vaju Ariel. Used under license of Shutterstock, Inc.

Even if you are already fully engaged in a career and are using your college coursework to grow in your career, you still need to engage in the process of career exploration and planning because you will want to determine your growth path in your organization or career. If you are using college education to help you switch or establish a career, this is even more important. You will need to decide what employment sector or type of industry you would like to work in, such as nonprofit, for-profit, education, or government. Thus, no matter how certain or uncertain you are about your career path, you still need to explore career options and start taking your first steps toward formulating a career development plan.

Becoming a 21st-Century Graduate

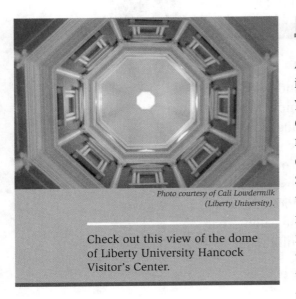

Photo courtesy of Cali Lowdermilk (Liberty University).

Check out this view of the dome of Liberty University Hancock Visitor's Center.

Although graduation seems to be in the far and distant future, it's never too soon to plan for the demands that will await you once you have your degree in hand. What will those demands be specifically? Well, that may be hard to anticipate right now when you think about how quickly our world is changing. When you consider the list of jobs in the Snapshot Summary that didn't exist 10 years ago, you can see how these careers express the global changes that have occurred in the past decade. While planning for the future seems to be full of uncertainties, you can work now with your advisor and the Career Center on identifying your abilities, interests, and values and then factor this information into your educational plan. Be sure to take full advantage of the curricular and co-curricular opportunities that align with the components of your plan. In doing so, you will prepare yourself to become a 21st-century graduate who is ready for an ever-changing world.

Jobs That Didn't Exist 10 Years Ago

Snapshot Summary

1. App developer

2. Market research data miner

3. Educational or admissions consultant

4. Millennial generation expert

5. Social media manager

6. Chief listening officer

7. Cloud computing services

8. Elder care

9. Sustainability expert

10. User experience designer

Source: Casserly (2012)

It is common for Americans to change jobs throughout their working lives. In fact, studies show that Americans change jobs 10 times in the two decades following college and that such change is even more frequent for younger workers (AAC&U, 2007). So, while you might be focused on a particular career, it's also important that you widen your focus and acquire a breadth of skills and knowledge that will make you marketable for a variety of career paths. The transferability of experiences offered by your major and the liberal arts are the keys to your success.

Not only are employers seeking job candidates with a strong foundation in their field, they want their new hires to have the 21st-century skills that will propel their companies and organizations forward. That is, their new hires need to be adaptable, innovative problem-solvers who have strong communications skills and are culturally competent when interacting with people from diverse backgrounds.

From *Thriving in College and Beyond*, 3/e by Joseph B. Cuseo, Aaron Thompson, Michele Campagna and Viki S. Fecas. Copyright © 2013 by Kendall Hunt Publishing Company. Reprinted by permission.

Dr. Elmer Towns, co-founder

"God has a plan for your life. I want to challenge you this year: Find that plan, and do it" (Liberty University News Service, 2014).

Strategies for Career Exploration and Preparation

Reaching an effective decision about a career involves the same four steps involved in setting and reaching any personal goal:

Step 1. Self-Awareness

Self-awareness is a particularly important step to take when making career decisions because your career choice says a lot about who you are, what you value, and what you want from life. Your career choice should be based on and built around your personal identity and life goals, not the other way around.

Dr. Elmer Towns

"What could God use you to do? What's your dream of doing something for God?" (McKay, 2009).

Alissa Keith

"In planning your career, follow your dream as long as that dream includes paying all your bills, living a contented life, and serving the Lord."

One way to gain greater self-awareness of where your career interests may lie is by taking psychological tests or assessments, such as Focus 2. This will allow you to see how your interests match you to certain career fields. When making choices about a career, in addition to your interests, abilities, and values, you should also be aware of your personal needs. A *need* may be described as something stronger than an interest. When you do something that satisfies a personal need, you're doing something that makes your life more personally satisfying and fulfilling (Melton, 1995). Psychologists have identified several important human needs that vary in strength or intensity from person to person.

Personal Needs to Consider When Making Career Choices

As you read the needs in this box, make a note after each one indicating how strong the need is for you (high, moderate, or low).

1. **Autonomy.** Need for working independently without close supervision or control. Individuals with a high need for autonomy would experience greater fulfillment working in careers that allow them to be their own boss, make their own decisions, and control their own work schedule. *moderate*

2. **Affiliation.** Need for social interaction, a sense of belonging, and the opportunity to collaborate with others. Individuals with a high need for affiliation would experience greater fulfillment working in careers that involve frequent interpersonal interaction and teamwork with colleagues or co-workers. *moderate to high*

3. **Achievement.** Need to experience challenge and a sense of personal accomplishment. Individuals with high achievement needs would feel a stronger sense of fulfillment working in careers that push them to solve problems, generate creative ideas, and continually learn new information or master new skills. *high*

4. **Recognition.** Need for prestige, status, and respect from others. Individuals with high recognition needs are likely to feel satisfied working in careers that are perceived by family, friends, and society to be prestigious or high-ranking. *moderate to high*

5. **Sensory stimulation.** Need for experiencing variety, change, and risk. Individuals with a high need for sensory stimulation are more likely to be satisfied working in careers that involve frequent changes of pace and place (e.g., travel), unpredictable events (e.g., work tasks that vary considerably), and moderate stress (e.g., working under pressure of competition or deadlines). *high*

Sources: Baumeister & Leary (1995); Chua & Koestner (2008); Deci & Ryan (2002); Ryan (1995)

In summary, four key personal characteristics should be considered when exploring and choosing a career: abilities, interests, values, and needs. These core characteristics are the pillars that provide the foundational support for making effective career choices and decisions. You want to choose a career that you're good at, interested in, and passionate about and that fulfills your personal needs.

Lastly, since a career choice is a long-range decision that involves life beyond college, self-awareness should involve not only reflection on where you are now, but also self-projection—reflecting on how you see yourself in the future. When you engage in the process of self-projection, you begin to see a connection between where you are now and where you want or hope to be.

Ideally, your choice of a career should be one that leads to the best-case future scenario in which your typical day goes something like this: You wake up in the morning and hop out of bed enthusiastically, eagerly looking forward to what you'll be doing at work that day. When you're at work, time flies by; before you know it, the day's over. When you go to bed at night and reflect on your day, you feel good about what you did and how well you did it. In order for this ideal scenario to have any chance of becoming (or even approaching) reality, you should make every attempt to select a career path that's is true to yourself and leads you to a career that's "in sync" with your abilities (what you do well), your interests (what you like to do), your values (what you feel good about doing), and your needs (what provides you with a sense of satisfaction and personal fulfillment).

Step 2. Awareness of Your Options

In addition to self-awareness and self-knowledge, making an effective decision about your career path also requires knowledge about the nature of different careers and the realities of the work world. The first place to go for information on and help with career exploration and planning is Liberty University's Virtual Career Center. Besides helping you explore your personal career interests and abilities, this is your campus resource for learning about the nature of different careers and for strategies on locating career-related work experiences.

Photo courtesy of Kevin Manguiob (Liberty University).

Students enjoy time at Snowlex, Liberty University's year-round ski facility.

Mary Dixon

"As Colossians 3:23-24 says, 'Whatever you do, work at it with all your heart, as working for the Lord, not for human masters, since you know that you will receive an inheritance from the Lord as a reward. It is the Lord Christ you are serving' (NIV). God has called you to a work that will bring about his kingdom. Seek his kingdom and then do all that He has given you to do. This is the service and the reward!"

Photo courtesy of Joel Coleman (Liberty University).

This bench in the rooftop garden of DeMoss Hall features beautiful details in the iron, while supplying a place for students to relax.

Personal Reflection

Project yourself 10 years into the future and visualize your ideal career and your ideal life.

1. What are you spending most of your time doing during your typical workday?

   Investigating, problem solving, making connections, bringing wrong to right

2. Where and with whom are you working?

   Where? Canada. Coworkers traveling

3. How many hours are you working per week?

   30 - 40 hours

4. Where are you living?

   In Canada with my husband

5. Are you married or in a committed relationship? Do you have children?

   Married. Children are on the way.

6. How does your work influence your home life?

   Raising my children. Being there for them physically & emotionally

Jennifer Griffin

Prov 3:6, "In all your ways acknowledge him, and he will make straight your paths" (ESV).

Career planning is an important part of being a student. Whether you're starting your college journey at 18 years old or 68 years young, it's important to consider how you will use your education in the future. The Lord has placed in you a desire and passion for particular interests. You may have a natural inclination toward numbers and math, working with children and adults, or maybe the Lord has blessed you with an inquisitive mind with an aptitude for the sciences. No matter what your interests, you can be used by the Lord in any career! It is likely you will have many different jobs throughout your lifetime and your career will be formed as you move from one learning experience to another. No matter your profession, you can be certain the Lord has a special role for you in His plan. How he uses you will take many shapes and sizes. It delights the Lord when we follow His plan for our lives, and develop the passions He gives us!"

Katie Robinson

"A college degree is more than a piece of paper or a lofty goal. Instead, students have the chance to learn more about themselves and use these lessons to help expand career opportunities. Perhaps, even, those lessons will help students discover areas of interest in careers that they hadn't previously thought to explore."

If you were to ask people to name as many careers as they could, they wouldn't come close to naming the 900 career titles listed by the federal government in its Occupational Information Network. Many of these careers you may have never heard of, yet some of them may be good career choices for you. You can learn more about the multitude of careers available to you in the following ways:

- Reading about careers (in books or online)
- Taking career development courses
- Interviewing people in different career fields
- Observing (shadowing) people at work in different careers

- Volunteering or service learning

- Part-time work

- Internships (paid or unpaid).

Resources on Careers

Your Career Center and the Liberty University Jerry Falwell Library are campus resources where you can find a wealth of reading material on careers, either in print or online. Listed below are some of the best sources of written information on careers.

Dictionary of Occupational Titles (DOT) (www.occupationalinfo.org). This is the largest printed resource on careers; it contains concise definitions of more than 17,000 jobs. It also includes information on:

- Work tasks typically performed by people in different careers.

- Background experiences of people working in different careers that qualified them for their positions.

- Types of knowledge, skills, and abilities required for different careers.

- Interests, values, and needs of individuals who find working in particular careers to be personally rewarding.

Occupational Outlook Handbook (OOH) (www.bls.gov/oco). This contains descriptions of approximately 250 positions, including information on the nature of work, work conditions, places of employment, training or education required for career entry and advancement, salaries, careers in related fields, and additional sources of information about particular careers (e.g., professional organizations and governmental agencies). A distinctive feature of this resource is that it contains information about the future employment outlook for different careers.

Encyclopedia of Careers and Vocational Guidance (Chicago: Ferguson Press). This is an encyclopedia of information on qualifications, salaries, and advancement opportunities for a wide variety of careers.

Occupational Information Network (O*NET) Online (www. online.onetcenter.org). This is America's most comprehensive source of online information about careers. It contains an up-to-date set of descriptions for almost 1,000 careers, plus lots of other information similar to what you would find in print in the *Dictionary of Occupational Titles*.

Dr. Jerry Falwell

"I have an obligation to my children and to their children, to see to it that when I am gone I have left behind a legacy called freedom, liberty, morality and decency" (Falwell, 1996, p. 70).

Dr. Jerry Falwell

"God never promised to keep you out of trouble; but He does promise to be with you through all your troubles" (Falwell, 1996, p. 98).

Terry

"Seek the Lord's will in your life; oftentimes, you'll find that it is both challenging and fulfilling in a way you've never known before."

Photo courtesy of Kevin Manguiob (Liberty University).

Faculty tour the new Jerry Falwell Library which was still under construction on August 30, 2013.

Maddy

Q: *Did you seek an exciting career, a challenging career, or to find God's will for your work life? What advice would you give new learners about this?*

A: "I think that when you determine God's will for your life, it will be an exciting career to you. Going through multiple majors has helped me see that once you've found what God wants you to be doing, it really does become really interesting and fun to study and become better at the necessary skills for that line of work. It may also be challenging, but if you have the zeal for it, the enthusiasm required to get past the tough spots comes with it."

In addition to these general sources of information, your Career Center and Liberty University Jerry Falwell Library have other books and published materials related to specific careers or occupations (e.g., careers for English majors). You can also learn a lot about careers by simply reading advertisements for position openings in your local newspaper or online at such sites as www.careerbuilder.com and college.monster.com. When reading position descriptions, make special note of the tasks, duties, or responsibilities they involve and ask yourself whether these positions are compatible with your personal abilities, interests, needs, and values.

Review Action Steps to Take for Your Future Career Growth

II Chronicles 15:7,
"But as for you, be strong and do not give up, for your work will be rewarded" (NIV).

Action Steps to Plan Now

Information Interviews

One of the best and most overlooked ways to get accurate information about a career is to interview professionals working in that career. Career development specialists refer to this strategy as information interviewing. Don't assume that working professionals aren't interested in taking time to speak with a student; most are open to being interviewed and many report that they enjoy it (Crosby, 2002).

Information interviews provide you inside, realistic information about what careers are like because you're getting that information directly from the horse's mouth. The interview process also helps you gain experience and confidence in interview situations, which may help you prepare for future job interviews. Furthermore, if you make a good impression during information interviews, the people you interview may suggest that you contact them again after graduation to see if there are position openings. If there is an opening, you might find yourself being the interviewee instead of the interviewer (and you might find yourself a job).

Career Observation (Shadowing)

In addition to learning about careers from reading and interviews, you can experience careers more directly by placing yourself in workplace situations and work environments that allow you to observe workers performing their daily duties. Two programs may be available to you that will allow you to observe working professionals:

- **Job shadowing programs.** These programs enable you to follow (shadow) and observe a professional during a typical workday.

T. Marcus Christian

"Career planning begins in your first semester of college. This is a time to explore the paths you hope to take with courses that may interest you. When you find that one set of classes that spikes your interest, you will finish school with a clear path and a smile."

Nathaniel Valle

"A professor once told me to 'think about your next step long before you have to walk.' As you think about that next step in your collegiate career, utilize the tools and knowledge you have gained in this course to plan beyond it. If you are already working in a professional career, consider how you can use INFT 101 to enhance your work environment and relationships."

Jenny Walter

"Now that you are actually in college, you want to choose the path of study you will walk down. Interests or advancement in your job can be a motivating factor in the course you will follow. If you are still unsure, looking at all of the different paths you can take with the various majors offered can help you decide which course of study to follow."

Hanna Bruce

"Get to know someone who works in the field of your prospective profession. Ask this person about the pros and cons of his or her line of work, specific requirements that may be needed for the position and if he or she has any advice to pass along. This may help you determine whether or not this career is right for you."

- **Externship programs.** These programs are basically an extended version of job shadowing that lasts for a longer time period (e.g., two or three days).

Information interviewing, job shadowing, and externships can supply great information about a career. However, information is not experience. To get career-related work experience, you have three good options:

- Internships
- Volunteer work or service learning
- Part-time work.

Internships

In contrast to job shadowing or externships, where you observe someone at work, an internship actively involves you in the work itself and gives you the opportunity to perform career-related work duties. A distinguishing feature of internships is that you can receive academic credit and sometimes financial compensation for the work you do. An internship usually totals 120 or more work hours, which may be completed at the same time you're enrolled in a full schedule of classes or when you're not taking classes. A major advantage of internships is that they enable students to avoid the classic catch-22 situation they often run into when interviewing for their first career position after graduation. The interview scenario usually goes something like this: The potential employer asks the college graduate, "What work experience have you had in this field?" The recent graduate replies, "I haven't had any work experience because I've been a full-time student." You can avoid this scenario by completing an internship during your college experience.

Internships are typically available to college students during their junior or senior year. Check with the Career Center to determine if this option may be available to you. You can also pursue internships on your own by consulting published guides that describe various career-related internships, along with information on how to apply for them (e.g., *Peterson's Internships* and the *Vault Guide to Top Internships*). Information on internships may also be available from the local chamber of commerce in your hometown or even the company you work for now.

Volunteer Work or Service Learning

Volunteering not only provides a service to your community, it also serves you by giving you the opportunity to explore different work environments and gain work experience in career fields that relate to your area of service.

For example, volunteer work performed for different age groups (e.g., children, adolescents, or the elderly) and in different work environments (e.g., hospital, school, or laboratory) provides you with firsthand work experience and simultaneously allows you to test your interest in careers related to these age groups and work environments.

Volunteer work also enables you to network with professionals who may serve as excellent references and resources for letters of recommendation for you. Furthermore, if these professionals are impressed with your volunteer work, they may become interested in hiring you part-time while you're still in college or full time when you graduate.

Personal Reflection

Have you done volunteer work? If you have, did you learn anything about yourself or anything from your volunteer work that might help you identify careers that best match your interests, talents, and values?

Not yet.

Part-Time Work

Part-time work can provide opportunities to learn or develop skills that may be relevant to your future career, such as organizational skills, communication skills, and ability to work effectively with co-workers from diverse backgrounds and cultures. It's also possible that work in a part-time position may eventually turn into a fulltime career.

Learning about careers through firsthand experience in actual work settings (e.g., shadowing, internships, volunteer services, and part-time work) is critical to successful career exploration and preparation. There is simply no substitute for direct, hands-on experience for gaining knowledge about careers. These firsthand experiences represent the ultimate career reality test. They allow you direct access to information about what careers are like, as opposed to how they are portrayed on TV or in the movies, which often paint an inaccurate or unrealistic picture of careers and make them appear more exciting or glamorous than they are.

Terry Conner

"It's never too late or too early to start thinking about your future employment. Seek out and research companies/industries that you think you'd be interested in joining. This serves a dual purpose; it can reinforce your desire to join that company and it can help you narrow the list of companies. Once you have this information you can then use the time to work on the skills that will make you more desirable to the company."

In summary, firsthand experiences in actual work settings equip you with five powerful career advantages. You can

- Learn about what work is like in a particular field.

- Test your interest and skills for certain types of work.

- Strengthen your resume by adding experiential learning to academic learning.

- Acquire contacts who may serve as personal references and sources for letters of recommendation.

- Network with employers who may hire you or refer you for a position after graduation.

Furthermore, gaining firsthand work experience early in college not only promotes your job prospects after graduation, but also makes you a more competitive candidate for internships and part-time positions that you may apply for during college.

Be sure to use university resources (e.g., the Career Center and Financial Aid Office), local resources (e.g., Chamber of Commerce), and your personal contacts (e.g., family and friends) to locate and participate in work experiences that relate to your career interests. When you land a work experience, work hard at it, learn as much as you can from it, and build relationships with as many people there as possible, because these are the people who can provide you with future contacts, references, and referrals. Research indicates that as many as 75 percent of all jobs are obtained through interpersonal relationships, i.e., "networking" (Brooks, 2009).

Step 3. Awareness of What Best Fits You

Effective decision making requires identifying all relevant factors that need to be considered and determining how much weight (influence) each of these factors should carry. As we've emphasized throughout this chapter, the factor that should carry the greatest weight in career decision making is the match between your career choice and your personal abilities, interests, needs, and values.

A good career decision should involve more than salary and should take into consideration how the career will affect different dimensions of yourself (social, emotional, physical, etc.) at different stages of your life: adulthood, middle age, and late adulthood. It's almost inevitable that your career will affect your identity, the type of person you become, how you balance the demands of work and family, and how well you serve others beyond yourself. An effective career decision-making process requires you to make tough and thoughtful decisions about what matters most to you.

Roger

"I was hired to teach a self-contained special education classroom at a public middle school. The amazing thing is that I was asked to come in for an interview three days before the start of the fall classes. My first day in the classroom was literally the first day of school! Since that day I received the educator of the year award for the entire school. I have had opportunities to take continuing education workshops and be certified as a highly qualified educator. I have had a positive impact on the lives of students with disabilities and have developed opportunities to bless fellow colleagues.

"But my greater joy is teaching as an online instructor for Liberty University School of Religion. I am truly blessed to interact with students from all across the country as well as students who are engaged with the military."

Step 4. Awareness of the Process

Whether you're keeping your career options open or you want to develop in your current position or career, you can start taking early steps for successful entry into, or continued growth of your career by using the following strategies.

Self-Monitoring: Watching and Tracking Your Personal Skills and Positive Qualities

Don't forget that the learning skills you acquire in college become the earning skills in your career after college. It may appear that you're just developing *academic* skills, but you're also developing *career* skills. When you're engaged in the process of completing academic tasks (such as note-taking, reading, writing papers, and taking tests), you're strengthening career-relevant skills (such as analysis, synthesis, communication, and problem solving).

The general education skills and qualities developed by the liberal arts component of your college education are critical to *career advancement* (your ability to move up the career ladder) and *career mobility* (your ability to move into different career paths). General educational skills enable workers to move into and take on different positions, which is important in today's work world. On average, Americans now change jobs ten times by the time they're 40 years old (Association of American Colleges and Universities, 2007). Specific technical skills are important for getting you into a particular career, but general educational skills enable you to move into different careers and move up the career ladder. These skills are growing more important for college graduates entering the workforce in the 21st century because the demand for upper-level positions in management and leadership will exceed the supply of workers available to fill these positions (Herman, 2000). The courses you take as part of your general education will prepare you for advanced career positions, not just your first one after you complete your degree (Boyer, 1987; Miller, 2003).

Students often think it's the final product (a college diploma) that provides them with the passport to a good job and career success (AAC&U, 2007; Sullivan, 1993). However, for most employers of college graduates, what matters much more than the credential are the skills and personal qualities the job applicant brings to the job (Education Commission of the States, 1995; Figler & Bolles, 2007). You can start building these skills and qualities through effective *self-monitoring*—keeping track of the skills you're using and developing during your college experience. Skills are mental habits, and like all other habits that are repeatedly practiced, their development can be so gradual that you may not even notice how much growth is taking place—perhaps somewhat like watching grass grow. Thus, career

Tim

"The career path that I have chosen and been called to is in religion. I am not quite sure what it will entail; however, I do know that it is something that I use almost every day. Each day I answer questions about different religions, God, and the Bible that Marines are curious about. I absolutely love talking about these matters with the Marines that I work with and I would love it if God opened the door for me to be a chaplain in any military service."

development specialists recommend that you consciously reflect on the skills you're using so that you remain aware of them and are ready to "sell" them to potential employers (Lock, 2004).

The key to discovering career-relevant skills and positive personal qualities is to get in the habit of stepping back from your academic and out-of-class experiences to reflect on what skills and qualities these experiences involved and then get them down in writing before they slip your mind. One strategy you can use to track your developing skills is to keep a *career development journal* in which you note academic tasks and assignments you've completed, along with the skills you used to complete them. Also, don't forget to record skills in your journal that you've developed in non-academic situations, such as skills used while performing part-time jobs, personal hobbies, and volunteer services.

Create Documents to Use in Your Future Job Search

Matthew 7:7,
"**Ask** and it will be given to you; **seek** and you will find; **knock** and the door will be opened to you" (NIV).

As you begin to consider the path ahead in your career development plan, it may seem that the career opportunities you are pursuing are still a long way off, and you may become discouraged. Do not let the steps in the process deter your progress: Keep moving forward! This verse can help you think of the steps you will take: Ask, seek, knock. **Ask:** Verbalize what you are pursuing. **Seek:** This is an action verb that indicates that you will actively pursue opportunities to build your skills and hone your strengths. **Knock:** Look around you for those who can help you secure the job you want. Ask for their help with references, a job internship opportunity, or networking for your success.

Self-Marketing: Packaging and Presenting Your Personal Strengths and Achievements

One way to help convert your college degree into gainful employment is to view yourself (a college graduate) as a product and future employers as customers who may be interested in purchasing your product (your skills and attributes). As a first year student, it could be said that you're in the early stages of developing your product. Begin the process now of developing and packaging your skills and attributes so that by the time you graduate, you've developed into a high-quality product that potential employers will notice and be interested in purchasing.

An effective self-marketing plan is one that gives employers a clear idea of what you can bring to the table and do for them. You can effectively market or advertise your personal skills, qualities, and achievements to future employers through the following channels.

Tracey Good

"As a Career Counselor, we meet with all majors and so would first encourage our students to take the Focus 2 Assessment. This will either help to confirm your major or will give them ideas on what types of jobs you could pursue within your area of strength. You will be tested on their interests (both work and leisure), personality, skills, and values."

Course Transcript

Your course transcript is a listing of all courses you enrolled in and the grades you received in those courses. Two pieces of information included on your college transcript can strongly influence employers' hiring decisions or admissions committee decisions about your acceptance to a graduate or professional school: (1) the grades you earned in your courses, and (2) the types of courses you completed.

Simply stated, the better grades you earn in college, the better are your employment prospects after college. Research on college graduates indicates that higher grades improve the following:

- The prestige of their first job
- Their total earnings (salary and fringe benefits)
- Their job mobility (ability to change jobs or positions) This relationship between higher college grades and greater career success exists for students at all types of colleges and universities; regardless of the reputation or prestige of the institution they attend (Pascarella & Terenzini, 1991; 2005).

Personal Portfolio

A portfolio could include such items as:

- Outstanding papers, exam performances, research projects, or lab reports
- Artwork and photos from study abroad, service learning, or internship experiences
- Video footage of oral presentations or theatrical performances
- Recordings of musical performances
- Assessments from employers or coaches
- Letters of recognition or commendation.

You can start the process of portfolio development right now by saving your best work and performances. Store them in a traditional portfolio folder or save them on a computer disc to create an electronic portfolio. Another option would be to create a website and upload your materials there. Eventually, you'll be able to build a well-stocked portfolio that documents your skills and demonstrates your development to future employers or future schools.

Tracey Good

"Have an end goal in mind. What type of job are you wanting to pursue? It's never too early to begin research within your field. We have a job database that is specific to Liberty University. It's our version of a monster.com and has jobs and internships from employers who are seeking Liberty talent. We have national and global positions listed. You can go to www.liberty.edu/lunetwork to join for FREE. You need to be aware of the job description of interest and know what skills you need to be achieving while taking your classes. This needs to be a part of your research process."

Tracey Good

"The Career Center also helps with resumes, interviews, graduate school preparation, and more. Our students can visit www.liberty.edu/careers to help with their specific career planning needs."

Personal Resume

Unlike a portfolio, which contains actual products or samples of your work, a resume may be described as a listed summary of your most important accomplishments, skills, and credentials. If you have just graduated from high school, you may not have accumulated enough experiences to construct a fully developed resume. However, you can start to build a skeletal resume that contains major categories or headings (the skeleton) under which you'll eventually include your experiences and accomplishments, as well as skills you developed and problems you solved. As you acquire experiences, you can flesh out the resume by gradually filling in its general categories with your skills, accomplishments and new credentials.

Jess Cromley

"One strategy that I always found helpful in my undergraduate program was to request 'informational interviews' with the people who worked in a job I found exciting or interesting. Being able to ask questions like 'What is a typical day' or 'What is the hardest part of your job' allowed me to consider the answers as way to determine if I could handle that in my own career."

Updating Your Resume

Here is a standard resume template that you can use as you add skills and experiences through college. Begin with the standard information and then, under each heading, list any experiences or skills that you've already acquired. Then, return to each heading and add (in a different color) any experiences or skills you plan to acquire during your college experience. Finally, review your entries under each heading and identify any experiences or skills that may result in work products or artifacts that you can include in a personal portfolio.

NAME
(First, Middle, Last)
Current Addresses: Permanent Addresses:
Postal address Postal address
E-mail address E-mail address (be sure it's professional)
Phone number Phone number

EDUCATION: Liberty University
Degree Name (e.g., Bachelor of Science)
College Major (e.g., Accounting)
Graduation Date
GPA

RELATED WORK: Position Title, City, State, Start and stop dates

EXPERIENCES: (Begin the list with the most recent position and dates held.)
(List skills you used or developed.)

VOLUNTEER (COMMUNITY SERVICE) EXPERIENCES:
(List skills you used or developed.)

NOTABLE COURSEWORK
(e.g., leadership, interdisciplinary, or intercultural courses; study abroad experiences)

PERSONAL SKILLS AND POSITIVE QUALITIES:
(List as bullets; be sure to include those that are especially relevant to the position for which you're applying.)

HONORS AND AWARDS:
(In addition to those received in college, you may include those received in high school if you are young)

PERSONAL INTERESTS:
(Include special hobbies or talents that may not be directly tied to school or work experiences.)

Nicole Lowes

"#1) Before deciding on a career path I would recommend that students do some 'Job Shadowing'. Spend a day or two with a professional in your field of interest. Students typically have a preconceived idea of what a career looks like (possibly because they heard about it from a friend, or see it on TV) when in actuality it is something very different. Students who take the time to job shadow sometimes realize that the career they thought they wanted is definitely not what they expected. This prevents them from changing majors multiple times throughout their college journey. (I.e., If someone wants to become a nurse to help people and then realizes they can't handle blood.)

#2) Once a student has decided on a career path it is important for them to research what it will take to actually work in that field. Many students believe that an undergraduate degree will get them the job of their dreams, which as well all know, is rarely the case. I think it is important for them to understand that most careers will take additional schooling beyond their initial BS degree. For instance, students think they can become a counselor with a degree in Psychology not realizing that it is going to take another 3 years for a masters and then 4000 hours of supervision. Or they think they can become a Physical Therapist with a degree in Health Science without understanding that Physical Therapy School is an additional 3-year program. So having the student understand what the full journey looks like to get them to the end goal is important.

#3) Once a student has decided on their career path, it is important for them to figure out what skills are necessary in that career so they can begin developing them in their college years. Does the chosen career take excellent writing skills, strong attention to detail, etc.? How can they begin developing those skills while in college to prove they are a worthy candidate for a position in the field of their choice once they have successfully graduated?

(continues on next page)

Letters of Recommendation (Letters of Reference)

Letters of recommendation can serve to support and document your skills and strengths. To maximize the power of your personal recommendations, give careful thought to (1) who should serve as your references, (2) how to approach them, and (3) what to provide them.

The Art and Science of Requesting Letters of Recommendation: Effective Strategies and Common Courtesies

1. Select recommendations from people who know you well.

2. Seek a balanced blend of letters from people who have observed your performance in different settings or situations:
   - The classroom
   - In the community (volunteer service, internship, etc.).

3. Pick the right time and place to make your request. Be sure to request your letter well in advance of the letter's deadline date (e.g., at least two weeks).

4. Waive your right to see the letter.

5. Provide your references with a fact sheet about yourself.

6. Provide your references with a stamped, addressed envelope.

7. Follow up with a thank-you note.

8. Let your references know the outcome of your application.

One of the best ways to acquire accurate information about a career that interests you is to interview a working professional in that career. This career exploration strategy is known as an *information interview.* An information interview enables you to (1) get an insider's view of what the career is really like, (2) network with a professional in the field, and (3) gain confidence in interview situations that prepares you for later future job interviews.

Steps in the Information Interview Process

1. Select a career that you may be interested in pursuing. Even if you're currently keeping your career options open, pick a career that might be a possibility.

2. Find someone who is working in the career you selected and set up an information interview with that person. To locate possible interview

candidates, consider members of your family, friends of your family members, and family members of your friends.

The Career Center on campus and the Alumni Association may connect you with graduates or professionals working in the local community near you, who are willing to talk about their careers with students.

The Yellow Pages or the Internet may also be used to locate names and contact information for interview candidates. Send candidates a short letter or e-mail asking about the possibility of scheduling a short interview, and mention that you would be willing to conduct the interview in person or by phone, whichever would be more convenient for them. If you don't hear back within a reasonable period (e.g., within a couple of weeks), send a follow-up message. If you don't receive a response to the follow-up message, then consider contacting someone else.

3. Conduct an information interview with the professional who has agreed to speak with you. Consider using the following suggested strategies.

Nicole Lowes (continued)

#4) Once a career path is chosen it is important to understand what is required in the transition between undergraduate programs and graduate programs. Many graduate programs require students to take specific courses before they are eligible for enrollment. So if a student chooses to go on to graduate school it is important for them to research that information during their junior/senior year to make sure they are meeting the requirements. I.e. Each Physical Therapy school requires different science courses as pre-reqs. It is important for student to know which courses they must take in order to be eligible for the school they desire to go to."

Tips for Conducting Information Interviews

- **Thank the person for taking the time to speak with you.** This should be the first thing you do after meeting the person—before you officially begin the interview.

- **Prepare your interview questions in advance.** Here are some questions that you might consider asking:

  1. During a typical day's work, what do you spend most of your time doing?
  2. What do you like most about your career?
  3. What are the most difficult or frustrating aspects of your career?
  4. What personal skills or qualities do you see as being critical for success in your career?
  5. How did you decide on your career?
  6. What personal qualifications or prior experiences enabled you to enter your career?
  7. How does someone find out about openings in your field?
  8. What steps did you take to find your current position?
  9. What advice would you give first-year students about what they might do at this stage of their college experience to help prepare them to enter your career?
  10. How does someone advance in your career?
  11. Are there any moral issues or ethical challenges that tend to arise in your career?

12. Are members of diverse groups likely to be found in your career? (This is an especially important question to ask if you're a member of an ethnic, racial, or gender group that is underrepresented in the career field.)

13. What impact does your career have on your home life or personal life outside of work?

14. If you had to do it all over again, would you choose the same career?

15. Would you recommend that I speak with anyone else to obtain additional information or a different perspective on this career field? (If the answer is "Yes," you may follow up by asking, "May I mention that you referred me?") It's always a good idea to obtain more than one person's perspective before making an important choice, especially one that can have a major influence on your life, such as your career choice.

■ **Take notes during the interview.** This not only benefits you by helping you remember what was said, but also sends a positive message to the persons you interview because it shows them that their ideas are important and worth writing down.

Final Note: If the interview goes well, you might ask whether you could observe or shadow your interviewee during a day at work.

From *Thriving in College and Beyond*, 3/e by Joseph B. Cuseo, Aaron Thompson, Michele Campagna and Viki S. Fecas. Copyright © 2013 by Kendall Hunt Publishing Company. Reprinted by permission.

BUILDING BLOCKS

In national surveys, employers rank attitude of the job applicant as the number one factor in making hiring decisions. They rate this higher in importance than such factors as reputation of the applicant's school, previous work experience, and recommendations of former employers (Education Commission of the States, 1995; Institute for Research on Higher Education, 1995; National Association of Colleges & Employers, 2012b). However, many college students think that it's the degree itself—the credential or piece of paper—that will get them the career they want (AAC&U, 2007).

Graduating from college with a diploma in hand may make you a more competitive job candidate, but you still have to compete by documenting and selling your strengths and skills. Your diploma doesn't work like a merit badge or passport that you flash to gain automatic access to your dream job. Your college experience opens career doors for you, but it's your attitude, initiative, and effort that enable you to step through those doors and into a successful career.

From *Thriving in College and Beyond*, 3/e by Joseph B. Cuseo, Aaron Thompson, Michele Campagna and Viki S. Fecas. Copyright © 2013 by Kendall Hunt Publishing Company. Reprinted by permission.

Back in Chapter 1, we mentioned that Dr. Falwell, the founder of Liberty University, set "big, hairy, audacious goals" from the time he was a young man up until the day he died. What career goals do you have in place now? Are they ones you feel God is leading you to pursue, or are they ones that originated with you? At times, it seems that God is calling us to tasks that are bigger than we are or are ones we are not capable of achieving. Are you familiar with the story of how God called Moses? We read the story in Exodus in the Bible's *Old Testament*. Moses, a son of Hebrew parents, was raised in the palace of the Egyptian pharaoh. He ran away from Egypt and spent 40 years away, tending his father-in-law's sheep. One day, God called Moses to a special job in a very dramatic way . . . He spoke to him from a burning bush! Imagine that! Do you suppose Moses set off right away to follow God's direction? Not quite, for Moses insisted to God that he was unprepared for the task of leading God's people out of Egypt, where they had been for 400 years. Rather than go straightaway and relay God's message to the Egyptian leader, Moses responded with a "Who, me?"

Photo courtesy of Dave Moquin.

Construction workers expand the top level of Williams Stadium, making it the beautiful, state-of-the-art facility it is today!

attitude! Eventually, Moses came around and followed God's direction. He became the leader of the exiles who left Egypt to go to the land God had promised their ancestors. From a humble shepherd to a leader of hundreds of thousands, Moses followed where God called him. Have you heard the expression, "God does not call the equipped, He equips the called"? Think on the story of Moses' call and reflect on how that "equipping" might play out in your life.

What tasks stand between you and completion of the career goals you have set? Do you have both a short-term plan and a long-term plan for the future? What steps will be required to move from where you are now to live out your plans? What obstacles do you see in your path? Are your plans not only God-honoring but also God-inspired? In Mark 3:35, Jesus says, "Whoever does God's will is my brother and sister and mother" (NIV). That is an exciting prospect. What does "doing God's will" look like for you? How does it reflect in your career plan? Are the characteristics you possess, along with your skills, relevant to the career choice you are pursuing? Are you able to connect your personality, skills, education, and drive to achieve the career goals you have set for yourself?

TOOL BOX

Career Center

The Career Center at Liberty University is your one-stop shop for all things to do with preparing yourself for a career. Here are just a handful of the services available to Liberty students through the Career Center:

- **Focus 2**—This program is designed to assist you in the process of assessing your interests, options, talents, and values. Liberty University students may register and use the tool for free. Once registered, you will work your way through a series of self-assessments, each designed to explore and expose different aspects of your interests, talents, and values. Upon completing the assessments, you will be able to explore a large database of degree and career options, each cross-referenced against your results in order to show you which ones are most compatible with your goals.

- **Resume Service**—Liberty offers a full line of resume assistance to active students and alumni. You can access sample resumes and cover letters, rubrics for grading the quality of your own resume, samples of resumes listed by major area of study, webinars on effective resume writing, software to assist you in writing the perfect resume, and even have an expert in the Career Center personally critique your resume.

- **LU Network**—Looking for an internship, full-time, or part-time position? Use the LU Network tool on the Career Center page, and you just might find the perfect position for you. LU Network is similar to other employment tools except the employers listed in this database are specifically looking for Liberty University graduates.

- **Phone Appointments**—All of the online tools are wonderful, but the Career Center at Liberty takes it a step further by offering personal meetings with online students by phone. Appointments last about 30 minutes and can range in purpose from reviewing the results and meaning of your Focus 2 assessment to conducting a mock interview.

On top of these great services, the Career Center also offers things like portfolio development, networking advice, graduate school preparation, and more.

Alumni Relations

Get involved early with the Liberty Alumni Association. The alumni site has listings of physical and virtual groups from around the globe. You can utilize these groups to connect and network with other Liberty alum who know just what it takes to be successful after graduation.

Portfolios

- **Cloud-based storage**—When developing a portfolio, consider the use of cloud-based storage options. These are free sites that store your files on the Internet and allow you to access them from anywhere in the world. You can use this space as a personal storage drive, but most will also allow you to share documents and folders with outside users, which is perfect for creating an online portfolio. Once you register you will be able to download a small software program that lets you use your cloud drive just like you would use any other storage folder on your computer. When it comes time to share your work, you can make an entire document or folder public so that anyone can view it, or you can limit who you share with by entering specific email addresses. Dropbox, GoogleDrive, and SkyDrive are three of the biggest names on the market right now.

- **Websites**—Another option for creating an online portfolio is to create a website. This can be a bit more complex than managing a cloud drive, but it also affords you the ability to create an aesthetically pleasing interface, which could be more appealing to prospective employers. Google Sites and WordPress are great free options for creating your first site. There is a learning curve, but these sites also offer tutorials to help you learn your way.

Resume Building

- **Course Selection**—As a Liberty student you can utilize the course catalog and your online ASIST account to locate and register for courses that will add to the "breadth of your experience." Do you need computer skills? Try signing up for INFT 110 or CMIS 210. Would additional language skills benefit you as you work toward a position as an inner-city teacher? Try one of Liberty's conversational language courses.

- **Syllabi**—Besides selecting courses that will broaden your skill set and appeal, you can also use the syllabi for those classes to help craft your resume. Each of the measurable learning outcomes in the course syllabus represents a skill that you may potentially acquire. Why not copy these into a working resume for later use?

Letters of Reference

- **Faculty**—An often-overlooked concept for online students is the power of a good letter of reference from an instructor. Develop a relationship with your professors and let them know who you are. Consider asking them if they teach classes other than the ones you are currently taking. If you develop a good relationship, it is likely they will remember you, increasing the chances that they would be willing to write a letter of reference for you.

Additional resources and links to specific sites, worksheets, and apps can be located by accessing the Breaking Ground website:

www.breakinggroundlu.com

References

Association of American Colleges and Universities (AAC&U). (2007). *College learning for the new global century.* Washington, DC: Author.

Boyer, E. L. (1987). *College: The undergraduate experience in America.* New York, NY: Harper & Row.

Brooks, K. (2009). *You majored in what? Mapping your path from chaos to career.* New York, NY: Penguin.

Crosby, O. (2002, Summer). Informational interviewing: Get the scoop on careers. *Occupational Outlook Quarterly, 32–37.*

Education Commission of the States. (1995). *Making quality count in undergraduate education.* Denver, CO: ECS Distribution Center.

Falwell, J. (1997). *Falwell: An autobiography.* Lynchburg, VA: Liberty House Publishers.

Falwell, J. (2014). *Press quotes.* Retrieved from http://www.liberty.edu/about liberty/index.cfm?PID = 26726.

Figler, H., & Bolles, R. N. (2007). *The career counselor's handbook.* Berkeley, CA: Ten Speed Press.

Herman, R. E. (2000, November). Liberal arts: The key to the future. *USA Today Magazine, 129,* 34.

Institute for Research on Higher Education. (1995). Connecting schools and employers: Work-related education and training. *Change, 27*(3), 39–46.

Liberty University News Service. (2014). *Chancellor Falwell announces Towns will step down for sabbatical.* Retrieved from http://www.liberty.edu/news/index.cfm?PID = 18495&MID = 97080.

Lock, R. D. (2004). *Taking charge of your career direction* (5th ed.). Belmont, CA: Brooks Cole.

McKay, Dominique. (2009). *Dr. Elmer Towns speaks at convocation.* Retrieved from http://www.liberty.edu/news/index.cfm?PID = 18495&MID = 5840.

Melton, G. B. (1995). *The individual, the family, and social good: personal fulfillment in times of change.* Lincoln, NE: University of Nebraska Press.

Miller, M. A. (2003, September/October). The meaning of the baccalaureate. *About Campus,* 2–8.

National Association of Colleges & Employers. (2012b). *Job outlook: The candidate skills/qualities employers want.* Bethlehem, PA: Author.

Pascarella, E. T., & Terenzini, P. (1991). *How college affects students: Findings and insights from twenty years of research.* San Francisco, CA: Jossey-Bass.

Pascarella, E. T., & Terenzini, P. (2005). *How college affects students: A third decade of research* (Vol. 2). San Francisco, CA: Jossey-Bass.

Sullivan, R. E. (1993, March 18). Greatly reduced expectations. *Rolling Stone,* 2–4.

Chapter 11

Your Degree: The Key

KEY CONCEPTS

In this chapter, you will:

- Reevaluate present and future goals.
- Reflect on your experiences within the course.
- Project new scholastic experiences.
- Identify keys that will make you successful.

THE KEY

When the builder finishes the building project and the client settles the debt, the builder presents the client with the key to the completed building. That key opens the door to the finished building, beautiful, fresh, and new. With the key in hand, the client can make this building his or her own by adding furnishings and personal effects. Getting your degree is just like the transfer of the key; once you have your degree, doors will open for you that would have otherwise been closed. Look forward to the day you receive your degree, and you can celebrate as Paul does in II Timothy 4:7–8, having "fought the good fight" and "kept the faith" (NIV).

© 2013 by Marie C Fields. Used under license of Shutterstock, Inc.

II Timothy 4:7–8,
"I have fought the good fight, I have finished the race, I have kept the faith. Now there is in store for me the crown of righteousness, which the Lord, the righteous Judge, will award to me on that day—and not only to me, but also to all who have longed for his appearing" (NIV).

THE CORNERSTONE: TRADITIONS

I Peter 5:2–7, "Be shepherds of God's flock that is under your care, watching over them—not because you must, but because you are willing, as God wants you to be; not pursuing dishonest gain, but eager to serve; not lording it over those entrusted to you, but being examples to the flock. And when the Chief Shepherd appears, you will receive the crown of glory that will never fade away. In the same way, you who are younger, submit yourselves to your elders. All of you, clothe yourselves with humility toward one another, because, 'God opposes the proud but shows favor to the humble.' Humble yourselves, therefore, under God's mighty hand, that he may lift you up in due time. Cast all your anxiety on him because he cares for you" (NIV).

As you pursue your degree and once you complete it, you will gain more and more responsibilities (at home, at school, and at work). With these responsibilities come opportunities to serve others by caring for them and living by example. John E. Johnson, Sr., one of the first graduates of Lynchburg Baptist College, tells the story of his graduation; his story evidences examples of the kind of servant leadership in Liberty University's founders that I Peter 5:2–7 describes.

Photo courtesy of Liberty University.

In 1973, Lynchburg Baptist College (now LU) held its first graduating ceremony (pictured here). One of the first graduates, John E. Johnson, shares his story of that first graduation; in the picture, he is located fourth from the left.

"Merriam-Webster's online dictionary states that tradition is 'a way of thinking, behaving, or doing something that has been used by the people in a particular group, family, society, etc., for a long time' (Merriam-Webster.com, 2013). Liberty University has several traditions, one of which I was inadvertently complicit in starting.

In the late 60s, I attended various universities and colleges before landing in Lynchburg, Virginia, in the summer of 1972 for my senior year at the small, fundamentalist Baptist college that Jerry Falwell had founded just the year before, called Lynchburg Baptist College. The thing that drew me and other enthusiastic young people to the school in those early years was not the facilities. We lived in cabins and barracks on Treasure Island in the middle of the James River; the church youth camp converted to house us as we attended classes in the Sunday school rooms at Thomas Road Baptist Church. We were transported back and forth in old rickety school buses and were offered bologna and peanut butter and jelly sandwiches as our meal plan. What attracted these early pioneers to LBC was the fact that where other schools were teaching students things that they could apply once they graduated and went out into the world, at LBC we were doing it through various opportunities to work in media, public speaking, performance, ministry, and hospitality.

Jerry was reaching the world with the gospel through the weekly televised broadcast of the "Old Time Gospel Hour," which was seen in every major city in North America. On the days when Jerry wasn't preaching from the pulpit of TRBC, he, along with gospel soloist Doug Oldham, the LBC Chorale, and a host of others would board the converted DC-3 or the Convair 580 and fly around the country, holding events and promoting the school. The students were enthusiastic and eager to be a part of the dream of becoming the largest Christian university in the world and in doing so, reaching the world for Christ.

That year went fast, and on the last Sunday of the school year, Jerry announced that the first class of LBC graduates would be graduating that evening and that all graduating seniors needed to meet at the front of the sanctuary at 4 o'clock for rehearsal. (We would actually receive our Certificates of Completion since LBC was not able to confer degrees until 1974.) Well, as a graduating senior, that was the first I heard about it! However, I didn't think it unusual since a lot of things happened fast and at the last moment back then. So, at 4 o'clock I walked in and sat on the front pew and watched eight students dressed in black robes complete with caps assemble on the platform.

The co-founder of the school, Dr. Elmer Towns, was directing the rehearsal, when he noticed me sitting on the front pew and asked, "John, what are you doing here?"

I said, "I came to graduate."

With an astonished look on his face, he responded, "Really!" I explained that this was my fifth year in school, and I was sure that I had more than enough credits to graduate.

He said, "Well, there is only one way to find out." He left the graduates to practice on their own while he and I raced up the hill to his office where he opened the lower right hand drawer of his desk and pulled my file out of the folder that held all of the student's files. He began adding all the credits from the transcripts of the four various schools that I had attended (Ohio University, University of Hawaii, Cedarville College, and now LBC), all the while apologizing that I had somehow fallen through the cracks, and he had somehow missed me in the process. In the end, he declared I had more than enough credits to graduate. He threw the file back in the drawer, and he and I raced back to join the others.

When we got back, it dawned on him, "You don't have a gown!" Whereupon, Vernon Brewer, a good friend of mine, who was also graduating, jumped up and exclaimed, "Hold on! I've got an idea!" He bolted through the door at the back of the platform and before long returned clutching Jerry's *baptismal robe in his hand, waved it above his head, and told me to try it on. It was a little long for me, so Vernon and I switched. Elmer said, "You must have a cap," so he offered me his. He said it would be okay if he went without one. I put it on my head, and I was ready to go!*

About that time, Jerry entered from his room in the back, dressed in his robe, cap, and stole. He noticed right away that Elmer wasn't wearing his cap and said "Elmer, where's your cap?" Elmer told him what had happened. Jerry immediately took off his cap, flung it across the platform, and said, "Well, Elmer, if you're not gonna wear one, neither am I!" It was a good excuse not to have to wear the old mortarboard, and he didn't. From that first graduation ceremony in May of 1973, at every graduation until his final commencement service in 2006, Chancellor Falwell went without his cap.

I often attend the commencement services at Liberty University, and whenever I do and notice Chancellor Jerry Falwell, Jr. without his cap, it takes me back to that first ceremony in 1973. I can still see Jerry, Sr. flinging his cap across the platform and saying, "Well, Elmer, if you're not going to wear one neither am I!" Is it a tradition? I don't know . . . but it continues!"

Photo courtesy of Liberty University; photographer: Les Schofer.

At Liberty University's 2003 commencement, Chancellor Jerry Falwell challenges graduates with an encouraging message.

Co-founders of Liberty University, Dr. Jerry Falwell and Dr. Elmer Towns, made a small decision that day in 1973 that impacted the lives of one of their graduates forever. By allowing a young man to wear a borrowed cap and robe so he could graduate in proper attire, they humbled themselves and showed camaraderie with each other by declining to don the graduation cap. This may have seemed like a small decision to these leaders, but to John, it became a lasting memory that he will cherish. Not only did these men teach the students how to be "young champions for Christ," they also lived it through their actions, "because they were willing, as God wanted them to be; not pursuing dishonest gain, but eager to serve; not lording it over those entrusted to them, but being examples to the flock" (I Peter 5:2–3, NIV). This tradition has transcended generations as President Jerry Falwell, Jr. leads the school with handpicked faculty unified to serve others in the vision of Liberty University. Take this tradition of service to heart everywhere you go as you touch the lives of others as a "champion for Christ!"

Photo courtesy of Liberty University; photographer: Les Schofer.

John E. Johnson and his wife, Paula, are pictured here with Jerry and his wife, Macel, at the opening of the Jerry Falwell museum. John and Paula met while attending school at LBC (now LU); now, they both work at LU and love to share their stories of LU's foundational years.

Reevaluate Present and Future Goals

Philippians 3:12-14,
"Not that I have already obtained all this, or have already arrived at my goal, but I press on to take hold of that for which Christ Jesus took hold of me. Brothers and sisters, I do not consider myself yet to have taken hold of it. But one thing I do: forgetting what is behind and straining toward what is ahead, I press on toward the goal to win the prize for which God has called me heavenward in Christ Jesus" (NIV).

Terry

Q: *Did you commit to your education one term at a time, or did you go all in from the beginning?*

A: "All-in from the beginning."

Q: *How did you feel when you earned your degree?*

A: "Relieved, not only had I accomplished something of significance, but also my family helped me, and that made it even sweeter."

In Chapter 2: Academic Goals: The Floorplan, we discussed the importance of determining a set of goals to direct you as you complete your courses (and ultimately, your degree). Take a minute to fill out the chart below, listing your original goals, noting what you have accomplished, steps it took to accomplish that goal, what goals are still outstanding, and what needs to be done to achieve those goals.

Personal Reflection

Original Goal	Was this a short-term or long-term goal?	Have you accomplished this goal? How?	Is this goal still outstanding? Why?	If not already met, how can you reach this target?

After completing this activity, reflect on what you have recorded. Then answer the following questions:

1. Did you notice patterns that have developed that help you master your objectives?

_____

_____

_____

_____

2. Did you notice patterns of obstacles that interfere with your goals?

_____

_____

_____

_____

3. Are your goals still worthwhile? If they are no longer worthwhile, how have they changed?

_____

_____

_____

_____

4. Take a minute to revise and make new goals as you look toward the future.

New goal	Is this a short-term or long-term goal?	What do you need to do to accomplish this goal? How?	What potential obstacles may interfere with this goal?	How can you overcome the obstacles? (This could be a practical suggestion or a motivating verse of scripture.)

Kristy Motte

"Don't forget the goals that you're seeking to attain through this degree—write them down. When things get tough, looking back on those goals will help you persevere and finish the race!"

Roger

Q: *How did you feel when you earned your degree?*

A: "Of all the schools I attended, this is the first time I really wanted to attend graduation and walk with my classmates. I was both very proud of my accomplishments and humbled that the Lord allowed me the opportunity to have a world-class education."

Terry

Q: *After earning your degree, what do you wish you had done differently?*

A: "While it was great completing the program quickly, I wish I had spent some more time on certain subjects. So, I would suggest smaller course loads to help retain the information."

Jenny Walter

"Once you have decided on a course of study, become familiar with your Degree Completion Plan (DCP) or the lists of courses required for your chosen major. Not only will your DCP keep you on track by helping your plan your course order, the DCP will keep you from taking unnecessary classes."

Roger

Q: *After earning your degree, what do you wish you had done differently?*

A: "I wish I hadn't accrued so much school debt."

Dr. Jerry Falwell

"There are far more valleys than mountain tops in the Christian life. God sends us two bad days for every good day in order to keep us looking towards Him" (Falwell, 1996, p. 471).

Cheryl

"As an adult learner, I am GRATEFUL I was able to complete my undergrad in a non-traditional format . . . one that afforded me the opportunity to attend from home."

Dr. Jerry Falwell

"There are some things money will do; there are some things human effort will do; there are some things human ingenuity will do; but there are some things only God can do" (Falwell, 1996, p. 266).

5. How do these new goals fit in with your time management plan that you established when reading Chapter Three: Time Management?

_____

_____

_____

_____

_____

Through this activity, you may have noticed that while you have achieved some goals, other goals went neglected or you determined that they were not necessary. In working through this, you may also have realized that you have new goals worth setting. Take a moment to celebrate the goals you have accomplished and the decisions you have made toward tweaking or setting new goals. Celebrate the strategies that you have put into place to conquer any obstacles that stand in your way and remember these words of encouragement from our founder, Dr. Jerry Falwell, "It is not the boulders ahead of us which wear us down. It is often the grain of sand in our shoe. God never puts more on us than He puts in us to bear up every burden" (Falwell, 1996, p. 427).

Reflect on Your Experiences Within the Course

Proverbs 1:5,
"Let the wise listen and add to their learning . . . and let the discerning get guidance" (NIV).

Throughout this course you have been exposed to a variety of information regarding:

- Goal setting.

- Time management strategies.

- Your responsibilities as a learner.

- Your learning as an adult (andragogy).

- Your learning as an individual (learning styles).

- Information literacy.

- Scholarly writing.

As you have applied the various techniques and information to different assignments in this course, you have done as Proverbs 1:5 advocates; you have added to your learning and you have received guidance! Reflect on the guidance and learning you have absorbed while taking this course. What different techniques/information did you embrace naturally? What techniques/information will you use in the future? Chart these in the table provided below. Also, consider revisiting the chart once you have completed the technique you planned to try out and record the results of your trial.

Terry

Q: *What was your scariest time in online college?*

A: "The scariest time was the initial class, fear of the unknown; once I settled down, everything was a breeze after that."

Photo courtesy of Aaron Traphagen.

Dr Jerry Falwell

"It is not the boulders ahead of us which wear us down. It is often the grain of sand in our shoe. God never puts more on us than He puts in us to bear up every burden" (Falwell, 1996, p. 427).

Personal Reflection

LEARNING OBJECTIVE	WHAT DO YOU NATURALLY DO?	WHAT NEW STRATEGY WILL YOU TRY?	REPORT: HOW DID THAT NEW STRATEGY WORK FOR YOU?
Goal Setting	*Short term goals*	*Long term goals*	
Time Management			
Adult Learning			
Learning Styles			
Information Literacy			
Scholarly Writing			
Study Strategies and Skills			
Career Planning			

Terry

Q: *Who provided support for you as you studied?*

A: "My lovely wife and our newborn baby (what a great motivator she was even then)."

Tim

Q: *Who provided support for you as you studied?*

A: "The best support I had while taking college courses was from my wife. She helped me in every way possible, from submitting my papers while I was away to reminding me of work that I needed to complete. This is why I love her so much, of course."

Shannon Bream, Liberty alumna and American journalist for Fox News in her address to Liberty graduates at the 40th commencement ceremony

"There will be joyous successes and beautiful families. There will be challenges and times when your burdens feel unbearable . . . But we know nothing is a surprise to the Lord. He has already woven a stunning tapestry of your life, but it's one you'll only get to experience a single thread at a time. It will require trust and patience and walking very close to Him. That is what we are called to do" (Menard, 2013).

Project New Scholastic Experiences

> Proverbs 16:3,
> "Commit to the Lord whatever you do, and He will establish your plans" (NIV).

Photo courtesy of Aaron Traphagen.

As you make plans for your academic future, what do you want to achieve? A degree, right? Or, is it more than that? Is it also the ability to qualify for a new job, advancement, or a raise? Is it the opportunity to be the first person from your family to graduate from college? Is it to set an example for the younger generation in your family, so that they see the importance of education at any age? Is it to follow your true calling? Whatever your reasons for pursuing a college education, commit your plans to the Lord and cover them in prayer, believing that he will do as Proverbs 16:3 promises. As you plan and pray, you must also prepare for the new scholastic experiences that will come your way.

As you make plans for your academic future, what do you want to achieve? Reflect on the answers to that question and beginning setting realistic goals.

In preparation for your future academic endeavors, consider the factors that will contribute to your success: goal setting, time management, and course selection and sequencing. Prayerfully consider the questions that correspond with each factor because your answers will drive the direction you take toward degree completion.

Personal Reflection

Set Realistic Goals

When do you want to complete your degree?

Before 2019

UNDER CONSTRUCTION

Dr. Harold Willmington

"We don't know what the future holds, but we know who holds the future" (Laird, 2012).

Alissa Keith

"No one cares more about your education than you do, so take the reigns and plan your own degree completion plan and complete what you started. Also, beware of those pesky pre-requisites."

T. Marcus Christian

"Think of degree completion as a race. Sometimes they are long with many hills, but there is always a finish line. Strive for that line, you will be glad you did."

Is this goal realistic when compared to the responsibilities you currently have in your life?

yes

Do your finances allow for you to complete your degree within this timeline?

Yes

Time Management

What time do you have to devote to your degree?

20 - 40 hours per week

How many courses can you reasonably take during a term without overloading yourself?

2-4 classes

If your degree is a priority, what might you have to sacrifice in order to complete it?

Work hours / social life / media

Course Selection and Sequencing

What courses are relevant to your degree?

In what order should you take the courses that are required for your degree?

_____

_____

_____

What other factors need to be considered to ensure that you meet your degree deadline: certification timelines or internships, for example?

_____

_____

_____

Nathaniel Valle

"If you spend time planning out your degree, you'll find it incredibly helpful—knowing what courses remain for your degree will lessen the chance that you sign up for an unnecessary course or miss a requirement. Most of you also have the freedom to take multiple electives, so planning your schedule ahead of time allows you to take courses outside of your major that interest you. Who knows? Maybe you will find English courses addictive!"

When making academic decisions regarding your course load for future terms, keep these factors in mind. Communicate these with your academic advisor, so he or she can help you make the best decision given the context of your situation. Also, share these concerns with your family and friends, so they can support you through your academic career. As poet John Donne wrote, "No man is an island." You do not have to go through this experience alone; your family, friends, advisors, and professors will be your cheerleaders, if you invite them to the game. When you graduate, it will be a shared victory—the sweetest kind, "And let us consider how to stir up one another to love and good works, not neglecting to meet together, as is the habit of some, but encouraging one another, and all the more as you see the Day drawing near" (Hebrews 10:24–25, ESV).

Identify Keys that Will Make You Successful

Joshua 1:7–9,

"Be strong and very courageous. Be careful to obey all the law my servant Moses gave you; do not turn from it to the right or to the left, that you may be successful wherever you go. Keep this Book of the Law always on your lips; meditate on it day and night, so that you may be careful to do everything written in it. Then you will be prosperous and successful. Have I not commanded you? Be strong and courageous. Do not be afraid; do not be discouraged, for the Lord your God will be with you wherever you go" (NIV).

As Joshua 1:7–9 says, obeying the Lord's guidance in your life will lead to success. The Lord's guidance can be found in scripture, in prayer, in daily devotionals, in church involvement and attendance, and in fellowship and relationships with other believers through wise council. Which of these have you already adopted as part of your walk with Christ? Which of these suggestions will you try? Recently, Willie Robertson, successful businessman and star of the hit TV show, "Duck Dynasty," came to

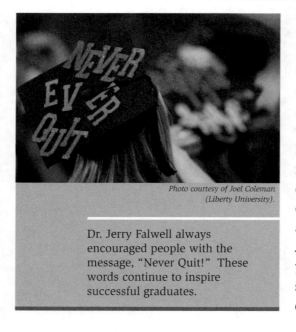

Photo courtesy of Joel Coleman (Liberty University).

Dr. Jerry Falwell always encouraged people with the message, "Never Quit!" These words continue to inspire successful graduates.

Liberty University's convocation. He shared this advice with the student body, "When you are moving toward God, you are moving in the right direction . . . My challenge to you is to not let the world's measuring stick show you what is successful. . . . Our family views success (as being) able to go around the country and share the message of the Lord and to talk about our faith" (Skinner, M. & Liberty University News Service, 2013). As you read further, you will discover many other practical tips that will bring you success in your college experiences; in your reading, look for things that you can incorporate into your routine that will help you grow and develop. Most importantly, just as Willie Robertson and Joshua 1:7–9 suggest, focus on the tips/keys that will put you on the path to a stronger relationship with Jesus and a strengthening of your faith because this will lead to a successful life.

Successful Beliefs

Stephen Covey's book *The 7 Habits of Highly Effective People* has been described as one of the most influential books of the 20th century.

In 2004, he released a new book called *The 8th Habit: From Effectiveness to Greatness.*

These habits are based on beliefs that lead to success.

1. **Be proactive.**

   Being proactive means accepting responsibility for your life. Covey uses the word "response-ability" for the ability to choose responses. The quality of your life is based on the decisions and responses that you make. Proactive people make things happen through responsibility and initiative. They do not blame circumstances or conditions for their behavior.

2. **Begin with the end in mind.**

   Know what is important and what you wish to accomplish in your life. To be able to do this, you will need to know your values and goals in life. You will need a clear vision of what you want your life to be and where you are headed.

3. **Put first things first.**

   Once you have established your goals and vision for the future, you will need to manage yourself to do what is important first. Set priorities so that you can accomplish the tasks that are important to you.

4. **Think win-win.**

   In human interactions, seek solutions that benefit everyone. Focus on cooperation rather than competition. If everyone feels good about the decision, there is cooperation and harmony. If one person wins and the other loses, the loser becomes angry and resentful and sabotages the outcome.

5. **First seek to understand, then to be understood.**

   Too often in our personal communications, we try to talk first and listen later. Often we don't really listen: we use this time to think of our reply. It is best to listen and understand before speaking. Effective communication is one of the most important skills in life.

6. **Synergize.**

   A simple definition of synergy is that the whole is greater than the sum of its parts. If people can cooperate and have good communication, they can work together as a team to accomplish more than each individual could do separately. Synergy is also part of the creative process.

President Jerry Falwell, Jr.

"Our ultimate purpose for our graduates is to know Christ and make Him known. We are now poised to carry out that mission in unparalleled ways" (Falwell, 2014).

Roger

"Success is obeying the Lord and submitting oneself to His control. I desire to let Him guide and direct my life and future. He has the authority and right to allow me to teach or to take that position away. I will strive to keep Him in the position of first place in my life. He must be before school, job, and family."

Katie Robinson

"James 1:12 states, 'Blessed is the man who perseveres under trial, because when he has stood the test, he will receive the crown of life that God has promised to those who love him' (NIV). So often, academics isn't about who has entered the classroom with the most knowledge or the most gifts. Instead, those who persevere through the many obstacles—and they will come—meet their educational goals. Anything that is worth having takes hard work."

Terry

Q: *How has receiving a degree at Liberty impacted your life?*

A: "Too many ways to list, but financially and work-happiness are the two most impacted areas."

Q: *What have been the keys to success in your life throughout your time at LU and beyond?*

A: "Much the same keys that made me successful in school: perseverance, determination, and the willingness to push forward when others would not."

Kristy Motte

"Remember the mantra of the late Dr. Falwell—'never, never, never quit!'"

Cheryl

"I know I can! This phrase has become more a philosophy than just a statement. My degree was hard. There were times I wanted to walk away! But, I didn't give up!

Situations in my life can be overwhelming (like taking my child to urgent care in the middle of the night, when I'm amazing crazy sick with the flu; or calling the ambulance to take my mother to the ER, every week for a year; or dealing with stage two cancer, wondering if it will crop up again; or trying to figure how I'm going to pay for my daughter's $2700 braces). But I remember that I not only kept moving forward with my undergraduate degree, but went on to earn straight A's in a master's degree program, as well.

I know I can! I remind myself of how far I've come, and have become my own cheerleader; reminding myself that I CAN do this (whatever the 'this' is at the time). I may not want to do the "this" of the moment; I remember that I took some classes at school that I did not like . . . but I did them. I am not a quitter."

7. **Sharpen the saw.**

Covey shares the story of a man who was trying to cut down a tree with a dull saw. As he struggled to cut the tree, someone suggested that he stop and sharpen the saw. The man said that he did not have time to sharpen the saw, so he continued to struggle. Covey suggests that we need to take time to stop and sharpen the saw. We need to stop working and invest some time in ourselves by staying healthy physically, mentally, spiritually, and socially. We need to take time for self-renewal.

8. **Find your voice, and inspire others to find theirs.**

Believe that you can make a positive difference in the world and inspire others to do the same. Covey says that leaders "deal with people in a way that will communicate to them their worth and potential so clearly that they will come to see it in themselves." Accomplishing this ideal begins with developing one's own voice or "unique personal significance."

From *College and Career Success,* 5/e by Marsha Fralick. Copyright © 2011 by Kendall Hunt Publishing Company. Reprinted by permission.

Brad Burgess, Liberty University Professor and Instructional Mentor for the College of General Studies, has worked with students and faculty alike, training them for success through a variety of tried and true techniques. In the following article, Brad offers tips for success, specifically in the areas of time management, accountability, diligence, and goal setting.

Tips for Success

Technology has created the opportunity to pursue a degree without ever having to physically attend a classroom. This flexible format helps to meet the needs of adults who may have busy lives with families, careers, and church obligations. Although the online classroom creates a great venue for learning, the online student needs to recognize that there can be pitfalls. Below are some basic tips for success for online students to consider as they pursue their degrees.

Time Management

The most important tip for success when pursuing a degree online is understanding the role of time management. One of the general pitfalls with time management is that a student will underestimate the time needed each week to successfully complete their studies. This can be a common problem, and students need to make sure that there is significant time available on a weekly basis to commit to homework, reading, writing papers, and taking tests. Education has to be a priority, and our priorities help dictate how time should be spent.

Action Plan

1. Closely examine your schedule and block out intervals of time throughout each week that can be committed to your studies.

2. Treat these allotted times as sacred and avoid the tendency to break these time commitments.

3. Set artificial deadlines for assignments at least 48 hours ahead of the actual due date. This will naturally build in some extra time just in case it is needed.

Accountability

Unlike a residential class, online classes do not have specific times to meet during a given week. Most students appreciate the flexibility the online environment offers, but this can also create a hardship because it may become easy to put off their studies. Knowing this, it is important to develop accountability within a student's weekly schedule. In many cases, it may be recruiting a spouse, family member, or friend that the student can interact with and be accountable to regarding his or her studies. The lack of a face-to-face environment can create a feeling of isolation, but successful students recognize that having individuals involved who hold them accountable will increase their opportunity for success.

Action Plan

1. Recruit one or two people who can be involved in your educational pursuits and keep you accountable.

2. Develop an extensive weekly plan that builds in time for school work and make this known to the individuals who are holding you accountable.

3. Give your accountability partners permission to hold you accountable, and make sure that you are on task with your studies. Allow them to exercise "tough love" as needed.

Dr. Elmer Towns

"See a vision, own a vision and share a vision. See what God wants you to do and then own it. I don't want you to just have a dream. I want you to become a dream" (McKay, 2009).

Cheryl

Q: *How did you feel when you earned your degree?*

A: "I felt like I won an incredibly long and challenging marathon. I felt: euphoric, accomplished, and proud that I hadn't given up. I DID IT!"

President Jerry Falwell, Jr.

"The common theme is always how many of them (our graduates) never could have obtained a college degree if not for Liberty University Online" (Menard, 2013).

Tim

"The best advice that I can give any military personnel is to take your time. Do not try to rush through courses and set up a full load of course work. Sometimes the courses can require a lot from you, the best thing to do is to take one or two at a time and work slowly. This will also help when it comes to field duty because you will not have as much work to catch-up on when you get back. I understand that you just want to get through college and get it over with. Slow and steady WILL win this race."

Terry Conner

"There is a saying on Mt. Everest, that when you reach the summit, you're only half-way done with the journey (understanding that you are only safe when you're back at base camp). Degree completion is like summiting, you've completed a tremendous feat, but you must then take the knowledge and skills you've attained and go fulfill God's purpose for you in your chosen profession."

Tim

"Tips for military personnel:

- Constantly remind your chain of command that you are taking college courses and that you have course work that must be completed.

- Take you course work to work with you. There are many times when you are just standing around, taking a two-hour lunch, etc. Do your homework during this time.

Find someone who is also taking college courses and build a support group; the encouragement that comes from friends and family helps."

Diligence

A great quality to enhance the opportunity to obtain a degree is diligence. The book of Proverbs has much to say about the importance of diligence, and this certainly applies to the online classroom. Proverbs 21:5 states, "The plans of the diligent lead surely to abundance, but everyone who is hasty comes only to poverty" (ESV). There can be a tendency to wait until the last minute and try to complete a week's worth of work in one day. This approach creates unneeded stress and is often a recipe for failure. A diligent person will review the weekly assignments early and make sure that he or she fully understands the instructions. In addition, the student will allow plenty of time to complete the work and will divide it up into achievable segments throughout the week.

Action Plan

1. Review weekly assignments early in the week to ensure that you understand what is expected and that you clearly comprehend the instructions.

2. Contact the instructor earlier in the week to clarify any issues. This will allow ample time for a response and make sure that you can easily submit assignments on time.

3. When you submit your work, always go back and verify that it has been submitted properly according to the instructions.

4. Recognize that diligence is a spiritual characteristic that demonstrates honor to God.

Long- and Short-Term Goals

Pursuing a degree is a long and sometimes tedious process. As with most things in life, when someone begins pursuing a degree, there is a tremendous amount of excitement and energy because it is new. Over time the newness wears off and the student can become discouraged. One of the ways to overcome this challenge is goal setting. In the case of online learning, it is important to have short- and long-term goals. The long-term goal is to earn a degree that will enhance one's vocation or ministry. The challenge with long-term goals is that they are "LONG" term. In this particular case it is good to periodically stop and remind yourself of the ultimate goal and how it will enhance the future.

Short-term goals work a little differently. In these cases a student is developing a shorter benchmark as the student works toward the long-term goal. It may be a short celebration or reward at the conclusion of each class. These are designed to recognize that a short-term goal has been accomplished, and although there may still be a long way to go, everything is moving in the right direction.

Action Plan

1. Periodically remind yourself of the ultimate goal of earning a degree and enhancing opportunities you may have in your vocation or ministry.

2. Regularly review your degree completion plan so that you can see that you are making progress.

3. Plan short-term celebrations when certain goals are accomplished. For example, you may decide to take an overnight trip with your family once you have completed four classes. This can be a nice motivation and helps remind you that you are accomplishing your short-term goals as you work toward the long-term goal.

The pursuit of a degree is a tremendous undertaking, which will require sacrifices of time and finances, but can also create a bright future with more opportunities. Students who succeed with an online degree recognize the commitment early on and work hard to achieve this lofty goal. My hope is that these tips for success will serve as a guide to help you earn a degree.

Dr. Jerry Falwell

"If God's people will see nothing but the goal line, will accept nothing but victory, will pay any price, will suffer any hurt and hardship, will refuse to be discouraged or disheartened, we cannot help but win; because we are charged with the power of God's Holy Spirit" (Falwell, 1996, p. 236).

Dr. John Hugo, composer of Liberty's theme song

"Champions arise and seek the prize of knowledge aflame!" (Hugo, 2014).

Just as Brad has offered some practical tips for success, Lisa Stephens Taylor, Professor and Instructional Mentor for the College of General Studies, has identified areas that can direct your spiritual walk as you balance a myriad of responsibilities, along with the pursuit of a college degree. Read her article regarding "Tips for Spiritual Balance" and take note of the areas that you want to become a permanent part of your routine.

Tips for Spiritual Balance

Finding the right balance between your studies, your personal life, and your spiritual development can be a tremendous challenge. During your studies, put forth effort to grow in the spiritual disciplines. Focusing on the following inward and outward disciplines can help you become stronger in your walk with Christ while also completing your studies here at Liberty University.

© 2013 by Edward Lara. Used under license of Shutterstock, Inc..

II Timothy 3:16-17, "All Scripture is God-breathed and is useful for teaching, rebuking, correcting and training in righteousness, so that the servant of God may be thoroughly equipped for every good work" (NIV).

Shannon Bream

"You are heading out into the world with your ambitions and hopes and dreams at a critical time . . . There is a lot of uncertainty, there is fear, and those who would like to create chaos and take innocent lives. . . . You will need to be strong, principled, and brave. And having earned an education that emphasizes not only facts and figures, but also absolute truths—I know you are ready" (Menard, 2013).

Dr. Jerry Falwell

"God has a vision for you. Don't settle for second best. Don't ever retire. Don't ever quit. Let your vision become an obsessive reality" (Falwell, 1996, p. 479).

1. **Pray.**
   The scriptures call believers to pray without ceasing (1 Thessalonians 5:17). Meeting with the Lord in an ongoing basis day-by-day opens the line of communication between yourself and Christ. Taking the time to pray will enable you to take your concerns to God, while also taking the time to listen to His response.

2. **Read the Bible Daily.**
   The Bible is our God-breathed book (2 Timothy 3:16). It is our sole guide for conduct, behavior, and belief. So much spiritual nourishment comes directly from time spent in individual, small-group, and large-group Bible study. Learn to spend time each day with God through daily study of the Bible.

3. **Meet With the Lord.**
   Too often, people believe that reading the Bible automatically equates with spending time with God. This is not necessarily the case. Find a quiet, uninterrupted place in order to spend one-on-one time with God through Bible study, prayer, and meditation on the Bible's truths. Through these, you come to have a true connection with God, and you can hear His voice as you meditate on the truth of His holy Word.

4. **Submit to the Word.**
   The Bible is true, and it provides us with guidance for right living, right relationships with one another, and a right relationship with God. In addition to reading the Bible, seek to live by its precepts. Doing so will provide you with guidance in how to manage your life and its challenges.

5. **Serve God and Others.**
   Christians are not only called to study the Bible, worship together, and pray. They are also called to serve. Giving is not only limited to financial giving, but also giving of our time and our abilities. Although you are busy as a student, do not forget to be actively involved in your local church, using your gifts to serve God, to serve the church, and to serve those who desperately need you in their lives.

6. **Integrate Your Faith Into Your Studies.**
   At Liberty, we encourage you to integrate your faith into your studies, just as your professors integrate their faith into how they teach you. Your academic studies should come alongside the growth of your faith and fuse together. History is full of men and women whose faith in Christ led to great learning, and whose learning led to achievements that have changed the world for the better. You are coming along in that great tradition. Use your faith and God's word as lenses for understanding all of the lessons before you. They will put the courses that you are studying in their proper context.

BUILDING BLOCKS

If you have read this far in this textbook, you probably understand that you are at a pivotal point in your education. Having come this far, you have had times of great success, perhaps some times of struggle, and perhaps even a few times that you did not make an attempt to struggle to build your success. Some of you will have had a hot and cold relationship with your coursework. You may have begun strong, but quickly burned out when the assignments were not to your liking or did not seem to be leading where you wished to go. Now is a good time to evaluate your work as you reflect on how you conducted your work this important term, as this course is the groundwork for so much that will come after it as you work toward your college degree.

Think back to the YOU who began the course. What do you see that has remained the same over the weeks you have been taking this course . . . and what has changed? Are the changes ones of attitude, work habits, or time management? These are the critical elements that will allow you to continue to build your success or that will drag you far from it. This chapter is the "key" chapter, but there are really multiple keys to your success. As you reflect on the YOU who is now completing the textbook, what lies ahead for you? Have you planned your next term's courses and are you eager to get them underway? In the New Testament book of Matthew, in Chapter 13, we read what is called the parable of the sower. It says:

> A farmer was sowing grain in his fields. As he scattered the seed across the ground, some fell beside a path, and the birds came and ate it. And some fell on rocky soil, where there was little depth of earth; the plants sprang up quickly enough in the shallow soil, but the hot sun soon scorched them and they withered and died, for they had so little root. Other seeds fell among thorns, and the thorns choked out the tender blades. But some fell on good soil, and produced a crop that was thirty, sixty, and even a hundred times as much as he had planted. If you have ears, listen!"
>
> (Matthew 13:3b-9, The Living Bible)

As you read that passage and evaluate yourself as a student, what sort of ground do you think you are? The title of this book is *Breaking Ground* because this is a course designed to help you lay the groundwork of online education in a way that will lead you to success. Have you "produced a crop," as the Bible passage puts it, with your work in this introductory course? Has your work been its best, leading you to ultimate academic success? We pray it has!

TOOL BOX

Accountability—As mentioned in the chapter, having an accountability partner can be a major factor in staying on task. Recruiting friends or family members who are close to you is a good idea, but you might also consider an online accountability partner who is going through the same experiences you are.

Was there another student, or group of students, who you made a connection with while in this class? Consider the idea of working together to keep yourselves moving forward toward your goals. This will not only benefit your time management but will also help to establish a sense of community.

Syllabus and Course Schedule—As you enter each new class, be sure to navigate to the Syllabus and Assignment Instructions folder in the Course Content area and download the syllabus and course schedule. These documents explain, in detail, what the learning objectives are for your class, how they will be attained and assessed, and what work will need to be accomplished each week. Reviewing these documents as you begin each of your next classes will help you to connect activities to learning outcomes and will allow you to plan an appropriate amount of time in your schedule each week.

Degree Completion Plan (DCP) Audit—You reviewed your DCP Audit earlier in the course, but don't let this be a one-time event. Log into your DCP Audit before the start of each new term. Watching your degree completion plan fill up as you progress through your degree can be a huge motivational factor, but it can also save you time, money, and frustration.

By checking your audit before each term, you can confirm that you are taking classes that will count toward your degree. You can avoid becoming a student who discovered that the class you just took won't count toward your degree by checking your audit ahead of time. Add another level of assurance by verifying your findings with your Academic Advisor. Your time and money are too valuable to waste.

End of Course Surveys—At the end of each class, Liberty University will ask you to complete a brief survey related to your experience with your professors and the course materials. Some students do not fill these out because they believe that professors will be able to see their comments and hold their comments against them when it comes to assign final grades. Rest assured, Liberty takes your privacy and your feedback very seriously.

Prior to final grade submission, your professors can view a list of who has or has not completed the survey, but they are not able to see your comments. This is used primarily so your professors can encourage those who have not completed the survey to do so. After final grades have been assigned, usually about two weeks after the course has ended, Liberty will release the survey results to your professors and their supervisors. This list does not contain any names, and there is no way for anyone to see who wrote what. All that is visible is the individual questions followed by a listing of anonymous responses.

Your professors and their supervisors will review the feedback of your entire class and utilize that information to make any necessary adjustments to the curriculum. This is your opportunity to help shape the future of your university. Take full advantage of it and offer your feedback at the end of each class.

Additional resources and links to specific sites, worksheets, and apps can be located by accessing the Breaking Ground website:

www.breakinggroundlu.com

THE ULTIMATE CORNERSTONE

Psalm 118:21-23, "I will give you thanks, for you answered me; you have become my salvation. The stone the builders rejected has become the cornerstone; the Lord has done this, and it is marvelous in our eyes" (NIV).

Throughout this textbook and this course, we have shared a lot of information with you to equip you for a successful academic career. As we conclude our time together, we want to share the most important message of all, which is the cornerstone of our faith—our forgiveness and salvation through Jesus Christ. Mark Tinsley, Army National Guard Chaplain and Department Chair for the College of General Studies, elaborates in the story that follows, "Our Altitude & Our Salvation."

Our Altitude & Our Salvation

I started flying airplanes when I was only 15 years old. In fact, I could fly solo in an airplane before I was legally allowed to drive a car in my home state of Virginia. As paradoxical as it sounds, my parents would drive me to the airport so I could fly alone in a plane. The situation with its waist-deep irony was quite humorous, even for a teenager. Still, it provided for some great stories among family and friends—stories that we still share with one another today, some 20–25 years later.

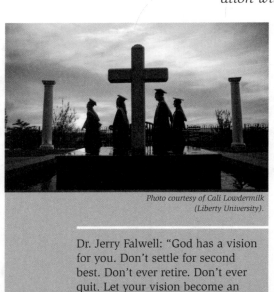

Photo courtesy of Cali Lowdermilk
(Liberty University).

Dr. Jerry Falwell: "God has a vision for you. Don't settle for second best. Don't ever retire. Don't ever quit. Let your vision become an obsessive reality" (Falwell, 1996, p. 479).

Regrettably, not all of my aviation experiences are so lighthearted in nature. I have been involved in several close calls around the country and one crash on the runway of the Raleigh-Durham Airport in North Carolina. Fortunately, the crash involved no injuries and was, when compared to other aviation accidents, rather minor. One of the close calls, though, was quite serious, and I avoided certain injury or death by only minutes.

A fellow pilot and I were flying from the Shenandoah Valley Airport in Weyers Cave, Virginia, en route to the Winchester Airport in Winchester, Virginia. The weather that day was cold and cloudy, so we had filed what is called an instrument (IFR) flight plan—a flight plan that allows properly-trained pilots to fly in bad weather.

Sometime soon after takeoff from Weyers Cave, we entered the clouds and began flying solely by reference to the cockpit instruments. Everything went well until we got closer to Winchester. During our flight north through Virginia, the weather had deteriorated significantly, and the temperature at our altitude had fallen well below freezing. Consequently, our wings started to accumulate ice—and lots of it. For those who are unaware, airplanes and ice do not mix. If a plane's wings accumulate too much ice during flight, then the airplane can become unstable and crash. After a few minutes of rapid ice buildup, the co-pilot and I realized we were in serious trouble.

We had two choices at that point in the flight. We could encourage the ice to melt by either climbing above the clouds where the sun was shining or descending to a lower altitude where the temperatures were most likely warmer. Since the route between Weyers Cave and Winchester is extremely mountainous, we would have preferred to climb to a higher altitude. Unfortunately, we had accumulated so much ice that the aircraft was too heavy to safely execute this option. We were left with only the descent. After obtaining approval from air traffic control to move to a lower altitude, we did so, praying all the while that temperatures would be high enough to melt the ice and that our controllers would safely guide us through the dangerous mountains of Northwestern Virginia.

Happily, the temperatures were indeed warmer, and the controllers did not disappoint in their ability to provide safe passage. After a few minutes at the lower altitude, we noticed ice starting to slough off of the wings and struts, and soon the plane was completely free of its burden. What is more, air traffic control maintained positive communication with us throughout the ordeal and constantly adjusted our heading, speed, and altitude to place us on final approach to the Winchester Airport within the shortest timeframe possible. When the wheels touched down on the runway, the co-pilot and I breathed a sigh of relief, thus concluding a one-hour flight that made us feel about 20 years older.

As I look back on this experience today, I realize just how fortunate we were. Had we decided to continue flying at our original altitude, our plane would have gathered excessive ice, causing it to become unstable. A crash would have likely ensued. Likewise, had we tried to climb to a higher altitude, the increased weight on the airframe would have prevented our ascent, and, again, we would have likely crashed. However, we made the right decision and descended to a lower altitude. Indeed, ours was the only safe and wise decision to make.

At the same time, I am reminded that neither my co-pilot nor I melted the ice that day. We simply made the decision to descend to a lower altitude. It was the natural laws of physics and thermodynamics that melted the ice. In other words, we decided to fly the plane at an altitude where the air was warmer, but it was the warm air—not the efforts of the co-pilot or me—that melted the ice. One might say that the "promises" of science were what saved us that day, even though our decision to move out of danger is what placed us in the right posture for positive change to occur.

When I read God's Word, I am amazed at how well this anecdote applies to the biblical concept of salvation. As sinners, we are flying at a dangerous altitude. The world around us is cold, and the icy burdens of life accumulate rapidly on our wings. We are seemingly helpless. We know we can't stay where we are, or we will surely die in our wretchedness and sin (Rom. 6:23); we are unable to climb by our own power to a higher altitude and, thus, save ourselves (Eph. 2:8-10); and we realize there are treacherous mountains below and, to go that direction means the assumption of considerable risk. So, what do we do? Where do we go?

In his grace and mercy, God does not leave us to wonder. Romans 5:8 reads, "But God shows his love for us in that while we were still sinners, Christ died for us" (ESV). Through his death on the cross at Calvary, Christ provides the warm air below. His sacrifice and atonement make staying at our present altitude a foolish choice and render futile any attempt at some sort of cavalier, self-directed climb. Christ alone is our Savior! In John 14:6, Jesus proclaims, "I am the way and the truth and the life. No one comes to the Father except through me" (ESV). The decision is singular and clear, and it is one that only we can make. We must power back and descend in order to place ourselves in the warmth below. If we do so, Christ promises to take away our icy-cold burdens. Romans 10:9, 13 states, "Because, if you confess with your mouth that Jesus is Lord and believe in your heart that God raised him from the dead, you will be saved. . . . For 'everyone who calls on the name of the Lord will be saved'" (ESV). That is to say, if we trust in Christ and give our lives over to him in full submission and obedience, we are promised ultimate deliverance from the trials and tribulations of this world. Indeed, as John 3:16 tells us, our faith is rewarded with eternal life.

Of course, trusting in God is not easy. Descending means coming in close proximity to the treacherous terrain of life. A life of faith is always wrought with rugged, dangerous peaks, deep, dark valleys, and raging rivers of temptation and worldly desire. What we have to remember, though, is that God has complete and perfect knowledge of this terrain. He is our air traffic controller, and He will guide us along a path that will bring us safely to our destination (i.e., eternal life with Him). Hebrews 13:5 quotes Deuteronomy 31:6 and records God's promise, "I will never leave you nor forsake you" (ESV). God is our trustworthy guide through all of life's dangers.

If you do not know Christ as your personal Lord and Savior today, the ice is building up on your wings, the air is cold, and you are in danger. You cannot stay where you are, nor can you climb out of the danger yourself. However, you do have an option. All you have to do is reach for the throttle, power back, and descend. Make a decision for Christ; warm air awaits you.

Dr. Jerry Falwell

"I believe in ignoring the walls that people build. Behind the facades that separate us, we are all alike. We all need to know that God loves us. We all need to know that in Christ God has forgiven our sins and our failures. We all need to know that through Christ we can begin again" (Falwell, 2008, p. 43).

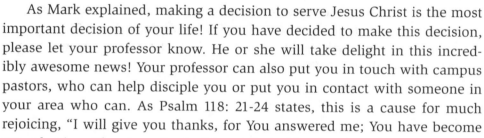

As Mark explained, making a decision to serve Jesus Christ is the most important decision of your life! If you have decided to make this decision, please let your professor know. He or she will take delight in this incredibly awesome news! Your professor can also put you in touch with campus pastors, who can help disciple you or put you in contact with someone in your area who can. As Psalm 118: 21-24 states, this is a cause for much rejoicing, "I will give you thanks, for You answered me; You have become my salvation. The stone the builders rejected has become the cornerstone; the Lord has done this, and it is marvelous in our eyes. The Lord has done it this very day; let us rejoice today and be glad" (NIV). Let the world know that you are now a true "champion for Christ!"

Photo courtesy of Joel Coleman (Liberty University).

Let the world know that you are now a true "champion for Christ!"

References

Falwell, J. (1997). *Falwell: An autobiography.* Lynchburg, VA: Liberty House Publishers.

Falwell, J. (2014). *Press quotes.* Retrieved from http://www.liberty.edu/aboutliberty/index.cfm?PID = 26726.

Falwell, M. (2008). *Jerry Falwell: His life and legacy.* New York, NY: Howard Books.

Fralik, M. (2011). *College and career success.* Dubuque, IA: Kendall Hunt Publishing Company.

Hugo, J. (2014). *Registrar: Liberty University Alma Mater.* Retrieved from http://www.liberty.edu/academics/registrar/?PID = 5648

Laird, B. (2012). *80 years dedicated to God.* Retrieved from http://www.liberty.edu/champion/2012/04/eighty-years-dedicated-to-god/comment-page-1/.

McKay, Dominique. (2009). *Dr. Elmer Towns speaks at convocation.* Retrieved from http://www.liberty.edu/news/index.cfm?PID = 18495&MID = 5840.

Menard, D. (2013). *40th Commencement: Celebrating historic accomplishments, continuous growth.* Retrieved from http://www.liberty.edu/aboutliberty/index.cfm?PID = 24995&MID = 91512.

Skinner, M. & Liberty University News Service. (2013, September 27). *'Duck Dynasty' star Willie Robertson calls students to be successful.* Retrieved from http://www.liberty.edu/news/index.cfm?PID = 18495&MID = 100031.

Tradition. (n.d.). In *Merriam-Webster.com.* Retrieved from http://www.merriam-webster.com/dictionary/tradition.